D1336868

THE MODERNIST GARDEN IN FRANCE ::

YALE UNIVERSITY PRESS
NEW HAVEN AND LONDON

THE MODERNIST GARDEN IN FRANCE : : DOROTHÉE IMBERT

This study was supported by a grant from
the Graham Foundation for Advanced Studies
in the Fine Arts.
Published with assistance from the Louis Stern
Memorial Fund.

Designed by Marc Treib

Set in Sabon and Gill Sans by Highwood
Typographic Services, Hamden, Connecticut
Printed in the United States of America by
Horowitz/Rae, Inc.

Library of Congress Cataloging-in-Publication
Data

Imbert, Dorothée.
The modernist garden in France / Dorothée Imbert.

    p. cm.
Includes bibliographical reference (p.   ) and index.
ISBN 0—300—04716—9
1. Gardens—France—Design. 2. Landscape
architecture—France. 3. Architecture,
Modern—20th century—France. 4.
Modernism (Art)—France. I. Title.
SB470.55.F8143 1993
712'.0944'0904—dc20   92—30514 CIP

A catalogue record for this book is available
from the British Library.

The paper in this book meets the guidelines for
permanence and durability of the Committee
on Production Guidelines for Book Longevity
of the Council on Library Resources.

10 9 8 7 6 5 4 3 2 1

for my parents,

Jacqueline Imbert

Jean-Bernard Imbert

PREFACE

It is in the garden that the modernist finds himself stuck. That is where his interpretation of functionalism breaks down. Walls, steps, balustrades, and pavements—even hedges and windscreens—are functional features that may be treated as such. Nobody will dispute my statement, however, that most of the garden that we see is pure decoration for its own sake. . . . We need only once glance at the modernist's pitiful attempts out of doors to know that he is stuck. In most cases he has thrown up his hands and done nothing. The few examples where any serious effort has been made are of such severity, or of such grotesqueness, as to have little resemblance to anything we should recognize as a garden.
H. B. Dunington-Grubb, "Modernismus Arrives in the Garden—To Stay?"

This acerbic commentary on modernism in landscape design reveals the ambiguity that undermined the definition of the French garden in the early twentieth century. Caught between the call for functionalism and the pursuit of aesthetics, their designers alternatively pro-

GARDEN BACKDROP.
Salon d'Automne,
Paris, 1921.
Robert Mallet-Stevens.
[Saint-Sauveur,
Architecture et décor des jardins]

x

posed, as viable landscapes, orchards, beehives, tennis courts, landing strips, solaria, or purely pictorial compositions. They employed *new* materials and invoked the *new* means of transportation and ways of life as justifications for their *new* order—whether formal or pastoral. The shaping of the modern garden also oscillated between two extremes: the ultradecorative, hardly recognizable as a landscape in its "severity" or "grotesqueness"; and the Virgilian ideal of untouched nature, in which the modernist seemed to have "thrown up his hands and done nothing."

The *style régulier*, or regular style, had reappeared in the gardens of the early twentieth century, supplanting the tendency to design in a naturalistic fashion. Henri and Achille Duchêne sought to retrieve France's cultural inheritance through their re-creation or re-invention of the grand formal gardens; Jean-Claude Nicolas Forestier, in his writings, gardens, and park designs, argued for an architectonic structure whose rigor was softened by vegetation; and André and Paul Vera translated the idiom of the *jardin à la française* into a reduced and simplified bourgeois garden.[1] These times thus witnessed both the last vestiges of aristocratic estate design and the first attempts to redefine a modern garden. In spite of differing approaches, however, the aforementioned designers all associated the formalism of the style régulier with the new landscape.

As if to answer André Vera's "Exhortation to Interest Architects in Gardens" (1923), a series of landscape works by Paul Vera, Jean-Charles Moreux, Pierre-Émile Legrain, and Gabriel Guevrekian marked the culmination of the collaboration within the fields of architecture, the decorative arts, and landscape design. Vera's writings and contemporary articles argued for a "synthetic" garden, reduced in size, and based on a formal structure that was primarily mineral and evergreen. Although as a whole they were frequently advertised as outdoor apartments providing a retreat from the speed-crazed city, several of these gardens were essentially pictorial compositions, reflecting the geometrization and "cubification" of a style applied indiscriminately to all the arts—from the interior *ensemble* to jewelry, automobiles, bookbindings, and fashion. As one contemporary critic observed, "When one may meet one's best friend buying a jade leather coat just to match the jade line on her new car, it is not surprising to find the garden coming into this ordered scheme of fitness."[2]

The Exposition of Modern Decorative and Industrial Arts, held in Paris in 1925, played an essential role in the development of the new French landscape. Although only original and modern submissions were to be admitted at the fair, the garden entries varied in both style and degree of innovation. Whether mere vegetal decorations for the exposition pavilions or strong conceptual statements, these landscapes ranged from Moorish patios and exterior showrooms for ceramics to aviaries and pure sculptural shapes. Among the most cited designs were the gardens by Robert Mallet-Stevens, Pierre-Émile Legrain and Gabriel Guevrekian. Exploiting new materials and formal vocabularies, their creators challenged gravity, the relation of time and movement, and a preconceived notion of nature and garden as a symbiotic system.

The designs presented at the section Art du jardin functioned as abstracts of the predominant garden trends of the 1920s and 1930s. Refuting nature's cycles and processes of maturation, these works objectified "instant-gardens" rather than true landscapes. Almost completely architectural, the hard-lined compositions attained their peak effect at the moment construction was completed rather than after the vegetation had been allowed to grow. Composed as graphic arrangements of mostly planar and barely volumetric elements, such gardens were extremely photogenic. If, as a journalist noted, "the spread of modern architecture has been hastened by the perfection . . . of the half-tone system of reproducing black-and-white photographs," the concise flat-patterned gardens of the 1920s also profited from the new reproductive medium.[3] Striking images such as Man Ray's photograph of the Noailles garden by the Veras and Moreux almost subvert the reading of the text. In fact, Peter Shepheard's slightly ambiguous description of this illustration in *Modern Gardens* has snowballed into a series of misattributions in subsequent literature—the true location of the garden was in Paris, not Saint-Germain.[4]

Whether conceived by an architect, an artist, or an *ensemblier*, the architectonic gardens followed the rules governing interiors more closely than those of horticulture. In this characteristic lies both their success, as an extension of architecture or decorative ensembles, and their weakness, as landscapes ill adapted to the demands of nature.

Later in this period, the French decorative arts evolved toward what one critic termed a "mod-

GARDEN FOR
JACQUES HEIM.
Neuilly, 1928.
Gabriel Guevrekian.
[Photo: Therese Bonney;
© 1993 ARS, N.Y. /
SPADEM, Paris]

ernized baroque."5 Cubistic excesses were tempered by restraint, and garden designers aimed at creating an aesthetic system that could be described as innovative, while remaining classical in tone. It was within these parameters that Paul Vera and Jean-Charles Moreux revised the iconography of the traditional French garden and challenged the preconceived use of materials in *tableaux* that reflected the unsettling play between artifice and nature.

Although aware of André Vera's writings, Le Corbusier seldom displayed any effort to imprint the landscapes around his villas of the 1920s with a recognizable order. Furthermore, as he displaced the architectonic center of gravity upward, with *pilotis* and roof gardens, he removed the necessity for a horizontal connection between architecture and landscape. Unlike most architects, who would attempt to extend an architectural order into the fields, Le Corbusier seemed to invoke William Kent, who had "leaped the fence and [seen] that all nature was a garden."6 Seeking a landscape that would be part of the architectural composition, Le Corbusier literally captured fragments of nature within the building, which in its turn was set against, or within, the natural elements of sun, air, and greenery. The scenery, whether urban or natural, was framed and borrowed, but the interaction with the landscape remained visual rather than physical. Although diametrically opposed in appearance, Guevrekian's decorative *tableau-jardin* and Le Corbusier's *paysage-type* nevertheless rested on the same pictorial principle—that of regarding the landscape as a once-removed image of nature.

If Le Corbusier effaced the perceptible impact of architecture on the natural order, André Lurçat attempted to strike a balance between the landscape of the roof terrace and the terrace garden. With his designs, the Hegelian cycle of formed and unformed landscape in the early part of the century was completed. At the next Paris exposition, in 1937, gardens appeared to have receded behind decoration, while landscape design evolved toward social and functional grounds. The predominance of floral displays throughout the fair revealed the severance of garden design from the fields of arts and architecture.

Permanent only in their immobility, the fragile two-and-a-half dimensional exercises of the interwar years resisted the fourth dimension,

time, only briefly. Within a decade, almost all of them had vanished, leaving behind only fragments of the larger design, as in the Gernez garden in Honfleur, by Paul Vera. Rare descriptions and a few drawings and photographs are virtually the only records of this brief, coherent —although localized—burst of landscape invention.

I make no claims to a comprehensive history of modernist garden design in this book. Focusing instead upon a twenty-year interval, roughly 1920 to 1940, I have attempted to present and analyze a selection of what I consider to be representative examples of modern thought in French landscape architecture. Modern not only in the use of such innovative media as concrete or electric light, these gardens also reflected new impulses within their cultural milieu and transformed landscape design precedents.

Some illustrations—such as the Noailles garden by Gabriel Guevrekian—recur in books and articles on the modern landscape. During my archival research in France, I discovered a considerable amount of graphic material that has seldom—if ever—been published since the 1930s. Because no design still exists in its entirety, apart from the re-created Noailles garden in Hyères, I would like to stress the necessity and importance of interpretation in this work. For example, the Tachard garden by Pierre-Émile Legrain warranted, in my opinion, a detailed examination of both the plan and the limited photographic evidence, as verbal descriptions remain both rare and vague.

Except for the more visionary, historical, or poetic writings of Achille Duchêne, J.C.N. Forestier, and André Vera, criticism and theory of that period were devoted mostly to a garden as an extension of the interior ensemble, a garden situated on the thin line between architecture and landscape. I have thus attempted to connect these designs with their creators, whether architects or ensembliers, in order to present a more comprehensive story. It has been my intention to serve as both detective and archaeologist, to establish a common structure among the recorded fragments in order to reintroduce these accomplishments to those currently involved with giving form to the environment.

ACKNOWLEDGMENTS

xiv

**GARDEN FOR THE
VICOMTE DE NOAILLES.**
Hyères, 1928.
Gabriel Guevrekian.
[University of Illinois,
Urbana Champaign]

This project being the scion of my thesis for a
Master of Landscape Architecture degree at the
University of California at Berkeley, I wish to
thank the members of my committee—Garrett
Eckbo, Michael Laurie, and Reuben Rainey—
for their guidance.

I am also grateful to the staff of the libraries
and institutions where I pursued my research,
among them, the Archives d'Architecture
Moderne, the Bibliothèque du Musée des
Arts Décoratifs, the Bibliothèque des Beaux-
arts, the Bibliothèque Forney, the Bibliothèque
Nationale, the Caisse Nationale des Monu-
ments Historiques, the Fondation Jacques
Doucet at the Bibliothèque d'Art et d'Arché-
ologie, the Fondation Le Corbusier—all in
Paris—and the Photothèque Albert Kahn, in
Boulogne-sur-Seine; in New York, the Avery
Architectural and Fine Arts Library at Colum-
bia University, the Museum of Modern Art, the
Watson Library at the Metropolitan Museum
of Art; the Garden Library at Dumbarton
Oaks, in Washington, D.C., and the Bancroft,
Doe, and College of Environmental Design

libraries at Berkeley. My thanks are directed in particular to Elizabeth Byrne and Susan Snyder, Linda Lott and Annie Thatcher, and Holy Raveloarisoa for their time and help.

In topical order, I wish to acknowledge Michel Duchêne and the Association Henri et Achille Duchêne for their generous loan of graphic materials. In my quest for documentation on Forestier, I relied on my brother Luca to climb Montjuïc in search of a better pergola, and on my friends Victor Carrasco and Mireia Belil to establish contacts in Seville and Barcelona. Toward John Dixon Hunt I feel most obliged, as he manifested an early interest in this project and provided continuous support. It was he who brought to my attention the Vera drawings then owned by Yu-Chee Chong Fine Art in London; Ms. Chong kindly loaned several reproductions from her collection. The Cooper-Hewitt Museum has since acquired these works, and it has been a pleasure to consult with Marilyn Symmes and Gail Davidson, the curators of Drawings and Prints. I am deeply indebted to the Musée d'art et d'histoire of Saint-Germain-en-Laye, where I studied documents from the bequest of André Vera, and more particularly to Mrs. Cécile Vincent, Ms. Christine Helfrich, as well as to Mrs. Janine Hébert and Mr. Michel Péricard. Mr. Courdille-Gernez kindly offered me a glimpse of his garden in Honfleur, which Paul Vera designed in the early 1920s.

Gilles Ragot, at the Institut Français d'Architecture, greatly facilitated my research on Jean-Charles Moreux by graciously providing his biographical notes on the architect; he also reviewed the chapter on Moreux in this book and supplied several images. Although limited in number, the Gabriel Guevrekian papers at the University of Illinois at Urbana Champaign contained some useful documents; I wish to acknowledge the cooperation of Maynard Brichford, University Archivist, and Professor Richard Betts. Cécile Briolle was extremely kind in sharing her knowledge and documents on the garden by Guevrekian for the Villa Noailles.

My gratitude also to Professors Alan Colquhoun, Nancy Troy, and especially Jean-Louis Cohen and Mary McLeod for their support, generous sharing the information, and critical readings of various chapters.

This list would not be complete without the mention of those who were essential in supplying a name, an image, a source, or a thought: Stanford Anderson, Georges Blaizot, Chuck Byrne, Carolyn Constant, James Elliott, Hartmut Frank, Philippe Garner, Nancy Goldman, Carol Greentree, Kai Gutschow, Nina Hubbs, Bernadette Imbert, Jacqueline Imbert, Jean-Bernard Imbert, Miwon Kwon, Florence Langer-Martel, Bénédicte Leclerc, Andrew Mead, Robin Middleton, Evelyne Possémé, Raymond Reece, Robert Riley, François Roubaud, Hervé Ruffier, Ellen Samuels, Anne-Marie Sauvat, Monique Schneider-Maunoury, Charles Stuckey, Steve Van Dyk, George Waters, Joachim Wolschke-Bulmahn.

I am indebted to the Graham Foundation for Advanced Studies in the Fine Arts, whose financial support aided in producing illustrations in this book. Many of the images were reproduced from contemporary periodicals such as *L'Architecte, Art et Décoration,* and *L'Illustration.* Dan Johnston, at the University of California Library Photographic Services, and Kevin Gilson either photographed and/or printed hundreds of these.

I also wish to thank Serge François and Denis Seigneur at the Ministère des Affaires Étrangères for allowing me to consider this topic with a foreign eye. The whole editorial board at Yale University Press deserves my gratitude, but it is certainly to Judy Metro that I owe the privilege of publishing these lines: she believed in this venture almost from the beginning and accepted most of my incongruities. Ken Botnick was also very helpful in the design process, and I remain in awe of my manuscript editor, Karen Gangel, whose patience is outweighed only by the precision of her eye.

To my skeptical family, certain friends, or *maestri* who do not fit in any particular category but who exert a stronghold on my thoughts, such as John Brinckerhoff Jackson and Spiro Kostof, and to the many who by their support, help, criticism, or simple understanding have made this book possible, I offer my most sincere thanks.

Last and foremost, to the one who could recite this text backward, the one who has threatened me frequently and flattered me shamelessly, the one for whom, by whom, and to whom this book is: Marc Treib.

HENRI DUCHÊNE; ACHILLE DUCHÊNE

A RETURN TO FORMALISM

1-1

Formal garden design regained favor at the turn of the century with a revised version of the *style régulier*. The regular style—frequently considered an epitome of gallicism, as in the *jardin à la française*—refuted all previous digressions into English, Chinese, romantic, and other naturalistic landscape fashions. Whether taken as a modification of French formalism or as a distortion of nature into an abstract pictorial composition, the modern regular garden contrasted sharply with the degenerate parodies of a landscape style that had characterized the latter half of the nineteenth century.

The forced nature of the *jardin de l'intelligence* (garden of reason) that had been transformed into the *jardin de la sensibilité* (garden of the senses) gave way to an idealized naturalistic landscape. Initiated during the second half of the eighteenth century, this reverse formalism dominated the course of the French landscape for over a hundred years. Although the differences in style were considerable, oscillations between the apparent order of the *régulier* and

1-1 CHÂTEAU DU MARAIS. TERRACES AND PARTERRES FOR THE COMTE BONI DE CASTELLANE. The grander scheme for the surroundings was left unexecuted. Essonne, 1896. Achille Duchêne, [Duchêne, *Les jardins de l'avenir*]

1-2 BOIS DE BOULOGNE. PLAN.
Paris, circa 1855.
Adolphe Alphand with Pierre Barillet-Deschamps.
[Alphand, *Les promenades de Paris.* Courtesy Dumbarton Oaks, Washington, D.C.]

1-3 PARC DE LA CHAUMETTE. PLAN.
Design in the *style composite,* balancing the formal garden with a curvilinear *parc paysager.* Seine-et-Oise, circa 1875.
Édouard André.
[André, *L'art des jardins.* Courtesy Dumbarton Oaks, Washington, D.C.]

1-4 THE SECOND EMPIRE JARDIN PAYSAGER.
[Duchêne, *Les jardins de l'avenir*]

1-2

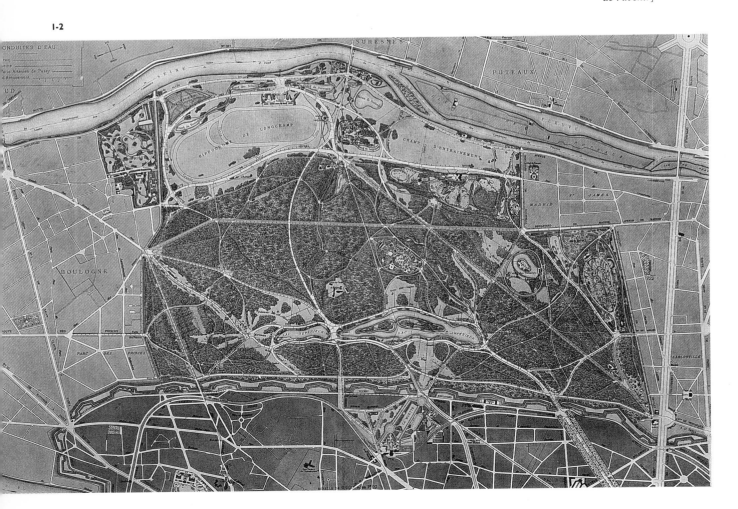

the naturalism of the *paysager* were neverthe-less rather smooth. Foreign influences which shaped gardens at the end of the eighteenth century were already manifest by 1709. That year Antoine Dezallier d'Argenville, in his trea-tise *La théorie et la pratique du jardinage*, recorded the shift from the elaborate to the simple and more natural, from the *parterres de broderie* to the *parterres à l'anglaise*.[1] Like this stylistic overlap, the renewed formalism of the late nineteenth century reacted against, but also drew obliquely from, the landscape style that had dominated the preceding period. Rarely, in fact, had there been a clear distinc-tion between the approaches; more typically, the design character resulted from a borrowing of elements, forms, and orders from various styles.

The influence of England was still evident when Napoléon III—returned from exile—commissioned a series of urban open spaces modeled after the London park system. The terrain of the Bois de Boulogne was graded and replanted, and its system of rectilinear allées altered to form a *parc paysager*. Begun in 1852 under the supervision of the engineer Louis-Sulpice Varé, the construction was completed by Jean-Charles-Adolphe Alphand and Pierre Barillet-Deschamps in 1858.[2] Alphand, engi-neer and director of parks for the city of Paris, dominated the urban public landscape of the late nineteenth century. Under his direction Barillet-Deschamps and Édouard André designed the Bois de Vincennes between 1860 and 1865, the new parc Monceau in 1861, the Buttes-Chaumont between 1864 and 1867, and the parc Montsouris shortly thereafter. The renowned Second Empire parks, squares, and promenades marked the transformation of the Anglo-Chinese style into a simplified *style pay-sager*, or landscape style.[3] The sophistication of garden design, however, did not equal its growing popularity and horticultural achieve-ments, and innumerable pastiches of nature appeared at the same time as the grand urban parks. [Plate I]

In an attempt to codify landscape design prin-ciples, Édouard André wrote *L'art des jardins: Traité général de la composition des parcs et jardins,* published in 1879. An advocate of a *style composite,* in which the jardin paysager followed a jardin régulier as an ideal expres-sion of the transition from architecture to nature, André acknowledged the legacy of the formal tradition, previously dismissed.[4] Both Alphand and André foresaw the decline of the

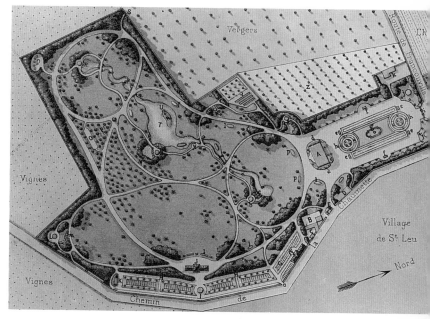

1-3

3

1-4

I-5 CHÂTEAU DE VOISINS.
TERRACES AND
PARTERRES FOR THE
COMTE DE FELS.
AERIAL VIEW.
Yvelines, 1919.
[Duchêne, *Les jardins
de l'avenir*]

I-6 CHAMPS-SUR-MARNE.
PARTERRES DE BRODERIE.
Early eighteenth-
century design by
Claude Desgots,
restored by Henri and
Achille Duchêne in
1895.
[Photo: Marc Treib,
1988]

I-5

landscape style that eventually led to the regular irregularities of the *jardin horticole*. Similar to the excesses that preceded the fall of the regular style, the stereotypical curvilinear layouts, and precious displays of flowers and exotic species, provoked a return to the hard line. Citing the historian Ludovic Vitet, André reasserted that gardens in which nature outgrew poetry, where freedom forbade order, would inevitably lead to an exclusive counterrevolution, thus replacing a gracious imitation of nature with the "monotonous and irksome prisons of the old symmetrical garden."[5]

As the Third Republic followed the Second Empire, the first tangible manifestations of a return to the regular garden appeared. Henri and Achille Duchêne redrew the erased parterres of the jardins à la française in direct opposition to the previous mannerism of floral fireworks on mottled lawns.[6] Answering the "interesting question" of restorations raised by Édouard André, the Duchênes proceeded to re-create André Le Nôtre's heritage, mixing "art and science in the happiest of proportions," possessing and respecting garden history, as well as a "deep architectural knowledge and a long practice of horticultural matters."[7] Although such projects may appear as distant from the small regular gardens of the 1920s as they were from their picturesque predecessors, these essays illustrated the French equation of formalism with its landscape heritage; in fact, such gardens reflected the decorative dimension and preceded André Vera's argument for a modern architectural garden.

Initiated by Duchêne père, the restoration of formal estate design is instead usually associated with his son, Achille, who joined the firm in 1878 and ensured the lineage of a tradition in landscape design that spanned nearly a century.[8] Dismissing the style composite favored by André as a hybrid "possessing none of the qualities of either of its parents," Duchêne nevertheless set his formal parterres within the broader scheme of the parc paysager.[9] He sought an "undisrupted harmony" in the flow from a geometric pool to a picturesque river; using this sequence to link the residence to the forest, he appeared to combine the syntax of both the regular and landscape styles.[10]

Achille Duchêne insisted on distinguishing his restorations from designs of the past, sometimes produced by "mere gardeners," and considered his compositions "more authentic than those of old days."[11] Although refined, the new schemes did re-create certain mistakes

1-6

1-7

intended to recapture the spirit of an earlier period. If decorative anachronisms needed to be avoided, tradition was to be kept alive by the renewal of its expressions, wrote Duchêne.[12] The domain of Champs-sur-Marne, east of Paris, is a manifestation of such an interpretation of history and its evolution. To adapt the morphology of an early eighteenth-century site design to contemporary use, the terrain was manipulated so that its *parti* could be viewed from the ground-floor terrace, the locus of modern living, rather than from the higher viewpoint of the *piano nobile* alone.

A similar interpretation was the garden for the château de Voisins that the comte de Fels commissioned from Achille Duchêne. The intention was to plan the estate in the French manner, had the revolution not interrupted the course of history and, by extension, the evolution of garden design. The count's demand for a formal and intellectual rather than romantic and emotional garden was answered with grounds where the logic and sense of French formality were mirrored in the parterres surrounding the house, albeit intimately linked to a park executed in the naturalistic fashion of the 1750s.[13]

Those remnants of Second Empire tradition that had influenced the designs of Henri Duchêne were corrected in the orthodoxy of the parterres in Achille Duchêne's subsequent renovation. At Vaux, for example, the statues that had embellished frontal stretches of lawn outlined with flowers were replaced by filigreed designs of boxwood and gravel. Rejecting the softer jardin composite for its ambiguity, he mastered the knowledge of modern horticulture without resorting to the "nursery sampling" of contemporary landscape architects.[14] The formal garden became an extension of interior decoration and architecture into the fields. The composition and axes incised on the land reflected those of the facade and allowed for perspectival distortion and the overlapping of planes. The "method of procedure was above all technical, as in the architectural and decorative part, everything is foreseen and calculated," recalled Duchêne.[15] Planned according to an axial system, elements such as parterres, *tapis verts*, pools of water, and canals were treated as graphic motifs within the general tableau; the degree of definition and sophistication increased near the residence. The immediate surroundings of the house, as out-of-door extensions of the reception rooms, flaunted utter decorative sumptuousness.

These splendid evocations of French formal rigor eventually evolved into simpler schemes in response to the decline in land ownership and patronage for garden art at the turn of the century. If parterres are still fashionable, Duchêne laconically commented, expenditures are tighter and detailed estimates have to be met.[16] A new type of garden of hard lines and perfect scale, which he termed *jardin d'architecture,* should clearly express its function as well as reflect the character and psychology of the owner. In addition to smaller urban compositions and roof terraces for apartment buildings, this supposedly more modest category nonetheless included the gardens for such estates as Blenheim and Voisins and the Renaissance parterres for the château de Chambord.

Achille Duchêne accused the automobile, airplane, telephone, radio, and cinema of playing a fateful role in the evolution of garden design as they propelled postwar France into a speed-crazed and transient society. Democratization and simplification appeared to exert an unfortunate leveling that, in Duchêne's mind, erased all nuances of elegance and signs of luxury. Lamenting the increasing rarity of new designs for private parks and the concurrent dismemberment of large estates, he saw the city rooftops covered with soot "as if to mourn the vanished gardens."[17]

In an attempt to answer the demand for smaller gardens, Duchêne stressed simplicity and functionalism. His brand of turn-of-the-century "architectural garden" was renamed "garden of tomorrow."[18] He redistributed the decorative motifs of the transformed leisure gardens to accommodate programmed activities, which he saw as characteristic of the new era: sheared hedges now enclosed a green theater; pools of water were modified to suit swimming; rooms were designated for resting and dancing; and purely ornamental beds were adapted to provide cut flowers. As he observed the decay of the large French estates and private parks, he addressed changes in the demands of the ruling class by designing smaller gardens with smaller means, justifying their formality and decoration with allusion to function. However conciliatory his condensed designs at first appeared, Duchêne's proposed activities remained elitist and his plans continued to rely heavily on symmetry. The relaxation in strength and elegance of his sobered compositions appeared to generate a formulaic plan. In fact, the "garden for the residence of an athletic family" was almost

1-7 VAUX-LE-VICOMTE. The parterres as renovated by Henri Duchêne in 1897 and by Achille Duchêne in 1910. [Association Henri et Achille Duchêne]

1-8 CITY GARDEN FOR A SOCIALITE. New York, 1910 [Duchêne, *Les jardins de l'avenir*]

1-8

1-9 "GARDEN FOR THE RESIDENCE OF AN ATHLETIC FAMILY"; "GARDEN FOR FLOWERS AND DOMESTIC HORTICULTURE." PLANS. Circa 1925. [Duchêne, *Les jardins de l'avenir*]

1-10
1-11 "GARDEN FOR THE RESIDENCE OF AN ATHLETIC FAMILY"; "GARDEN FOR FLOWERS AND DOMESTIC HORTICULTURE." PERSPECTIVE VIEWS. Circa 1925. [*Jardins d'aujourd'hui*]

1-12 MAISON DE VIE SOCIALE. Diagram illustrating the aims and services provided. Circa 1925. [Duchêne, *Les jardins de l'avenir*]

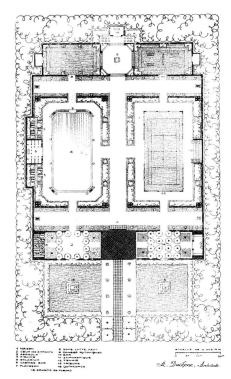

1-9   1-10

1-11

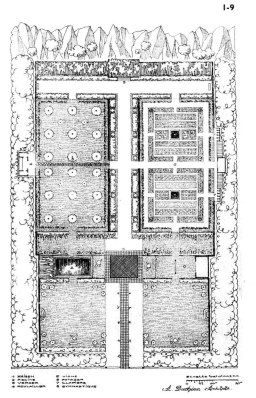

La Maison

interchangeable with the plan of a "garden for flowers and domestic horticulture": these two schemes, similar in proportion and line, differed only in that the orchard and flower beds replaced the swimming pool and tennis court.[19]

Achille Duchêne's "social aesthetics" came to full form with the economic crisis of the 1930s and extended beyond the realm of garden design. His "Maison de vie sociale," whose "aims and services" he illustrated in *Les jardins de l'avenir* of 1935, was a utopian system organized to preserve the individual's physical and moral integrity through education and leisure.[20] As the prospect of private patrons vanished, Duchêne turned his attention—at least in projects—toward communities; the scale of such landscapes, he believed, implied the availability of powerful resources and would result in grandiose designs.[21]

Duchêne's views of a future utopian society within a natural order were meritorious: they reflected a complete reversal of aim and his genuine search for a definition of the modern (private as well as public) landscape, a structured landscape that would sustain both physical and educational necessities. Simple social values overlaid aesthetic ones in the project for a family of artists, complete with a bird garden for decorative purposes and a bee garden whose colonies provided a sociological model and thus invited contemplation. However graciously Achille Duchêne followed or even instigated the shift to a modern twentieth-century garden, his solutions remained tinged by reduction rather than by innovation. A systematic symmetry and a rigid vocabulary revealed his difficulty in translating the sumptuous scale of private estates and their intricate parterres de broderie into a concise urban modern garden. In returning to past tradition, Henri and Achille Duchêne—ironically perhaps—had set the stage for and prompted one of the most radical movements in modern garden design. Their manipulation of a formal tendency into an elegant revival of the jardin à la française also reassessed the role of the garden as a complement to the decorative scheme of the house rather than as grounds for sentimental or exotic experience. But this translation of *Grand Siècle* vocabulary failed to evolve into a true transformation. For Duchêne, the unfortunate leveling of a new art-consuming society meant reducing gardens to the status of accessory goods, susceptible to the rapid shifts of fashion. Considering the art of

the garden to be redeemable only by a social perspective, he failed to adjust to the renewed formalism and the spur of inventiveness that marked the gardens of the 1920s and 1930s. He dismissed these compositions as "illogical, bizarre, curious and puerile."[22] In spite of such prejudice, however, his prediction of their being merely a passing fashion was correct: within a decade virtually all these modernist designs had vanished.

As revised by the Duchênes, the syntax of the traditional regular garden suggested a renewed formalism that found its expression in the arts of the modern period rather than in the parterres of the past. This resurgence of geometric order prompted the design of gardens that would achieve, however briefly or superficially, this long-sought confederation of the fine and decorative arts.

I-12

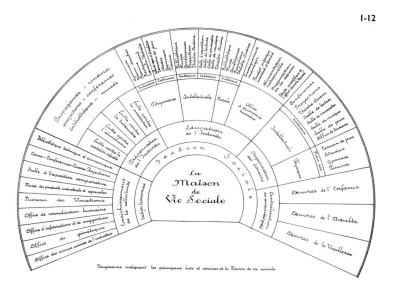

Diagramme indiquant les principaux buts et services de la Maison de vie sociale

J.C.N. FORESTIER
PLANTS & PLANNING

2-1

As a successor of Adolphe Alphand and a contemporary of Achille Duchêne, Jean-Claude Nicolas Forestier (1861–1930) held a strategic position within the formal debate that absorbed garden designers at the turn of the century. Forestier was undoubtedly a descendant of the Second Empire tradition of urban parks executed in the landscape fashion. In addition, his work paralleled the return to formalism found in Duchêne's restorations of aristocratic estates. But Forestier did not adhere entirely to either of these design tendencies. Eschewing either extreme, he drew from, and was the link between, the two primary styles: the *paysager* and the *régulier*. In his position as administrator as well as designer, he dominated the evolution of the garden in France from the *jardin horticole* of the Second Empire to the cubistic/modernist exercises of the 1920s.

Like Duchêne, Forestier designed many private gardens for an aristocratic clientele. He rehabilitated extensive historic landscapes such as Le Nôtre's parc de Sceaux, while at the same

2-1 BAGATELLE.
THE IRIS GARDEN.
Paris, circa 1906.
J.C.N. Forestier.
[Photo: Marc Treib,
1992]

time tackling the problems and realities of a garden reduced in both scale and refinement. Forestier conceived of the garden as more than just a luxurious work of art. To play a beneficial social and aesthetic role, the garden had to address the definite needs of the client and user. To prove its validity as a "necessary annex to the factory as well as to the château," he designed a garden for the Sant Adrià de Besòs thermal power station near Barcelona.[1] The strong resemblance of this plan to his gardens for the sultan in Casablanca revealed that Forestier derived the morphology of his designs from a consideration of climate and its corresponding plant palette rather than from strict adaptation to function. Instead of creating a new landscape idiom for a different use, he relied upon a sober formality to remedy the ugliness of the industrial surroundings. In spite of Forestier's lofty intentions, the Sant Adrià project ultimately failed to define a new industrial garden. Its design was, in fact, a typical Mediterranean scheme for an aristocratic estate, reduced in scale and detail and reapplied to the semipublic spaces of a shoreline factory.

Unlike Achille Duchêne, who never mastered the shift from private estate to urban or social garden, Forestier did succeed in implementing his theories in various urban planning schemes. Duchêne's public landscape involved a revision and anticipation of a new social order that reflected his highly structured "Maison de vie sociale" of the future, a vision that sometimes bordered on the utopian.[2] The more pragmatic and politically astute Forestier, on the other hand, always followed a realistic program; climatic zone and context determined the specific forms of realization. Successfully translating his inheritance of Alphand's public parks into a modern — although not ground-breaking — vocabulary, Forestier quietly addressed the transformation of society.

Forestier considered that the modern garden, necessarily limited in size by the contemporary condition, could afford neither the great axial perspectives of the *jardin à la française* nor the ampleness of the naturalistic English park.[3] Although he acknowledged as positive the attempts of contemporary landscape architects like Duchêne to return to the design tradition of Le Nôtre, Forestier explored the reformation of garden design in a different manner. At first sight it appears that Forestier redefined the modern landscape through a merely formal transformation, but in fact he considered the

new discoveries in horticulture as a constant factor and an essential driving force in his designs. "On the large estates of olden days, reverent restorations were often well done," he admitted, "[but] they were ill adapted to the display of thousands of magnificent new plants created by clever horticulturists."[4]

Schooled within the Alphand tradition, Forestier could not conclusively repudiate the Second Empire jardin horticole in spite of its excessive "curvilinear layouts," "insipid undulating lawns," and tiresome "punctuations of circular or oval flower beds."[5] [Plate I] He dismissed peremptory stands regarding any single design vocabulary; a design language, he argued, ought to be derived only from the context of a particular project. Many people of taste have obstinately rejected the past vogue for wavy contours, he wrote in his book on the use of turf, almost as an apology. When used properly, undulating lawns should be considered an appropriate and effective design element for very large gardens, even if to some people there are negative connotations. He noted that they create "pleasant light effects" and can be used "to screen sandy areas and the limits of the garden from sight, to emphasize clumps of vegetation on higher grounds, to increase the apparent extent of lawns and to bring variety to flat sites."[6] Forestier refuted a design style and a plant palette determined by the fashion of the period. In his use of traditional elements, he stressed evolution over revolution, and as a complement to Humphry Repton's precept that "good taste will make fashion subservient to good sense," Forestier resorted to taste and feeling to give reason to things that escaped rules.[7] For its simplicity, he favored the regular over the landscape style but drew as well from the romantic garden and its infatuation with horticulture.

Educated as an engineer and a sylviculturist, Forestier joined the administration of the Paris Parks and Promenades in 1887, four years prior to Alphand's death.[8] He became superintendent (*conservateur*) of the Bois de Vincennes in 1889, and of the Bois de Boulogne thereafter; he assumed the direction of the western sector of the Paris Promenades in 1898. Having encouraged the city of Paris in 1905 to purchase Bagatelle, thus preventing subdivision, Forestier was subsequently favored with the administration and transformation of its gardens.[9]

The Anglo-exotic grounds of Bagatelle bore the marks of many political regimes and stylistic

2-2 PROJECT FOR A
THERMAL POWER
STATION.
PLAN AND SECTION.
Sant Adrià de Besòs,
1916. J.C.N. Forestier.
[Forestier, *Gardens*]

2-3 PATIO DE LOS
2-4 CUPRESOS,
GENERALIFE,
GRANADA, AND
GENERALIFE SECTION
OF MONTJUÏC,
BARCELONA.
The Andalusian
courtyard is barely
modified to
accommodate a
secluded pool on the
Barcelona hillside. 1918.
J.C.N. Forestier
[Forestier, *Gardens*]

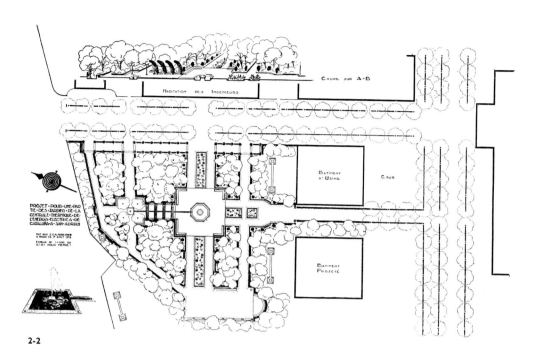

2-2

2-3

2-4

trends.[10] Designed by Thomas Blaikie around 1780, the gardens featured, among other curiosities, a house made of roots and stones for a resident philosopher, a pavilion in the Indian style, and a tomb for a pharaoh.[11] Following the extensive alterations to the Bois de Boulogne between 1853 and 1858, Bagatelle had been reshaped by Louis-Sulpice Varé with a Second Empire imprint that diluted the effect and reduced the number of *fabriques* by casting them into a broader network of elliptical paths and undulating lawns.[12]

In his subsequent renovation of Bagatelle into a public garden, Forestier did not dismantle its anglicized frame; rather, he overlaid it with a sober French formality. Although he believed that the source of artistic beauty lay in the understanding of rhythm, Forestier did not allow abstract aesthetic ideas or the rigor of drawing to override nature. Design schemes needed to remain supple so that plants can serve functions different from those of a pillar or a wall.[13] His ideal landscape followed an "architectonic sketch" (*canevas architectonique*), in which he manipulated nature like a raw material. Forestier sought a garden as a work of art: a tableau that belonged not to nature but to the immediate surroundings of the house. A graphic composition, the archetypical garden was simply traced. The somber masses of high vegetation, the colored flats, the heavy lines of hedges, and the moiré of the short-napped lawns were balanced along its principal axes.[14]

At Bagatelle, Forestier composed a formal rose garden, a garden for perennials, and yet another for Japanese irises. The perennial garden was not merely a selection of specimens arranged according to scientific classification but a design determined by plant color and structure, grouped to paint an aesthetically pleasing picture. The tableau Forestier realized at Bagatelle has been frequently, if simplistically, described as impressionistic. Forestier admired the garden of Claude Monet at Giverny, which he termed "a spot of ravishing beauty," although it followed no particular school of design.[15] Monet's collection of nympheas also appeared to share certain features with the water garden at Bagatelle, and perhaps the painter influenced the conception of color in the plantings of Forestier, the *jardinier-artiste.*[16]

In the introduction to *Les promenades de Paris,* the *ingénieur-jardinier* Adolphe Alphand had already renewed the call for a garden as a

work of art brushed on nature's raw canvas.[17] The human order, he wrote, was inlaid within the generating lines of the landscape to correct the imperfect aspects of nature, even if these improvements were not at first perceived by the human eye.[18] Alphand's idealized picture of a calculated casualness differed considerably from the garden sought by his successor. Forestier, in fact, wove the vegetal fabric within an architectonic frame, providing, as a result, a composition of "ordered natural things" through which one could still read its precise structure.[19]

Chromatic as well as graphic, the designs that Forestier plotted in his ink sketches or on the site unfolded poetic tales of garden history. While traveling along the Mediterranean rim, he explored the possibilities of that "climate friendly to the orange blossom" which spanned the French Riviera, southern Spain, southern Italy, and northern Africa.[20] In his notebook on gardens entitled *Jardins,* published in 1920, he dissected the influence of the Persian paradise garden into two main streams: the Greco-Roman and the North African–Spanish, both of which he would employ in his designs.[21] In Morocco, he drew a planning report for open spaces and public gardens and designed a project for the sultan's estate in Casablanca.[22] From the Moorish garden Forestier acquired a hierarchical ordering system, creating the rigor and exactness of a whole within which flowers and shrubs were casually arranged. He then overlaid this structure of line and color with the olfactory dimension. Chroma and fragrance, in fact, became principal criteria for his selection of plants. Juxtaposing striking contrasts in hues and textures, he added horticultural depth to the formal lines of the design. A vivid account from "Les jardins arabes en Andalousie" reveals the intensity of Forestier's floral vision:

> Near a very white wall are brought together the dark foliage of the fastigiate cypresses and the tender flowers of the peach, almond, and apricot trees, or the crimson blossoms of the bougainvillea, of red *Tecoma capensis;* around [the] dark spindles [of the cypresses], roses wind. . . . Anemones or tulips are framed by thick myrtles; oleanders spill over a white marble base and spread their fresh flowers against a whitewashed wall, on top of which bursts the light blue mass of *Plumbago capensis* or the deep and violent blue of ipomoeas (*I. leari* and *I. rubrocerulea*). Blue, so rarely found in flowers, is the dominant color for the tiles of the garden, and nothing equals its harmonious and sumptuous vividness against the

green foliage, the white walls and marble, and the brown-red bricks, or next to Bengali roses and white anthemis, adjacent to the dazzling pink of *Hibiscus rosa-sinensis*, the triumphal yellows of gazanias, chrysanthemums, sunflowers, Persian roses and the crimson or vermilion red of bougainvillea.[23]

One discerns from this text Forestier's search for a brilliant and rich visual effect in planting plans. But in addition vegetation provided a cyclical order through its fragrance, an integer of the garden's composition that evidenced the hours of the day and the changing seasons:

> [In winter,] the orange, jasmine and . . . mimosa are enveloped in a fragrant atmosphere. Then come the rose, honeysuckle, broom . . . Yerba de Santa Maria (*Tanacetum balsamita*), and *Mirabilis jalapa*. . . . On warm nights, little insignificant shrubs called "Dama di Noche" (*Cestrum nocturnum*) spread their triumphant and intense perfume of heliotrope; to this penetrating combination is added the peppery scent of carnations, perceived from far away in the warm air. In autumn, following the Dama di Noche come the sweet-smelling yellow flowers of the *Cestrum aurantiacum*, then those of the loquat . . . and the leaves and flowers of lavender! of rosemary! of lemon verbena![24]

Whether in a small theoretical garden project or a large public park, Forestier thoroughly exploited—as complementary elements—the relationship between the architectonic skeleton and the poetic aspect of each plant. With a knowledge that encompassed technology and horticulture as well as landscape composition, he was able to bridge the gap between the detail-oriented sensitivity of a jardinier-artiste and the expansive scale of the land engineer and city planner. Forestier defined himself as a man of cities, which in his view—without irony—meant a man who appreciated open air and trees. The garden or park functioned as a suture to the architectural blocks; the promenade, on the other hand, served as a link between the knots of the urban fabric.

In addition to his appointment as director of the Paris park system, he maintained a private practice and produced several urban planning schemes abroad.[25] Among these projects were the plan for the beautification of Buenos Aires, based on a system of parks and promenades, and an urban extension for Havana that attempted to alleviate congestion in the historic Spanish city while joining the central area with the suburbs. During the early decades of the century, Forestier also acted as a planning consultant for the cities of New York, Lisbon, Mexico, and Santo Domingo.

2-5 CHAMP-DE-MARS. VIEW FROM THE EIFFEL TOWER. Paris, 1908. Jean-Camille Formigé and J.C.N. Forestier. [Photo: Marc Treib, 1991]

2-5

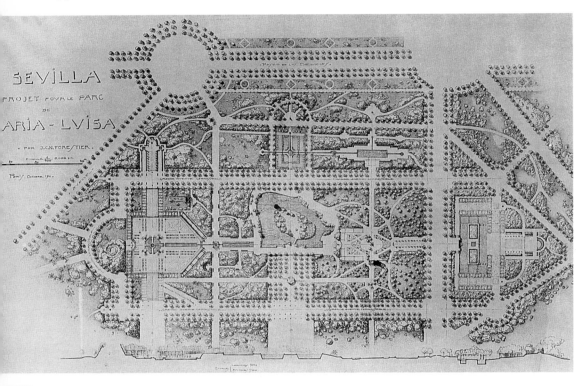

2-6 PARQUE DE MARÍA
LUISA. PLAN.
Seville, 1911.
J.C.N. Forestier.
[Gromort, *Jardins
d'Espagne*]

2-7 PARQUE DE MARÍA
2-8 LUISA.
THE NYMPHEA, OR
WATER, GARDEN AND
THE ROSE, OR SUNKEN,
GARDEN.
J.C.N. Forestier. Plans
measured and drawn
by G. F. Ingalls and
J. F. Whitney.
[Ingalls, "The Maria
Luisa Park in Seville"]

2-7

2-8

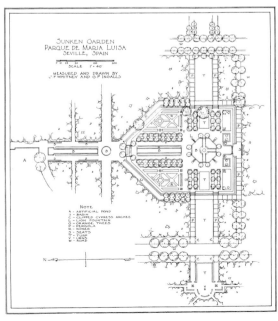

A didactic constant underlay several of Forestier's public projects. Since 1907, the formal rose garden at Bagatelle—site of an annual competition—had served as a ground for experimentation on new species. His introduction of new plants to Spain and the design of exposition grounds all manifested his interest in horticultural display and spatial perception.[26] In 1908, following his success at Bagatelle, Forestier transformed the Champ-de-Mars (the grounds surrounding the Eiffel Tower that since 1867 had served as the site for Universal Expositions) into a public park.[27] The French segment of his career closed with the planning of an academic village, the Cité universitaire, south of Paris. Here the individual national pavilions, hygienically arranged within a sports park, would form a virtual open-air museum of modern architecture.[28] Of Forestier's principal works, planning and garden design were perhaps most successfully combined in his contributions to several international expositions, whether as designer, as in Seville and Barcelona, or as coordinator and site planner in Paris in 1925.

THE GARDEN AS A GROUND FOR AN EXPOSITION

SEVILLE, 1914. To celebrate the close relationship and respective influences between Spain and the American continents, a Hispano-American Exposition was planned for Seville in 1914.[29] As municipal and regional showcases, international expositions often acted as the driving force for implementing major urban interventions. No exception to this trend, the Seville exposition generated a plan for extending the city that included the design of a large public park as one of its principal projects. Assigned a fraction of the San Telmo gardens, the park was to serve as both recreational open space for the city and grounds for the exposition. If the site boundaries for the Hispano-American event shifted slightly accordingly to urban politics and land expropriations, the Parque de María Luisa remained a constant within the development scheme. Located on land previously owned by the House of Montpensier, the park was named after María Luisa Fernanda de Borbón, duchesse de Montpensier and sister of Isabella II, queen of Spain. The plot lay adjacent to the Prado de San Sebastián—site of the Feria de Avril—and abutted the Guadalquivir River, symbolic link of the city with the Americas.[30] On 1 April 1911, Forestier, now celebrated for his designs at Bagatelle and the

Champ-de-Mars, was entrusted with the design of the Parque de María Luisa.

Although Forestier's project was always considered a central element of the master plan, it appears to have exerted little influence on the design of the contiguous exposition site. The plan of the architect-in-chief, Aníbal González, traced a sequence of knots along the Canal Alfonso XIII, spine of the city's new development. The land allotted for the exposition's temporary pavilions barely connected with the principal lines of the Parque de María Luisa. As a concession to Forestier's *parti*, the Royal Pavilion and the Plaza de Honor, bordered by the Palace of Fine Arts and the Palace of Industrial and Decorative Arts, were aligned with one of the park's secondary axes.[31]

The plan Forestier proposed in 1911 wrapped the existing irregular clumps of mature trees within a rigid structure of allées. The scheme thus seems to invert his design for the Champ-de-Mars, where the central and formal *tapis vert* was trimmed with curvilinear paths and informal plantings. The regularity of the María Luisa plan, in contrast, actually decreased toward the center. The picturesque ornamental lake floated as a central void within clumps of vegetation and mannerist irregularities; only its eastern side was straightened by the edge of the main axis.[32] This informal core was, in turn, framed by a system of rectilinear allées, a grid of kiosks, trees planted in quincunx, and geometrical parterres. Forestier regarded this formal structure as the proper backdrop for the monumentality of the permanent exposition buildings and a structure that still respected the existing planting.[33] Such genial contrast revealed Forestier's quest to unite poetry and architecture—as well as nature and art—by combining simplicity with ingenuity, rules with fantasy, and rigorous axes with *laisser-aller*.[34]

Although Forestier exported his theories and plans throughout the world, it is in Spain that one can fully measure the validity of his contribution to the development of the new formal garden.[35] In all his Andalusian designs, the French landscape architect recalled Moorish antecedents yet maintained a delicate balance between historical references and twentieth-century materials.[36] In the Parque de María Luisa, the Arabic-Andalusian tradition enriched the hierarchical axiality required by the gardens for the exposition. The poles of the north-south axis were anchored by two extremely architectonic spaces. Both the elaborate rose garden, at one end, and the nymphea garden, at the other, abounded with trellises, arbors, and raised or sunken tiled pools: all these structures reflected Forestier's endeavor to resist the inherent ephemerality of gardens.[37] [Plate II]

In designing the Parque de María Luisa, Forestier drew inspiration from the Generalife, the Alhambra, and the Alcázar.[38] Using elements of Moorish gardens, such as *azulejos*, sunken rills, and simple geometrical pools, Forestier attempted to reconcile the conflict between the intimacy of the enclosed private garden and the openness of an exposition park.[39] He solved the problem of increased scale by multiplication rather than by transformation. "To build a garden on a big scale, this square unit of design is multiplied, the . . . alleys are broadened and the shape of the pools is varied," stated Forestier.[40] The garden historian Georges Gromort, on the other hand, criticized Forestier's approach because the organization of the site was far too apparent. A sophisticated interpretation of the secluded space of Moorish gardens would have gained in detail what it lost in intimacy. Forestier's enlarged versions of these historical patterns lacked the complexity and the enclosure essential to keep the eye from wandering across the landscape, wrote Gromort, who felt that the experience of sequential discovery would have been more sympathetic to the tradition of walled spaces.[41]

The plan, with its regular structure of linked courtyards and basins intersecting with elliptical paths, repeated the play of elements of a hybrid semiformal French park. The Parque de María Luisa appeared Mediterranean primarily in its planting and materials, which ranged from lush vegetation and palm trees to Moorish patterns of ceramic tiles. The paths of the *hortus conclusus* were outlined with hedges of myrtle, veronica, euonymus, or box, and its beds appeared to be carelessly scattered with flowers and shrubs, thereby avoiding tiresome repetition.[42]

The validity of the Andalusian borrowings was verified when a series of *glorietas*—either monuments or benches—were later dedicated to the honor of regional authors.[43] Within these figurative homages the stroller could find the writer's oeuvre and use the park as an open-air library. Thus the French landscape architect provided the setting for a Spanish reading room in which the specificity of the word literally overlaid the evocation of the garden.

18

2-9

The Parque de María Luisa, a composite of French Second Empire and Sevillan styles, was inaugurated on 18 April 1914, the first day of the Feria. In 1922, in recognition of his valuable contribution to Seville's extension plan, Forestier was awarded the title of Director Técnico de los Jardines.

But Forestier's urban project for Seville was not limited to the design for the park. In 1924, he submitted a planning scheme for the temporary pavilions in the southern section of the Exposición Ibero-Americana.[44] Adopted by the governing committee, the design was later adapted by Aníbal González. Although the English-style vegetation of the old San Telmo gardens remained apparent in the regular structure of the Parque de María Luisa, the plan for the Ibero-American Exposition was a Beaux-Arts scheme set in an elongated rectangle of unrelenting formality. The rigid planting served as the articulating skeleton for a cruciform axial system rather than as a backdrop for the monumental spaces and architectonic elements. The only naturalistic touches were plantings along the edge of the site that disguised the irregular lot line. If Forestier's 1924 plan expressed few references to the garden tradition of Seville, his perspective view further denied any interpretation of Spanish, Moorish, or Mudéjar precedents. It illustrated, instead, an international formalism in response to the exhibition and its variegated architecture. More ambitious, if not more original, than the Parque de María Luisa, the exposition design promulgated a model of urban planning in which vegetation functioned as a structural matrix rather than as mere infill between buildings.

The Ibero-Americana fair was inaugurated on 9 May 1929, fifteen years after the dedication of Forestier's work on the Parque de María Luisa. The success of the park, which was immediately praised and widely celebrated as a superb example of both regional and modern urban landscape architecture, led Forestier north to another Spanish public commission — in Barcelona.

2-9 PARQUE DE MARÍA LUISA.
THE FOUNTAIN OF THE LIONS NEXT TO THE ROSE GARDEN.
J.C.N. Forestier.
[Gromort, *Jardins d'Espagne*]

2-10 PROJECT FOR THE IBERO-AMERICANA EXPOSITION.
Seville, 1924.
J.C.N. Forestier.
[Hemeroteca Municipal, Seville]

2-10

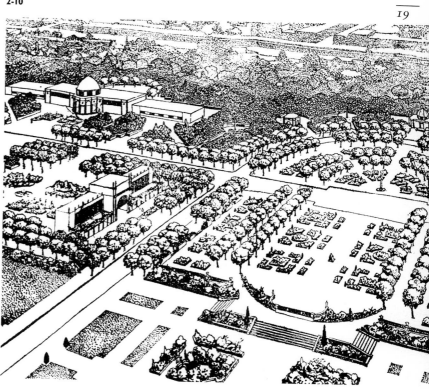

2-11 GARDEN FOR THE
CASA DEL REY MORO.
PLAN.
Ronda, 1912.
J.C.N. Forestier.
[Gromort, *Jardins d'Espagne*]

2-12 GARDEN FOR THE
CASA DEL REY MORO.
AERIAL VIEW.
J.C.N. Forestier.
[Gromort, *Jardins d'Espagne*]

A GARDEN TERRACE TO THE CITY

BARCELONA, 1915–1923. On 19 May 1929, almost simultaneously with the Ibero-Americana opening celebration, the Barcelona Exposition was inaugurated. Its committee, established two decades earlier in 1907, had initially planned the event to take place in 1914, but the project was successively postponed because of economic and political difficulties.[45] Originally conceived as a universal exposition in tribute to Catalan commercial and industrial growth, it was revived in 1917 and divided into two main sections: the Exposició Internacional d'Indústries Elèctriques and the General Espanyola.[46] Its site, the hill of Montjuïc, provided Barcelona with an opportunity to reorient itself toward the developing western sector of the city.[47] For the future network of trams, train lines, and funiculars, Montjuïc and the Plaça d'Espanya would act as an urban and circulation node. A park was developed on Montjuïc in an attempt to alleviate the severe lack of green open space within the city.

Having attained recognition in Andalusia with the garden for La Casa del Rey Moro in Ronda and the Parque de María Luisa in Seville, Forestier realized several projects in Catalonia. His designs for Barcelona included the Ferrer-Güell estate, the grounds of the Hotel del Lléo, the garden for the marquès d'Alella, and the museum square in the Parc de la Ciutadella.[48] In addition, the industrialist-politician Francesc Cambó invested Forestier with his major public statement in Barcelona: the landscape design of the exposition grounds on Montjuïc.[49]

Like the Seville expansion plan and exposition project, the Monjuïc park and gardens were put forward as an incentive for developing the system of open space within the city. Forestier's impact on Barcelona extended beyond his design for these gardens, however. His presence coincided with the interurban development plan (Pla d'enllaços) of 1917; his intervention appeared to have influenced the proportion of open spaces within the plan; and his administrative status in the Paris park system prompted the transformation in 1918 of the old Servei de Jardins into its present structure of Direcció de Parcs Públics.[50] Furthermore, Forestier was credited with founding in Barcelona the first Spanish school of horticulture.

The architect Josep Amargós i Samaranch had proposed the initial planning project for the hill of Montjuïc in 1894, although construction did not begin until 1915.[51] Responsible for the initial earthworks and circulation infrastruc-

2-12

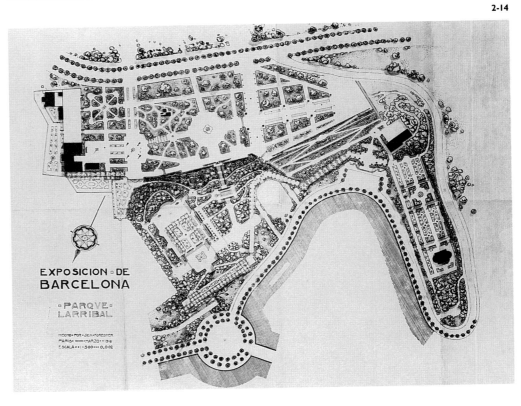

ture, he died in 1918, leaving Forestier in charge of the master planning for the park and gardens. The latter closely collaborated with the architects Josep Puig i Cadafalch and Nicolau Maria Rubió i Tudurí until 1923, at which time General Primo de Rivera came to power and Cadafalch resigned.

If Montjuïc was intended to serve a similar purpose as the Parque de María Luisa, their schemes were diametrically opposed. Although acknowledging its surrounding urban structure, the Seville project could function equally well as a self-sustained environment. A centripetal promenade in form, the park derived its character from plantings, architectonic spaces, or a particular tile design. The Parque de María Luisa thus acquired through elegant details and hierarchical sequences what the Montjuïc design extracted from dramatic scenery and rugged topography. The program for the Barcelona exposition called for a series of monumental pavilions and processions that subjugated the morphology of the site. Forestier displayed his command of hillside engineering in the exposition projects for the Parc Laribal, the gardens of Miramar, and the amphitheater. These landscape designs appeared more as natural protrusions, merely outlined by a mineral edge, than as rigidly manipulated grades.⁵² Terraces, stairs, or promenades traced the contours of the land and projected outward to the harbor or the city. "Views—wide panoramas or small pictures close at hand—demand either a foreground or a frame which hold important roles in the garden background," Forestier wrote.⁵³ On Montjuïc he provided those frames and reinforced the axes with trees set in an architectonic space. Girdling the hillside, these stairs, terraces, and allées, lined with trees or covered by trelliswork and punctuated by pavilions, formed an architectural promenade that revealed and addressed the surrounding panorama. [Plate III]

Although Forestier relied on a consistent vocabulary throughout his career—fountains and pools, pergolas and roses—only few Andalusian traces tinted his design for Montjuïc. For the section of the Parc Laribal he termed the Generalife, Forestier designed a courtyard "inspired" by the Patio de los Cupressos at the Generalife in Granada. Approaching plagiarism, Forestier minimally modified his sketch of the original Court of the Cypresses and appropriated its boxwood hedges, pools, and water jets. As a concession

2-13 MIRAMAR GARDENS. AERIAL VIEW OF SECOND PROJECT. Montjuïc, Barcelona, circa 1923. Nicolau Rubió after J.C.N. Forestier. [*Quaderns d'Arquitectura i Urbanisme*, March–April 1982]

2-14 PARC LARIBAL. PLAN. Montjuïc, 1916. J.C.N. Forestier. [Administrative Archives, Barcelona]

2-15 GARDEN FOR JOSEPH GUY. PERSPECTIVE. Béziers, 1918. J.C.N. Forestier. [Forestier, *Gardens*]

J.C.N. FORESTIER: PLANTS & PLANNING

23

2-15

2-16 GARDEN FOR THE
HOTEL DEL LLÉO.
PERSPECTIVE, DETAIL.
Barcelona, 1919.
J.C.N. Forestier.
[Forestier, *Gardens*]

to contextualism, he replaced the white stuccoed enclosure with low walls of rough stone used throughout the Montjuïc design. A palisade of tall cypresses ensured seclusion. Certain of the architectural elements of the Parque de María Luisa—such as a pergola supported by brick pillars—also appeared in the gardens of Montjuïc. The design of the hill evoked a more western-European influence, however; its terraced elevations recalling Italian Renaissance gardens, and its formal parterres citing French counterparts rather than Moorish predecessors. In Montjuïc, nature either suggested a pattern or served as a mass against which to set the architectonic structures. In the Parque de María Luisa, on the other hand, vegetation outgrew and softened the architectonic canvas and the rigor of its composition. Forestier shifted the character of his design from Moorish to Latin in Barcelona, trading the azulejos for stone, the quiet sunken rill for the bursting fountain, the clipped hedge for a classical procession of cypress, and the palm tree for the obelisk. For this city that regarded itself as the "Paris of the South" rather than as part of the Iberian peninsula, Forestier restricted the presence of African-Spanish influence, instead exploiting the parallel, but distinct, Greco-Roman tradition.

Forestier never exported French gardens abroad, wrote Henri Prost; rather, he was an ambassador of knowledge extracted from the French tradition. In fact, he appeared to belong to the country in which he was operating at the time.[54] It is ironic, perhaps, that Forestier influenced the evolution of the French formal garden through his Spanish designs. The projects for Andalusia, Catalonia, or even southern France distilled the essence of Mediterranean character, while the archetypical layouts presented in his *Jardins* suggested a more northern Gallic temperament.[55] Apart from Moorish elements, the garden for the "climate friendly to the orange blossom" provided an alternate solution to the problem of formality on a reduced scale. The tension between architectonic lines and poetic vegetation was derived from the delicate balance characteristic of Forestier's southern designs, then transposed to other latitudes. Within this softened formality, the choice of plant material and architectonic forms suggested regional variation. Further north, the jardinier-artiste diluted his palette of colors and fragrances and traded ceramic tiles for sandstone. Although "not easy to fit into a rustic or picturesque garden, and

. . . not sufficiently big and elegant for the vast, exact, pruned and pompous estates of the seventeenth and eighteenth centuries," the pergola comfortably supported plants intended to grow naturally in a formal scheme. This structure was a ubiquitous element in Forestier's designs, but its density and ornament varied with function and climate: in the south, compact grapevines provided shade and fruit; at Bagatelle, the beams of the rose pergola were widely spaced, letting in the sunlight necessary to grow a tunnel of blossoms.[56] Garden structures, whether arbors, fountains, rills, or benches, figured as local idioms in the composition. As in the romantic garden, nature provided the backdrop; the character of the architectural elements, on the other hand, set the particular tone of the scene.

Forestier's attitude toward nature and structure is best revealed through his criticism of the "exactness" of certain landscape designs. The modern garden, he wrote, "returns to a clear, geometric composition without subjecting itself to the symmetrical severity and ample forms of our seventeenth century."[57] In his designs plants partially erased, rather than reinforced, the rigor of the plan. This play between the grace of the vine and the strict line of the post situated Forestier precisely at the juncture of the jardin à la française and the cubist/modernist garden.

26

GARDENS AT THE EXPOSITION

3-1

PARIS, 1925. For the American critic and landscape architect Fletcher Steele, the "real impetus to gardening in the new manner" was objectified in the forms of the Exposition Internationale des Arts Décoratifs et Industriels Modernes, held in Paris in 1925.[1] Gardens were displayed throughout the fair as part of an urban *ensemble;* while complementing the architectural submissions, they appeared as extensions of interior decoration. As supervisor of the newly created landscape section, J.C.N. Forestier induced designers to redefine the concept of the garden, and several landmark designs resulted directly from experimentation with materials such as concrete and glass, with media such as electric light, or with the manipulation of earth. The products of architects and designers, these gardens ranged from decorative patterns applied to the landscape to those truly innovative projects that would influence landscape architecture during the following decades, both in France and abroad. Even though significant gardens were created before and after the expo-

3-1 JARDIN DES OISEAUX. Exposition Internationale des Arts Décoratifs et Industriels Modernes, Paris, 1925. Albert Laprade. [Marrast, *1925 Jardins*]

3-2 FOUR COSTUMES FOR THE BALLET *LA CRÉATION DU MONDE.* 1923. Fernand Léger. [*Les ballets suédois*]

3-2

sition, the fair can be justly regarded as a
pivotal point in the development of the new
French landscape, both in its promulgating of
original designs and as an expression of the
stylistic, cultural, and social dichotomies
inherent to the 1920s and 1930s.

Participation in the exposition guaranteed
garden design a position under the aegis of
modernism, countering the stylistic inertia that
had plagued the profession throughout the late
nineteenth century. In this one instance landscape architecture joined the other arts at the
forefront of aesthetic development.

At the turn of the century, Henri and Achille
Duchêne had successfully engineered the
return to formal garden design. In the renewed
jardin régulier lay both France's past and
future—a theme that pervaded the writings of
André Vera. Landscape, like the products of
craft and industry, offered a propagandistic
vehicle for expressing Gallic culture. Resting
on the premises of stylistic originality and heritage, the resurgence of France's supremacy in
the decorative arts also hinged on issues of
economy and production.[2] The 1925 exposition was thus based upon France's fear of
losing its artistic hegemony and commercial
welfare; it was the outcome of a maturation
process that had extended over two decades
of French domestic and foreign politics.

The success achieved by the German decorators
at the 1910 Salon d'Automne constituted a
"foreign threat" that prompted René Guilleré's
alarmed report on the need for an international
decorative arts exposition.[3] His tale of France's
domination in matters of taste since the Middle
Ages—with a brief concession, of course, to the
Italian Renaissance—paralleled Vera's rejection
of internationalism and Jean-Charles Moreux's
argument for the *jardin à la française* as the
paragon of landscape design. Guilleré was also
well aware of the economic problems that
accompanied the loss of such cultural supremacy.[4] Other countries were surpassing France:
even in copying antiques. An original "modern" style was urgently needed to stimulate
trade.

On 12 July 1912, the House of Deputies
approved the proposal for an international
exposition to take place in Paris in 1916, to be
sponsored by the Ministry of Commerce. A
preliminary program was adapted from the
Turin exposition of 1902, which had required
original and aesthetically innovative submissions: the brief specified that participants

present "newly inspired works of a true originality" and cautioned that any "copy, imitation or counterfeit of any historical or past style" would be rejected.[5]

The outbreak of war between Germany and France on 28 July 1914 destroyed prospects for the exposition, and art turned instead to chauvinistic propaganda. André Vera's 1912 inducement to revere the artistic forms that he termed "the appanage of our race," and "the glory of our country" was sustained in the wartime effort to distinguish France's Latin heritage from pan-Germanic stock.[6] The Treaty of Versailles, signed on 28 June 1919, formalized the end of hostilities. As early as 29 July 1919, a decree revived the project for an exposition to be held in 1922.[7] Considering the burden of 1,350,000 deaths, 600,000 invalids, the devastated regions north and east of Paris, and a huge debt to Great Britain and the United States, France's interest in such an international exposition may have seemed ludicrous. Lulled by the illusion that war indemnities would be settled, however, the French lavishly budgeted expenses for reconstruction.

Reacting against the emotional anxieties of the *grande guerre,* French society celebrated the *années folles.* Traditional values disintegrated all through the 1920s, affecting entertainment, fashion, taste, and design. Short hair, short skirts, lascivious Argentinian tangos, the foreign beat of jazz, the nihilistic Dada or the absurd Surrealist movements, and the insouciant nouveaux riches collectively depicted an illusion of prosperity in opposition to the reality of economic and political stagnation. The state, despite the instability of its governments, strengthened its role in the field of artistic production and diverted popular dissatisfaction by offering the festive prospect of an international fair.[8]

The need for economic recovery was urgent, and although Guilleré had implied that the event should be more aesthetic than mercantile, an international exposition would also stimulate exports to countries with "swollen dollars and regilt pesos,"[9] in the area where France should have always excelled: taste and luxury.[10]

Initially conceived to demonstrate a never-lost dominance in the decorative arts, the 1925 exposition became a declaration of the country's postwar economic recovery. Slighting France's broadly advertised hospitality toward

its allies and enemies, Germany, financially impaired, declined the invitation to exhibit in Paris.[11] Discarding such economic "pretexts," critic Yvanhoé Rambosson attributed the rival's absence to the certainty of France's artistic superiority.[12] Nobly wounded, though victorious in the martial arts, France now intended to dominate the arts of peace.[13]

L'Exposition Internationale des Arts Décoratifs et Industriels Modernes became the official title recorded in the 1922 statutes.[14] Carefully plotted to respect the protocol of participating nations, the site plan for the exposition allotted the four most prominent sites to France's principal wartime allies: Great Britain, Italy, Belgium, and the United States. But Herbert Hoover, then Secretary of Commerce, declared the United States incompetent in the field of modern decorative arts and withdrew America's participation.[15] Twenty-one other countries accepted France's invitation, however.[16]

The exposition was inaugurated—although not yet completed—on 28 April 1925.[17] The French section, the foreign section, and the areas allotted to the gardens and circulation were to occupy equal thirds of the seventy-acre site.[18] The fair spanned the Seine on the pont Alexandre III, linking the esplanade des Invalides and a portion of the quai d'Orsay on the Left Bank to the Grand Palais, the Cours-la-Reine, and a portion of the cours Albert Ier on the opposite bank. This location was chosen for being "large enough to accommodate an important event and yet restricted enough to guarantee a rigorous standard of selection."[19] A perfect showcase for the French nation, this tract offered aesthetic quality, accessibility, and the availability of the existing Grand Palais, a vestige of the 1900 Universal Fair.[20] Although the location precluded permanent structures such as housing or a park, it nevertheless offered a green framework of existing trees.

The configuration of the site not only governed the planning and appearance of the architectural entries but also determined the nature of its gardens. The two main areas of the exposition appeared to belong to different climatic zones. Although the trees of the *quinconces* surrounded the esplanade, the central expanse provided no shade for the hapless visitor.[21] Little vegetation could be planted in asphalt and sand; furthermore, the structure of the railway station immediately beneath the esplanade could not support the amount of soil necessary to grow additional trees. On the opposite

bank, however, the triangle formed by the Cours-la-Reine, the avenue Alexandre III, and the Champs-Élysées resembled a park, with its allées of mature horse chestnuts. The alignment of trees dictated the configuration of the exposition gardens. The deep shade created by the lush plantings provided a pleasant relief from the summer heat, although it limited the selection of flowers.[22]

The exposition committee adopted a classification in which products were to be exhibited within five groups and further subdivided according to the materials used.[23] The principal divisions were:

Group I. Architecture
Group II. Furniture
Group III. Ornament
Group IV. Arts of the Theater, Street, and Garden
Group V. Education

All products were to be presented in real-life settings in which each element contributed toward creating a cohesive ensemble.[24] Architecture and gardens would function as paradigms of this modern environment. Open spaces, restaurants, cafés, and bakeries were arranged in clusters to exemplify idealized urban settings. Products that could not justify an individual pavilion were to be displayed in "harmonious ensembles" within galleries on the esplanade des Invalides or in the Grand Palais.[25]

Louis Bonnier, director of the agency governing architecture, parks, and gardens, and Charles Plumet, chief architect, implemented the master plan. The constructions on the esplanade presented the efforts of French commerce and were arranged to leave unobstructed the view of Mansart's dome of the Invalides. Georges Le Fèvre, a contemporary critic, vehemently deplored Plumet's master plan. He condemned the forty-two-foot height limitation—which only the chief architect was permitted to exceed—and the resulting field of low pavilions that transformed the esplanade into a seeming necropolis.[26] Condemnation of the plan was not universal, however. If Le Fèvre regretted Plumet's not having retired earlier from active practice, many critics praised the architect's ability to accommodate all the fair's utilities and program requirements while creating a "picturesquely ordered" plan.[27]

The exposition revealed the moral and social crisis pervading postwar France. Although advertising for the fair had promised beautiful

Exposition Internationale des Arts Décoratifs et Industriels Modernes. At the top is the dome of the Invalides; and at the other end, the pylons announcing the pont Alexandre III; the four towers by Charles Plumet are in between. [*La Revue de l'Art Ancien et Moderne,* 1924]

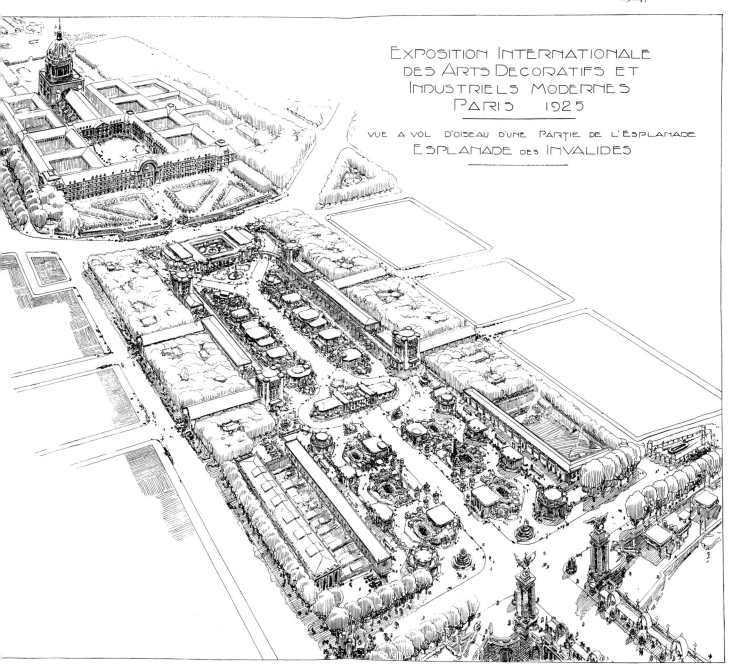

EXPOSITION INTERNATIONALE
DES ARTS DECORATIFS ET
INDUSTRIELS MODERNES
PARIS 1925

VUE A VOL D'OISEAU D'UNE PARTIE DE L'ESPLANADE

ESPLANADE DES INVALIDES

GARDENS AT THE EXPOSITION

31

yet cheap mass-produced objects, "for every carpenter's interior" there were "one hundred fashionable interiors for actresses."[28] Social or utilitarian art came wrapped in an art deco package of precious woods, marble, silver, and gold. Utility was buried beneath a "captivating debauch of exotic refinement but false luxury."[29]

As a vehicle for elevating quotidian taste, the exposition's success was limited. The noted fashion designer Paul Poiret moaned that the fair—open only from April to October—could not possibly reach its targeted audience, who abandoned Paris every summer. Years later he recalled that "at most one could see, between nine and eleven, a horde of concierges and clerks, attracted by the light, crowd and noise. I was wrong to count on a luxury clientele that flees these sorts of working-class pleasures; it just did not come."[30] But the rich *did* come. In fact, it was one of the gardens at the fair—the Jardin d'eau et de lumière—that prompted the vicomte de Noailles to commission the famous "cubist garden" for his villa in Hyères. With its Hôtel of a Rich Collector and Apartment of an Ambassador, the exposition embodied the clash between the impoverished middle strata and the nouveaux riches, whose affluence coincided with the indigence and suffering caused by the war and its aftermath.

3-4

3-5

To Le Corbusier, 1925 simultaneously marked the apotheosis and the decline of the decorative arts. "The almost hysterical rush of these last years toward quasi-orgiastic decor is simply the last spasm of a predictable death," he wrote.[31] And he compared the extravagance of such lavish materials with the decadence of postwar society.[32]

The eclecticism of the exposition revealed the plurality and latitude of *le style 1925*. Tendencies hovered among ascetic "architectural Lutheranism"[33] and its uncompromising attitude toward historical styles; neotraditionalism; and geometric patterns applied to decorative objects, fashion, interiors, and gardens. Guillaume Janneau described the designs of Süe et Mare, André Groult, and Émile Ruhlmann—neotraditionalist artists—as "a singular mixture of daring curiosity and selected culture," reflecting André Vera's call to maintain a national tradition that ideally would resume the ruptured lineage of design in the Louis-Philippe style.[34] The neotraditionalists considered themselves contemporary but not modern, explained Janneau, predicting that designers such as Francis Jourdain, Pierre

3-4 MODELS IN FRONT OF THE PAVILLON DU TOURISME. Representing the fashion house of Heim, they wear dresses by Sonia Delaunay; the car is painted with patterns derived from Delaunay fabric designs. [Courtesy Archives Famille Delaunay]

3-5 HALL OF A MINISTRY OF FINE ARTS. Michel Roux-Spitz. [*L'Architecte*, 1925]

3-6 THE BAKERY AT THE VILLAGE FRANÇAIS. A. Levard. [*L'Émulation*, February 1926]

3-6

Chareau, Pierre-Émile Legrain, Eileen Gray, and René Herbst, who sought a sharper definition of innovation, would adopt the epithet "modernes."[35] Disillusioned by the outcome of the 1925 exposition, these artists joined Robert Mallet-Stevens, Hélène Henry, and Raymond Templier to found the Union des Artistes Modernes (U.A.M.) in 1929. Their aim was to "endow XX° century man with a framework . . . capable of satisfying all material and intellectual requirements" and to promote the art of the everyday product.[36]

There was no lack of chauvinism in accounts of the Village français. The original title, Village moderne, had been changed because little evidence of modernity underlay its design.[37] Vaunted as an anthology of regional architecture, with "immutable necessities" and a "lovely multiplicity of aspects," the pseudovernacular agglomeration relied on rural imagery alone.[38] The fair was intended as a national event at which the French village and the regional pavilions—or on a more minor key, the colonial section—appeared as a tribute by the grateful mother country to its citizens: "*À ses citoyens, la Patrie.*"[39]

Whether because of their country of origin or the tenor of their ideas, certain artistic movements were conspicuous by their absence; for example, neither the German Bauhaus nor the Dutch De Stijl was represented. Le Corbusier and Pierre Jeanneret opposed the polite academicism and popular modernity that ruled the exposition. Named after the magazine published between 1920 and 1925 by Le Corbusier, Amédée Ozenfant, and Paul Dermée, the Pavillon de L'Esprit Nouveau was conceived as a polemic for standardization, in which every element of the living environment would be produced by industry, not by decorators. Circumventing the chief architects' demands, Le Corbusier and Jeanneret erected a single standard unit, a cell from the Immeuble-villa, which was itself an element from the greater Plan Voisin, named after the automobile and airplane manufacturer Gabriel Voisin.[40]

Le Corbusier's aesthetics of the standard object barely concealed his elitism, however: the exposition unit prominently featured a maid's room, for example.[41] Nor was it to be just anybody's house; on the contrary, it was "the apartment of an ordinary man concerned with well-being and beauty."[42] Although their vocabularies were diametrically opposed, Le Corbusier and Ruhlmann, who was "forced to work for the rich because the rich never imitate

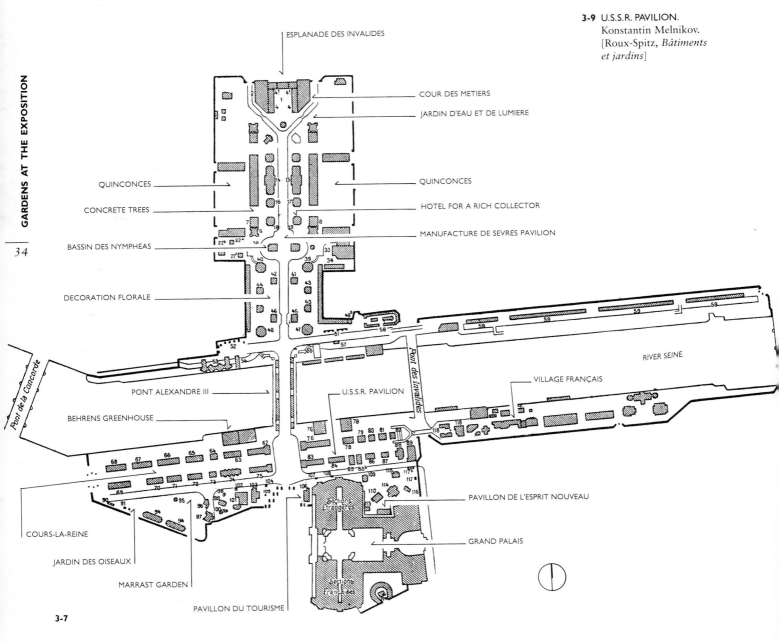

3-7 SITE PLAN OF THE
EXPOSITION.
[*Art et Décoration*,
May 1925]

3-8 PAVILLON DE L'ESPRIT
NOUVEAU.
Le Corbusier and
Pierre Jeanneret.
[Roux-Spitz, *Bâtiments
et jardins*]

3-9 U.S.S.R. PAVILION.
Konstantin Melnikov.
[Roux-Spitz, *Bâtiments
et jardins*]

ESPLANADE DES INVALIDES

COUR DES METIERS

JARDIN D'EAU ET DE LUMIERE

QUINCONCES

QUINCONCES

CONCRETE TREES

HOTEL FOR A RICH COLLECTOR

MANUFACTURE DE SEVRES PAVILION

BASSIN DES NYMPHEAS

DECORATION FLORALE

RIVER SEINE

VILLAGE FRANÇAIS

PONT ALEXANDRE III

U.S.S.R. PAVILION

BEHRENS GREENHOUSE

Pont de la Concorde

Pont des Invalides

PAVILLON DE L'ESPRIT NOUVEAU

COURS-LA-REINE

Sections Etrangères

GRAND PALAIS

JARDIN DES OISEAUX

MARRAST GARDEN

Sections Françaises

PAVILLON DU TOURISME

3-7

the middle-classes," aimed at a similar clientele while educating the masses from the top down.[43] By enlarging the scope of housing toward urbanism, however, Le Corbusier addressed, in this time of reconstruction, issues broader than the mere decoration of a "hatbox."[44] Considered one of the only true modern architectural designs exhibited, the Pavillon de L'Esprit Nouveau stood oddly on a lawn, its garden forming a counterpoint to the overall regular style of the fair. Although most entries boasted ceramic patterns, brilliant horticultural varieties, architectonic layouts, and rigorous plans, Le Corbusier accompanied the *tracé régulateur* of his facade with an underdesigned naturalistic yard. For this rare opportunity, in which a designer was able to complement a housing unit with a garden, Le Corbusier opposed the sophistication of the pavilion with only a lame image of nature. The shrubs and sparse flowers were scattered irregularly on the lawn; their configuration did not compete with the elevation of the cell. Rather than extending the plan of the unit to the site, Le Corbusier instead brought the garden inside. The terrace repeated the same pattern. Forestier rendered the verdict: "Without apparent order, rustic shrubs and a few flowers were planted side by side."[45]

The Italian pavilion, designed by Armando Brasini, occupied a site of honor. Dwarfing the British structure, it was described as "a mausoleum built by a speculative builder in readiness for the death of a Fascist demagogue."[46] Adjacent to this utmost retrograde entry was the Soviet pavilion, announcing a new political order with a strikingly innovative architectural manifesto.

France had recognized the Soviet Union and established diplomatic relations with the new republic in October 1924. In these times of political and social unrest, however, the French fear of Bolshevism was likely to influence critiques of the Soviet offering. Set in opposition to the reactionary Italian arch, obsessed as it was with antique Rome, the U.S.S.R. pavilion—"original, and distinguished in character from the usual European architecture"—was intended to manifest this "new civilization unlike any that preceded it."[47] The architect, Konstantin Melnikov, diagonally sliced the glass parallelepiped with an oblique stairway, thereby achieving the effect of unstable equilibrium.[48] Most critics found the U.S.S.R. pavilion to embody an amusing or pathetic decor that reflected the flimsiness of the new political sys-

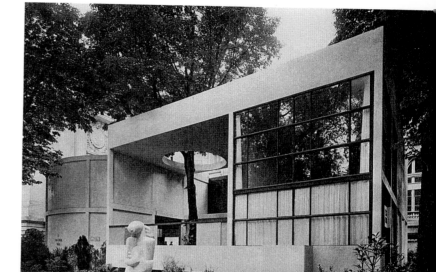

3-10

tem it represented: the oblique stairway was designed for cripples, they wrote, and would perform ideally as a set for a new Caligari. The pavilion as a whole stood, on the other hand, as a stylization of a guillotine, with "the jambs, the gallows, the basket indicated by the glass shell, and the blood shed all over."[49] In spite of these public disclaimers, the Soviet pavilion was not without admirers: Melnikov was awarded a Grand Prix by the jurors.[50]

Although Germany did not officially participate in the exposition, Peter Behrens designed a greenhouse overhanging the Seine, complementing the Austrian pavilion by Josef Hoffmann. From the outside, the greenhouse appeared to be a simple glass box filled with mist. The crystalline volume was outlined by sophisticated geometric patterns of slender mullions. The visitor who stepped inside experienced luxuriant subtropical vegetation, complete with fountain and pool, aquarium, and terrarium. As a contrast to the delicate prism structure, the plan and interior views revealed the rusticity of stone pavers and blocks.[51] With a predictable lack of objectivity, the French critics compared this elegant structure—which they termed an "engineering product"—to the Hoffmann pavilion in order to demonstrate what they considered the fundamental difference between German and Viennese designs: that Austrian grace was "far closer to Paris than to Germany."[52]

Despite a seemingly rigorous master plan, the pavilions as a group failed to create the desired urban ensemble. In his description of the hybrid architectural styles, a critic expressed gratitude for the existing trees:

> For it is the nature of exhibitions to be heterogeneous and composed of loose ends, and trees will cover a quantity of sins in a cloud of green. . . . There is a graceful bizarre Austrian building, all in white; a red-brick Dutch house fronted by a water garden; a rather successful Czechoslovakian extravaganza clothed in enormous crimson glazed tiles; a sweet Swedish temple which discovers with exquisite nicety a modern form within a traditional convention; . . . a Russian pavilion composed cubistically of plate glass and steel; a Polish building; a Swiss, a Turkish, a Yugo-Slav, and a Chinese. Picture them side by side, discovered to the eyes; then be grateful for the trees.[53]

Robert Mallet-Stevens's Pavillon du tourisme occupied a prominent place physically as well as in reviews. Located near the main entrance to the exposition, the tower of the pavilion dominated this portion of the grounds. The purity of the rectangular volume was enhanced by its contrast to the elaborate wrought-iron Porte d'honneur, the macabre ostentation of the Italian pavilion, and the bulk of the Grand Palais.

Throughout the exposition, Mallet-Stevens erected monuments to concrete—whether pavilion, kiosk, interior, or garden—intended to demonstrate the potential and inherent modernity of the material.[54] Although the Pavillon du tourisme was often dismissed as "an architecture of false technique," where method was the pretext instead of the means, Mallet-Stevens was also praised for his virtuoso manipulation of concrete, through which the "decorative effect was obtained by the accentuation of structural forms."[55] To some visitors, the tower planes suggested the stabilizers of a dirigible, while the interior bas-reliefs and glazed stripes represented the image of a world to be viewed at a speed of 80 miles per hour.[56]

Sculptors Jan and Joël Martel designed the dynamic bas-reliefs that represented contemporary means of transportation: the train, automobile, ocean liner, and airplane. Louis Barillet, a master glazier, rendered the principal cities of France in cubistic black-and-white stained glass; the furniture was designed by Pierre Chareau, and the floor pattern by Armand Nau. At night, the minimally rendered clock faces were illuminated, while the chimes played modern compositions by Francis Poulenc and Arthur Honegger.

Praised by Melnikov for his mastery of forms and construction techniques and his avoidance of the luxurious tendencies of modernity, Mallet-Stevens did not completely oppose the "dazzling Parisian chic," as the architect of the Soviet pavilion claimed.[57] Fashion models wearing dresses created by Sonia Delaunay appeared to confirm Mallet-Stevens's genial modernity when they posed for posterity in front of his Pavillon du tourisme and the garden he had designed on the esplanade.

3-11

3-12

3-13 THE SCULPTORS JAN AND JOËL MARTEL. [*L'Art et les Artistes*, 1935–36]

3-14 MODELS WEARING DRESSES OF SIMULTANEIST FABRICS BY SONIA DELAUNAY. Behind them is the garden by Robert Mallet-Stevens featuring concrete trees by Jan and Joël Martel. [Courtesy Archives Famille Delaunay]

3-13

3-14

INSTANT GARDENS

Robert Mallet-Stevens joined Jan and Joël Martel to create a garden on the eastern section of the esplanade des Invalides. More an experiment in a contemporary construction medium than a recuperation of the traditional garden, their design differed starkly from any landscape to which the visitor was accustomed. The extensive network of utilities and rail lines beneath the esplanade severely restricted the scope of any new planting.[58] To overcome these restrictions, the designers constructed two raised planters based upon a parti of positive and negative planes of lawn and flower beds. Forestier described the garden as a composition of "simple lines and precise volumes" achieved through "powerful reliefs, little color, but crisp contrasts."[59] Mallet-Stevens constructed as a nearly perfect exercise in "cut and fill" a modern and condensed version of the *boulingrin*, at the bottom of which spread sheets of flowers.[60] Four mature, perfectly identical trees sprung from these giant boxes edged with *Sempervivum*.[61] Austere and contemporary, the garden was planted with trees cast in concrete by Jan and Joël Martel. Planes of cement were attached to each cruciform trunk at an angle of approximately forty-five degrees, recalling on a smaller scale the clock tower of the Pavillon du tourisme. In their planar abstraction, the articulated masses suggested, rather than imitated, living foliage.

As a radical reinterpretation of French formal landscape design, this composition—captioned Jardin de l'habitation moderne in a periodical of the time—elicited both commentaries and critiques. To Ferdinand Bac, the concrete trees planted around "craters formed by artillery shells" represented a landscape from "an extraplanetary world."[62] The "antiphysics paroxysm" of such stylized vegetation was illustrated by the vignette of a puzzled gardener debating whether or not to water these "four heavily abstracted palm trees of poured concrete."[63] The contributions of the Mallet-Stevens and Martel team to the landscape of the exposition were less favorably termed "unfortunate" and "a joke"; the trees deserved to be mentioned, remarked one detractor, only "for their success in causing hilarity and bewilderment."[64] The press attributed several motives for their design. One garden journalist surmised that these "amusing trees of concrete in cubist lines" were surrogates for the original plantings that had died and could not be replaced in time.[65] Fletcher Steele provided

Devant l'arbre cubiste : l'arroseur perplexe. — *Croquis de J. Touchet.*

3-16

3-15

another justification for these unusual specimens:

> The original intent was to have real trees trained and clipped to predetermined shapes. It was impossible to get just what was required without more time and money than was available. . . . Half a dozen minds and hands working together produced the concrete trees, and unfortunately, at the same time, a norm by which unthinking people judged the whole effort as merely a trick on the part of artists to attract attention by eccentricity. As a matter of fact, with vines all over them, as was intended, the concrete trees were not one whit less absurd than a red cedar trunk with stubby branches sticking out in all directions to catch climbing roses which one can see in many a New England garden.[66]

While both accounts credited J.C.N. Forestier, supervisor of the garden section at the exposition, as their source, Forestier himself offered yet another explanation. Mallet-Stevens and the Martels, he wrote, were "very talented artists," and their quest for perfection had led to construction rather than to horticulture:[67]

> Four tall trees were required for this small garden, and we could not plant them in June; furthermore, their shapes and sizes needed to be strictly identical. . . . With audacity, Mr. Mallet-Stevens resorted to reinforced cement. . . . A puerile copy of nature, like that of artificial flowers, was to be avoided. . . . The design frankly expressed the material's characteristics while its overall perception was that of a tree. . . . [The original] intention to paint [the trees] was abandoned. . . . It is rather difficult to comprehend the extent of ingeniousness and art that is required to complete such a work.[68]

Although Forestier conceded that the merit of the Jardin de l'habitation moderne might lie in its execution rather than in its providing a new garden type, he judged the result "undeniably interesting."[69] Such commentary revealed the breadth of Forestier's attitude toward innovative landscape idioms. He also stated that gardens should not merely be constructed, just as they should not merely be planted.[70] Although he was referring to the dichotomy between the *régulier* and the *paysager* styles, the precept could justifiably apply as well to the garden by Mallet-Stevens and the Martels. Despite the flower beds, supposedly sunken for protection from the wind, the design perfectly expressed the idea of a constructed/sculpted architectural garden, with its trees forming an exact quincunx. Although Forestier himself would certainly have relied on the poetry of plants and colors to soften the straight lines, he

nevertheless valued the bold use of concrete, which he considered "the material of the machine age."[71] Perhaps this very material lies at the origin of the nature expressed in the Mallet-Stevens garden. When the architect wrote, "Abruptly, everything changed. Reinforced concrete appeared revolutionising the processes of construction. . . . Science creates a new aesthetic, forms are profoundly modified," one senses that the condemnation of his Pavillon du tourisme as a pretext for building technique was not totally unwarranted.[72] On the other hand, concrete allowed Mallet-Stevens and the brothers Martel to suggest, rather than to replicate, nature and thus to create an abstraction of foliage as might a painter or a sculptor.

As a totality, the garden section at the exposition presented little more unity than its architectural counterpart, whose lack of homogeneity in style and color was often blamed on space limitations. The further fragmentation of the residual areas for gardens induced Forestier to commission several artists—mostly architects, in fact—to design these landscape vignettes. As curator of the Paris park system, Forestier ensured the safety of existing vegetation; as chief of the garden section, he assigned the available plots to various *jardiniers-artistes*.[73]

Forestier encouraged, although with some trepidation, the garden designers he commissioned to "unbridle their imagination" and reinvigorate the modern landscape.[74] He realized, however, the inherent contradiction that underlay the concept of a temporary garden; the "light and mottled atmosphere" of a landscape required several years and could not be achieved within the time constraints imposed by the exposition. Constructed during April, May, and even as late as June, in a period of only eight to ten days, the gardens were intended to last six months.[75] It was clear that such creations, essentially serving only a visual function, were considered an appendix to the exhibit of decorative arts and architecture. The time parameter being a constant for all these projects—and they were all to be dismantled with the exposition—the manner of acknowledging their temporality became the variable.

"Instant gardens" countered the limited time of exposure with the intensity of medium, whether architectural or vegetal. Some designs relied on the dazzling chromatic effect of flowers, continually replanted as they wilted, which differed little from horticultural displays, such as that of the Société "Pour les jardins," whose dainty floral decoration was said to resemble a wedding buffet.[76] Others used trellises, pergolas, and porticoes to outline, or even simply suggest, the garden.

The common denominator for all the landscape designs along the Cours-la-Reine was a background of trees. Forestier planned the northeastern triangle of the exposition site as an exterior ensemble highlighted with various artists' decorative compositions.[77] Whether or not the individual fragments successfully fitted together, Forestier's overall reading of the site is discernible in his description of this ensemble. To enhance or balance the calmness of the allée, he manipulated colors, contrasts, horticulture, and topography as distinct but interrelated layers:

> In the light areas, the contrasts of colors mixed with the gold of the statues and mosaics were strong. In the green-shaded alley under the horse chestnuts, on the other hand . . . the blues [dominated]—hortensias and cinerarias. The promenade, which would have seemed too short if open, was enclosed at its ends: on one side was the [sculpture] . . . *les Illusions et le Regret*, resting against a background of tall thujas irregularly spaced like Italian cypresses; and on the other were three cement steps lined with dark blue terminated by a stela. . . . In order not to disrupt the calmness of this resting place composed of blue, green, and shade, the benches . . . were black. But a fountain by Roux-Spitz . . . with its tubs of pink hortensias heightened the ensemble with a touch of color.[78]

On the eastern side of the Cours-la-Reine, Joseph Marrast executed one of the most lauded designs of the exposition. [Plate IV] Marrast had worked as an architect and a planner for Henri Prost in Morocco; his *1925 Jardins* remains the essential record of the garden section. Within the rows of existing trees, he laid out a two-level axial pool lined with benches and tall amphoras. The enclosure provided by the mass of foliage was further defined by mounds of flowers. Although the general idea was supposedly derived from the French tradition, embellished with some Italian touches, the upper pool was designed after a distinctively Moorish pattern.[79] With a pervasive color scheme of gold, blue, and green, with red benches, Marrast played the chroma of the potted flowers and their reflections against the stark cypresses and deep shade of the existing horse chestnuts.[80] Forestier appreciated Marrast's entry because of its use of cement for pools, stairs, and even vases—proof that this

3-17 COURTYARD GARDEN BEHIND THE HÔTEL FOR A RICH COLLECTOR.
Jules Vacherot and André Riousse.
[*L'Architecte,* 1925]

3-17

3-19

3-20

material, when skillfully used, could rival the time-honored beauty of marble, brick, and stone.[81] Alluding to the proper Mediterranean references, the garden on the Cours-la-Reine achieved a balance of vegetation and hard lines that was unanimously recognized as an adequately contemporary landscape. So successful was Marrast's "Latin" design, in fact, that it was re-created, complete with statue, in Palm Beach, Florida, less than a year later.[82]

Other Oriental connotations were found in the Jardin des oiseaux, located a few pavilions away; the architect of this garden, Albert Laprade, had also worked in Morocco, joining the Agence Prost in 1915, one year before Marrast's arrival. The Garden of Birds Laprade designed was framed by architectural structures on three sides, thus seeming to draw its references from a secluded Moorish patio rather than from an expansive French garden. Laprade's project was named after its five cubic aviaries painted in gold and inhabited by exotic and colorful specimens. The cages, the dominant volumes in an otherwise planar design, were displayed on a geometric parterre that alternated blue ageratums and pink and white begonias with rills of water lined by cream-colored and celadon tiles. Reflecting its author's "passion for flowers cast in architecture" and the influence of the Spanish and Moroccan gardens,[83] the Jardin des oiseaux was another of the landscape scenes that met with almost unanimous critical acceptance.[84]

Unlike the gardens on the Cours-la-Reine, those on the esplanade could not be superimposed upon a green vegetal background. There, Albert Laprade realized another supposedly Moorish-inspired piece on the central axis between the pont Alexandre III and the dome of the Invalides. Whereas the Jardin des oiseaux decorated a semienclosed space, the Bassin des nymphéas, or Pool of the Water Lilies, floated in the vastness of the esplanade, barely framed by frail arches in an almost pathetic attempt to form a "courtyard in a public square."[85]

To address the daunting monumentality of the surroundings, most garden artists reinforced the edges of their designs with ceramics and masonry. The "broad white roadway unrelieved by trees" appeared tiresome to one critic, who used the linguistic metaphor of bad punctuation: "The commas, in the shape of the pylons at each end of the bridge, and the colon, in the shape of the Sèvres pavilion, are inadequate to carry the load of the sentence as far as the full stop, which is the dome of the Invalides."[86] Focusing inward, enclaves such as the Pavillon de la Manufacture de Sèvres or the Cour des métiers resorted to vegetation as mere accents on tiles, vases, and fountains.

The twin pavilions of the Manufacture de Sèvres were situated just north of the Bassin des nymphéas and were marked by eight monumental stoneware vases.[87] [Plate V] Here the architect Henri Rapin appeared to extend his Study for a Ceramics Amateur outdoors. Paralleling Mallet-Stevens's demonstrations in reinforced concrete, Rapin's courtyard garden expressed the decorative potential of porcelain. Without proposing a radically new garden vocabulary, he established an unusual relation between the exterior design and the program of the adjacent pavilion. The garden itself showcased recent technical innovations from the Sèvres factory: the four corner pools were outlined by soft siliceous porcelain and contained translucent fish and turtles of porcelain, which were illuminated at night. White and turquoise glazed stoneware edged the bridges; the central fountain featured steps of celadon tiles.[88] Rapin distributed vegetation parsimoniously in his "abotanical garden": a columnar tree in each corner, the ubiquitous begonias and water lilies in the center of the pool, and green vegetal dots lining the passage between the two wings executed by Pierre Patout.[89] The mineral elements, varied and sophisticated, predominated, culminating in a lavish "ceramic carpet."[90]

The Cour des métiers, or Courtyard of Trades, was the final stop on the same north-south axis; its name implied a restrained use of plants. Charles Plumet had designed the Palais des métiers, a sort of monument to crafts climactically positioned at the base of the Invalides. In its atrium, Plumet made an explicit reference to the cloister, in which a fountain substituted for a well, and the motifs of clipped boxwood were flattened into floral parterres. Although no Mediterranean idiom was apparent, the Cour des métiers shared the same chromatic palette recurring throughout the exterior ensembles of the exposition: gold, black, blue, and green.

These similarities in color, as well as in the use of concrete, mosaics, pergolas, and the references to Moorish and Spanish sources, were often attributed to the influence of Forestier.[91] Ironically so, for he would himself denounce the banality and the excessive use of pseudo-neo Arabic gardens and Spanish patios that

44

3-21

"do not belong in such an exposition."[92] Instead, Forestier argued for a formal casualness displaying the regularity of the French tradition and the irregular planting of the ancient paradise garden.

The architectural elements that appeared frequently throughout the exposition gardens were even more essential along the esplanade. Pergolas and arches were used to strengthen the impact of designs diluted by excessive space. The architect Jacques Lambert resorted to vertical constructions as the central features of his Décoration florale. Commissioned to camouflage the vents of the subterranean railway station, he arranged potted garnet-red geraniums in cascading tiers threaded with royal blue flowers and dominated by four vermilion octagonal masts. These pylons crowned with tulip or lotus buds were occasionally described as "red asparagus."[93] Despite its awkward aspect, however, at night Lambert's composition was said to offer "the effect of a garden from an Oriental tale bathed in lights as soft as they are pretty."[94]

Like Mallet-Stevens, Lambert constructed an instant garden of replaceable flowers, whose radicalness lay only in its decorative gesture. Although they were dramatic statements and daring chromatic accents within the washed-out tonality of the esplanade, Lambert's over-scaled versions of garden bibelots failed to question the image of a modern exhibition landscape. In contrast, the concrete grove issued a challenge to received ideas about the garden that still stands unequalled. As an extreme reinterpretation of the contemporary garden, the Martel trees represented a nature made not with horticultural pigments but with an almost mechanized vegetation.

Predictably, the gardens or courtyards most generally accepted by the critics and the public were those that acknowledged tradition by coating history with a gloss of modernity. The gardens on the Cours-la-Reine provided physical amenity: greenery, shade, water, color, rest. Several of them also added a zest of foreign influence to this foolproof recipe, thereby suggesting a sense of innovation beyond what they truly possessed.

If, as Aldous Huxley has claimed, "tradition is the nearest approach to a substitute for talent," borrowing from foreign sources seemed preferable to a drastic reinterpretation of that very tradition.[95] As long as the final product retained a basis in French roots, exoticism was

3-21 COUR DES MÉTIERS.
One of the towers promoting French restaurants and wines can be seen in the background.
Charles Plumet.
[*L'Architecte*, 1925]

3-22 DÉCORATION FLORALE.
Jacques Lambert.
[Marrast, 1925 *Jardins*]

GARDENS AT THE EXPOSITION

45

3-22

permissible.[96] Laprade revealed Moroccan influence when he quoted colored ceramics, flowing water, and masses of flowers of a single hue. Praised for his understanding of a "measured modernism," he translated such Moorish antecedents to the Parisian settings without eccentricity.[97]

Of all the landscapes of the fair, the most radical in appearance was the Jardin d'eau et de lumière in front of the library, at the southern end of the esplanade. [Plate VI] Designed by Gabriel Guevrekian, the Garden of Water and Light in its eccentricity directly opposed the cautious modernism of Laprade's Bassin des nymphéas. Forestier described the Jardin d'eau et de lumière as the "most curious bit of garden," answering his wish for a modern landscape composed with Persian elements.[98] The triangular site was enclosed on two sides by glass partitions; in its center were four triangular pools arranged on three tiers. Over them, a faceted stained-glass sphere, illuminated from within, rotated on an axis. The formula of ageratum, begonia, water, glazing, and electric light used here—the ingredients of garden tradition and modern technology—was applicable to any of the instant gardens.

In his manipulation of textures and planes and the juxtaposition of vibrant colors, however, Guevrekian achieved a dazzling translation of the paradise garden. He invoked his Persian memories only to dismiss them, wrote Forestier in his praise of the design.[99] As a garden that was to be experienced only visually, the Jardin d'eau et de lumière literally rendered Forestier's view of nature as a *tableau d'art*, while achieving the effects of the Delaunays' Simultaneist paintings in two and a half dimensions.[100] The Guevrekian garden was praised by some as the prettiest garden of the fair, but its intensity and avant-garde character also drew condemnation. Although critics frequently suggested a parallel with Persian gardens, one fairly conservative writer accused Guevrekian of departing from the compositional rules of acceptable garden forms. "The Garden of Water and Light was certainly not inspired by any ancient garden," he asserted, and moreover "did not follow any garden convention."[101] Far from substituting tradition for skills, Guevrekian, as an artist of extraordinary talent, successfully "neglect[ed] tradition with impunity."[102] Forestier, to his credit, publicly expressed his support for Guevrekian's "great and original ingeniousness" at attempting to formulate a new landscape design.[103] Although it was clearly a "constructed garden," he praised the "curious" and "singular" exercise of the architect for adding electric light to the modern palette—seen rather frequently in the various gardens—of cement, ceramics, glass, and new horticultural varieties.[104]

The Jardin d'eau et de lumière and the Pavillon de L'Esprit Nouveau, described earlier in this chapter, suggested the extremes in attitude toward garden design at the fair. Guevrekian composed a fragmented yet formally synthetic tableau. Le Corbusier's landscape design, in contrast to his radical architecture, reverted to a miniaturized pastoral dream.

L'ART DU JARDIN AT THE GRAND PALAIS

The realized Moorish patios, bird gardens, ceramic and porcelain exterior showrooms, stylized "asparagus," and cubist concrete trees reflected the general heterogeneity of the fair. Submissions for exhibition also included existing gardens, however. Under the direction of Jacques Gréber, photographs and plans of these gardens were displayed in a small gallery on the second floor of the Grand Palais.[105] Representing not instant but permanent landscapes, they mirrored the same stylistic tendencies of the gardens at the exposition. Although analysis today is limited by the few references or reproductions published in contemporary periodicals or Marrast's *1925 Jardins*, the designs appeared to range from untainted French formalism to more architectonic gardens of minerals and meager vegetation. When Forestier wrote a brief review of the modern gardens at the exposition in *L'Architecte,* he cited the works of André Vera and Pierre Legrain.[106] Both designers utilized a formal plan, and each represented a different angle in his reading of the modern garden.

Vera, known for his article "Exhortation aux architectes de s'intéresser au jardin," presented the garden he designed in collaboration with his brother, Paul, in Saint-Germain-en-Laye.[107] A classic modernist exercise, the garden adapted the vocabulary of the jardin à la française to a reduced scale and a new horticultural palette. A clear regular structure that did not need to borrow from exotic sources, this garden simply translated analytical seventeenth-century principles into a contemporary format.[108]

Pierre-Émile Legrain, already a celebrated bookbinder and furniture designer, widened his range of talents to garden design, providing

3-23 LA THÉBAÏDE.
FLOWER GARDEN
AND *GLORIETTE* UNDER
THE SNOW.
Saint-Germain-en-Laye,
circa 1921.
André and Paul Vera.
[Courtesy Janine
Hébert]

3-23

3-24 *GLORIETTE* WITH
FABRICS BY SONIA
DELAUNAY AND A
BAS-RELIEF BY
HENRI LAURENS.
Jean-Charles Moreux.
[*Les Arts de la Maison,*
Autumn 1925]

3-24

a comprehensive design, interior as well as exterior, for Jeanne Tachard in La Celle-Saint-Cloud. The exactness of the plan was attained essentially through a manipulation of plants, not unlike the Vera garden. Legrain's green vocabulary, however, drew more from the cubistic patterns that dominated the decorative arts of the 1920s than from the French formal heritage. Treating the garden as a graphic composition, he created a skewed version of the jardin régulier in which the shrubs were clipped at an angle, the sheared allée played against a zig-zag strip of lawn, and the flowers were arranged in tilted panes.

This type of redefinition, or purposeful diversion, of the syntax of the classical garden was also seen in a little garden room built in the Grand Palais by the architect Jean-Charles Moreux, who gave it the title Gloriette. Although this small pavilion belonged primarily to the category of interior design, the conception suggested more a garden brought indoors. A shelter for sitting in the park, it was furnished with a rattan table and armchairs, upholstered in a fabric designed by Sonia Delaunay, and a fountain of colored cement. The pattern of polychromed paving was repeated in the wall design; the overall tone of the room was, not surprisingly, green. This curious little exercise received only scattered comments in the press although it was a noteworthy indication of a trend toward a contemporary rendering of the French classical tradition.

Such a collection of high-style exteriors was bound to reinforce the image of an exposition catering to the rich. Thus, the intention to "display art in life . . . in the reality of the everyday object" and not "works of exception" failed.[109] To be more democratic the exposition could have included a vegetable garden, challenged one critic. But the lack of space that precluded such working plots also prevented the comprehensive design of a public park.[110] Instead, the fair presented gardens or sculptures that were luxurious outdoor artifacts; whether fabricated of flowers or concrete, they illustrated the imbalance of a stilled, temporary permanence. The designer Ferdinand Bac presented a quite contrary opinion, seeing the exposition as the paragon of a garden city. He equated the "compartmented gardens," distilled from former aristocratic estates, with the diminutive landscapes of the exposition, whose designed terrain reconciled present and future. Witnessing "old Europe expiring at the threshold of

garden cities," he placed "immense social meaning" on the exposition.[111]

The solemn and monumental aristocratic garden—now destined for the middle class—needed to become intimate and bourgeois.[112] Characterized in the press as "fragmentary decorations," the exposition gardens were conceived as private environments, even though they were visible or accessible to visitors. While the efforts to create an alternative contemporary landscape were partially stunted, the result, thought some, "was really not bad."[113] The garden section of the fair should be considered neither a starting point nor a conclusion, stated one reviewer, who justly predicted that 1925 would become a precious point of reference in the future.[114] As a critical juncture in the path that transformed the jardin régulier into a garden form that echoed modernist architecture and cubism, the occasion brought together the talents of individuals who would dominate French garden design in the following decade.

The accomplishments of the 1925 fair reveal a broad range of garden designs: one of the final imprints left by J.C.N. Forestier, for which he received the Légion d'honneur; an aristocratic and quasi-anachronistic project by Achille Duchêne; a unique design by Pierre Legrain; one of the rare examples of gardens by Le Corbusier; the concrete garden of Robert Mallet-Stevens and the brothers Martel; the modern / classicist exercise of André and Paul Vera; the classic / modernist garden room of Jean-Charles Moreux; and the first landscape signal emitted by Gabriel Guevrekian.

In attracting the attention of the public to a field of endeavor usually reserved for private eyes, the garden section sparked an interest that generated a series of momentous designs in the decade following. The 1920s, years of illusion, preceded the great delusions of the 1930s. The 1925 exposition opened a critical chapter in garden history that would be concluded in 1937 at the next international exposition in Paris.

50

JARDIN RÉGULIER;
JARDIN D'ARCHITECTURE

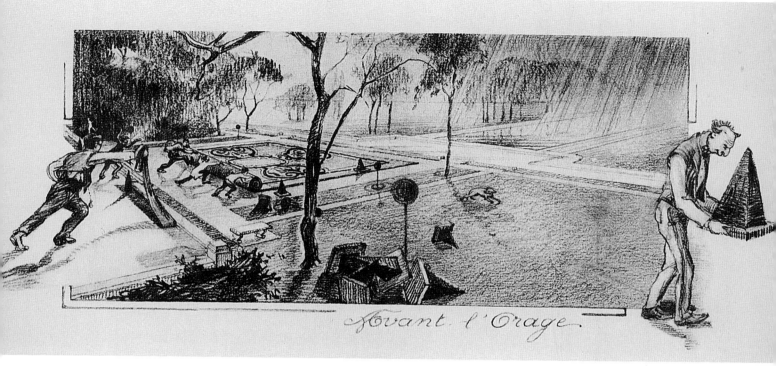

4-1

The *style régulier,* André Vera continually asserted, was a new system to supplant the faded irregularity of the *jardin paysager*; a new system to establish the garden as a modern outdoor apartment. Although Vera the critic is essential to the study of early twentieth-century garden design, his views regarding the *jardin régulier* do not appear to be idiosyncratic to this period. The debate between the advocate of a Virgilian nature and the land *topiarius,* who strove to impress an idealized geometric order upon the earth, had resonated throughout the course of garden history. Whether schisms or parallels, the forces of Reason, Nature, and Art were often invoked. In the seventeenth century, the French transcribed a belief in methodized nature into the formal garden. In the eighteenth century, both the English and French set their architecture of pure, classical forms within a poetic landscape that attempted to replicate nature untouched. Such pronouncements are too simple, however. Each of these attitudes presents a contradiction, and thus an enigma: the rigorous French

4-1 "BEFORE THE STORM."
Achille Duchêne.
[Duchêne, *Les jardins de l'avenir*]

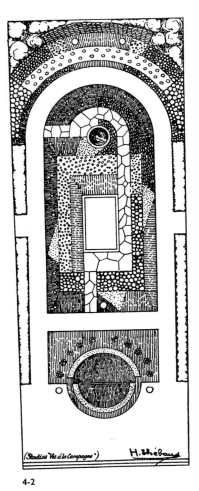

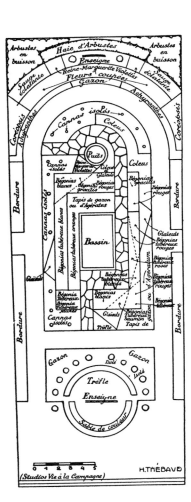

4-2

4-2 EXPOSITION GARDEN.
PLAN AND PLANTING
SCHEME.
Circa 1930.
Henri Thébaud.
[*Jardins d'aujourd'hui*]

formal compositions of the seventeenth century were supposedly modeled after nature; the enlightened eighteenth century extolled mathematics yet resisted geometric figures in the shaping of landscape.[1] Continually, one finds disparities between concepts of nature and their application to garden making; these paradoxes did not disappear in 1900.

In spite of their problematic conceptual underpinnings, the highly formal gardens of the interwar years, like their seventeenth-century counterparts, were in total accord with architecture and the decorative arts. Unlike the designs that preceded them, however, the patterns of the modernist landscape seldom invoked nature as their prime source of inspiration. Indeed, the gardens of the 1920s were closer to architecture than to nature, and few projects introduced vegetation in its natural state within the garden walls. In many ways, these gardens were the repudiation of the romantic model, and their authors cited speed, economy of maintenance, and modern materials as the factors generating the morphology of their designs. In the most radical examples, vegetation did not soften the regular canvas, as it had in the landscapes of J.C.N. Forestier. On the contrary, plants were constricted by the architectural elements that outlined the plan and framed the volume of the garden. As a result, structure and composition were rendered coincident.

The *style paysager*, elegantly used in the public parks of the Second Empire, was not easily transferred to smaller private gardens. Lacking the scale necessary for a bold gesture, these reduced fragments of landscape often created a parody of nature, replete with mock meandering rivers and rocklike grottoes. Against the *jardin horticole*—which was the ultimate degeneration of the style paysager—rose the formal style régulier, tinged by a veneer of instant modernity.

L'Art du jardin, a section introduced at the 1925 Paris Exposition, confirmed the acceptance of garden design as a decorative art independent of, and at times only remotely related to, the practice of horticulture. Although its director, Forestier, was an engineer-forester, most of the section's gardens were designed by architects.

The international exposition revealed many of the dichotomies and divergences within the fields of decorative arts, architecture and, to a lesser degree, garden design. Paralleling the academic caution that dominated the architecture of the exposition, in which the new was "subject to the old, or at least to the outlines of the old," the products of the so-called modern landscape sought a link between the past and present through a renewal of tradition.[2] Set against a background of postwar chauvinism, the exposition simplistically equated the resurgence of the formal garden with France's patrimony.

With roots in the landscape ideal of England, any new garden in the picturesque style should be considered as "an act of sabotage against the National Revolution," declared Vera. First publicizing his attack on internationalism in 1912, Vera continued to pursue this theme through the Second World War.[3] He repeatedly admonished architects to abandon any foreign influences, whether English or Chinese, Japanese or German. Gardens should be "marked by a character neither dwarf, which is Japanese, nor colossal, which is German, but rather human, which is truly French."[4] Although several of the designs presented at the exposition betrayed North African origins, references such as these might not have seemed anti-nationalistic, for they could be interpreted in terms of France's dominion over its colonies. This refutation of exoticism in the early 1900s inverted the late eighteenth-century shift from French formalism to the Anglo-Chinese fashion. Although inherited laws of garden design were seldom defied, certain designers attempted to reinvent a landscape vocabulary by exploring the potential, or limitations, of vegetation, gravity, and graphic composition.

Despite their varying levels of innovation, the gardens of the 1920s and 1930s as a group formed a distinct argument for a regular style. Whether termed modernist, cubist, or simply modern, these designs countered previous garden traditions while revealing the need for aesthetic cohesion among the arts.

Vera's incitement to return to gardens in the formal manner was only cautiously innovative, but his call to involve architects in their design was a sign of the times. Le Corbusier had praised him for writing a book (*Le nouveau jardin*) whose content and spirit addressed a single category of people, most likely architects.[5] Leon Henry Zach, an American landscape architect, attributed the "over-plentiful use of architectural and geometric forms" and the "bizarre effects" obtained in these gardens to the fact their designers—Tony Garnier, Laprade, Mallet-Stevens, and Le Cor-

4-3

4-3 CITY GARDEN IN A RESIDENTIAL NEIGHBORHOOD. PLAN. Circa 1929. Jean-Jacques Haffner. [Haffner, *Compositions de jardins*]

busier—were all trained as architects.[6] [Plate VII] Apart from Mallet-Stevens's garden of concrete trees at the 1925 exposition, however, the aforementioned architects treated landscape as part of their architectural ensembles, with a rather nonradical voice. Nevertheless, the gardens produced between the wars shared an iconography that was applied to all the decorative arts—and for this, they warrant careful study. As extensions of architectural design into the landscape, they were characteristic of the early twentieth-century trend toward the designed *ensemble*. Jean Badovici described decorated interiors, or ensembles, as compositions in which furniture elements were "entities extending one another," whose geometric shapes merged with the lines of walls.[7] It was thus only a short step to bring this concept out to the garden. The idea of the garden as an outdoor room could be traced back to the Renaissance, if not to Rome itself. The garden of the 1920s, however, was truly contemporary, as it extended outward the domain of the interior ensemble, including its sharply redefined vocabulary. The critic Guillaume Janneau saw the common origin of Cubism, Orphism, Purism, Dada, and Surrealism in a similar perception of the world's unity, and, as a result, "Negro sculptures . . . reinforced concrete, naval and aeronautical architecture, all contributed to modify our sensibility profoundly and gave us the *taste for clearly defined forms*."[8] Architects decorated or composed gardens as they would interiors. Such materials as oilcloth or vellum were diverted from their more common applications and used as coverings for a wall or a stool. Similarly, concrete reinforced the structure of the garden, glass whimsically defined its fountains, and mirrors effaced its boundaries. Whether interior or exterior, the ensemble transformed fragmentary decoration—whose strength derived from the beauty of each distinct element—into a composition of masses and surfaces arranged to form an interrelated and balanced totality. Previously, the jardin horticole had featured floral mosaics on perfect lawns framed by dark groves of exotic trees. Against it, the new jardin régulier presented an image of nature arranged according to graphic rules rather than those of horticultural specificity.

"The formal treatment of gardens ought to be called the architectural treatment of gardens, for it consists in the extension of the principles of design which govern the house to the grounds which surround it," wrote the English

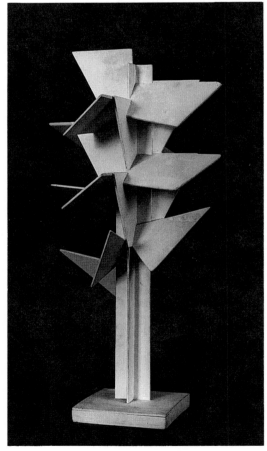

4-4

54

architect Reginald Blomfield in 1892.[9] Twenty years later, André Vera validated this precept in *Le nouveau jardin*, arguing that the park ought to be assigned to the *paysagiste*, or landscape gardener, while "naturally" the garden should be designed by the architect.[10] In the preface, Vera also stated how gardening, "humble" and "docile," should follow the evolution not only of architecture but also of painting, sculpture, and furniture design.[11] Correlations between landscape and art had almost always existed, but during the 1920s, garden forms were treated as direct translations of contemporary decorative trends to an unprecedented extent—one since then unmatched.

In conjunction with his numerous writings, André Vera—with his brother, Paul—executed a garden in Saint-Germain-en-Laye that did not transfigure, but simply revised, the French formal vocabulary. When Vera attempted to establish precepts for the modern garden in *Le nouveau jardin* and *Les jardins*, the plans and views he presented as examples of modern gardens were charming but rather conservative in addressing the transformation of the *jardin à la française*. "Le nouveau style," an article published the same year as *Le nouveau jardin*, argued for a modern idiom in furniture design derived from the last truly French stylistic tradition, that is, the nineteenth-century school of Louis-Philippe.[12] Similarly, the modern garden ought to borrow from the last truly French traditional landscapes—the designs of Le Nôtre—to establish "solid precepts of composition" and the art of arranging the elements according to a mathematical ratio.[13] All of Vera's creations were "submitted to French discipline," whether the engravings of the conceptual projects in his books, or concrete designs like the garden in Saint-Germain.[14] Moreover, when Vera wrote that the garden should be "a refined version of nature, that is to say, nature shaped into intelligible forms," he completed a full circle with the seventeenth-century concept of a nature imprinted by reason.[15] Fletcher Steele criticized Vera's designs as "rest[ing] on French classic garden principles and refus[ing] to look odd or inappropriate."[16] In spite of the traditional vein visible in Vera's applications of his garden theory, his writings reflected and analyzed the spirit of the times and thus provided one of the sole justifications for the more radical examples of gardens designed during the first decades of this century.

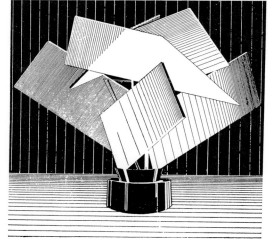

4-5

4-4 MAQUETTE FOR A TREE CAST IN CONCRETE. Painted wood. 1925. Jan and Joël Martel. [Courtesy Florence Langer-Martel]

4-5 STUDY FOR AN ALABASTER LAMP. Pierre Chareau. [*Les Arts de la Maison*, Winter 1924]

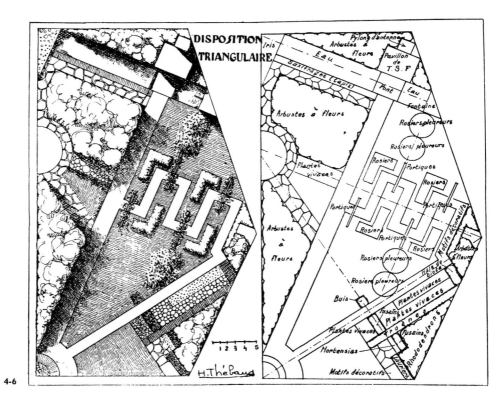

4-6

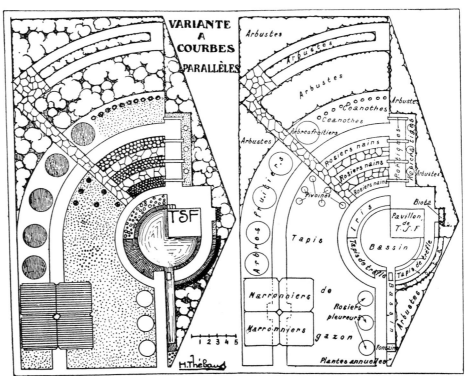

4-6 TWO PROJECTS IN "A
DECORATIVE MANNER
APPROPRIATE FOR AN
ERA INFATUATED WITH
COLOR."
PLANS AND PLANTING
SCHEMES.
Circa 1930.
Henri Thébaud.
[*Jardins d'aujourd'hui*]

4-7 GARDEN PROJECT.
4-8 Pencil and ink studies
for *Les jardins*. Circa
1913. Paul Vera.
[Collection of Cooper-
Hewitt Museum,
New York.
Courtesy Yu-Chee
Chong Fine Art,
London]

4-7

4-8

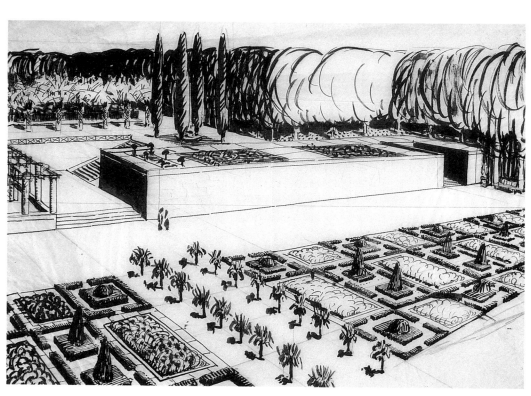

André Vera was a vehement advocate for the return to the formal garden, but his predilection was not based on chauvinism alone. As the amount of land surrounding the house diminished during the contemporary era, simplicity became essential. The naturalistic style was out of fashion, he believed, just as picturesque architecture, impressionist painting, the realist novel, and free verse were out of fashion.[17] In an address to architects entitled "Exhortation aux architectes de s'intéresser au jardin," he emphasized the mineral element rather than the horticultural and stressed the importance and innovative quality of materials such as glass mosaic, cast masonry and, naturally, reinforced concrete. The garden featured red cement vases, freshly whitewashed concrete columns, and tile aggregate; the white steps and ceramic tiles were washed, but not aged, by rain. Thus, the garden achieved a "new, clean, even hygienic aspect: a sign of modernity."[18] The weeping willow, winding path, and false ruin, timeless in their dreamlike artificiality, gave way to another ideal of permanence: the mineral garden, a synthetic version of trimmed nature. The gardener might have been led astray on a meandering path through the circular or oval flower beds, but the architect would fully control a garden whose composition was subordinated to the module of the house.[19]

A certain degree of intuition and care was still required, however. If mathematics ruled the garden, as Vera recommended, an abuse of geometry was condemned as evidence of the architect's insensitivity to nature.[20] "The excessive indulgences on paper to the T-square, triangle, and compass" were considered a recurring flaw in the architectural garden, in which plants were used only as a painting medium. The simplified horticultural palette of the modern garden, with expanses of monochromatic species treated as textured planes of color, reinforced the cliché of the architectural garden as a two-dimensional design that showed little respect for the beauty of plants as living specimens.[21] Conceived in planes, the garden was given volume by extruding the flat surfaces of the plan into an axonometric view.

In an attempt to unravel the genesis of design forms, an American critic, Robert Wheelwright, paired architecture with painting, and landscape architecture with sculpture.[22] He explained that architects draw their ideas as a series of planes on a sheet of paper, whereas landscape architects consider the potential of a piece of land as sculptors gauge a block of

4-9

4-9 PERGOLA BORDERING A SUNKEN PARTERRE. Illustration for *Les jardins*. Circa 1913. Paul Vera. [Collection of Cooper-Hewitt Museum, New York. Courtesy Yu-Chee Chong Fine Art, London]

stone. However simplistic, and despite definite exceptions, this statement does summarize the architectonic layers of the 1920s landscapes.

The gardens of this inquiry were limited in size, located in the immediate vicinity of the house, usually enclosed by walls or fences, and executed mostly by architects. Flat designs, constructed in a modern, régulier, or cubist style, they acquired the status of pictorial tableaux rather than of true, multi-dimensional landscapes. The transitions between the terrace of Le Nôtre and the distant hunting grounds, between architecture and nature, had been grandly and exquisitely developed in the seventeenth-century gardens of France. In contrast, during the twentieth century all the intermediate shades of formality so carefully drawn in parterres, pools of water, and quincunx groves dissolving into the horizon had disappeared. The designs of the 1920s and 1930s were reduced to the state of graphic plinths for the house and compressed into a single layer the image of the garden and the minerality of the terrace. The new gardens were not accepted without challenge, however. Most criticism focused on the rigorous geometries of their patterns; what most distressed garden critics was the pervasive triangular shape lacking historical precedent. Whether reinterpreted through selective exaggeration or merely refurbished with a hint of modernity, the elements of the French formal vocabulary were still perceptible beneath the surface.

From medieval times, arbors, bowers, or *gloriettes* had provided shade in the jardin régulier. In its modern form, the trellis reappeared flattened against a whitewashed garden wall. Simplified to a square grid, its structure repeated the pattern displayed in the *salle fraîche*.[23] Although the new trellis was enhanced by vegetation, it did not exist to support the vine, and the frame never disappeared under foliage. Jean-Charles Moreux, one of the main protagonists of the modern garden, set latticework over the pruned hedge, as if to remind the viewer of the control exerted by the human mind over nature and to outline the transition, or border, between the architectural structure and the manipulated vegetal domain. Ironically, in a later project, Moreux reverted to a Renaissance image of the gloriette, rendered contemporary only by its reinforced-concrete frame.[24]

The general perception that nature had been subdued by the tyranny of the formal garden was furthered by the imbalance between min-

4-10

4-10 *GLORIETTE.*
Villandry.
[Photo: Dorothée
Imbert, 1989]

eral and vegetal elements in several of these designs. In his eulogy to the French regular garden, Moreux praised the variety of stone and marble and the convenience of brushed concrete—which looked like sand but did not need to be raked.[25] Mosaics, paving, and gravels dominated the compositions of the 1920s. But even a case as extreme as the Noailles garden, designed in Paris by Paul Vera, André Vera, and Jean-Charles Moreux, still revealed a French character despite its bold manipulation of patterns and materials. Recalling the designs of late sixteenth- and seventeenth-century parterres, in which colored stones enhanced the calligraphic patterns of trimmed boxwood, the Veras and Moreux translated the memory of these gracious stamps into a fragmented play of bright and dark lines. The angularity of these motifs was replicated in the surrounding mirrors, which Moreux described as replacing the illusory tapestries that were traditionally hung in copses.[26] If the *parterres de broderie* were so named for the resemblance between their filigree motifs and embroidered fabrics, the Noailles garden appeared to transcribe the shattered geometry of a textile pattern by Sonia Delaunay into a barely vegetal tableau. André Vera cited the modern woman's dress for the chromatic composition of bed plantings, and silk sweaters as the stencil for a Greek border in boxwood.[27] In this appropriation and translation, the modern garden layout, influenced if only distantly by contemporary art, mirrored the geometry and color schemes of dresses as well as cars, book covers as well as carpets.

In his writings, Vera tempted architects with the image of a garden-machine, cohesive with no superfluous elements.[28] Ironically, the Corbusian *machine à habiter* itself was seldom set in a landscape of architectonic character. Furthermore, the implication of a strictly functional garden did not acknowledge aesthetics, the primary value of these regular designs. Seemingly ludicrous terms when applied to the garden, *machine* and *hygiene*—like references to speed, aviation, or streamlining—were catchphrases that connoted modernity and little else. The beauty of the machine had been evoked in the previous century by the poet Charles Baudelaire when he described the "mysterious and complex grace" of the moving carriage or ship.[29] The machine aesthetic and the need for addressing contemporary functions were common themes pervading the writings and works of the Italian Futurists as well as those of French architects such as Le Corbusier and Pierre Jeanneret. More often

4-11

4-11 *SALLE FRAÎCHE.* Château de Maulny, Sarthe, 1930. Jean-Charles Moreux. [Moreux, *J.-Ch. Moreux*]

4-12 PARTERRE FOR THE HÔTEL DE NOAILLES. DETAIL OF PLAN. Paris, 1924. André and Paul Vera. [Musée d'art et d'histoire, Saint-Germain-en-Laye]

than not, however, their application to the garden seemed extremely strained.

Vera had initially advertised the sharp-edged mineral garden as a low-maintenance landscape, so simple a maid could care for it;[30] by 1943, however, he viewed positively the structures of the garden as a source of work for both artists and artisans. To promote the "Revival of French Arts," Vera wrote,

> Our regular garden will not lack terraces, stairs and steps, gloriettes, porticoes, and galleries along enclosing walls, benches, trellises and lattices, lamps and ironwork fences, spouts, pools and fountains, stone or brick paving, statues and bas-reliefs, marble or pebble mosaics on the walls of the galleries, as well as paintings, frescoes and etchings, panels of millstone, faience or ceramic tiles. . . . Thus, in the regular garden, all the trades will find work . . . some as architects, sculptors, painters, fresco painters, mosaicists, ceramists; others as ironworkers, carpenters, trellis makers, cement and stone masons.[31]

By considering the garden part of the architect's jurisdiction, Vera intended a decorative unity between the interior and its extension, the apartment out-of-doors.[32] "The object of formal gardening is to bring the two into harmony, to make the house grow out of its surroundings, and to prevent its being an excrescence on the face of nature," Blomfield had declared in *The Formal Garden in England*.[33] Vera shared the English author's beliefs but furthered them by suggesting that as a projection of the facade onto its soil, the garden was imprinted with movement, for example largo or staccato, similar to that regulating the architectural elevation.[34]

Just as the reduced scale of the garden demanded a new clarity, so did the pressures of modern living impose new requirements for the maintenance and enjoyment of exterior space. The speed and cleanliness characteristic of contemporary life justified a simple layout for the garden; compact and direct, it was designed for the man or woman of the 1920s who viewed the world at 80 miles per hour. The composition shifted from analytical to synthetic. The whorls of the parterre de broderie were rectified with the straight edge—and simplified. The splash erased the arabesque, wrote Vera, and the new garden will be without transitional spaces; instead, there will be "rooms balancing and opposing one another."[35] The realization of these garden plans in three dimensions retained the imprint of their origins as graphic compositions: these architectonic

4-12

gardens appeared as extensions of the building plan or mirrors of its facade. The few trees within the garden usually served as punctuation marks, elements that might have thrown the rigorous composition into imbalance unless sheared and used as green walls. [Plate VIII]

Thus, apart from the early examples of gardens in the regular style, such as those of Forestier or André and Paul Vera, vegetation played only a minor role. Instead of overpowering its limited dimensions with a swarm of plants, the little garden kept greenery to a bare minimum. Flattening and trimming the textures and masses of the volumetrically rich *jardin paysager*, the modern jardin régulier became a two-and-a-half dimensional still life. In the anglicized landscape of the previous century, "the ornamental construction desired a frontal or three-quarter light, the trees and woods needed to be backlighted, and the waters became more brilliant in the evening."[36] By contrast, the new regular garden was designed to produce an immediate impact. Inviting neither contemplative strolling nor melancholy, its compactness and contemporaneity displayed all its elements as in a picture frontally viewed, without surprise effects. The rejected English, romantic, or picturesque garden of textures became a garden of surfaces, with panes of mirrors and planes of lawn, latticework and water. Sophisticated ordering, contemporary materials, and electric illumination replaced the drama of changing light, and the subtle variations of natural processes over time gave way to kinetic statues or water jets. The Gothic ruin or other *fabrique* reemerged as a radio pavilion; the irregular stone path, a straight walkway bordered by white concrete curbs.

4-13

4-13 GARDEN FOR THE DUC DECAZES.
Arcachon, 1926.
Charles Siclis.
[*L'Illustration,*
28 May 1932]

4-14 *"MA JOLIE."*
Paris, Winter 1911–12.
Oil on canvas.
Pablo Picasso.
[The Museum of
Modern Art, New York.
Lillie P. Bliss Bequest]

The gardens of Gabriel Guevrekian or Jean-Charles Moreux and Paul Vera at first appear to be extraneous, if not antithetical, to received ideas of landscape. Sharply delineated and extremely flat, they paired the evergreen quality of plants with the permanence of mineral materials, thereby achieving a composition closer to a still life than to nature. To extend the metaphor, the image became that of an *abstract* still life. Vegetation, water, ceramics, and glass all played a plastic role in the *tableaux-jardins* where the concern for graphic balance outweighed the beauty of any individual plant. If at times they mirrored the seclusion and geometry of the Persian paradise garden, the new gardens did not engage nature as a symbolic system. Symbolism and iconographic references played no part in their design. Materials were chosen for their physical characteristics rather than for their semantic associations, and meaning derived from the contemporaneity of the form and the intrigue of the textures. It was, thus, not analytic but synthetic. Vera believed that the garden should be conceived as a decorative piece, the "naïve expression of a very simple emotion."[37] Such a composition drew not a realistic but a sublimated image of nature, one in which plants were implied and glass fountains suggested a spring.

The "circumscribed and mutilated nature," which, in the eighteenth century, René-Louis de Girardin had condemned as "sad and boring," was revived by the radical geometry of the gardens of the interwar years.[38] Vegetation in the French formal garden evolved from use as a tool of reason mirroring the implied perfection of nature to use as a pictorial abstraction. Whereas eighteenth-century landscapes cited the seventeenth-century paintings of Claude Lorrain and Nicolas Poussin, the early twentieth-century gardens reflected the influence of cubism on the decorative and applied arts. These zig-zag, primary geometries or asymmetrical designs—simplifications of the earlier artistic movement—were, and still are, termed cubist gardens.

Juan Gris described cubism as "simply a new way of representing the world. . . . Not a manner but an aesthetic, and even a state of mind; it [was] therefore inevitably connected with every manifestation of contemporary thought."[39] In fact, cubism had shattered the one-point perspective of representational Renaissance painting and, by extension, had influenced sculpture, architecture, and vir-

4-14

tually all the decorative and applied arts. Besides affecting parallel artistic trends, cubist works received scathing or rave reviews in the popular press, which stimulated the curiosity of the public and even created a taste for cubistic artifacts. While cubism as a pictorial movement faded, "it was seized by fashion design, which is always hungry for inspiration." Léon Deshairs claimed that the decorators at the 1925 Exposition were "intoxicated by whimsical geometry." Deshairs questioned the validity of applying these patterns indiscriminately to fabrics, carpets, and tapestry; to bas-reliefs and bookbindings: "What is this fashion worth?" he asked rhetorically. "What the artist is worth," he replied insightfully.[40]

The challenge that cubism imposed on perceptual and representational axioms varied widely. Most often, the new school of painting induced neither structural nor conceptual changes, but merely cosmetic applications of motifs. The Maison Cubiste of Raymond Duchamp-Villon is frequently cited as one of the first examples of cubism translated directly into architecture. Commissioned by André Mare in 1912 for the Salon d'Automne, the project revealed the usual schism between intention and realization, despite the polemic it provoked at the time.[41] In reality, Duchamp-Villon's design was little more than a cubistic facade applied to an ordinary bourgeois house from the turn of the century. His ambition, instead, was to find a vocabulary for the modern times, a new architectural style that would not merely transpose lines and forms into other "materials, but rather "interpret in lines, planes and synthetic volumes, [and] in balance" the relation of elements to one another.[42]

Almost as an illustration of Vera's assertion that gardening should not precede but follow the evolution of architecture and its allied fields, the garden was the last to fall under the influence of the new school of painting. Cubism and its diffusion exerted an incentive to "conceive systematically in terms of pure surfaces and volumes, that is of spaces."[43] It is rather difficult to evaluate the direct impact of cubism upon landscape architecture, because the designs underscored by the laconic caption "Cubist Garden" were created almost a decade after the passing of cubism's formative period.[44] Furthermore, critical writings on the subject remain rather sparse.

Whether the landscape counterparts of the Maison Cubiste reconciled the principles of

4-15

4-15 MAISON CUBISTE. MODEL.
Presented at the Salon d'Automne, 1912. Raymond Duchamp-Villon.
[*Raymond Duchamp-Villon*]

painting with the reality of a garden structure is questionable, as it is doubtful that any of them addressed the spatial and perceptual challenges of cubism. Like paintings, the gardens of Moreux and Vera, Guevrekian, and Legrain were tableaux that manipulated geometries and colors to contract planes into an illusory dynamism. Although certain of these designs simply transposed traditional lines into contemporary materials, others transformed the structure of the garden to become more than a pattern stenciled on the surface. Composed essentially of flat and controlled forms rooted firmly on the ground plane, these gardens nevertheless bore in their spatial dimension the essence of both their strength and failure as cubist exercises—the same contradictions that plagued the conception of cubist sculpture.

The transparency of overlapping planes that characterized cubist paintings had proven difficult to translate into sculpture.[45] The fragmentation and compression of foreground into background, and the simultaneous representation of multiple points of view characteristic of early cubism, introduced the fourth dimension —time—into a two-dimensional medium.[46] But the three-dimensionality of sculpture undermined any ambiguity in perceiving depth. The haziness of the painted boundaries became hard-edged, and the defined and opaque segments prevented the immobile viewer from perceiving the subtle fusion of foreground and background.

Like the palpable three-dimensionality of sculpture, the garden allowed movement and a true change of viewpoint. Representation of time and varied perception were ludicrous, at least to some degree. Therefore, if one were to search for a parallel to cubist structure or aesthetics in the field of garden design, its most likely illustration would be a bas-relief. These flat-patterned and heavily geometrized landscapes could be perceived as a sequence of planar compositions read as decorative walls or floors rather than as vegetal spaces.

Cubism had substituted conceptual for visual sensations by painting the subject not the way we see it but the way we know it, that is, from several points of view simultaneously. It is "necessary to paint three figures to portray every physical aspect of a woman, just as a house must be drawn in plan, elevation and section," wrote Georges Braque in 1910.[47] In the manner of cubist bas-reliefs, gardens were composed of tilted surfaces and articulated planes to present different angles from limited

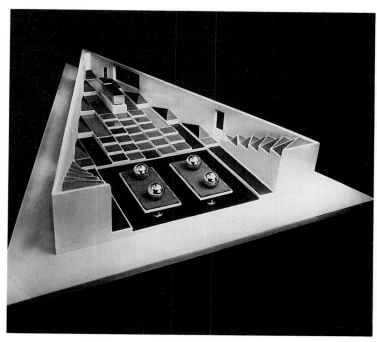

4-16

4-16 GARDEN FOR THE VILLA NOAILLES. MODEL. Presented at the Salon d'Automne, 1927. Gabriel Guevrekian. [*Les Arts de la Maison,* Winter 1926]

4-17

4-18

points of view. As a palliative to the contraction of depth forced by a constricted site, the instant garden presented all its facets at once, to let the viewer grasp the nature of space without entering the garden. By a quasi-elimination of the subject, the picture-garden became an entity independent of nature. If the gardens realized by Guevrekian or Legrain borrowed from a cubistic sensibility, they rejected both its lyricism and formal disorder. However ironic, Guevrekian's gardens were mostly symmetrical, while Legrain's composition remained decidedly formal in spite of its asymmetrical balance.

Vibrant in color and strikingly contrived in their geometry, gardens such as those by Gabriel Guevrekian at the 1925 Paris Exposition, or in Hyères for the vicomte de Noailles, appeared as stilled images that could only suggest time and visual movement. Instead of a nature decomposed, like Paul Cézanne's, into "cylinder, sphere and cone" they represented an obsessive compilation of triangles and squares.[48] Resorting to a chromatic palette closer to the more optically resonant Orphism, Guevrekian juxtaposed complementary colors that vibrated in Simultaneist combinations.[49] In the Noailles garden, he played with angled planes of groundcover that alternated two different shades of green to create the illusion of varying light. With modulated shadows and an architecture of geometry, such gardens conceptually resembled paintings by Juan Gris projected into three dimensions. The proportional system of Gris organized the pictorial field to illustrate the "contrast between an anecdotal world of appearance and a realm of metamorphosis"; Guevrekian's rigidly symmetrical gardens, however, presented a still life fixed in time.[50] Such a garden expressed less the variations than the invariables. Imagined as a dynamic tableau, but realized as a permanent installation, it nonetheless tolerated the passage of time only briefly.

The manipulation of vegetation as an architectonic material was hampered by just the same difficulties faced by the contemporary Czech cubist furniture designers who "ventured to the very boundary of the static." The surfaces bent into "sharp profiles and cut with deep incisions" that described their furniture would serve equally well to depict Guevrekian's Noailles garden.[51] Like the steel plates that strengthened the difficult connections between the diagonal planes of the cubist couch, Guevrekian's angled planes of masonry retained the soil. The limited tolerance of vegetation to formal manipulation paralleled that of upholstery cloth stretched over concave or convex surfaces. For that same reason, the fragmented garden of Guevrekian, and the obliquely terraced lawns of Legrain, required assiduous maintenance to defy gravity and other natural laws governing the growth of plants.

With a few photographs as the sole remaining traces of these gardens, our analysis of them is bound to be influenced by the shortcomings of this two-dimensional medium.[52] On the other hand, such representations might conceal the disturbing stillness of their reality and heighten their radicality. The Noailles garden in Hyères, for example, featured an architectonic use of vegetation, permitting little movement and evolution, apart from the short life cycle of tulips. Orange trees, bounded panels of groundcover, dense masses of low flowers, and slender tulips (a perennial favorite of architects) differed from the mineral patterns only in texture.[53] In these constructed gardens, the importance of ceramic tile and water equaled or surpassed that of flowers and ground covers.[54] In describing the influence on our perception of the "Cubist's conquest of space," Sigfried Giedion could very well have been discussing the balance among the elements of a garden of the 1920s: "the interplay of imponderably floating elements irrationally penetrating or fusing with each other, as also the optical tensions which arise from the contrasts between various textural effects (the handling of color qua color, or the use of other media, such as sand, bits of dress fabrics, and scraps of paper, to supplement pigments)."[55] Like fragments of caning in the cubist collage, plants—that is, plants in a recognizable form—appeared as foreign elements that unsettled the boundaries between picture and reality.

Of the four maxims devised by Dezallier d'Argenville in 1709, most formal gardens of the 1920s did not respect the first: art did not yield to nature. The treatise had recommended borrowing from art "only what could set off nature to advantage."[56] The so-called cubist garden stood in perfect opposition to the natural condition, as it borrowed only those aspects contributing to its pictorial composition. Gardens like that for the Villa Noailles were *tableaux-objets*. They represented nature as an abstraction paired with a play of surfaces and artificial color. Here and there were some recognizable elements we usually associate

4-17 *HEAD OF A BOXER.* Stone relief, polychrome. 1920. Henri Laurens. [The Museum of Modern Art, New York. Gift of Mrs. Marie L. Felchaeusser]

4-18 SOFA. Softwood, upholstered. 1914. [Museum of Decorative Arts, Prague]

4-19 GARDEN FOR THE VILLA NOAILLES. (Photograph retouched) All other views show the garden with the pool in disrepair. Hyères, 1928. Gabriel Guevrekian. [*L'Illustration,* 28 May 1921]

4-20 GARDEN FOR JEANNE TACHARD. STEPS AND INCLINED TRIANGLES OF LAWN LOOKING TOWARD THE *SALLE FRAÎCHE.* La Celle-Saint-Cloud, circa 1923. Pierre-Émile Legrain. [*L'Amour de l'Art,* December 1924]

4-19

4-20

with the natural world, such as a pair of orange trees or several squares of tulips. As an illustration of Ozenfant's definition of a tableau-objet, the plants recalled these "shapes issued from existing objects" that "occasionally . . . subsist, only to play upon our sensitivity, with their shapes or associated colors."[57] The pictorial garden did not arouse our emotions for its reproduction of an exterior scene, the wilderness from which it was secluded, but for its interior strength as a tableau-objet.

Cubism could very well be applied to planar decoration, wrote Henri Clouzot, a contemporary critic, but it should not be considered for a chair or any other functional object.[58] The medium of architecture, however, with its overlapping planes and chromatic intersections, did present an alternative to the categorical dismissal of a cubist space. Giedion described Le Corbusier's Villa Savoye as conceived in a space-time frame, thus making it "impossible to comprehend . . . by a view from a single point."[59] Similarly, the "extensive transparency" of Walter Gropius's Bauhaus allowed the "interior and exterior to be seen simultaneously, *en face* and *en profil*, like Picasso's 'L'Arlésienne.'"[60]

Gardens, on the other hand, approached the premise of cubism more literally. Two-and-a-half dimensional compositions, they treated volumes as a sequence of planes rather than as spaces. But one should not dismiss them as mere fashionable patterns, for several of them presented distinctly differing images depending on the angles from which they were viewed. As tableaux-jardins, these self-contained pictorial images rarely addressed the empirical experience of a stroller, but the viewer could "feel these planes shifting forward and back, taking their appointed distances until after time the painted world into which we are drawn becomes almost more actual than the real world."[61]

These projects of the 1920s succeeded, if only briefly, in linking design and art with the garden. Commissioned as tableaux or sculptures, these landscapes lasted about as long as murals exposed to the inclemency of weather or fashion. They presented nature in an abstract bas-relief, as an independent entity, which, in spite of its spatial shortcomings, was highly successful as a visual construct. If the decorative work was described as a dependent organ, and the cubist tableau as an organism that carries in itself its raison d'être, then the cubist garden was an extremely fragile organism.[62]

Paradoxically, most garden theory and criticism seems to have been generated by the less radical designers of the period. Duchêne, Forestier, and André Vera published extensively on the evolution of garden design, whereas Guevrekian, Legrain, and Paul Vera remained almost mute on their conception of the modern landscape. In describing the design process, André Vera announced the predominant view of the garden as an essentially visual phenomenon. The parterres in his books appeared as tableaux in which plants were used primarily as a chromatic medium or to express the variations of a brushstroke. He recommended avoiding complication and establishing "frank juxtapositions" of materials and colors to awaken the senses with the play between muted hues of one color and the bright tonality of another.[63] Throughout his literary career, André Vera maintained a rather conservative view toward art and design, best revealed in his residence at Saint-Germain. His 1912 article on the "new style" condemned internationalism and advised resuming the French heritage that had been interrupted after the last monarchy. It is ironic that the same writer could extol the power of history and tradition while describing garden design as an abstract, graphic, two-dimensional composition. Perhaps Vera realized that the successful return to formalism required the architect, whose involvement he had to coax. In spite of the poetic scenarios with which he justified his views, the garden Vera proposed—if intimate in scale and traditional in manner—remained primarily a pictorial composition.

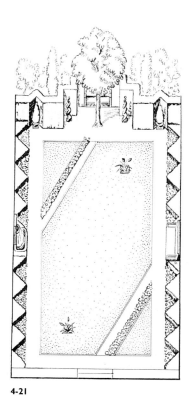 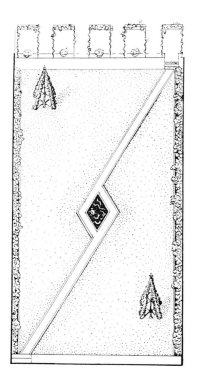 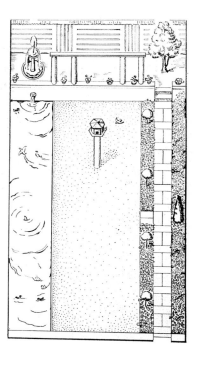

4-21

4-21 THREE SCHEMES FOR A
LITTLE URBAN
GARDEN. PLANS.
Paul Vera
[Musée d'art et
d'histoire, Saint-
Germain-en-Laye]

ANDRÉ VERA; PAUL VERA; JEAN-CHARLES MOREUX
MODERNITY & TRADITION

5-1

In the 1929 article "New Styles in Gardening" Fletcher Steele claimed that the innovation found in André and Paul Vera's garden compositions fell short of that achieved by other designers such as Gabriel Guevrekian or Pierre-Émile Legrain. Steele saw the Veras as being "strongly influenced by modern thought" yet dismissed them, feeling "inclined to think of them rather, in company with M. Gréber and M. Forestier, as modern rather than modernistic."[1] André Vera's contribution to landscape criticism is clear; his position as a designer, with his brother, Paul, is perhaps more ambiguous.

The vague definition of *modernity* is partly responsible for this ambiguity. The 1925 Exposition des Arts Décoratifs revealed all the degrees of innovation and the range of attitudes toward contemporary design. "We still thought in 1924," wrote a disenchanted critic, that *modern* was synonymous with "rational, appropriate, constructed, practical and solid." As a condemnation of the overly decorative tendencies evident in the exposition, he con-

5-1 GARDEN FOR JACQUES ROUCHÉ.
Paris, circa 1931. Paul Vera and Jean-Charles Moreux.
[Institut Français d'Architecture]

5-2

5-3

cluded that "the modernist hen [has] given birth to a duck with pretty feathers; [whereas] a superb rooster [was wanted]."[2]

In his "Considérations sur l'esprit moderne," Guillaume Janneau distinguished less radical contemporary designers such as Louis Süe and André Mare or Émile Ruhlmann from Pierre Chareau, Eileen Gray, or Pierre Legrain, who sought beauty in construction rather than in applied decoration.[3] Paul Vera was not among the latter group, and his frequent contribution to the Compagnie des Arts Français, founded by Süe and Mare in 1919, revealed his greater sympathy for a more traditional modernism rather than for one that championed the machine and the ocean liner.

The careers of André Vera (1881–1971) and Paul Vera (1882–1957) are so closely intertwined that it is difficult to isolate their respective roles in various projects. Paul was actively engaged in the decorative arts. His diversified production included screens, clocks, rattan chairs, woodblock engravings, decorative panels, sketches for canvas and tapestries, and gardens. André Vera insisted, not without bias, that such versatility was not evidence of instability but a sign of his brother's manic pursuit of excellence, which required him to bring the same attention and craft to an etching, a painting, or a parish garden.[4] Except for the conception of two gardens and hypothetical tales of vegetal tableaux, André Vera devoted himself to a literary career in landscape architecture and urbanism. In addition to several articles, he wrote *Le nouveau jardin* (1912); *Les jardins* (completed in 1914 and published in 1919); *Modernités* (1925); *L'urbanisme ou la vie heureuse* (1936), which included the earlier essays "Exhortation aux architectes de s'intéresser aux jardins" (1923) and "Nouvelle exhortation aux architectes de s'intéresser aux jardins" (1924); *L'urbanisme* (1946); and *L'homme et le jardin* (1950).

Despite Steele's categorization of him as a "modern" rather than a "modernistic" designer, André Vera should, in fact, be credited with the most extensive and focused writings on the early twentieth-century garden. J.C.N. Forestier also published several books and articles on the state and design of the modern garden, but he differed with André Vera on various points. Although he almost systematically favored regular designs, Forestier dismissed any notion of a truly universal style. Furthermore, he rejected the legitimacy of art theory applied directly to the landscape.

5-2 STUDY FOR A FABRIC
DESIGN.
Paul Vera.
[*Les Arts de la Maison*,
Autumn 1926]

5-3 "JARDIN D'AMOUR."
The apple trees are
pruned in the form of
goblets, and the
pergolas are covered
with wisteria.
Illustration by Paul
Vera, wood engraving
signed Verdeau.
[Vera, *Les jardins*]

5-4 PARTERRE.
Ink wash sketch for *Les
jardins*. Circa 1913.
Paul Vera.
[Collection of Cooper-
Hewitt Museum,
New York.
Courtesy Yu-Chee
Chong Fine Art,
London]

5-4

According to Forestier, garden design was
"directed by general formulas transmitted
through tradition. These rules [were] modified
by the desire for innovation and by the needs of
daily life which [shaped] the physiognomy of
each period's works."[5]

André Vera, on the other hand, relentlessly
argued for the regular style, free of the social
and functional conscience of the period. "The
question of whether your garden must be
régulier or *paysager* is not worth posing any-
more: it must be *régulier*," he declared.[6] It was
in their Saint-Germain estate that André and
Paul Vera crystallized the rejection of the
picturesque layout.

Vera heralded the garden of the postwar years
as a symbol of France's reconstruction, both
material and moral. Displays of brilliant and
shiny vegetation formed "flamboyant flares of
lyricism," and a profusion of red foliage was
meant to "warm the heart." The sober ornamentation of flower vases resting on slightly
curved columns expressed "abundance" as well
as "naïveté," "youth," and thus "promises";
the copies of antique torsos, in calm poses,
brought dignity to the estate, for "to the local
peasants, the garden needed to appear as
belonging to a familial abode, not a casino."[7]
To erase the damage the country had suffered
in war, a new order was necessary. To retrieve
an image of France unsullied by foreign influences, the rediscovery of tradition and its
regional roots was essential.

To answer the call he himself had raised, André
Vera proposed a vernacular modernism that
praised labor and reflected his strict religious
morals. The garden he described in an article
titled "Modernité et tradition" presented a
grove of pruned and fruit-bearing trees as a
metaphor for cultivating social values.[8] He recommended—then and again after the Second
World War—that one choose the trees from
regional species, not for a picturesque effect,
but to reinforce a bond with the provinces of
France, singly and collectively. If Vera dis-
carded cedars of Lebanon and catalpas because
of their foreign origin, he nevertheless relied
heavily on thujas, from North America, China,
or Japan, and privets, from China.[9] Later, he
would imperatively recommend the selection of
foreign coniferous species for public parks.[10]
Despite his inconsistent refutation of exoticism,
Vera cited the exhortation of Pius XII "to
develop the deep sense of [one's] past and land"
to promote regionalism and modernity.[11]
Modeled on morals, Vera's garden reflected the

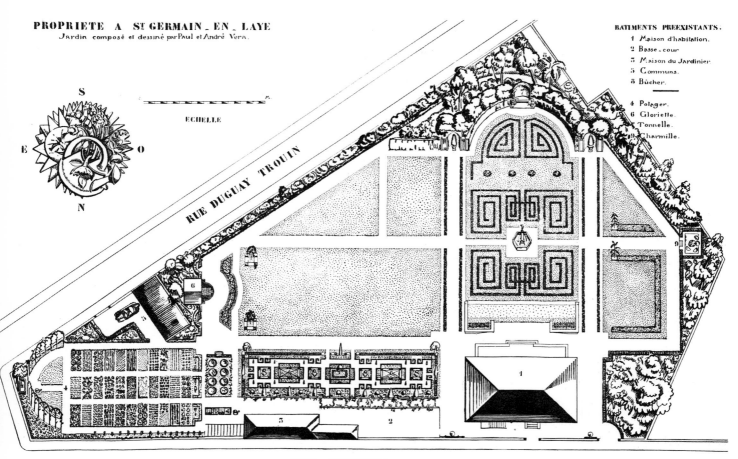

PROPRIETE A St GERMAIN - EN - LAYE

Jardin composé et dessiné par Paul et André Vera.

ECHELLE

BATIMENTS PREEXISTANTS.

1 Maison d'habitation.
2 Basse - cour
3 Maison du Jardinier
5 Communs.
8 Bûcher.

4 Potager.
6 Gloriette.
7 Tonnelle.
9 Charmille.

RUE DUGUAY TROUIN

RUE QUINAULT

5-5

enclosed and inwardly focused cloister of the Middle Ages rather than an invitation to foreign experience.

Vera's design not only was sharp and crisp—as a reaction against the "Sybaritism, individualism and weakness" of "romantic evil"—but also acknowledged activities, whether leisure or labor. The young bourgeois who had experienced the action of war, according to Vera, might feel the need for exercise. Thus, they would welcome areas for playing tennis or throwing the discus. Officers would ride horseback on a track geometrically composed of white stripes and red sand, lined with green lawn, and adorned with statues.[12]

Like the medieval garden, several of the landscapes Vera proposed were more than purely visual in function. Juxtaposing the yard with the pleasure garden, he extended the spatial hierarchy of the house outdoors. Divided in rectangular compartments, the layout of the garden mirrored the rooms of an apartment and the contiguous domestic quarters.[13] The garden room (*salle fraîche*) was served by corridors of pergolas; the lawn it faced was a carpet graced with lines of boxwood, furnished with controlled shrubs, and delineated by sheared green walls. At the other end, the service alley and chicken coop—which preferably sheltered only white species—were conveniently hidden by a portico overgrown with vines.[14]

A perfect illustration of these design principles was the garden for La Thébaïde, a retreat for meditation located in Saint-Germain-en-Laye.[15] André Vera acquired the estate in 1920 and with Paul designed the garden shortly thereafter. As an essay in permanence, the garden was intended to provide visual interest during each season. The central expanse of lawn was enclosed by evergreen trees, bordered with *Euonymus fortunei radicans,* and imprinted with rigorous geometric motifs of boxwood. Praising the variations in hues throughout the day, Vera affirmed that the garden, although monochromatic, was not monotonous.[16] This symphony of greens was set against a background of varnished red lattices.[17] The structures were balanced by a colorful flower garden, bordered by varieties of silver and yellow boxwood. [Plate IX] He recommended that flower beds be arranged in the garden with the same circumspection that governs the setting of stones in a necklace or touches of color in a painting.[18] Although Vera was inspired by the purest Gallic tradition, he

5-5 LA THÉBAÏDE.
SITE PLAN.
Saint-Germain-en-Laye,
circa 1921.
André and Paul Vera.
[Marrast, 1925 *Jardins*]

5-6 LA THÉBAÏDE.
CENTRAL PARTERRE
WITH BOXWOOD
MOTIFS.
Circa 1921.
André and Paul Vera.
[*L'Architecte*, 1924]

ANDRÉ VERA; PAUL VERA; JEAN-CHARLES MOREUX: MODERNITY & TRADITION

75

5-6

5-7 "JARDIN DE L'AVIATEUR."
AERIAL PERSPECTIVE.
Paul Vera.
[Vera, *Les jardins*]

5-8 GARDEN FOR PAUL-ÉLIE
GERNEZ. PARTIAL PLAN.
Honfleur, circa 1923.
Paul Vera.
[*L'Architecture
d'Aujourd'hui,* April
1937]

acknowledged the legacy of romanticism. He described the new jardin régulier as composed of elemental shapes and planted with the variegated foliage and long-blooming species bequeathed by our curious romantic ancestors. Thus the modern garden was rendered brighter than any of its formalist predecessors.[19] At La Thébaïde, the gardener's contribution was limited to execution rather than to creation.[20] Since vegetation was used to reinforce an enclosure, to garnish, or to color, the design of the garden could be placed in the hands of the architect. To reinforce the pattern of evergreens, the Veras used concrete as a would-be mineral equivalent in permanence. The corners of the embroidered lawn were marked by blocks of stone-aggregate concrete, which through frequent whitewashings maintained a new appearance. At the center of the parterre a concrete statue of Jupiter crowned a fountain. Its hexagonal pool was cast in concrete, as was the column supporting the statue. The contradiction between the classical image of a gilded Jupiter and the contemporary nature of its structural material best expressed the dichotomy between tradition and modernity that characterized the Veras' gardens.[21]

This veneer of contemporaneity overlaid upon the permanence of classicism constituted the essence of the Veras' modernism. In the reduced and simplified twentieth-century garden, the brothers arranged replicas or casts of antique statues, as if to remind the viewer that beneath the newer ideas of the garden as machine or garden as ocean liner was the foundation of the garden as a classical conception.[22] In this regard, they succeeded in combining the two necessary dimensions of the artwork that Baudelaire described as the substance of modernity: "the transitory, the fugitive, the contingent, half of art, [with its] other half: the eternal and the immutable."[23]

Ordered by a *tracé régulateur* of squares, double squares, rectangles, triangles, and multiples, the garden would strike a common chord, which André Vera saw as a complement to the architectural harmony praised by Eupalinos.[24] The perfect example of a garden ruled by mathematics and the compass was to be found in the designs of André Le Nôtre: "All of [his plans] are submitted to mathematics. . . . Everything is calculated. The numbers . . . generate numbers. Is it not opportune to return to these traditional principles when we truly desire, by taste and necessity, a bare style? Mathematical beauty requires no ornamenta-

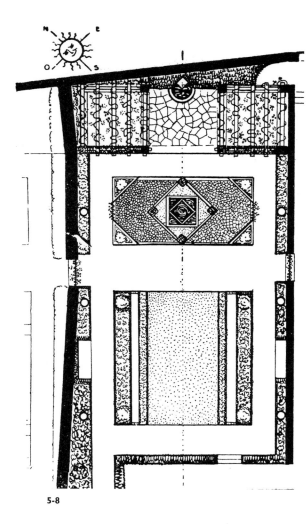

5-8

tion. . . . Harmony creates the appearance of plenty, which brings joy and serenity of mind. With green open spaces, you provide health; with flowers, trees, and shrubs blooming successively, you provide hope; with mathematics, you provide peace."[25]

Although André Vera revered the richness of the French classical tradition, he was nonetheless aware of the transformations that had occurred during the first decades of the twentieth century. The diffusion of electricity, air and automotive travel, radio and cinema, radically influenced the quality of living and the perception of the world. The faster pace of modern life required the "composition of a decorative piece to be synthetic, rather than analytic, as it had been during the centuries of leisure."[26]

The series of gardens André Vera published in *Le nouveau jardin* or *Les jardins*, which Paul Vera illustrated, also juxtaposed classicism with modernity. An overall symmetry balanced the weight of the various green rooms, which were designated for such fashionable activities as tennis, vegetable gardening, or aviation. A bird's-eye view of the "Jardin de l'aviateur" revealed that the aviator had "exerted his power . . . on a few acres and completely subdued them. His Daedalian tyranny being recent, his authority [was] still severe. The composition of the garden [was] rigorous: the interlocking surfaces [were] indissoluble, the proportions [were] exact and the oppositions clear."[27]

The Architecte de jardins Paul Vera first materialized the imagery of his engravings in Honfleur, where he created a garden for his friend the painter Paul Élie Gernez.[28] Period photographs, a plan, and an extant portion of the original garden indicate a nearly perfect combination of geometry and regionalism. Paul Vera executed its design in two parts: the first can be dated around 1923, the second, sometime before his 1930 design for a public garden, also in Honfleur.[29]

In spite of the ubiquitous pruned yews and square pools, a marine atmosphere pervades the Norman design. [Plate X] "Adapted to the climate of the estuary," André Vera remarked, the garden is disguised in neither the English nor the Japanese style; rather, it is "dressed in the costume of Honfleur."[30] Garden ornaments sheathed with seashells, paths paved with pebbles, and nautical references to mermaids and dolphins evinced a vernacular tone as they glis-

5-9 PUBLIC PARK.
SITE PLAN.
Honfleur, 1930.
Paul Vera.
[Musée d'art et
d'histoire, Saint-
Germain-en-Laye]

5-10 GARDEN FOR PAUL-ÉLIE
GERNEZ. SEASHELL
AND CEMENT
ORNAMENT.
Honfleur, circa 1923.
Paul Vera.
[Courtesy Janine
Hébert]

5-11 "TRÈS GRAND JARDIN
EN TERRASSES."
PLAN.
Paul Vera.
[Vera, *Le nouveau
jardin*]

78

5-10

5-9

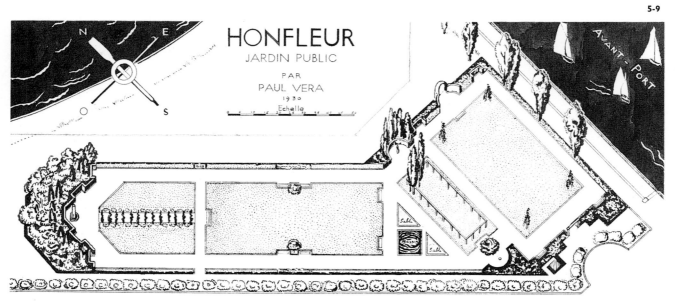

tened under the more-than-frequent rain. André Vera described the plants as *rustiques,* hardy and fitting the simplicity of the countryside. The winter attire of lawn, spindle trees, yews, boxwood, and ivy was enlivened by hydrangeas and flowering perennials during the summer. The two garden rooms each bore a distinct character. The "salon," with its pool, frescoes, and ornamental shellwork, appeared exuberant in comparison to the sober composition of the cloister.

The layout of this charming and almost monochromatic mixture of yews and seashells still reflected the rigorous geometrical composition of the garden of Saint-Germain-en-Laye in that both plans were ruled by multiples of the same unit. A similar classic modernity was apparent in the garden's details. The central pool of water—formed by a series of concentric squares, each rotated forty-five degrees—was neatly outlined with pebbles and bricks. The tone was underscored by the contrast between the timeless quality of seashells and the modernity suggested by the concrete in which they were set.

André Vera himself frequently argued for a regional garden, but his imaginary landscapes appear universally applicable. Whether intended for the suburbs or for the mountains, for an aviator or for lovers, the layouts were similar in line and featured the same orchards, vegetable gardens, beehives, and tennis courts.[31] His only concession to a mountainous location was to step the garden in terraces, although even here the arrangement of rooms and galleries, axes and pools, grandly ignored their site. This "Très grand jardin en terrasses" functioned like other walled gardens, with its own internal sources of distractions, food, and beauty.[32]

The specificity of order, however, was found in the relation of garden to building. Subordinating the secondary to the primary element, that is, the landscape to the architecture, Vera dissected the ground and the elevation of the garden into a succession of proportions derived from the plan and facade of the house.[33] Thus several of the gardens planned or constructed by André and Paul Vera mirrored an extreme contextuality not to the outside world but to the interior living arrangement. In plans or dimetric projections of the Noailles, Rouché, or André projects, the membrane between the inside and the garden is represented as a dividing and dictating line, the doors, windows, and steps of the terrace determining the patterns

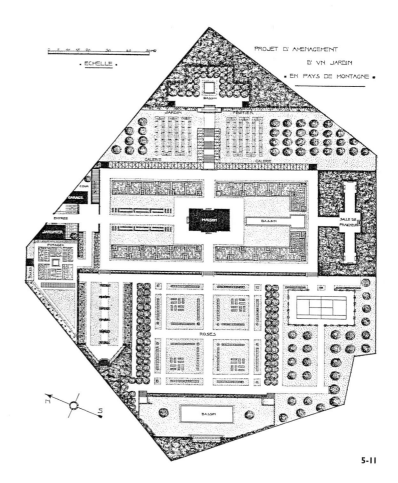

5-11

and walks on the ground, the position of focal points, and the elevation of the garden wall. All served to bind interior and exterior.

André Vera appealed to architects to attain this tight correlation of garden, house, and decorative arts. He dismissed landscape architects, to whom "statuary is nudity gamboling on the lawn" and whose imprecision countered the contemporary fascination with measure.[34] Landscape architects were to restrict their design activities to parks, for they were prone to revert to the once-fashionable style paysager. And "since independence, Sybaritism, dilettantism, inertia, weakness, negligence, indifference, caprice, dispersion, acceptance of incertitude . . . will not need be represented in any of our works," wrote Vera, "in the garden, we shall no longer see sinuous lines, serpentine alleys nor undulated lawns, rounded contours . . . and exotic pursuits."[35]

Prior to his "Exhortation to Interest Architects in the Making of Gardens"[36] Vera had entreated these designers to consider "a garden [that] will be extended through enumeration, a whole developed in dependent parts . . . [featuring] stepping levels, terraces, horizontal parterres, angles, straight allées, lines of trees of one species—grafted, pruned and sheared . . . [where] canals and pools will be dug according to geometric outlines and be neatly bordered with stones or lawn."[37]

Although Vera was an advocate for an architectonic garden that expanded the interior order into outdoor rooms through a rigorous mineral structure, his writings still reflected a deep sensitivity to the poetic and cyclical aspects of nature. Little desire for permanence informed his account of the "Jardin d'amour," published in 1914.[38] [Plate XI] A possible dedication to the brotherly love between André and Paul, it revealed an understanding of vegetation that might appear contradictory in light of the bareness of the garden the Veras later drew for the vicomte de Noailles. Not unlike Forestier's tale of Andalusian gardens, published in 1921, André Vera's description of aromatic plants was detailed and delicate:

> We remain at length on our bench; we are still there when the sun sets and the heat is softer: it is the hour of perfumes. . . . The fragrant alyssum that discreetly and suavely frames the other flowers, the sweet woodruff, the *daphné bois-joli* that bears a gay name, the flag iris, the Persian lilac and the Varin lilac, which we prefer to every other lilac because they withstand pruning, [and] the fragrant grape hyacinth and narcissus blossom in the spring;

while the blister cress, the stock, the yellow day lily . . . continue to flower into summer. Then the Centaurea . . . the dragon's heads, the lavender, the white lily, the sweet marjoram so familiar to troubadours . . . the different varieties of carnations, the phlox, the climbing and dwarf sweet pea, whose blooms resemble attentive butterflies, the reseda and the rosemary, both of provincial style, the exuberant valerian and the modest verbena, all flower only during the summer months. But the *Amaryllis belladonna*, the asclepias, the *Cestrum nocturnum* . . . the ardent crimson-black sneezeweed, the heliotrope . . . the Cruckshanks lupine . . . the *Phlox paniculata* with its innumerable marveled eyes, the *rose à-parfum-de-l'Hay*, the *rose roseraie-de-l'Hay*, the fragrant white tobacco plant . . . and the fragrant iberis keep flowering until the end of September. Because our flower beds are lined by a trellis covered with white jasmine and honeysuckle, because our bench is encased within privet hedges which we clip only after their strangely fragrant bloom has past, all the air we breathe is scented.[39]

Although André Vera had formerly approached the question of plants in the modern garden—recommending monochromatic expanses of flowers, in the manner of both contemporary fashion and the seventeenth-century garden—he rarely defined vegetation with the subtlety offered in his description of the "Jardin d'amour." In fact, Vera more characteristically praised such plants as ivy, boxwood, and *Euonymus fortunei* for their evergreen and malleable character, perhaps implicitly acknowledging the limitations of architectural formalism. Whether the result of an excessive trust in the capacity of architects to think in a space-time framework or a lack of confidence in the design capabilities of landscape architects, the architectonic gardens executed during the early twentieth century endured the loss of the subtle horticultural palette of designers like Forestier. The refinement of olfactory composition attained in the "Jardin d'amour," mirrored by the poetic nature of the imaginary places illustrated in Paul Vera's engravings, was seldom encountered in the modern visual garden.[40] La Thébaïde linked art and nature with poetry: it was successfully "constructed with plants and science."[41] The "rationalized garden" described as the encounter between art(ifice) and nature prevailed with "red- and yellow-colored gravels, crushed marble, refuse from the foundry: black, shiny, unalterable as jet," and little fragrance.[42] In spite of their traditional roots, the later gardens of André and Paul Vera seemed to play art against nature. Vegetation

5-12 LA THÉBAÏDE. THE
FLOWER GARDEN.
Saint-Germain-en-Laye,
circa 1921.
André and Paul Vera.
[*L'Architecte*, 1924]

5-12

withered. The 1924 garden for the vicomte de Noailles, in Paris, more closely resembled an outdoor parquetry than a landscape from the traditional mold.

THE MIRROR IN THE GARDEN: LE JARDIN NOAILLES

PARIS, 1924. Situated on the Place des États-Unis, the nineteenth-century hôtel of Charles and Marie-Laure de Noailles reflected all the brilliance of discriminating and ambitious art patronage. Although André and Paul Vera cosigned the plans for the garden in 1924, Jean-Charles Moreux, a close friend of the brothers Vera and a frequent collaborator with Paul, is sometimes credited with its design, completed in 1926. No drawings for the Noailles garden are found in the Moreux archives, and contemporary photographs of the garden usually cite Paul Vera as the sole designer. Features such as the fence lined with mirrors, however, suggest Moreux's participation in the project.[43] This garden, which was highly atypical of works by the Veras, might have resulted from their collaboration with Moreux or from the directives of their clients.

The Noailles garden—which could be better defined as an esplanade—exuded a sober luxury: its five-thousand-square-foot area in the center of Paris was composed as an extravagant tableau in spite of a Spartan use of color and plants. Not intended as a garden in which to stroll, it functioned primarily as a picture to be seen from the windows of the hôtel. Its subtle variations of minerals, glittering under the city's frequently overcast skies, provided a nearly perfect example of a dry garden. Vegetation was restricted to low, trimmed boxwood and controlled ground covers; the remainder of the garden was given over to a diversity of gravel, brick, pebbles, and stone. The only seasonal change of color—apart from the deciduous trees surrounding the garden—was a spring planting of monochromatic flowers that replaced certain of the mineral panels. Ironically, this graphic composition, in which vegetation provided merely a texture or color accent, was designed for a man whose horticultural passion was later recognized internationally.[44]

In spite of the inherent flatness of its design, the perceptions of this picture garden—like the projects of Gabriel Guevrekian or Pierre Legrain—varied markedly with the point of view.[45] From ground level, the colors and patterns of the paving and vegetation merged into one another, both floating on the lighter hue of

5-13 THE NOAILLES GARDEN. PLAN.
Paris, circa 1925.
André and Paul Vera.
[*Les Arts de la Maison,* Winter 1926]

5-14 THE NOAILLES GARDEN IN WINTER.
The bench in the far corner is by Paul Vera. In time, vines would have framed the mirror-clad enclosure and created the illusion of a *fenêtre en longueur.* Place des États-Unis, Paris, circa 1926.
André and Paul Vera; Jean-Charles Moreux.
[Lurcat, *Terrasses et jardins*]

5-13

5-14

the gravel. The sole anthropomorphic references within this *tableau-jardin* were the figurative statue reflected in the mirror-lined wall and two sculptures by Henri Laurens that flanked a bench by Paul Vera, which anchored the farthest corner of the site. I refer to this type of composition as a tableau-jardin, for in addition to being a picture in itself, the design also suggests the application of the cubist *tableau-objet* to the form of the garden. A painting or image is a physical entity complete in itself, which need not relate to the surrounding decor.[46] The mirrors in the Noailles garden reflected the hôtel, its inhabitants, and the tree trunks that rhythmically lined the limit of the space. The reflective wall also brought the sky into the garden, its soft brilliance contrasting with the dense shade of the summer foliage that screened the buildings beyond the garden.

Few descriptions of the Noailles garden provide an accurate account of the plants and materials employed, as if the lines of the pattern were more important than the vegetation or the elements by which they were rendered. Rectangular grey stones in a basket-weave pattern framed the garden's panels of fragmented shapes that alternated plantings of grasses and blue lobelia with red bricks, yellow stones, and black-and-white checkerboard mosaics.[47] Seen from above, the reflection of the wedge-shaped mosaics appeared as a continuation of the pattern on the public sidewalk beyond the wall. Because of its two-dimensional treatment, the essence of the garden was reduced to an image of nature, and with its frame of stone paving, that image became a tableau. For its seemingly fragmented representation, the tableau was interpreted by contemporary observers as cubist.

Although photographs taken obliquely suggest a garden composed of multiple perspectives and contradictory vanishing points, the plans and design sketches by André and Paul Vera depict a rather different conception. The state of unrest of the trapezium-shaped lot was, in fact, regularized by a continuation of the hôtel's terraces into the garden. The width of the steps determined the size of the parterres, each presenting a specific pattern to the window it addressed. The photographic view, in which no line paralleled another, distorted the forced perspective shown in plan. As an advocate of a traditional modernism, André Vera had recommended designing the garden with "precision" and "mark[ing] with care the entrances of parterres with a noticeable threshold, with narrow trees, with stelae, statues, or other signs, as one would mark the principal points of [the] layout."[48] The protrusion of the hôtel steps and terraces addressed two sets of triangles symmetrically arranged along an axis perpendicular to the facade, their sharp angles converging toward statues and tree trunks. Although seemingly an independent abstraction, the Noailles design expressed Vera's concept of a garden that actively interacted with the house like a mortise and tenon.[49] The location of the allée dividing these parterres was determined by the gap between the terraces; the path was terminated by a statue. Preliminary sketches by André and Paul Vera reveal the subdivision of the three decorative parterres into triangles. As a matter of fact, the hypotenuse of the figure was corrected to develop a design of interlocking equilateral triangles. The simple lines and Greek patterns traced on the garden at Saint-Germain were transposed into the more modern motifs of triangulated spirals and zig-zags. With a few squares, a lozenge, circles, and several triangles, the Veras delineated a geometric composition that clearly translated contemporary fabric patterns for women's garments into designs for parterres.[50] Despite the vibrancy of the zig-zags, the relationship between solid and void of this early scheme was rather static, the motifs appearing as a series of fashionable carpets displayed beneath the windows. On the other hand, the geometric vocabulary of the realized design was limited to the triangle, equilateral or other, thus creating a bold effect in spite of a prevalent symmetry. Although drawn as regular forms, the wedges of boxwood stenciled on the gravel appeared as fragments of a large mirror that had been shattered on the paving, dramatically reflecting the physical lines of rupture.

When one considers Paul Vera's artistic signature, the ground pattern of the Noailles garden appears radical, its unstable gestalt further fragmented by the reflections in the mirrored wall. It is tempting to see a reference to cubism in the inclusion of mirrors within an essentially pictorial garden composition. As pokes at reality, Juan Gris added fragments of newspaper, fabric, or even mirror to his paintings. In both *Le Lavabo* (formerly known as *Table de Toilette*), painted in 1912, and *The Marble Console*, executed two years later, Gris included a piece of mirror because "it could not be imitated."[51] Similarly, the mirror in the Noailles garden reflected the rather unsettling play between artifice and nature.

5-15 THE NOAILLES GARDEN
SEEN FROM THE UPPER
FLOOR.
The mirror-lined door is
open.
[Photo: Man Ray;
© 1993 ARS, N.Y. /
ADAGP, Paris]

5-15

    Ce matin
  La tête dépasse
 Un coup de poing enfonce le paysage et
l'esprit
  Le pan du jardin bascule et va tomber
de l'autre côté du mur
      Le gong éclate
 Le soleil
  Les débris de verre
  dans l'œil du promeneur
 Gong

Pierre Reverdy,
"L'imperméable,"
in *La peau de l'homme,*
1926

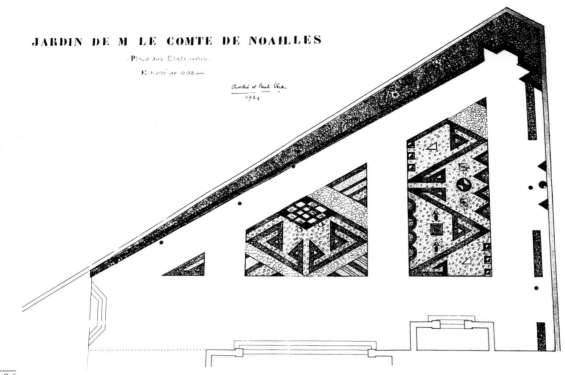

JARDIN DE M LE COMTE DE NOAILLES

.Place des Etats unis.

Echelle de 0.02 om

André et Paul Véra
1924

5-16

86

5-17

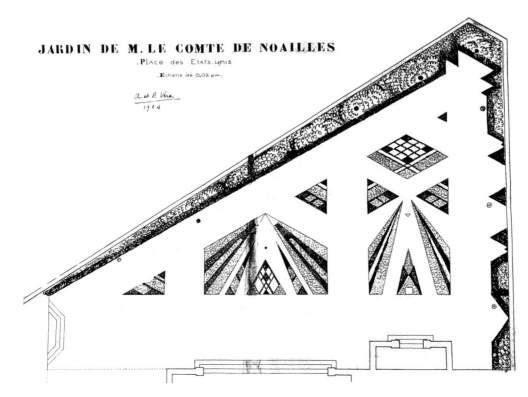

JARDIN DE M. LE COMTE DE NOAILLES

.Place des Etats unis

.Echelle de 0.02 pm.

A. et P. Véra
1924

The mirrors lined only a limited strip of the hypotenuse of the garden. More than merely a device to increase depth, the use of reflection was a conscious design gesture. The illusionistic ribbon window framed by ivy created a tension and an ambiguity that would have been undermined by the reflection ad infinitum had mirrors lined both walls. The optical displacement of the hôtel's facade to the limit of the site was a perfect expression of the garden as an extension of the interior. By walling the garden with the image of architecture, the parterre belonged to the living room, like a carpet brought outdoors.

Alberti saw Narcissus as the first painter, writes John Berger: "The mirror renders the appearances of nature and simultaneously delivers them into the hands of man."[52] The image of nature replicated by the mirrors of the Noailles garden was an artist's pictorial ideal. The illusion of nature was rendered with planes, colors, and lines, as in a painting, except that at the hôtel de Noailles, this image was manipulated and modernized. The mirror addressed the many textures of the garden just as the real, extraneous element articulated the painted surfaces of a cubist tableau. A giant *papier-collé*, the Noailles garden joined the pictorial reality of the parterre with the virtual world of the mirror.[53] It became a reality twice removed: an image of an image that further fragmented the pattern and eschewed historical perspective by doubling the vanishing points. Through these devices, the garden embodied a grotesque version of Renaissance space.

As a tableau-objet, the garden exemplified an inherent reality apart from quotidian existence until confronted by human presence. The mirrors allowed the spectator to include his or her own image within the tableau-jardin without disrupting the unstable equilibrium between a two-dimensional picture and a three-dimensional human figure. Thus in the tableau of the Noailles garden, the image of man was at least optically reunited with the image of nature.

5-16 THE NOAILLES GARDEN. VARIANT PLAN. 1924. André and Paul Vera. [Musée d'art et d'histoire, Saint-Germain-en-Laye]

5-17 THE NOAILLES GARDEN AS REALIZED. PLAN. 1924. André and Paul Vera. [Musée d'art et d'histoire, Saint-Germain-en-Laye]

5-18 *THE MARBLE CONSOLE.* 1914. Juan Gris. [Private collection] "A surface can be transposed on a canvas, a volume can be interpreted, but what about a mirror, a changing surface which even reflects the spectator? One can only apply the real thing." (Juan Gris to Michel Leiris, *Juan Gris*)

5-18

5-19 JEAN-CHARLES MOREUX IN HIS ATELIER.
On the wall is an axonometric view of a project for low-cost housing on the outskirts of Paris, 1927.
[Photo: Therese Bonney; © 1993 ARS, N.Y. / SPADEM, Paris]

5-20 HOTEL SHEPHEARD'S. DANCE FLOOR.
Cairo, 1947. Jean-Charles Moreux.
[Institut Français d'Architecture]

5-21 *SALLE FRAÎCHE* FOR L. L. WEILL.
Poigny, circa 1932. Jean-Charles Moreux.
[Institut Français d'Architecture]

JEAN-CHARLES MOREUX

Remembered as the "last man of the Renaissance" and as a humanist "not quite at home in the twentieth century," Jean-Charles Moreux (1889–1956) balanced a wide range of professional interests within a primarily architectural practice.[54] He seems to have possessed astute political skills: he was entrusted with protecting the artistic patrimony of the eastern front after the First World War, taught at the Beaux-Arts in Dijon (in the Occupied Zone) in 1940, and held a position in the Department of Reconstruction the following year.[55] His prolific architectural career appears to have spanned the years before, during, and after the Second World War relatively unscathed, at least quantitatively. Moreux participated in, and curated, several expositions and salons, either as architect, or as interior, furniture, or garden designer. He not only propagated his ideas through periodicals, such as *L'Amour de l'Art*, of which he was an editor, but also lectured on the art of the garden and published his landscape designs extensively.[56] Moreux was a member of the Union des Artistes Modernes (U.A.M.) and was later named chief architect for public works and national monuments.[57] Seemingly contradictory, these positions in fact revealed the same blending of modernity and history that formed the foundation of the Veras' doctrine. As a collector of astrolabes, telescopes, minerals, and birds, Moreux was compared to eighteenth-century amateurs; considering himself a humanist, he explained that a search for an ordered nature should not eclipse the human side of things.[58] For having asserted that architecture should not ignore the past and that the modern should not be adopted uncritically, just because it is new, Moreux was described as being closer to Andrea Palladio and Claude-Nicolas Ledoux than to his contemporaries.[59] Le Corbusier's work was a case in point. Moreux confessed that "like everyone else, I first built on pilotis, but I soon realized that after one cube came only another cube, and that was very boring."[60] The emerging International Style was conceptually impoverished, because it sufficiently acknowledged neither recent history nor the human dimension.

In his work, Moreux established a certain equilibrium between tradition and contemporaneity. An ideological sympathy and a common design vocabulary strengthened his friendship with the brothers Vera. As a result of this professional bond, the respective contribu-

5-19

tions made by each of these three designers on collaborative projects are not easily distinguished. For example, the attribution of the grounds of La Thébaïde in Saint-Germain to Moreux is rather hazy. As in the case of the Noailles garden, the only traces of the design process remain in the Vera archives; however, this does not preclude a contribution, if only technical, by Moreux.[61] Although the architect decorated several of the rooms in La Thébaïde, the drawn plan of the garden reads only: "Jardin composé et dessiné par Paul et André Vera." In sum, then, it is best not to attempt to pick apart these works but to treat them simply as fruitful collaborations. Tentatively credited as a landscape architect as early as 1920 or 1924, Moreux created gardens until 1954.[62] This continuous involvement with landscape design distinguished him from other designers like Pierre-Émile Legrain and Gabriel Guevrekian, who either fleetingly or only periodically focused their attention on the garden.

Even within the realm of landscape architecture, Jean-Charles Moreux greatly varied his approach from project to project. Although the garden of the twentieth century should be in the *style régulier,* he believed, it could alternate among the *jardin à la française,* the *jardin à l'italienne,* and the *jardin espagnol.*[63] Cross-cultural references abounded in his work: for example, in 1947 an Italianate garden was laid out on the grounds of the Hotel Shepheard's in Cairo. Moreux described its dance floor as a "composition with four lobes . . . flanked by 'salles fraîches'"—references to the seventeenth century. The tile pattern replicated the design of the Chapel of Anet, built by Philibert de l'Orme during the late Renaissance.[64] Like his choice of styles, the scale of Moreux's contributions was also flexible: rattan armchairs in a *gloriette,* salles fraîches, a private wharf, a swimming pool, furnished balconies and garden terraces, exposition gardens, small private city and country gardens, large estates, and public squares.

Like the Veras, Moreux favored the style régulier over the picturesque. In the text for the Rotterdam exhibition on "The French Garden from the Middle Ages to Our Day," which he curated, Moreux outlined the historical evolution of the French formal garden. He extolled the geometry and symmetry that had characterized these gardens until the fateful date of 1763, when "English fashion, with its Chinese jardins paysagers, upset the noble equilibrium of the jardin à la française . . . . The garden of

5-20

5-21

the senses superseded the garden of the mind." Fortunately, Moreux concluded, "this romantic wave was short-lived and barely [altered] the beautiful trajectory of the jardin régulier, the glory of France."[65]

Moreux's design vocabulary derived from several distinct formal sources. From the Middle Ages, he borrowed the geometric layout of squares delineated by paths, with pools or fountains at their intersections; this Oriental flavor reflected the contribution of the Crusaders. More or less literally, he applied the motifs of the jardin à la française to his compositions. Although the Noailles parterre was an extravagant marquetry[66] of boxwood inlaid with flowers and gravels of different colors, the garden designed by Moreux with Paul Vera for Jacques Rouché was a quieter design, a modest reform of the *parterre de broderie*. Moreux later designed Grosvenor Gardens in London, which prominently featured a cursive fleur-de-lys—a rather direct application of a classically French garden motif to a mid-twentieth-century public square. The architect also reinterpreted the grandiose unity of land and sky found in Le Nôtre's gardens, in which planes of water were used as "immense reflectors" bringing sky to earth while the surface of canals also duplicated the verticality of trees.[67] In his more modest, but equally pictorial, compositions, Moreux skipped the metaphor entirely and applied the mirror directly to the garden.

In the purest French tradition, Jean-Charles Moreux restated the need to extend to the garden the geometry and harmony characteristic of formal architecture. The principles he employed in building could be applied as well to the landscape. Optical corrections, human scale, and the use of the module, colors, and relief enriched the general composition. Moreux advocated a *jardin sec*, or dry garden, for it was "a garden without weeds, without gardener. A garden always clean and gay."[68]

5-22

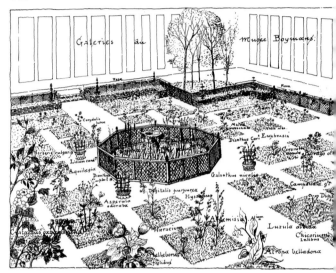

5-23

CÔTÉ-COUR; CÔTÉ-JARDIN: THE GARDENS FOR JACQUES ROUCHÉ

PARIS, 1930.   Director of the Théâtre des Arts during the 1910s, Jacques Rouché had become head of the Opéra by the time Paul Vera and Jean-Charles Moreux designed his garden. Like Charles de Noailles, Rouché was an enlightened patron of the arts and founding benefactor of the U.A.M.[69] Under his direction, the Théâtre des Arts had sought and implemented aesthetic unity on the stage.[70] Sets and costumes, for example, were designed by the same artist in close collaboration with the director of the play. The stage was conceived as a stylized pictorial frame in which decor and costumes fused to form an integrated whole.[71] Rouché commissioned Vera and Moreux, who framed his hôtel with a refined scenographic garden.

The English conventions of "stage right" or "stage left" also apply to French theater, except that orientation is indicated by either the *côté-cour* (courtyard side) or the *côté-jardin* (garden side) of the traditional hôtel. For Rouché, Vera and Moreux designed an urban garden composed of two independent but connected landscapes for a côté-cour and a côté-jardin. Both were dictated by geometry. Apart from some contained planting, one garden was entirely mineral; the other admitted only a minimal amount of vegetation into its sanctum.

The côté-cour was enclosed by buildings on three sides and bordered on the fourth by a low wall with a latticed partition above it. Receiving little light, this courtyard utilized few plants and was tiled almost entirely in white. The composition of the whole was divided according to the positioning of the windows and French doors of the hôtel. At the intersection of the views from the living and dining rooms was a single jet of water. The longitudinal axis led to a Greek statue, mounted away from the wall to intercept the view from one of the dining room windows, while the other transverse line ended with bonsai set on stepped ledges. Aligned with the living room was a Greek pattern composed of polished limestone floating on a darker ground of decomposed and compacted greenish-grey porphyry. The hygienic white ceramic tile facing the corner planters added a modernistic note that completed the unsettling eclecticism of this dry garden. The gilded bronze replica of the *Charioteer of Delphi* stood against a black polished marble stela—an illusory cutout in the white tiled wall that suggested greater depth.

5-24

The black-and-white composition of the côté-cour reflected rigor and stillness. The frozen meander framed by a pair of umber tree trunks addressed the raised hand of the charioteer, his movement captured in bronze.

With no furniture and a ground plane painted with tiles, stone aggregate, and evergreen shrubs, there was little to suggest motion in this austere pictorial composition. The pencil-like jet of water that animated the pool in the center of the courtyard was the sole exception to this stillness; aquatic creatures in black-and-white mosaic perpetually circled the squirting water.[72] In preliminary sketches, Paul Vera had studied various combinations of squares, although all layouts respected the alignment and dimensions of the openings they faced. The size, angle, and number of pools changed, but the positive/negative play of the central motif remained a constant. The permutations included (Scheme A) a tripartite arrangement of square modules rotated at an angle of forty-five degrees to the sides of the garden, framing potted plants and a pool. Less awkward was the continuous stream of mosaic fish and eels moving in a zig-zag from positive to negative (Scheme B), or the simple elegance of a stretch of square white tiles from which were cut out four units that played the game of opposites between black and white, plants and water (Scheme C). This tile-clad monochromatic shrine to exotic species and sculpture was paired with a second graphic composition glimpsed through the passage to the côté-jardin.

Paul Vera made sketches for both sections of the Rouché garden; Moreux executed the construction documents for the côté-jardin. The côté-cour was an almost exact realization of Vera's drawing (except for the reversed order of the stepped ledges on the side wall). The côté-jardin, as built, reflected more clearly the style of Moreux: the trellis partitions and the articulated mirrors are characteristic of his work during this period. The studies Vera composed for this section were far more conservative than the executed design.[73]

As formal as, although perhaps more playful than, the côté-cour, the côté-jardin was the exterior complement of the hôtel's dining room. Reversing the black/white ratio of the courtyard, in which the white tiles of the Greek meander were set against the darker aggregate, this section of the garden played a dark mass of vegetation against the lighter surface of white decomposed marble and sand. Here, Vera and

PETIT JARDIN A PARIS
PAUL VERA J.C. MOREUX
1930

Salle à Manger

Salon

5-25

5-26

5-25 GARDEN FOR JACQUES
ROUCHÉ.
CÔTÉ-COUR. PLAN.
Paris, 1930. Paul Vera.
[*L'Architecture
d'Aujourd'hui*, April
1937]

5-26 THE *CÔTÉ-COUR*.
The gilded replica of the
Charioteer of Delphi
is set against black
marble; the gravel is
gray-green prophyry. To
the right is a glimpse of
the *côté-jardin*.
Circa 1931.
Paul Vera and
Jean-Charles Moreux.
[*L'Architecte*, 1932]

5-27 THE POOL OF THE
CÔTÉ-COUR.
FULL-SCALE MOCK-UP,
DETAIL.
Ink wash. 1930.
Paul Vera.
[Courtesy Janine
Hébert]

5-28 THE *CÔTÉ-COUR*.
SCHEMES A,B,C.
1929–30. Paul Vera.
[Musée d'art et
d'histoire, Saint-
Germain-en-Laye]

5-28

A

B

93

5-27

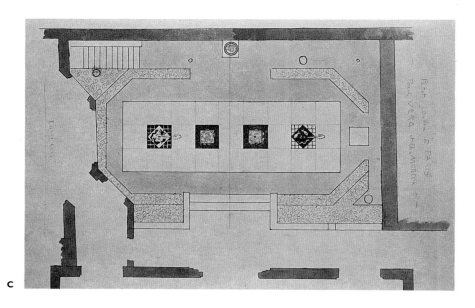

C

5-29 THE *CÔTÉ-JARDIN,*
LOOKING TOWARD
THE HÔTEL.
Paris, circa 1931.
Jean-Charles Moreux
and Paul Vera.
[Institut Français
d'Architecture]

5-30 THE *CÔTÉ-JARDIN,*
LOOKING TOWARD
THE MIRRORED
PARTITION.
The lateral niches are
painted light green, and
the columns supporting
silver spheres are
stuccoed with dark
green cement; the
trellises frame sheared
privets.
[*L'Architecte,* 1932]

94

Moreux composed a jardin régulier in which
all parts—a carpet of lawn, gravel, low
trimmed shrubs, and a fountain—were con-
tracted into a narrow elongated plan. A
lightning bolt of boxwood imprinted upon the
tapis vert enlivened the inherently static composition. A negative shadow of white marble
chips bordered by begonias set off the boxwood from the lawn. As a geometric version of
yin and yang—nature's equilibrium—studs of
clipped boxwood were inserted on alternating
sides of the central zig-zag; a frame of light
gravel expanded the limits of this geometrically
embroidered carpet.

The glass fountain, the focus of the garden,
was skewed forty-five degrees from the main
axis and opposed its translucent lightness to
the solidity of a masonry base. The motif of a
square within a square within a square
recurred in the designs of both Paul Vera
(Saint-Germain and Honfleur) and Jean-
Charles Moreux (the terrace of the Maison
Brugier and the Yvon garden).[74] The fountain
was internally lighted at night. Its chrome volutes whimsically suggested a frozen squirt of
water, a permanent jet that echoed the sus-
pended dynamism conveyed by the helicoidally
clipped yews.

The varying tonality and articulation of the lateral trellises modulated the elongated shape of
the garden, softening the effect of the alternating panels of light green wall and dark masses
of sheared hedges. This play of positive and
negative was also apparent in the parterre, the
ground, and the black marble benches.

A parallel can also be drawn between the
scheme for Mr. and Mrs. André's garden by
Paul Vera and the outdoor room of the côté-
jardin. The André project was a typical *décor
de fond de jardin,* a decor at the end of the garden. [Plate XII] The center was left open but
for a carpet of lawn; all ornamentation was
displayed against the wall, creating a peripheral strength similar to that of the Rouché
garden. In fact, the André design also recalled
the walls of the dining room at La Thébaïde,
decorated by Jean-Charles Moreux in 1926.
The André project was the perfect expression
of an apartment extended by the displacement
of its envelope to the limits of the garden. The
green wall of sheared shrubs replaced interior
wood paneling; the exterior niches showcased
statues instead of paintings.

The limited space of the garden for Jacques
Rouché almost demanded the use of axial symmetry. The côté-jardin, however, eschewed

5-29

5-30

complete rigidity with design puns such as the zig-zag boxwood pattern, the mirrors that articulated the end wall, and the dark green cement columns crowned with chromed spheres that caught the last reflections of light at the end of the day.[75]

In optically furthering the property line, the mirrors facing the narrow side of the garden functioned as a modern ha-ha. Not only did they enlarge the appearance of the garden by duplicating its dimensions, they also effaced its border. Existing trees and latticework layered the background to which two illusory allées seemed to lead. The angled mirrors suggested a tripartite, neobaroque composition in which the oblique views were marked by thresholds and framed by niches. The pair of mock openings repeated the same optical adjustments used in devising a dark frame around the statue of the charioteer in the côté-cour.

As a play between positive and negative architectonic modules, in which plants were treated as materials rather than as living organisms, the côté-cour allowed little change. The côté-jardin, on the other hand, constituted a dynamic design whose animation had been abruptly interrupted; it was a frozen gesture, a scene in which the actors were perpetually about to reappear from behind the modulated stage.

The Rouché garden did not imitate nature; instead, nature appeared in metaphors. Mirrors replaced allées, glass imitated water, and movement was imminent in the lightning pattern or the helicoidal shrubs. As a synthetic work, the garden was reduced to a cipher: a few lines, suggestive colors, and familiar textures were sufficient to evoke the presence of nature. Unlike its pendant, the côté-jardin suggested a human scale in its recessed benches. The illusion of depth was unidirectional, however: when seen in reverse, that is, from the mirrored panels looking toward the hôtel, the garden appeared drastically foreshortened and static. Furthermore, the visitor was estranged from the almost theatrical decor: set against this refined play of artifice, the figure became the principal natural element of the composition. Repeating the schism inherent in juxtaposing a human body against a stylized theater set, the perception of the garden as a pictorial entity was enhanced. Like the Noailles garden, the Rouché côté-jardin was a difficult tableau to traverse, yet it was a graphic garden that had shunned the fragmentation of the cubistic vocabulary.

OTHER PROJECTS

In many other designs for gardens, squares, terraces, and salles fraîches, Moreux mitigated his rather modernistic use of geometry and materials with an almost naïve classical eclecticism in which nature was severely tamed. An account of a garden presented by Moreux and Paul Vera at the 1924 Salon d'Automne described the balance between nature and formalism: "This rectangular garden first appears to be symmetrically arranged. In actuality, clever disruptions in the symmetry of its details keep the eye from 'learning' the garden layout too soon and tiring of it. The large central expanse of lawn is broken by oblique motifs which divert thoughts from too rigorous an axis. The garden does not follow the seasons, the seasons will follow the garden. It is composed of nonflowering evergreens, spindle trees, and boxwood; only potted plants 'comprise the seasonal decor.'"[76]

Moreux's mirror and mineral compositions did not always neglect horticultural concerns, however. His garden in Ardèche offered a delicate plant palette ranging from grey to dark green. The lavender, santolina, thyme, yews, and cypresses complemented the dry stone walls and water of this "jardin espagnol" with geometric Moorish patterns, the sum of which created stasis and symbiosis.[77]

Prior to the Rouché garden, Moreux had already used a folded screen of mirrors in his project for the hôtel de Rothschild in 1927. The addition of a swimming pool and exercise room to the Second Empire residence was sheathed by a contemporary facade that did not contrast too violently with the style of the previous century. Described as being of Palladian proportions, the new elevation featured cylindrical columns that framed a central niche, which was decorated with a fresco by Giorgio De Chirico illustrating a pair of horses trampling a broken Doric column.[78] Flanking the central part of this composition were two wings clad with mirrors that reflected multiple views of the existing jardin à la française. The unsettling juxtaposition of a neoclassical fragment with slick panes of silvered mirrors was exaggerated by the articulation of the reflective partition. The new wing would not simply disappear. Instead it destroyed the forward view of a French formal garden by collaging its duplicated fragments under the mass of existing foliage.

5-31 HOUSE WITH GARDEN
IN SAINT-GERMAIN-EN-
LAYE. MODEL.
Salon d'Automne, 1924.
Jean-Charles Moreux
and Paul Vera.
[Delisle, "J.-Ch.
Moreux"]

5-32 THE ARCHITECT'S OWN
GARDEN WITH A POOL
OF MOORISH
INSPIRATION.
Malet-Largentière,
1938. Jean-Charles
Moreux.
[*Gardens and
Gardening, 1939*]

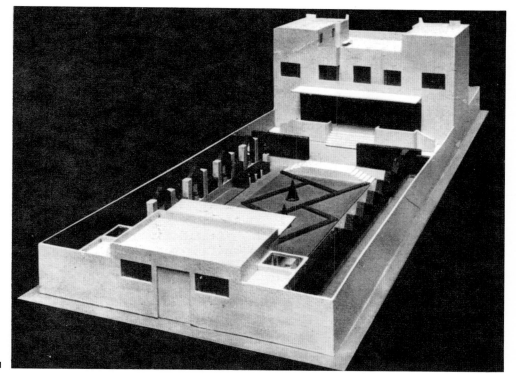

5-31

5-32

5-33

Like André Vera, Jean-Charles Moreux extended the proportions of his architectural elevations into the garden and explored the geometry of the square at length. Characteristically, the garden realized in Cherbourg for Eugène Yvon in 1932–33 relied on the theme of the quadrant. Although the garden was located in a northern province, the main feature of the composition was a series of three squares recalling a Moorish sequence of fountains, the interval between them collapsed in space. In spite of this "tyranny of the square" reminiscent of motifs of the Viennese Secession, Moreux argued against a "banal and styleless Esperanto" and praised a "Geography through Architecture."[79] Like Paul Vera's design in Honfleur, this Norman garden—striped with sand from the sea and paved with green and pink schist—relied on vernacular materials. As the generator of forms or as regulating geometry, the square recurred in several of Moreux's other projects, such as the trellised salle fraîche for the château de Maulny in 1930, or the small balconies designed for Count Orlowsky between 1931 and 1933, in collaboration with Paul Vera.

These sober geometries—whether squares or diagonals of squares—marked Moreux's compositions with an even rhythm overlaid with a rational modernity. The modern garden for which he argued had as a source the jardin régulier: it was characterized by simplicity, fantasy, and a regard for materials and plants.[80] "France needs to recover its first-place rank in the art of designing gardens in the formal style," he later wrote.[81] Throughout the 1930s Moreux proposed his revisions to the formal garden. Perhaps slightly static, but not without visual strength, was the "garden" designed for François David-Weill in Paris, consisting of a terrace framed with evergreen vegetation, in which the only blush of modernity was the brushed concrete paving. The roof terrace for Mr. J. Bloch-Lesné, on the other hand, was an exercise in regularization. Here, Moreux attempted to provide diversified spaces by adapting a highly irregular perimeter to the requirements of outdoor living. Although the roof terrace was open to the sky and to the view, an axonometric drawing conveyed Moreux's intention to create sheltered sitting areas, furnished with busts and sculptures, and the ubiquitous square pool; the existing chimneys provided the vertical accents. Moreux also paid close attention to the color scheme of this exterior apartment. The ground was light concrete, and the planters pale pink brick; the

5-33 HÔTEL DE ROTHSCHILD. STORAGE AND EXERCISE PAVILION WITH ARTICULATED MIRROR FACADE. Paris, 1928. Jean-Charles Moreux. [Martinie, "Deux récentes réalisations de J.-Ch. Moreux"]

5-34 TERRACE IN FRONT OF THE BRUGIER RESIDENCE. The design also included a garden to the rear of the house and a solarium. Saint-Cloud, 1927. Jean-Charles Moreux. [Moreux, "Un hôtel particulier à Saint-Cloud"]

5-35 GARDEN FOR EUGÈNE YVON. SEQUENCE OF POOLS. Cherbourg, 1933. Jean-Charles Moreux. [Laprade, "L'œuvre de J.-Ch. Moreux"]

5-35

5-34

pedestals, tables, and low walls were cast in white cement; and the pool, framed by white and pink bricks, was tiled in black ceramics. The vegetation was mostly evergreen, consisting of thujas, yews, cotoneasters, and deciduous Japanese maples. As if to exemplify Moreux's view of the roof garden as an important component of the architectural facade, the masonry and paving of the terrace extended the tonality of the building with a chalky hue tinged with pink.[82] A palette of blue bulbs or perennials, such as flax, delphinium, iris, campanula, lupine, and lobelia, provided color and harmony and linked the garden to the sky.[83]

The revisions of the historical jardin régulier that Moreux first explored during the 1920s and 1930s became mere quotations during the ensuing decades. Perhaps this change from reinvention to alliteration was due to the change in the nature of his private commissions. The call for urban gardens in the modern idiom gave way to restorations of jardins à la française or formal gardens "in the style of." The gardens for the château de Quintin—designed between 1943 and 1946—linked two châteaux and two eras, the seventeenth and the eighteenth centuries. Moreux drew large and small tapis verts, a *vertugadin*, a hemicyclical garden "in the manner of Jean Marot," and a parterre de broderie.[84] Also in 1943, Moreux drafted, with little irony, a jardin à la française in forced perspective.[85] His hypothetical Jardins théoriques of 1949–50 were less redefinitions of the modern garden than reduced formulas of traditional parterres or bosks for contemporary needs.

Moreux's return to the jardin à la française could be interpreted as resulting from a shift in client demand. A comparison of his two public gardens—square Croulebarbe and Grosvenor Gardens—reveals his continued drift toward traditionalism and his seeming disillusionment with contemporary forms.

The square Croulebarbe, also known as the jardin des Gobelins or square René-Le-Gall, is located near the Mobilier National, designed by Auguste Perret. Conceived and executed by Moreux between 1936 and 1939, this square allied historicist references, the "jardin régulier," and "jardin vert" with the modern style of an area for play. The jardin régulier, to use Moreux's term, was a formal sitting room outlined with sheared boxwood and furnished with four gloriettes, which faced a rustic obelisk. Whereas the reinforced-concrete gloriettes replicated the latticed structures in the

5-36

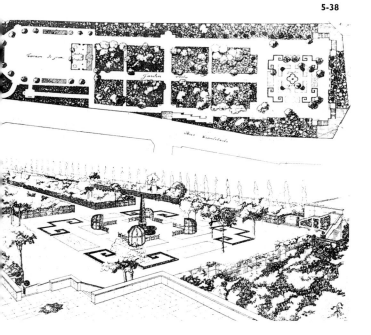

5-38

5-40

5-39

5-36 ROOF TERRACE
FOR J. BLOCH-LESNÉ.
VIEW OF THE
DESIGN AS BUILT.
Paris, 1934.
Jean-Charles Moreux.
[Moreux, "Jardins
réguliers"]

5-37 CHÂTEAU DE QUINTIN.
SITE PLAN.
Brittany, circa 1944.
Jean-Charles Moreux.
[Institut Français
d'Architecture]

5-38 SQUARE CROULEBARBE.
PLAN AND
PERSPECTIVE.
Paris, 1936–39.
Jean-Charles Moreux.
[*L'Architecture
d'Aujourd'hui,* April
1937]

5-39 SQUARE CROULEBARBE.
THE *JARDIN RÉGULIER.*
1938.
Jean-Charles Moreux.
[*L'Illustration,*
28 May 1938]

5-40 SQUARE CROULEBARBE.
CONCRETE *GLORIETTE*
INSPIRED BY THOSE AT
VILLANDRY.
[Photo: Dorothée
Imbert, 1991]

ornamental vegetable garden at Villandry, the figure of the planted medallion in the center of the jardin régulier recalled the shape of a pool at the Orto Botanico in Padova.[86]

The jardin vert linked this regular pole to the playground. This promenade followed the course of the subterranean river Bièvre and was shadowed by the dense mass of the existing trees. Moreux balanced the order of the jardin régulier with the austerity of the porticoes surrounding the playground. The ground plane of the square Croulebarbe lay well below the street grade, and Moreux dramatically orchestrated the play of stairs and ramps connecting the two levels. At one end of the site twin sets of stairs anchored the corners of the jardin régulier; at the opposite end another entrance funneled visitors into the playground. Between the two, Moreux set a series of parallel flights of steps, bordered by a ramp for baby carriages. The concrete stairs were inlaid by Maurice Garnier with figures of rocks and pebbles; the handrails were crowned with massive cement spheres. In this garden Moreux juxtaposed aesthetic and social concerns. With such a framework for play, commented Albert Laprade, "the working-class children . . . are immersed in a beauty bath, [which is] more efficient than one might think."[87] In designing an elegant project that was not destined for the upper classes, Moreux overlaid three types of gardens within a single public square. Utilizing the existing trees of the jardin vert, he acknowledged the history of the site and the underground river; with the concrete gloriettes of the jardin régulier, he addressed France's garden heritage; with his consideration of use and structures for play, he mirrored the needs of the present.

With the square Croulebarbe, Moreux had verified that "on a small scale, [the English garden] was the shame of our squares, [being] both inconvenient and ridiculous."[88] Similarly, André Vera had condemned the romantic and melancholy mood of a "vegetal exoticism," characterized by the same perfect absurdity as a recently outmoded fashion, its obsolescence evident but its charm not yet recognized."[89] Perhaps the later designs of Moreux reflected the quest for a past that was sufficiently remote to be acceptable.

Moreux constructed another public square, in London, a few years after the jardin des Gobelins, and centuries apart in style. Designed in 1948 and completed in 1952, the remodeling of Grosvenor Gardens, or square

5-41 SQUARE CROULEBARBE. CORNER STAIRS LEADING TO THE *JARDIN RÉGULIER.* [Photo: Dorothée Imbert, 1991]

5-42 SQUARE CROULEBARBE. STAGGERED STAIRS WITH RAMP. PERSPECTIVE. Ink on vellum. 1937. Jean-Charles Moreux. [Institut Français d'Architecture]

5-43 SQUARE CROULEBARBE. STAGGERED STAIRS WITH RAMP. [Photo: Dorothée Imbert, 1990]

5-41

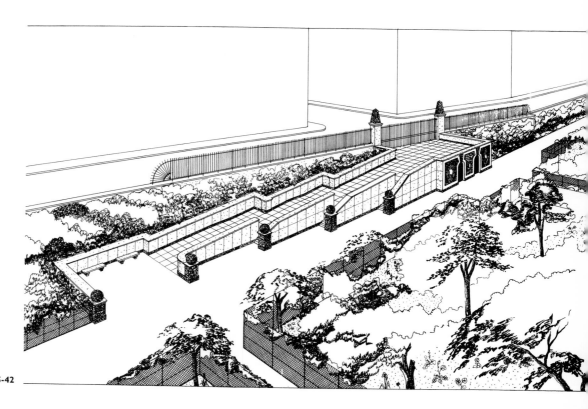

5-42

5-43

Maréchal Foch, fully illustrates the shift that had occurred in Jean-Charles Moreux's design sensibility. Built to honor Ferdinand Foch, Marshal of France, Great Britain, and Poland and a hero of the First World War, the garden filled a triangular site fronting Victoria Station. To evince the spirit of France, Moreux chose an arabesque pattern set amid existing trees, symmetrically arranged along a central axis that extended from the statue of Foch to the opposite tip of the site.[90] In the original project, the scalene triangle of lawn was embroidered with a "double palm" pattern of boxwood, whose volutes were terminated by jets of water. These vertical accents created two perspectival lines further emphasized by the decreasing heights of the jets from the base of the triangular site to its vertex. As a more economical option, Moreux proposed substituting conical yews for the water accents. Neither option was implemented. Instead, circular flower beds were planted, weakening the intended optical illusion; the boxwood pattern became a paved path. In a note, Moreux insisted that the beds contain only one type of flower, "in accordance with the spirit of Le Nôtre."[91]

The architect believed that an "arabesque de broderie" with moving waters, seen through a "filigreed fence," constituted an appropriate backdrop to the statue of Foch. In an article titled "Victorian Curves," a contemporary critic disagreed: "But Foch, in whose honor all this will be, does not, I think, really approve. He turns his back on the work and continues gazing towards Victoria Station; such stuff is all very well for Landscape gardeners; but to a Marshal of France the shortest way between two points is still a straight line."[92]

Obviously, Moreux did not consider the modern jardin régulier to be a background befitting a marshal. Whether a *clin d'œil* or a mastery of historicism, the optical amusement of his intended design for Grosvenor Gardens evidenced little invention.

By the 1950s Moreux had traveled beyond the concept of a modern garden as a simplified French formal vocabulary adapted to contemporary materials and habits. Instead, he searched history for the "vigor and beauty that was the appanage of French gardens across past centuries."[93] He still opted, however, for a reinterpretation of this history—a position supported by André Vera's assertion that there was no modernity without tradition and no tradition without modernity.[94]

5-44 GROSVENOR GARDENS. BOXWOOD ARABESQUE WITH GRADUATED WATER RILLS. PLAN.
The statue of Maréchal Foch stands at the base of the triangle. Ink and pencil on vellum. London, 1949. Jean-Charles Moreux. [Institut Français d'Architecture]

5-45 GROSVENOR GARDENS. AERIAL VIEW.
Circa 1952. Jean-Charles Moreux. [Institut Français d'Architecture]

5-44

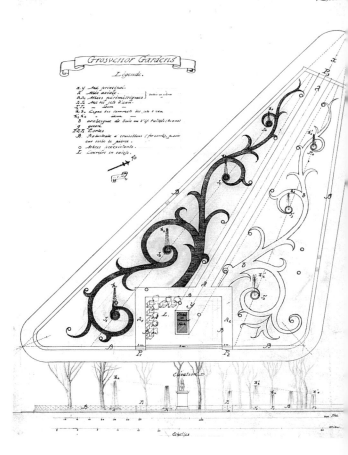

Grosvenor Gardens

5-45

5-46

5-47

In addition to designing such formal exercises Moreux had followed André Vera's incentive to construct gardens "to adorn leisure rather than to stave off idleness."[95] At the château de Maulny, for example, a concrete wharf on the river Sarthe was executed in a "simple, appropriate, exact, and distinguished style" suited to yawls and canoes.[96] His concern for aesthetic formulas and decorative patterns shifted toward the new utilitarian garden. In 1935, Achille Duchêne himself described the gardens of the future as *jardins d'utilité* and assigned them to three groups: artists and intellectuals, sportspeople, and "those who are concerned . . . with the strictly practical aspect of flower crops and domestic horticulture."[97] Jean-Charles Moreux and Paul Vera echoed the call for such utilitarian gardens in their contemporary proposal for the parc de Sceaux, the potential site for the garden section of the forthcoming 1937 International Exposition. The series of small gardens they designed reflected an economic concern for practical beauty. In addition to water, bird, and alpine gardens, there were orchards and vegetable plots and gardens for the working class. In their project for the Jardins ouvriers, Moreux and Paul Vera demonstrated their worth as "refined high-class artists": taking into account the economic aspect of small gardens, they designed a system of units set in clusters of four, at the intersection of which were a communal water source and shelter. Several of their other gardens proposed for the exposition functioned as educational vignettes. The Jardin de fleurs, conceived for an "enlightened amateur," featured flower pots arranged on tiers for greater access to sunlight and easy maintenance.[98] A Jardin d'oiseaux, according to Moreux, offered both "ornamental and didactic" qualities.[99] Visitors actually passed through the aviary rather than contemplating the cages from the exterior, as in Laprade's Garden of Birds at the 1925 Exposition. The variegated and somewhat irrational Jardin alpestre—a true exposition garden—was a strange concoction divided into geographical zones. On one half of the site, a picturesque landscape supposedly based on an alpine theme featured spruces, meadows, and rocks. Just across a path, a dry plot of cacti ironically included a formal pool for marsh plants. In these designs Moreux and Vera proposed a catalog of elementary case-study landscapes applicable to the life-style of the 1930s.[100] The projects for Sceaux were left unexecuted, and

Moreux instead realized the garden for the U.A.M. pavilion on the Seine.

Throughout his long career—in garden designs ranging from still tableaux to restorations of classical parterres—Jean-Charles Moreux attempted to reconcile regionalism with modernism and, to a certain extent, plants with geometry.[101] In the catalog for the 1948 Rotterdam exposition on "The French Garden from the Middle Ages to Our Day," the few lines Moreux dedicated to the modern garden are quite revealing. Questioning the validity of a true twentieth-century garden, and placing its design in the hands of the urbanist, he refused to acknowledge any attempts during the past decades to define a modern architectural garden.[102]

To the eternal question regarding the influence of architecture on garden design, Moreux replied clearly and concisely that there could be little interaction between the two fields, if only because "the so-called 'modern' architecture [had] yet to be defined." He dismissed attempts to "introduce unusual gardens in the 'cubist' sense" for being "as out-of-date as a fabric or an ornament designed on cubist lines." Gardens follow neither styles nor the times. For Moreux, as for Reginald Blomfield fifteen years before, there were "only two forms of gardens; the formal garden, which is the point of contact between the house and nature, for it is a product of them both; and the landscape garden which is an imitation of nature." Then he added laconically, "The general rule will always be: to use both common sense and imagination, and this applies to all gardens the world over."[103]

5-48

5-49

5-46 CONCRETE WHARF ON THE RIVER SARTHE. Château de Maulny, 1930. Jean-Charles Moreux. [*L'Illustration*, 28 May 1932]

5-47 PROPOSAL FOR EXPOSITION GARDENS IN THE PARC DE SCEAUX. SITE PLAN, DETAIL. 1935. Jean-Charles Moreux and Paul Vera. [Courtesy Janine Hébert]

5-48 JARDINS OUVRIERS FOR THE PARC DE SCEAUX. 1935. Jean-Charles Moreux and Paul Vera. [Courtesy Janine Hébert]

5-49 JARDIN D'OISEAUX FOR THE PARC DE SCEAUX. 1935. Jean-Charles Moreux and Paul Vera. [Courtesy Janine Hébert]

5-50 JARDIN ALPESTRE FOR THE PARC DE SCEAUX. 1935. Jean-Charles Moreux and Paul Vera. [Courtesy Janine Hébert]

5-50

PIERRE-ÉMILE LEGRAIN

GARDEN DESIGN AS APPLIED ART

6-1

A brilliant illustrator, Pierre-Émile Legrain (1889–1929) became a central figure in the French world of applied arts during the 1910s and 1920s. Merging modernism with *art nègre* and Oceanian influences, he redefined the aesthetics of interior and furniture design. Throughout his career he demonstrated a versatility and a capacity to adopt new techniques and materials, as well as to divert traditional ones. Imbuing his elegant illustrations with the materiality of his furniture, he reformed the idiom of bookbinding. Despite a wide range of interests, he developed an acute sense of craft and, above all, a distinctive personal vocabulary that was later to be termed the *style Legrain*. The radical forms of his creations, supported by extensive journalistic coverage, indelibly marked design production of the early twentieth century—all within Legrain's brief career of two decades. Similarly, his design of a single garden, or more specifically, its photographic views, would later influence the course of modernist landscape architecture in the United States.

6-1 BOOKBINDING FOR *L'IMMORALISTE*. (André Gide, 1902) 1924. Pierre-Émile Legrain. [*Les Arts de la Maison*, Autumn 1924]

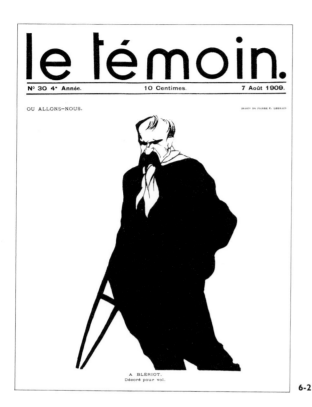

6-2

6-3

Educated at the Germain Pilon School of Applied Arts, Legrain had to abandon his formal studies before completion because of both financial and health reasons.[1] By 1909 he was contributing illustrations to *Le Témoin,* a satirical periodical established three years earlier by Paul Iribe, where he also served as typographer and layout artist.[2] His collaboration with Iribe, often seen as a dependence, continued when Iribe opened a small design shop in the faubourg Saint-Honoré.[3] There, many diverse projects including furniture, decorative objects, books, jewelry, fabrics, dresses, theater sets, and costumes were created.[4] The designs were destined for highly receptive clients such as Louis Vuitton, Paul Poiret, Paquin, Lalique, and the renowned fashion designer Jacques Doucet.

Exempted from military duty during the First World War, both Legrain and Iribe avoided the hiatus that occurred in most artistic developments, continuing their editorial and graphic collaboration with another periodical, also satirical: *Le Mot.*[5] Their association ended in 1919, however, when Paul Iribe left for the United States. In 1912, during his partnership with Iribe, Legrain met Jacques Doucet. An arbiter of taste and a major collector, Doucet played a prominent role in Pierre Legrain's artistic development, both as a client and as an intermediary with other patrons.

Fully committed to contemporaneity, Doucet in 1912 auctioned a splendid and celebrated collection of artwork from the eighteenth century, as well as the hôtel-musée that housed it.[6] While the public was consecrating impressionism as a new classicism, the adventurous designer was collecting paintings by Picasso, le Douanier Rousseau, Matisse, Modigliani, Ernst, and De Chirico.[7] Believing that artworks and the environment in which they are displayed should share a common aesthetic, Doucet transformed his apartment into a showcase befitting the modernity of his new collection. He considered Louis XIV frames —whether originals or reproductions—illsuited to contemporary paintings, and in 1927 commissioned several designers to create his new studio—from the furniture to the picture frames and the garden.[8] Legrain orchestrated the efforts of Rose Adler, Miklos, Jean Lurçat, and Eileen Gray, among others, who together composed a strikingly unusual interior ensemble; the sculptor Henri Laurens contributed a portico and a cubistic fountain to the adjacent garden.[9]

Jacques Doucet's artistic interests also extended to books and manuscripts. His initial collection of works on eighteenth-century art was steadily expanded, both in volume and scope. Between 1912 and 1917 he amassed more than 100,000 books, 15,000 manuscripts, 150,000 photographs, 2,000 portfolios of etchings, and enough prints to fill two rooms; he entrusted this remarkable collection to the care of 25 librarians.[10] Doucet realized that writers and painters pursued similar aims through different means. Thus, to parallel his collection of contemporary art, Doucet created a library of literary manuscripts by such avant-garde authors as Guillaume Apollinaire, Max Jacob, Pierre Reverdy, and André Breton.[11]

Doucet considered the bookbinding style of that period "too precious, too nuanced, [and] too rich" for the writings he collected. Seeking both originality and simplicity, he commissioned Pierre Legrain to encase the works of such authors as André Gide and Francis Jammes.[12] Just as he reframed paintings by Braque, Picabia, or Miró in glass, enamel, leather, or metal, Legrain dressed the texts of contemporary authors with exquisite refinement.[13] As a novice and amateur, he was able to disregard the traditional rules and techniques of bookbinding and to avail himself of unusual materials.[14] Legrain's book covers were highly praised at the Salon des Artistes Décorateurs of 1919; a new style had been launched and a swarm of imitations followed.[15]

Legrain shunned affected and facile ornament. He sheathed books in *partis* expressing a sober geometry, with broad surfaces and typefaces attuned with the spirit of the book. Legrain was categorized among the "real modernists [who sought] to convey the character of the text, not through any real object, but by the abstract expression of the form and color of the design"; a bookbinder who "learned from Cubism and the expressionist schools the arrangement of geometrical forms in asymmetrical patterns to symbolize a mood or attitude."[16] [Plate XIII] Legrain's designs—whether an interior, a furniture piece, a bookbinding, or a landscape—were frequently labeled cubist. He himself credited art nègre as having exerted a major influence on his sensibility.[17] With the same "discreet search for sumptuousness" expressed in his ensembles, he chose rare and unusual materials for his bookbindings.[18] With "audacious logic," he incised woods and a variety of leathers, such as yellow China shark, galuchat, or lacquered skins.[19]

6-4

6-2 COVER FOR THE PERIODICAL *LE TÉMOIN*. The design celebrates Louis Blériot's first flight over the English Channel. Pierre-Émile Legrain. [Bibliothèque Forney]

6-3 STUDIO FOR JACQUES DOUCET. THE VESTIBULE. Paintings by Picabia and Miró, a carpet by Jean Lurçat, and a lacquered armoire by Pierre-Émile Legrain. Neuilly, circa 1928. [Joubin, "Le studio de Jacques Doucet"]

6-4 VILLA PROJECT FOR JACQUES DOUCET. MODEL OF THE ENTRANCE. Marly, 1924. Henri Laurens. [Courtesy Quentin Laurens]

6-5 BOOKBINDING FOR *LE CANTIQUE DES CANTIQUES*. 1929. Pierre-Émile Legrain. [Courtesy Librairie Blaizot, Paris]

6-5

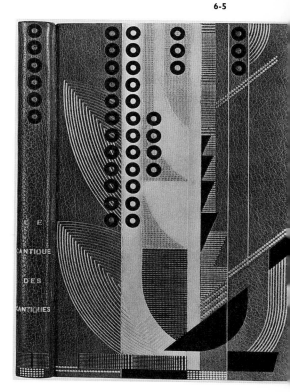

Legrain achieved fame mainly through his book dressings, as they were often called—and justifiably so, since many of his 1,236 book-bindings (or more) were executed for a fashion designer. Yet his versatility extended far beyond interiors and book covers. He demonstrated an eclectic interest in various applied arts, producing a wide range of creations that included a black-and-white design for the automobile maker Louis Delage; a glass piano for Pleyel; a case for a Kodak camera, and one for Lucky Strike cigarettes; a dress for Paquin; stage sets; and even a garden.

Pierre Legrain was truly an *ensemblier* whose design territory was nothing less than the whole. An *ensemble* is defined as a composition whose elements create general harmony through emulation and avoid competing for attention with one another. Gaston Varenne, a contemporary critic, noted that Legrain excelled at creating "atmospheres," "rhythms in space," and interiors that expressed "total unity and harmony."[20] In his introduction to *Objets d'art,* Legrain stated that "a form appropriate to its use equalled beauty." Nevertheless, after attending to the "tools for sleeping, tools for eating and tools for producing," the "obstinate reverie" and the "object of art" remained.[21] Legrain's individuality pervaded his complete oeuvre, although each of the pieces also reflected the character, and perhaps the influence, of his clients.

In fact, the furniture he designed for Jacques Doucet—whose interiors were dismissed on several occasions as too eclectic—addressed the patron's "preference for the elaborate over the simple."[22] As if to reflect the cubist and art nègre collections in Doucet's studio, Legrain proposed a composition in which the art of the Far East was coupled with the most modern cubism. The ensembles he designed for the artistically inclined milliner Jeanne Tachard, in contrast, fully embodied Legrain's synthetic process, which expressed strength by utilizing a compact and sober vocabulary.[23]

Some considered Legrain's furniture pieces excessively unusual in form and material; his bookbindings, on the other hand, were unanimously celebrated and frequently imitated. Yet it is because of his only garden that Fletcher Steele would write in 1930: "Pierre Legrain died recently. He was perhaps the greatest loss that modern garden design could have suffered."[24]

6-6

6-6 CHAISE LONGUE FOR MRS. DOUCET. Paris, circa 1925. Pierre-Émile Legrain. [Musée des Arts Décoratifs]

6-7 *TOMB FOR AN AVIATOR.* Montparnasse Cemetery, Paris, circa 1924. Henri Laurens. [Photo: Dorothée Imbert, 1989]

6-8 VILLA TACHARD. INTERIOR, LOOKING TOWARD THE GARDEN. La Celle-Saint-Cloud, circa 1924. Pierre-Émile Legrain. [*Vogue,* 1 June 1925]

LA CELLE-SAINT-CLOUD, CA. 1924. Jeanne Tachard shared with Jacques Doucet a close friendship as well as a pronounced taste for the avant-garde.[25] Although renowned as a collector of African sculpture, she also patronized contemporary artists.[26] Among the works she commissioned is the headstone for the Tachard family grave in the Montparnasse Cemetery.[27] Henri Laurens sculpted this refined work in 1924. Its title, *Tomb for an Aviator*, most likely commemorated Tachard's son, Louis, who died at the end of the First World War.[28] The chiseled mass elegantly united the tension and strength of a dying bird/airplane with the calmness of a reclining humanlike figure.[28]

Devoted exclusively to the style Legrain, Jeanne Tachard commissioned him to design several pieces of furniture and various interior ensembles. Her two apartments on rue Émile-Menier in Paris reflected Pierre Legrain's usual unusual touch. There, he freely experimented with materials removed from their normal context to create a structure that evoked a cubism with Egypto-Negro-Japonesque overtones. Legrain acknowledged his exotic references by noting that the "centuries of Ramses, of Pericles, the Ming dynasty, and aristocracies" left traces found in all decorative objects and buildings.[29] For these interior compositions Legrain chose such diverse materials as palm wood and Makassar ebony, metal, leathers, parchment, silver-plated glass, and oilcloth.[30] Everything in the Tachard apartments was of Legrain's design: the furniture, the vertical and horizontal planes, the bathroom accessories, even the bird cage and aquarium.

It is through the remodeling of Jeanne and André Tachard's country estate, however, that Pierre Legrain's role as an ensemblier reached an apotheosis. If the interiors he created for Jacques Doucet involved a collaboration with several other artists, the Tachard villa in La Celle-Saint-Cloud, outside Paris, was designed exclusively by Legrain. He orchestrated the entire composition, from the overall sequence of rooms to the minute detail of door handles. In addition to creating the interior, Legrain laid out the grounds and designed the outdoor furniture.

Descriptions of the house, with its movable partitions, suggest a feeling of temporality.[31] The sensation of time was further enhanced by the juxtaposition of elements from different periods. Inside, Legrain set his client's African

6-7

6-8

artworks against pristine monochromatic surfaces and amid his so-called "space odyssey furniture."[32] He played on the apparent dissonance between the modern spirit expressed by the slickness of metal and the "primitive" texture of rough palm wood—a conscious reference to the adjacent African artifacts. Like those of a movable stage set, sliding partitions created an ephemeral spatial structure reminiscent of Japanese architecture. Through a curtain of vines, the veranda looked out on the ultimate picture: the garden.

Legrain refurbished the Tachard residence in the early 1920s and received recognition for his arrangement of the grounds at the Exposition des Arts Décoratifs et Industriels Modernes, where he presented various photographs and a plan.[33] Legrain was awarded a silver medal in the garden section; his landscape design was published in Joseph Marrast's 1925 *Jardins* and several contemporary magazines. The Tachard garden was also reviewed abroad, and as a result of American reports, Legrain greatly influenced a trio of students at the Harvard Graduate School of Design in 1937: Garrett Eckbo, Dan Kiley, and James Rose.[34] Although the Tachard garden appears to be Legrain's only essay in landscape architecture, its innovative yet simple register provoked praise, imitation, and criticism. Leon Henry Zach discussed the Tachard garden without directly citing its designer in a 1932 article on the natural limitations of formalism. To Zach, the modernist landscape designer "provide[d] interest with certain harmonious relations produced by repetition (sometimes too much), or by sequence (sometimes harshly, as in the famous example of the saw-tooth edged path), or by balance (occult preferred to symmetrical)."[35] The "saw-tooth edged path" was an obvious reference to the zig-zag bordered allée in the Saint-Cloud garden, while the critic paraphrased Steele's description of "formal elements arranged in occult unsymmetrical balance."[36] The dynamic triangulated shape became a motif frequently applied to the modernist American garden. Whether opposed to a biomorphic curve or set against a straight line, zig-zags were to appear often in the projects of California landscape architects such as Thomas Church and Garrett Eckbo.[37]

Considered a paradigm of modernism, the Tachard garden was in fact an exquisite wrapping of a prior naturalistic landscape, and as such, it appeared as the logical conclusion to Legrain's play between old and new. The African statues, almost atemporal, were displayed against a modern interior, itself placed within the shell of a suburban half-timbered house, which in its turn was framed by a contemporary dressing of a mature landscape.

In his account of the gardens at the 1925 Paris exposition, J.C.N. Forestier wrote, "Anyone who traces, draws, constructs, or plants with skill, with individual temperament and technique, can compose a special work that, small or large, is personal. . . . [A garden] like that of Legrain for Madame Tachard . . . proves [the point]."[38] The Tachard garden was certainly personal, the graphic elements of its plan echoing Legrain's book covers or his interior designs. The segmented vocabulary common to each followed an invisible but discernible structure. Léon Rosenthal claimed that "the rules after which the architecture of binding was founded," such as "symmetry and repetition," were "laws that [Legrain] repudiated."[39] Similarly, the plan of the Tachard garden eschewed both symmetry and a predictable reading. Shadows were not rendered; as a result, the shapes of the beds, walks, and hedges became abstractions. Each element was differentiated from the others only by a variation in geometry or texture. Even the villa's footprint appeared as a graphic element in the general composition.

The imaginary landscape of the "Jardin de l'aviateur," by André Vera, shared few visual similarities with the Tachard plan. One can nonetheless draw a parallel between the two gardens. In spite of the overall conventional lines, Vera's aerial view of the landscape expressed the salience of plans in the architectural garden as well as a fascination with aviation. Louis Blériot had traversed the English Channel in 1909, and the successful flights of Roland Garros captured the imagination of the public in the following decade.[40] Aviation became a popular theme during the 1920s and was enthusiastically illustrated or symbolized by designers and artists such as Le Corbusier, Guillaume Apollinaire, and Robert Delaunay.[41]

Seen in its two-dimensional representation, the landscape would have been a perfect garden for the aviator Tachard, and Vera's description could apply equally to Legrain's design: "The contrasts of surfaces, volumes, and colors are undeniable. . . . The lawns are weighed by sheared shrubs. . . . As the aviator rises in his airplane, this formal garden reminds him of his determination. But the regularity of the garden

6-9 TACHARD GARDEN. THE ORCHARD, LOOKING TOWARD THE VILLA. [Rambosson, "Un jardin de Pierre Legrain"]

6-10 TACHARD GARDEN. THE ROSE GARDEN. The steps lead to the orchard and vegetable garden. [Rambosson, "Un jardin de Pierre Legrain"]

6-9

6-10

is not manic: against straight shapes are free ones."[42]

From the air, the Tachard landscape resembled (and was often described as) a bookbinding, reflecting all the compositional rules of Legrain's covers.[43] The allée extending along the edge of the plan could be taken as the spine of the volume; its zig-zag pattern certainly fit comfortably within Legrain's repertoire of forms. Moroccan leather was rendered by the flatness and homogeneity of the lawn, and the embossed gilding by the slightly protruding earthwork and flower beds.[44]

Although the only remaining drawn record of the garden is a plan, period photographs reveal subtle changes in level. In his description of the garden, Legrain established the importance of grading. "Earthwork," he wrote, "constitutes the essence of the garden and its true value."[45] In a play of steps and embankments, sheared hedges and outlined planters, Legrain conjured the effect of an enlarged bas-relief or an exaggerated book cover. As light struck the various angles and tonalities of green, shifts of textures and planes emerged and could be read in much the same manner that one would perceive the subtle contrast of leathers and the embossed figures on a Legrain binding.

The house divided the rectangular plot into halves. The plan prominently illustrated the garden for living and pleasure below the house but merely implied the functional orchard and vegetable garden above it. Legrain positioned the access to the house along the lot line, which allowed him to manipulate the grade of the lower expanse of the garden as an independent entity. The villa sat on a plinth that unfurled with three shallow steps of grass. Across a broad lawn, the incline reversed, with a play of stepped wedges of grass. This raised boundary partially hid the garden wall but left revealed views of the adjacent Vaucresson hills.[46] Correcting an insignificant declivity with a successive descent and ascent, Legrain created a slightly sunken garden etched with lines and accents of grading and planting.

Although graphically striking, the design also considered function in its visual refinement. As a reflection of the interior design, the grounds marked the different living areas with changes of material. "Our old friend the axis" was either implied or shattered in the modern garden, commented Fletcher Steele, striking an analogy with the arrangement of the contemporary room: "Each [element] takes part in a

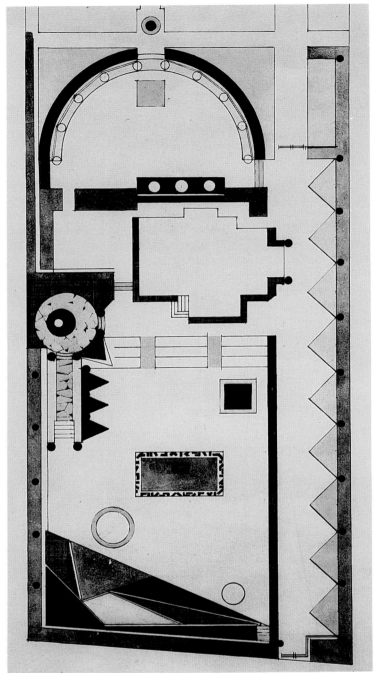

6-11

6-11 TACHARD GARDEN.
ANNOTATED PLAN.
Pierre Legrain.
[Dorothée Imbert]

6-12 TACHARD GARDEN.
THE SUNKEN LAWN
ROOM.
[Rambosson, "Un jardin
de Pierre Legrain"]

6-13 TACHARD GARDEN.
HAZELNUT TREE WITH
CONCRETE PLANTER.
[*Vogue*, 1 June 1925]

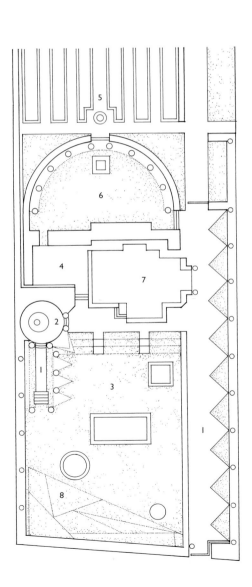

1 Green Corridor
2 *Salle Fraîche*
3 Sunken Lawn
4 Exterior Dining Room
5 Kitchen Garden
6 Rose Garden
7 House
8 Wedges of Lawn

slightly formal grouping. . . . The whole room composes. Yet the rigid axis of the French salon does not exist. A similar effect is more and more sought out-of-doors."[47] The search for an atmosphere in which each element was inherently linked to the next and "nothing would catch the eye" governed the interior scheme for the Villa Tachard. Legrain recast the once-anglicized landscape into a new composition of "rigorous discipline."[48] He applied to the garden the same considerations that ruled his interior assemblage. The private as well as the service areas of this open-air apartment were arranged with varied textures, colors, and shapes: (1) green corridors, (2) a *salle fraîche*, (3) a sunken lawn room enclosed by hedges and furnished with tree specimens, (4) a dining room, and (5) a kitchen garden.

The orchard, which was not drawn on the presentation plan, comprised a strict succession of espaliered lines. In spite of the simplicity demanded by function, Legrain interpreted the "obsolete and expired" formula of the boxwood border with a neat and contemporary cement curb variegated by intermittent red bricks.[49] But for a few white strokes, red was the only recurring color in the predominantly green scheme.

Below the kitchen garden was a semicircle of climbing red roses enclosed by a white fence and set against a dark background of cypress. The symmetry and formality of this space contrasted with the asymmetrical balance of dissimilar elements governing the remainder of the plan. Legrain explained that this part of the design was a "sacrifice to charm": June was so beautiful, he said, it deserved a rose garden.[50] Perhaps roses called for a little *jardin régulier* as André Vera might have imagined. Hoops covered with climbing species alternated with rambling roses trained on stakes. When in bloom, they floated over the lawn like large red spheres. With its preciousness, formality, and marks of pure color ranging from green, white, and red to almost black, the rose garden resembled a picture from the Viennese Secession.

To the left of the house — as seen on the plan — was an exterior dining area. A simple rectangular surface, paved with red crushed brick, it was furnished with a table bound — like a book cover — in varnished, stitched leather and a large cement bench with an adjustable back.

The lower, and main, expanse of the garden displayed an arrangement of plants, paving,

6-13

6-14 TACHARD GARDEN.
THE *SALLE FRAÎCHE*.
A cement bench circles
the trunk of a pear tree.
[*Vogue*, 1 June 1925]

6-15 TACHARD GARDEN.
THE "LOST AXIS."
[Marrast, *1925 Jardins*]

and modeled contours that perfectly illustrated Steele's "occult unsymmetrical balance." Even a slight manipulation of any of these elements would have disrupted the precarious equilibrium of the picture, surrendering it to a familiar banality. The triangulated edge of the periphery vibrated and exaggerated the perception of distance. The trees scattered on the grass carpet were arranged as though they were rocks in a Japanese garden: it was virtually impossible to view them all at the same time. As a result, the planters hovered upon the lawn, uncertainly held in tension by their respective square and circular shapes.

Léon Rosenthal's characterization of Legrain's style of bookbinding was equally applicable to the garden for Jeanne Tachard: "an ample concept, with broad bare surfaces, and frank oppositions; an extremely sober decor." It felt "immediate yet very distant" and appeared to be the result of reduced means: "succinct on the surface, and very refined all the same."[51]

The disposition of trees and shrubs in the depressed portion of the lawn exemplified the elegance of Legrain's diversion of the existing garden and his command of perceived depth. A square bench, of white cement incised with black lines, anchored the trunks of a large hazelnut. Although the tree was placed on axis with a set of stone steps, formality was eroded by the eccentric positioning of the plant within its frame. In opposition to the rigor of the aligned or sheared foliage along the garden edges, plants of various shapes and sizes were arranged on the central lawn. The multi-trunked hazelnut resembled a vegetal fountain; its white concrete base was echoed by the painted trunk of a small erect tree in the distance. A far corner of the lawn was punctuated by a dwarf tree whose rounded crown recalled the shape of a taller single-trunked variety on the other side of the lawn. The height of trees decreased with distance from the house, a device that enhanced the apparent depth of the garden. Elements and shapes reappeared from front to back, however, so that the composition was not simply a forced perspective.

The circle recurred as a geometrical motif throughout the Tachard garden. Legrain graphically treated planters, tree trunks, benches, space, and sculpture in a similar manner. To the left of the house a series of eccentric circles created a visual accent weighed down by a surrounding dark shadow. This abstracted salle fraîche was, perhaps, an updated remnant of the previous English garden. A circular space

framed a large wild pear tree within a template of varying patterns. The salle fraîche was almost entirely enclosed by clipped shrubs and sheltered by a broad tree canopy; only a triangular bed of white begonias marked its access. Within the space, Legrain wrapped the tree trunk with a slightly bulging circular bench, cast in cement and varnished with vermilion China lacquer. The irregular pattern of joints that etched the bench was repeated on the ground, using circular stones. This fashionable arrangement of *opus incertum* encouraged grass to grow between the stone flags. The deep shadow of this green room paved with dark gray cement and heightened simply by a touch of red created an atmosphere of "passionate intimacy," according to one critic.[52] A path parallel to the public access led from the salle fraîche to the vertex of the stepped panes of lawn in one corner of the garden. This narrow and raised stretch of flags was also bordered by a zig-zag pattern of triangular panes of begonias punctuated by yews.

The tangential axis, that is, the main access to the Tachard residence, acted as an independent gallery. Extending from gate to gate—from the road to the orchard—it skirted all sections of the garden, as well as the house itself. A distorted reference to the vocabulary of the baroque French garden, this allée—which Fletcher Steele termed the "lost axis"—focused not on a statue or urn but on the void of the gate. The imbalance of this path—lined on one side by clipped shrubs and on the other by a wall of vegetation—was increased by the vibrating effect of a saw-toothed fringe of lawn. The border of the garden was treated as a highly articulated layered sequence. Not merely a green wall, the trimmed masses of the horse chestnuts and the hedge appeared to frame an elongated window rhythmically divided at regular intervals by mullionlike tree trunks. The zig-zag border kept the stroller at a distance; the play in heights and textures along the lot line disguised the exact limits of the site.

Although Legrain's garden approached architecture, there was little resemblance between his design and other jardins réguliers, whether Mediterranean, like those of Forestier, or Gallic, like those of Vera. In a dynamic balance of elements, Legrain composed a garden in which order reigned but symmetry was banned. Whereas Vera continuously cited Le Nôtre in his homages to the regular style, Legrain professed an architectural garden and "above all, the *oblivion of Versailles*."[53] Arranging the ele-

6-16

ments from the existing picturesque landscape within a formal structure, he created a highly original ensemble. There was no "old new" in the Tachard house and garden.[54] Just as he disregarded the rules of classical bookbinding, Legrain reinterpreted the historical baggage of landscape architecture. Varenne established a parallel between Legrain's and Le Nôtre's assertions over nature: "Nothing would be as curious as to try to compare the need for discipline that crosses the art of our time with the one witnessed by our great classical century," he wrote; and "no result would be more different. Nature tamed by the will of that seventeenth-century man [Le Nôtre] remains magnificent and majestic in its rectilinear alignments." In the Tachard garden, "nature is instead fragmented, it draws angles, broken lines, it multiplies the planes and reliefs."[55] With a modeled, asymmetrical composition Legrain not only severed his design from the regular style but also avoided the static—if visually striking—atmosphere of pictorial gardens. The pristine and mineral designs of Paul Vera and Moreux and the geometric extravagances of Gabriel Guevrekian's plastic challenges to gravity confined the viewer to a fixed set of perspectives. The sense of depth enhanced by the mirrors in the Rouché garden was nullified when one viewed the composition from the reverse angle. The visual delight of the Jardin d'eau et de lumière by Guevrekian was iconic and not to be traversed, while his garden in Hyères essentially presented only two discrete images. Legrain proposed, instead, a geometric ensemble with multiple perspectives. Paralleling ideas advanced in Theo van Doesburg's manifesto of Neo-Plasticism, the harmony of the garden rested on an unstable equilibrium in which a *balanced relationship of unequal parts* replaced symmetry and "the equality of these parts [rested] upon the balance of their dissimilarity, not upon their similarity."[56]

Legrain described the recast Tachard garden as "a rectilinear plan that yielded only to portions that were exceptionally picturesque."[57] Eschewing the established rules of French formalism, he modified the regular structure by creating dynamic visual forces derived from the relation between independent elements. Even the more traditional spaces avoided complete predictability through the use of a design pun or formal distortion. The Secession-like rose garden framed an Oriental headstone; the pear tree in the circular salle fraîche sat slightly off center in the bench that surrounded it; the

6-16 TACHARD GARDEN. THE ZIG-ZAG-BORDERED PATH LEADING TO THE *SALLE FRAÎCHE*. [*Vogue,* 1 June 1925]

6-17 TACHARD GARDEN. VIEW FROM THE HOUSE TOWARD THE WEDGES OF LAWN. [*Vogue,* 1 June 1925]

6-17

lawn steps at the opposite end of the garden
repeated those of the house, but they were set
at an angle. The layout seemed to be on the
brink of falling into place: the zig-zag
appeared about to straighten; the trees floated
on the lawn, ready to settle into some ideal
position. The structure of the garden was far
from obvious—there was no symmetry, no
tangible axis, no focal point; and yet, there
seemed to be an inescapable order throughout.
In the rear of the garden, the triangular wedges
of lawn spiraled up to a crest, shifting the
usual center of gravity and implying yet
another vanishing point.

Descriptions of this garden as a "product of
logic" and a "vibrant and gay scene" of "high-
allure decor" suggest not a fragmented image
but an exquisite relation among elements and
spaces.[58] The chromatic theme of reds that pervaded the rose garden, the brick paving, and a
bench revealed Legrain's attention to detail.
This synthetic conception of color also governed the design of the interior. Inside the villa,
"each room [was] a single color—walls, floor,
ceiling—and [was] harmonized with the contiguous rooms. . . . The boudoir [was] citrus
yellow from vault to flagging. The hall [was]
entirely white. . . . Here and there a black and
a red armchair; a band of gold around the vast
fireplace constitute[d] the essential spots."[59]

With the same concise vocabulary and assertive
tone, Legrain specified "axioms" for ordering
the garden, one of which controlled the role
of vegetation. Flowers were not to alter the
structure or body of the garden, that is, the
evergreen skeleton: "A garden should not live
only from one month to the other and die
during the cold periods. Therefore, lawn,
privet, yew, cypress, and araucaria should be
intensively used. These will constitute the
permanent base upon which will be grafted
the floral cloaks of spring and summer.
However, the body will always remain
intact."[60]

If Legrain terraced and disregarded gravity by
tilting lawn surfaces, fragmenting and faceting
the ground plane, he was nevertheless characterized by Steele as a "horticulturist [who
understood] the limitations of plants."[61] Having brought his interior precepts outward, he
planted a cutting garden to provide flowers to
grace the inside of the villa. He held that glad-
iolus, lupine, delphinium, and flowering
trees—such as hawthorn, apple, and plum—
established only the temporary moods of the
garden.[62] Given his acceptance of vegetation,

6-18 BOOKBINDING FOR
*LES AVENTURES DU
ROI PAUSOLE.*
(Pierre Louÿs, 1911)
1924.
Pierre-Émile Legrain.
[Courtesy Librairie
Blaizot, Paris]

6-18

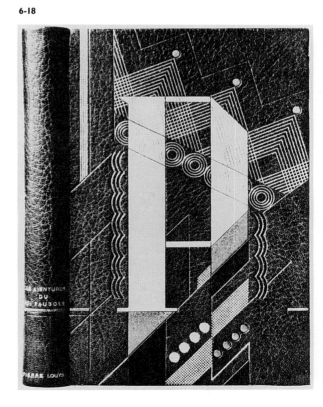

Legrain did not directly apply the plan's severe geometric abstraction to its three-dimensional realization. Although Legrain respected the individual characteristics of plants, he shaped his landscape primarily with planes, stenciled, extruded, and inclined at various angles. The conical profile of the shrubs was projected as a zig-zag pattern on the ground, and the circles in plan reappeared in elevation as the pruned crowns of small trees.

Like Legrain's designs for furniture and book covers, the Tachard garden reflected an admiration for angles, geometry, and the segmented line. References to cubism were, and still are, frequently cited in regard to his designs, whether in frames, furniture, bookbindings, or in "cubistic landscape architecture on the outskirts of Paris."[63] But Legrain's affinities with cubism or its derivations should not suggest that he consciously pursued the same aims as cubist painters. In fact, it might be more appropriate to consider Legrain's cubistic vocabulary as a solution rather than as research. Varenne saw in the ensemblier's empathy toward cubist theories a source for "a thousand good suggestions and a thousand possibilities to escape routine."[64] Criticizing modern binders for their use of geometric mosaics and combinations of lines, dots, and circles, Georges Cretté also traced such trends back to cubism, asserting that "the thing was in the air; it developed simultaneously in every department of decorative art."[65] Legrain, however, transcended the mere appliqué of cubistic patterns in his interior or garden designs. Although he directly cited African artifacts in his furniture, the sources for the Tachard garden were less obvious.[66] The parallel drawn between its plan and a book cover dissolves with the effects of nature and time, and the design becomes closer to a living sculpture than a two-dimensional composition. Fletcher Steele remarked that after "nature had stepped in and softened all the edges . . . the result failed to look much different from anything the rest of us might do."[67] His art has been linked directly to synthetic cubism, but like Gaston Varenne, I would position Legrain's creations more specifically in the wake of cubism.[68] Legrain did not coerce nature into the ideal permanence and rigor of modernism; rather, he attempted to translate, if somewhat literally, a two-dimensional decorative pattern into the space and volume of the garden.

The grounds of the Tachard estate illustrated Legrain's design principle that the "'decorative anecdote' must be radically abolished."[69] It was a garden in the best modernist spirit; a garden positioned between functionalism and aesthetics; a garden complementing the interior arrangement; a garden in which details simply succumbed, along with the "writing" and the proportions of the elements, to the overall atmosphere of the tableau.[70] Legrain applied to the land the precept that governed his ensembles, whether graphic or volumetric. While seeking a harmony with no dominant note, he also achieved a composition in which no detail was ignored.[71]

The garden for Jeanne Tachard reflected the same style that Legrain had applied to all the products of his artistic oeuvre. It was, according to Varenne, "the first attempt daring to harmonize, to such a degree, the garden with the interior and the furniture."[72] Fletcher Steele surmised that "from time to time [Legrain] really [liked] to see a plant have its own way," certainly "a fatal weakness [for a] modernistic garden designer."[73] I would prefer to see in the Tachard garden a graphically refined plan as well as a visually striking and highly unusual modern landscape. Intended as an extension of the house, it displayed simple shapes that resembled a book cover when seen from above. To those stepping within its gates, however, it presented a three-dimensional garden evolving with the seasons. This in itself was far more than most other modernist garden designers would ever offer.

124

GABRIEL GUEVREKIAN

THE MODERN PARADISE GARDEN

7-1

To define the position of Gabriel Guevrekian within the modernist architectural movement is as difficult as attempting to retrace his cultural origins or his path across countries.[1] Of Armenian descent, Guevrekian was born in Istanbul on 21 November 1900. Fleeing persecution, his family established itself in Tehran, where Gabriel acquired Persian citizenship and spent the first ten years of his life. In 1915, after moving to Vienna, he entered the architecture department of the Academy of Applied Arts. Although not a student of Josef Hoffmann, Guevrekian worked in his office; Oskar Strnad introduced him to theater and set design.[2] The academy educated a generation of "architect-artists," individuals on the edge of cultural and artistic trends who responded to the evolution of fashion. Having temporarily settled in Paris in 1921, Guevrekian briefly joined Henri Sauvage's office before collaborating with Robert Mallet-Stevens on several architectural projects. In 1928 he attended the first meeting of CIAM (Congrès International d'Architecture Moderne) as its secretary and in 1932

7-1 JARDIN D'EAU ET DE LUMIÈRE. Exposition des Arts Décoratifs et Industriels Modernes, Paris, 1925. Gabriel Guevrekian. [Roux-Spitz, *Bâtiments et jardins*]

appeared at the Austrian Werkbund as the architect of a pair of semidetached single-family houses. A year later he left Paris for Manchuria, and more promising economic prospects, but reached only Tehran, where he remained four years. There, he became a prolific architect, thriving within the architectural milieu and among the upper-class clientele of Iran. But he never again equaled the intellectual accomplishments and innovation of his Parisian years.[3]

To measure the extent of Guevrekian's contribution to modernism one must rely on reports from that period, since his own writings on the subject are practically nonexistent. Apart from some modest interiors, Guevrekian's architectural production in Paris appears rather limited: he designed a music store, Le Sacre du Printemps, in 1923 and a villa for the fashion designer Jacques Heim in 1927. Articles on the architect's participation in many salons and expositions brought him recognition, but his most noticed—and most publicized—contributions were in the field of garden design.[4]

The three landscapes he realized in France—whose geometries were variously interpreted in contemporary periodicals as "Persian," "cubist," and "modern"—marked a radical approach to modern garden design and deserve careful analysis.[5]

THE JARDIN D'EAU ET DE LUMIÈRE

PARIS, 1925. At the Exposition des Arts Décoratifs et Industriels Modernes, Guevrekian represented Austria as a juror in both the architecture and the music sections; he also designed a fashion boutique for Jacques Heim and Sonia Delaunay on the pont Alexandre III and a garden on the esplanade des Invalides.[6] Despite its being a reiteration of the Simultané store presented at the Salon d'Automne of 1924, the boutique appears to have been one of the rare modern touches on the festooned bridge.[7]

The Jardin d'eau et de lumière was the most noticeable, and most noticed, contribution Guevrekian made to the exposition. In keeping with its extreme character, this design provoked both rave reviews and severe condemnations. To most critics, the Garden of Water and Light appeared unrelated to any trend in landscape design. Praised by some as the prettiest design of the exposition, it was criticized by others as being overly avant-garde—an ambivalence that also greeted such projects as the pavilion of the U.S.S.R.[8] In spite

7-2

7-3

of popular criticism, and like Konstantin Melnikov, Guevrekian was awarded a Grand Prix by the jurors.[9]

The Jardin d'eau et de lumière was commissioned by J.C.N. Forestier, with the specification that the garden be conceived "in the modern spirit with elements from Persian decor."[10] Dictated by planning and technical constraints, garden sites at the exposition were limited in size and contrived in shape. More often than not, the projects resembled restricted horticultural samples or decorative fragments rather than designed landscapes.[11] Guevrekian's miniature garden opposite the exposition library was no exception. Named after its central feature—a tiered pool crowned by a luminous, electrically propelled sphere—the Jardin d'eau et de lumière was a perfect illustration of a *tableau-jardin*. Intended only as a visual experience, the triangular vignette was framed on two sides by partitions of small glass triangles ranging in color from pink to white. The ground plane was successively faceted as if to protect the flower beds, which, in their turn, embraced the sunken fountain with its stepped basins. Using repetition and dissection, Guevrekian exploited the primary constraints of his site and the concept of an exposition garden in a brilliant *exercice de style*.

The triangular motif appeared simultaneously in elevation (as screens), in plan (as pools of water), and in tilted planes (as flower beds). The polished glass triangles and pools played against the even lawn, and the undulating flower beds created a subtle variation of textures. In contrast to these soft surfaces translated by the delicate grain of the black-and-white photograph was the blatant color scheme depicted in Guevrekian's rendering.[12] [Plate XIV] Robert Delaunay's blue, white, and red circles painted on the bottom of a three-tiered pool evoked a patriotic air.[13] The large-scale harlequin pattern played orange pyrethrum against the complementary blue ageratum. In turn, the green of the banked lawn was carved from the field of deep red begonias.[14]

Guevrekian's garden appeared to be a direct realization of his rendering published in *1925 Jardins*: an overscaled cubist painting in which the depth of field was frontally compressed.[15] As if propped against an easel, plants and water were tilted or articulated to counter their inherent flatness. Conceived as exposition decor, the Jardin d'eau et de lumière used vege-

tal means to create a pictorial bas-relief. With the exception of the fountain and sphere, the design was limited to two and a half dimensions: the plants—dwarf cultivars or low ground covers—contributed mainly texture and color. Guevrekian's manipulation of earth seemed to exemplify the criticism that modernist architectural gardens created volume by tilting planting beds at "odd angles" rather than by an "adroit choice of plant materials."[16] In fact, it appears that Guevrekian acted as an art director for this modern Persian icon rather than as its landscape architect, and that a horticulturist selected the "brightly colored and extremely dwarf" plants.[17] The vibrant composition, with its recessed and inclined flower beds, validated landscape architect Fletcher Steele's observation that "horticulture as such is important not for the love of plants, but for what one can do with them."[18]

It was an instant garden striving for illusory permanence. The Jardin d'eau et de lumière, which was completed in the middle of July, needed to remain in bloom during the next three months. Guevrekian presented a landscape painted with concrete and colored glass in which time did not pass; a landscape that expressed motion not through the natural cycle of plants but through its jets of water and revolving glass sphere.

Perhaps the optical vibration of the complementary color planes succeeded in creating a dynamism that paralleled the *simultanéisme* promoted by Sonia and Robert Delaunay. In their paintings, the contrast of difference was exchanged for a contrast of resemblance. To the Delaunays, line was limiting. Color, on the other hand, brought forth form, movement, and depth: not a perspectival or a successive depth, but a simultaneous one.[19] Although it is difficult to ascertain whether Robert Delaunay exerted any influence on the Jardin d'eau et de lumière beyond the tricolor cockades painted on the bottom of the pools, the "(juxt)opposition" of solid planes of color appeared to cite Simultaneist principles.

Concrete, electricity, and monochromatic expanses of flowers geometrically arranged were the tools of modernity that recurred in varying degrees of formal innovation throughout the section Art du jardin. Guevrekian's orientalized modernism was a radical departure from the prevailing Mediterranean atmosphere. Treated as purely visual components, the plants in the Jardin d'eau et de lumière were used *"en masse* like paint."[20] The startling effect of this brilliant contrast was exceeded only by the compilation of the garden's triangles. The globe calmly revolving in the center of the composition responded to the dynamism of the corkscrew fountain that sprayed water horizontally from the vertex of the plot; both of these elements were executed in stained glass by Louis Barillet.[21] At night, the sphere projected luminous images and light rays onto the pools of water below. "Rather a night-club trick than a serious attempt at garden decoration," muttered Fletcher Steele, somewhat sarcastically. In spite of its position in the center of the site, Steele saw the sphere as "completely successful in focusing the interest and relieving by its unexpected location what would otherwise be an altogether stiff pattern."[22]

Although Forestier denounced the imitation of Arab gardens and Spanish patios as having "no place in this exposition," such Mediterranean references appeared to the audience as righteously French.[23] The Jardin d'eau et de lumière, on the other hand, with its obsessive geometry and intense colors, was set apart as cubist or Persian.[24] Perhaps in this garden Guevrekian reconciled the symbolism of the paradise garden, with its girdled layout divided by water channels, and cubism, which had fractured the structure of Western perspective.[25] Although rigorously composed, the Garden of Water and Light nevertheless differed from the regular style expressed in the designs of André and Paul Vera and Jean-Charles Moreux. Guevrekian did not resort to geometry simply to regulate vegetation: geometry *was* the landscape. His garden was an homage to geometry, which Apollinaire had described as being "to the plastic arts what grammar is to the art of writing."[26] Displayed among the Provençal gardens with neoclassical references and art déco bric-a-brac, the Jardin d'eau et de lumière merited the widespread attraction and curiosity it provoked. Among its admirers was Charles de Noailles.[27]

The vicomte de Noailles, by right of inheritance a major patron in the world of art, had a passion for gardens and a taste for modernity.[28] A year before the exposition, he had commissioned an abstract garden of boxwood and colored gravel for the grounds of his hôtel in Paris. In a letter to Robert Mallet-Stevens, the viscount praised the Jardin d'eau et de lumière: "I very much liked this garden at the Decorative Arts [Exposition] and would gladly

7-4 VILLA NOAILLES. VIEW FROM THE SWIMMING POOL TERRACE, LOOKING EAST. Hyères, 1927. Robert Mallet-Stevens. [Lurçat, *Terrasses et jardins*]

7-5 VILLA NOAILLES. THE INDOOR SWIMMING POOL. [Lurçat, *Terrasses et jardins*]

7-4

7-5

129

7-6 VILLA NOAILLES.
AXONOMETRIC
DRAWING.
[Courtesy Agnès Fuzibet
and Cécile Briolle]

7-7 VILLA NOAILLES.
VIEW FROM THE PATH
LOOKING TOWARD
THE JACQUES LIPCHITZ
STATUE AT THE TIP OF
THE GARDEN.
The wall to the right
retains the maquis.
Circa 1928.
[Deshairs, "Une villa
moderne à Hyères"]

7-8 VILLA NOAILLES.
THE LAWN TERRACE
PLANTED WITH
ORANGE TREES AND
ITALIAN CYPRESSES.
The wall frames views
of Hyères and the
Mediterranean.
Robert Mallet-Stevens.
[Lurçat, *Terrasses et
jardins*]

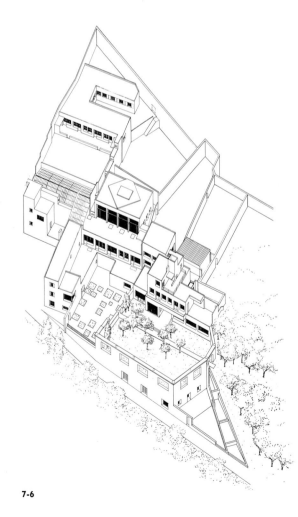

7-6

ask [Guevrekian] to design one for here, if you
think this kind of thing would amuse him."²⁹
"Here" referred to the site in Hyères on which
Mallet-Stevens was designing a villa for
Charles and Marie-Laure de Noailles.

A "CUBIST GARDEN" FOR THE VILLA NOAILLES

HYÈRES, 1927. In 1924, after having apparently
consulted both Mies van der Rohe and Le Corbusier about designing a modern villa for their
estate in the south of France, the Noailles settled on Mallet-Stevens as their architect.³⁰ A
fashionable ensemble in modernity, the Villa
Noailles was the outcome of Mallet-Stevens's
collaboration with such contemporary design
luminaries as Pierre Chareau, Theo van
Doesburg, Jan and Joël Martel, Djo-Bourgeois,
Henri Laurens, and Gabriel Guevrekian.

An elongated shape arranged in tiers on the
steep terrain, the house had commanding views
of Hyères and the Mediterranean Sea far
below. With an indoor swimming pool, an outdoor gymnasium, and its principal elevation
facing south to the bay and the low winter sun,
the villa was an homage to health, sunlight,
and innovation. Each of the several gardens
surrounding the villa bore a distinct character.
A cloister was laid out among the ruins of the
old château Saint-Bernard to the north of the
villa.³¹ On the western side of the main building was the Cour des pieds carrés, a paved
courtyard in which trees alternated with
squares of flowers or lawn.³² To the east of the
estate was a more naturalistic maquis planted
with pines and olive trees. The terraced
southern slope featured several ornamental
gardens.³³ Adorned with orange trees and Italian cypresses, the front lawn was enclosed by
walls whose cutout windows framed the view
of the bay and surrounding landscape. Wooden
shutters allowed the viewers to either hang or
take down the sights, as if they were giant post-
cards.³⁴ Two openings on the eastern wall
framed a view of the garden below, designed by
Guevrekian.

The model of the garden for the Villa Noailles
was exhibited at the Salon d'Automne of 1927
and appeared as a near relative of the Jardin
d'eau et de lumière.³⁵ [Plate XV] The severe
geometry and level of abstraction of the model
drew sharp commentaries from its reviewers.
According to a contemporary journalist, the
outcome was a "garden that looked like anything but a garden": this "bunch of little
triangles, green or blue" and "the barren
geometry of the planters" created a "curious

and sinister effect." Wondering if the designer intended to put flowers in this landscape, the author concluded such a natural addition would be rather a nuisance.[36] To another critic, Guevrekian "violated nature so much that, most likely, he had topped Le Nôtre."[37] In the model, a series of colored squares stepped down from the tip of the triangle toward four reflecting spheres, while triangles climbed in a zig-zag pattern toward the other corners. The spheres were interpreted as reflecting devices in which "all the colors of the garden merged harmoniously."[38] As the Jardin d'eau et de lumière was a direct translation of a graphic rendering, the Noailles model was an honest representation of a geometric tour de force in which "dirt [was] moulded in strangely scalloped terraces. Where [earth would not] hold, concrete [was] called in to help, and little compartments of rigid shapes and sizes raised above each other singly or in tiers [were] filled with water, bedding plants, turf, or colored stones."[39] By presenting the garden in isolation, however, the model failed to acknowledge the variations and optical effects resulting from shape or color juxtaposed against a changing background, whether a white- or sand-colored wall, a blue sky, or pine and olive trees.

Considered a milestone of early modernism, the villa resembled a contemporary castle rising from the ruins of an old one.[40] Its stark volumes, firmly anchored to the land, formed a rock terrace that dominated the site. Guevrekian's design terminated the linearity of the scheme with an elongated isosceles triangle.[41] With the Noailles pennant floating at the top of the tower, the villa from below resembled a ship stranded on the hillside. Reinforcing the maritime association, Jacques Lipchitz's figurehead, *La joie de vivre* (known as *Joy of Life*), anchored the bow of the site.[42] Illuminated at night, the sculpture was compared to a "luminous idol" that fishermen entering the harbor could see in the distance, perceiving it as they might a lighthouse.[43]

Between the grayish-green Mediterranean hills and the cerulean southern sky, Guevrekian painted his tableau with a chromatic and vegetal palette completely alien to the surrounding landscape. He "felt that almost complete seclusion was desirable, because elsewhere from the villa glorious Mediterranean views lie spread before one in every direction. Here he wanted close enclosure and attention directed to artifice, yet without confinement."[44] He reinforced the intensity of his design with a shift between

7-7

7-8

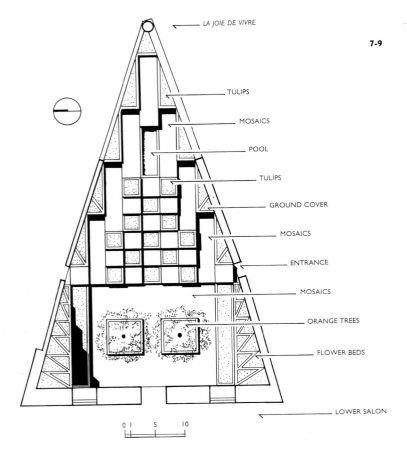

- LA JOIE DE VIVRE
- TULIPS
- MOSAICS
- POOL
- TULIPS
- GROUND COVER
- MOSAICS
- ENTRANCE
- MOSAICS
- ORANGE TREES
- FLOWER BEDS
- LOWER SALON

7-9

0 1   5   10

7-10

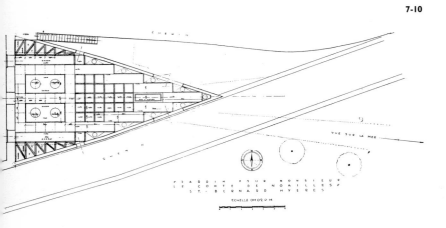

the rough tan stucco surface of the villa and the stark whitewashed garden enclosure. In spite of its contrasting forms and colors, the garden established a relation between the site and the villa's architecture, the former determining the overall triangular shape, the latter, the points from which the garden would be seen. As a pattern extending outward from the interior, the garden was purely decorative. A pristine ornament framed by crisp walls, Guevrekian's landscape was both "architecture, and a response to architecture."[45] The geometric composition vibrated with texture and color. The glazed tiles, the mirrorlike water basin, the glossy leaves of the orange trees, and the animated reflection of the gilded bronze statue all shimmered with light. The mosaics set yellow against blue, red, gray, and mauve hues, while the tulips floating on their fragile stems formed a separate plane that cast shadows on the adjacent tiles.

The richness of color and bold geometry of the garden contrasted with the almost classical lawn terrace on one side—with its cypress and orange trees—and the scrubbiness of the warm gray pines and olive trees on the other. Apparently oblivious to the colors of the native vegetation and the tonality of the villa walls, Guevrekian formed his garden as a hyphen between architecture and nature, linking the two elements while dividing them. Like the Jardin d'eau et de lumière, this garden had little connection to its surroundings. Unlike the exposition garden, however, the Noailles tableau-jardin offered to the eye three very distinct, if static, images.

Seen from the upper lawn terrace, Guevrekian's design was flattened into a tableau. This angle, similar to the photograph of the model exhibited at the Salon d'Automne, revealed the structure of the design. With little distortion, the view from above presented the sum of the parts and their distinct colors and geometries. The converging walls forced the side planters into inclined triangular planes, their different tones of green creating the illusion of an artificial shadow cast upon the darker side of the beds.[46] A peripheral looping path was implied by a staggered sequence of rectangles tiled in red, gray, yellow, and blue.[47] The central panel played tulips and mauve ceramic tiles. At the base of the triangle, the tips of two dwarf Chinese orange trees floated above a tessellated surface of black glass. The visual axis, strengthened by the rectangular pool and the depressed central spine, culminated with *La joie de vivre* at the vertex of the triangle.[48]

7-9 VILLA NOAILLES.
ANNOTATED PLAN OF
THE GUEVREKIAN
GARDEN AS BUILT.
[Dorothée Imbert after
Cécile Briolle and
Agnès Fuzibet]

7-10 VILLA NOAILLES.
GARDEN. PLAN.
Early scheme with four
orange trees and a
flower bed instead of the
pool. Circa 1926.
Gabriel Guevrekian.
[Rémon, "Jardins de
Guevrekian"]

7-11 VILLA NOAILLES.
VIEW OF THE GARDEN
FROM THE LAWN
TERRACE.
1928. Gabriel
Guevrekian.
[Lurçat, *Terrasses et
jardins*]

7-11

7-12 VILLA NOAILLES.
VIEW OF THE GARDEN
FROM THE LOWER
SALON.
[Deshairs, "Une villa
moderne à Hyères"]

7-12

The garden was also visible, and accessible, from the lower salon, a vaulted remnant of the convent. From there Guevrekian's design appeared as an exercise in one-point perspective. Framed by the orange trees, the converging checkerboard pattern enhanced the perception of depth and focused the view on the whimsically rotating vanishing point created by the Lipchitz statue. Each of the squares, whether of mosaic or tulips, was bordered in white cement, as if to delineate man's influence and nature's composure. The garden ascended toward the apex, behind which the statue thrust skyward. The model and the plan presented the garden as totally enclosed but for the side doors and two windows. Placed near the tip of the triangle, one of the windows was intended to frame a view of the sea and to establish a thematic link between the garden pool and the bay.[49] When constructed, however, the far end of each side wall was lowered. With a third of the frame removed, the sense of artifice was weakened, but the contrast, and the connection, between the tableau-jardin and the native landscape was reinforced.

When Lipchitz first exhibited *Joy of Life*, an abstract dancing figure with a large guitar, it bore the inscription "J'aime le mouvement qui déplace les formes."[50] Charles de Noailles described "statues [as] an excellent thing in the garden, they are halfway between man and matter, a perfect intermediary between nature and humanity."[51] Completing an electrically controlled rotation every four minutes, *La joie de vivre* came one step closer to man. Lipchitz considered this statue a turning point in his career, "a culmination of all my findings in Cubism but at the same time an escape from Cubism."[52] To others, it simply did not belong as the focal point of a modern garden. The critic P. Morton Shand saw it as "a man laboriously divesting himself of the convolutions of his own entrails after committing hara-kiri with insufficient technical precision."[53] Although Guevrekian had not included a statue in his original scheme, the articulated pool of water crowned by a bright red vertical element—perhaps a fountain—created a visual accent that relieved the otherwise rather planar design. The garden as built, with *La joie de vivre*, cited the Jardin d'eau et de lumière and its glass sphere. Animated and illuminated with electricity, both elements marked centers of gravity: the rotating globe reinforced the centripetal character of the exposition garden, while the Lipchitz statue, located at the tip of the triangle, suggested a connection with the surrounding countryside.

Photographs taken from the vertex of the triangle—the third principal view—presented a stilled picture. The reversed perspective flattened the composition, drawing closer the quiet anthropomorphic elevation of the villa and diminishing the perception of both the checkerboard and the slope. The link between the lower orange trees and those on the upper terrace—visible through the openings—implied that the triangular garden continued above, beyond the wall. This view exuded a calmness unsettled only by the inclined triangular beds that climbed toward the upper terrace along the garden's side walls. As if defying gravity within a stuccoed frame, the tiers of blue flowers formed two unstable ladder-paths seemingly taken from Dr. Caligari's cabinet. Zig-zagging upward, they suggested that the constricted vegetation could escape to the surrounding landscape.[54] In the background, the hillside balanced in mass the tower of the Villa Noailles. The garden itself breathed seclusion; the side doors were not perceptible within the angled walls. For the resulting feeling of calm; for its protective enclosure; for its pool; for the warmth of its colored tiles; for its orange trees and tulips, the Noailles garden was perceived as a modern evocation of paradise, a "stylization of the gorgeous effect of some Shiraz garden ablaze with flagged borders of richly patterned Persian tiles."[55] Weaving the Persian tradition with Western accents in the garden at Hyères, Guevrekian was seen as "entirely original"; "his adoption of an Eastern suggestion had to be harmonised with Western ideas, so that it should not look merely like a period or a puzzle."[56]

In contrast to the gardens of Le Corbusier, Pierre Jeanneret, Mallet-Stevens, and André Lurçat, which he dismissed as "commonplace" and "show[ing] an utter lack of interest or understanding of plant life," Fletcher Steele praised the designs of Guevrekian. In Steele's opinion, Guevrekian explored "the myriad ways [vegetation] might reënforce [his] ideas."[57] As a literal expression of an architectural landscape, the Noailles garden modeled plants to fit the geometry of its masonry frame. Steele described the garden in Hyères as a composition of "little compartments of rigid shapes and sizes . . . filled with water, bedding plants, turf, or colored stones as the distribution of colors may require."[58] Rigorously formal, the garden of artifice was affected only by environmental factors. The configuration of the walls, supposedly a protection against the prevailing winds, also reflected light and heat on the sequestered vegetation.[59] Growing at various rates according to exposure, the plants refused to obey the totalitarian symmetry the designer had wished to impose.

Mirroring the control of mind over nature, Guevrekian's landscape was a jardin de l'intelligence. Shaped with mineral elements such as cement and glass, with bulb flowers and plants tolerant of pruning, it was another permanent-instant garden—a constructed landscape that left little margin for evolution. In the winter, colors and textures shimmered as the tulips bloomed and the mosaics and water caught the weak rays of the sun. By summer the tulips had vanished.

Steele characterized Guevrekian's design as a "composition in geometry" which proved that "even gardens can be rudely simplified to the elementary spheres, cylinders, cones."[60] Instead, his garden appeared to exemplify the criticism attributed to architectonic gardens. Built with sheets of color, water, and plants, Guevrekian's creation was a "planar construction" rather than a volumetric landscape.[61] Ultimately, the garden in Hyères read as an outdoor translation of the flattened rendering for the little Cut-flower Room created by van Doesburg inside the villa.[62] Offering few tactile experiences, the garden was to be admired for the brilliance of its hues and the grace and discipline of its flowers. As a walled garden, in the sense of a paradise or a medieval cloister, it represented an idealized nature protected from the wilderness. As a tableau, the garden presented an image of nature frozen in time. From the moment of its construction until its complete deterioration, the estate's five gardeners worked to maintain its original quality and precise design.[63]

In spite of its hard-lined structure, Gabriel Guevrekian's garden resisted the assaults of nature only briefly. By 1934, the chromatic fantasy had been recast as a perennial monotony of aloe.[64] A succulent of the lily family, "showy, easy and drought tolerant," and well adapted to the dry climate and soil of Hyères, aloe was a low-maintenance substitute for tulips.[65] Other than the overall geometry and the walls, few traces of Guevrekian's scheme were left in the refurbished design. Four equal tiers, planted with rows of succulents, replaced the subtle rises of four inches for each square of the checkerboard. In the foreground, a more

7-13

7-13 VILLA NOAILLES.
VIEW OF THE GARDEN
FROM THE VERTEX
OF THE TRIANGLE.
[Lurçat, *Terrasses et jardins*]

7-14 STILL FROM *DAS
KABINETT DES DOKTOR
CALIGARI.*
1919. Film by Robert
Wiene, with sets by
Hermann Warm, Walter
Reimann, and Walter
Röhrig.
[University Art
Museum / Pacific Film
Archive, University of
California, Berkeley]

traditional Provençal tile replaced the black mosaics, and the planting beds were shifted to facilitate access to the garden through the side doors. The spikiness of the new vegetation left no ambiguity about whether the garden was intended as a tableau to be viewed or as a place to stroll. A photograph of this design, whose caption read, ironically, "garden [that] fits exactly the architecture of the house," shows the Villa Noailles with a year-round, low-maintenance, and low-intensity visual landscape.[66] Convenience was achieved at the expense of elegance.

Owing to complete neglect, no trace of any garden within the walls remained by the end of the 1930s. The estate, which was bequeathed to the city of Hyères in 1973, seemed doomed to total ruin. In the past few years, however, the villa and the triangular garden have been partially restored to their original designs.[67] [Plate XVI] Probably the first true re-creation of a modernist garden, its new form is marred by several deficiencies. If the statutes governing French historical monuments saved the estate from complete oblivion, they also required the installation of a sprinkler system whose hard water has obscured the colored tiles under an opaque layer of calcium and may have adversely affected the survival of the orange trees. The absence of the statue, the tyranny of the gardeners, and the need to present a display of blooms year round resulted in a composition that mutes the brilliance and strength of Guevrekian's original tableau-jardin.[68] In spite of these shortcomings, however, the triangular garden still offers striking views today, over sixty years after its creation.

Guevrekian may have intended to express isolated artifice in his design for the Noailles, but the walled garden nevertheless drew force from its dramatic contrast to the surrounding landscape. It is therefore odd that some reviewers considered the garden a formal solution suitable for any small site, labeling it a "forerunner of numerous other efforts at landscape gardening within a highly restricted area."[69] It was described as "an amusing feature, a novelty . . . [which] would do equally well for the garden of a small town house and would be extremely convenient as well as beautiful."[70] As an outcome of its being "a treatment full of suggestion for many a tiny London garden," A. E. Powell designed a pale replica of the Guevrekian garden near Bristol, but crucial differences between the designs weakened the English imitation.[71] Instead of using high side

7-14

7-15

7-16

walls, Powell timidly framed his triangle with a low hedge. Adorned by a more-modest statuette, the vertex of the garden was enclosed by a lattice fence in an attempt to keep the garden from flowing, unnoticed, onto the nearby field. Reduced to a mere geometric exercise, the vapid English re-creation evoked none of the essential tensions that Guevrekian had established between the Noailles garden and the landscape of Hyères.

Although Guevrekian's garden was physically accessible, it was essentially a pictorial and contemplative work. The polished or rippled textures, the juxtaposition of contrasting colors and differing intensities of reflection, the tilts, slight extrusions and depressions of planes, all joined to create an illusory depth that engaged only the sense of sight. Most published accounts represented Guevrekian's design with one or two images, which illustrated "a flat garden for one point of view and a sloping garden for the other."[72] Despite the suggestion of a jagged path, nothing invited a leisurely stroll through the checkerboard maze; indeed, its diminutive size precluded it.

Overlaying the exaggerated perspective with a cubistic geometry, a fragmentation in planes of light and shade, and color vibration, Guevrekian created a faceted painting that is still considered a cubist garden. Perhaps the lone three-dimensional element in this delicate bas-relief, *La joie de vivre*, best expressed the cubist character of the Noailles garden. Presenting all its contours to the stationary spectator, the automated sculpture was the only element that marked the passage of time in this stilled likeness of nature.

7-15 VILLA NOAILLES. POSTCARD VIEW OF THE ALOE GARDEN FROM THE LOWER SALON.
[Courtesy Cécile Briolle]

7-16 VILLA NOAILLES. THE TRIANGULAR GARDEN PLANTED WITH ALOE.
Circa 1933.
Designer unknown.
[*Gardens and Gardening, 1934*]

7-17 VILLA NOAILLES. THE GUEVREKIAN GARDEN RESTORED.
VIEW FROM THE LOWER SALON.
[Photo: Marc Treib, 1991]

7-18 GARDEN AFTER GUEVREKIAN'S DESIGN FOR THE VILLA NOAILLES.
Near Bristol, England, circa 1935. A. E. Powell.
[Tunnard, "The Functional Aspect of Garden Planning"]

7-17

139

7-18

A TERRACE GARDEN: THE VILLA HEIM

NEUILLY, 1927. Contemporaneously with the garden in Hyères, Guevrekian created his most complete ensemble: a villa in Neuilly for the fashion designer Jacques Heim.[73] Set between street and park, the building's impervious north facade contrasted with an "architectonic landscape of flowered terraces, propitious to games or meditation" to the south.[74] Reminiscent of Henri Sauvage's terraced apartment blocks, the park side of the villa descended step by step, and floor by floor, from the roof terrace to the paved section of the garden below. [Plate XVII] Because the ground floor was assigned to service—garage, kitchen, and servant quarters—the Heim garden was primarily intended to be seen from the living quarters on the upper floors. From above, the garden appeared to be an extension of the terraces.[75]

A master of both architectural and garden design, Guevrekian erased the boundaries between ground and terrace levels by interchanging their principal elements—grass and paving, shrubs and concrete. The brackets that framed the garden room below were repeated on the third-floor balcony, and the basin on the living room terrace countered a pool in the eastern corner of the garden.[76] The garden also reiterated the subtle variations of textures etched on the upper floors.

To mitigate its distance from the garden, the fourth-floor exterior was the most lavishly planted. There, wrote Guevrekian, "all means (lawn, pergolas, flower containers) were employed to make a real hanging garden."[77] In reality, the concrete and tile far outweighed vegetation. A fragment of lawn carpeted a "green room"; delicate vines were trained against one wall and across a pergola of metal pipe; a few planters softened the edge of the balcony. The Villa Heim was thus crowned by an archetypical modernist roof terrace, with greenery borrowed visually from the adjacent landscape of the parc de la Folie Saint-James.

As an architectonic composition set against the naturalistic background of the eighteenth-century park, the succession of delicate textures and engraved terraces reiterated the apparent antagonism between the artifice of the Noailles garden and the landscape around it.[78] Although created during the same years, the gardens for Noailles and Heim differed considerably in both approach and form.

The garden in Neuilly illustrated, perhaps unintentionally, André Vera's preference for

7-19

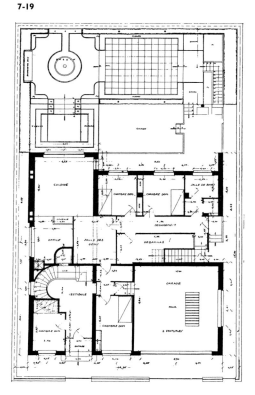

7-19 VILLA HEIM. THE GROUND LEVEL SHOWING THE SERVANTS' QUARTERS AND GARDEN PLAN. 1927. Gabriel Guevrekian. [*L'Architecte*, 1929]

7-20 VILLA HEIM. VIEW FROM THE UPPER TERRACE. Neuilly, 1928. Gabriel Guevrekian. [Zahar, "La maison de Mr et Mme Heim"]

7-20

7-21

7-22

dividing the modern garden into rectangular compartments similar to the rooms of an apartment.[79] The ground level of the garden reflected the interior plan with independent but connected outdoor rooms. Its spiraling succession of spaces, ending with a sunken garden, hardly implied convenience, however. Less traditional than Vera's plans, Guevrekian's exterior apartment appeared as a visual rather than spatial sequence in which one outdoor room graphically balanced the other. Guevrekian described his composition of brick, lawn, and mosaic as visually enlarging and enriching this modest garden.[80]

If the functional organization of the garden had faults, the geometries were carefully proportioned: the interlocking planes derived from subdivisions of the golden rectangle and continued the spiral initiated on the roof terrace. Attention to detail was revealed in the progressive increase in steps from one garden room to another; the shift from herringbone to basket-weave patterns in the paving; and the play between the pink and blue found in the glazed ceramics of the pool, the tonality of the bricks, and the blue benches framed by rose bushes.[81]

Although the Heim garden lacked the strength and concentration of both the Jardin d'eau et de lumière and the Noailles garden, it nevertheless formed a thoroughly orchestrated ensemble. The multiplication of geometric motifs that had dominated the triangular designs here simply modulated the basically sober composition. Rejecting the planes of pure color of his previous landscapes, Guevrekian designed the garden in Neuilly using planes patterned with lines. Both the exposition and the Hyères gardens responded to specific demands; Forestier had insisted that the Jardin d'eau et de lumière be modern and Persian, and Charles de Noailles had commissioned a pictorial design using the exposition garden as a point of departure.[82] The architectonic landscape for Jacques Heim, in fact, could be positioned on the thin line that distinguishes a tableau-jardin from a true garden. Graphically composed, it nevertheless considered functional questions—the garden as an extension of indoor living. In its sobriety the Heim garden revealed both its strength and its limitations.

For its marked interaction between interior and exterior design, the Villa Heim was considered Guevrekian's most complete achievement, but it also signaled the decline of his formal and plastic explorations in garden architecture. The

7-21 VILLA HEIM.
THE FOURTH-FLOOR
TERRACE WITH
PERGOLA AND
"GREEN ROOM."
[Chavance, "Guevrekian,
architecte et décorateur"]

7-22 VILLA HEIM.
THE SECOND-FLOOR
TERRACE.
[Lurçat, *Terrasses et
jardins*]

7-23 VILLA HEIM.
THE GARDEN,
LOOKING WEST.
[Lurçat, *Terrasses et
jardins*]

7-24 VILLA HEIM.
GARDEN PLAN WITH
CONSTRUCTION LINES.
Each area is based on
the golden section and
corresponds to the
planning of the house.
[Dorothée Imbert]

7-25 VILLA HEIM.
THE GARDEN,
LOOKING EAST.
[*L'Illustration,* 28 May
1932]

7-23

7-24

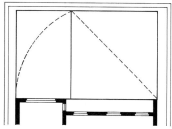
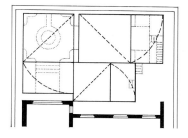

7-25

7-26 VILLA HEIM.
VIEW FROM THE GARDEN
TOWARD THE HOUSE.
[Photo: Therese Bonney;
© 1993 ARS, N.Y. /
SPADEM, Paris]

7-27 VILLA SIASSY.
PLAN OF GROUND
FLOOR AND GARDEN.
Tehran, 1935.
Gabriel Guevrekian.
[Guevrekian, "Maisons
en pays de soleil"]

7-26

rooftop he designed for Charles de Beistegui in 1929, only two years after the Noailles garden, was little more than a sequence of terraces outlined with sculptured vegetal elements.[83] Although the project overlooked the Champs-Élysées and was commissioned by a flamboyant art patron, it bore no sign of extravagance. There was no apparent interaction here between the tiled spaces of the roof and the skies and monuments of Paris. Hardly provocative, the Guevrekian design for the Beistegui penthouse remained far behind Le Corbusier's surrealistic homage to the city.[84]

The gardens Guevrekian realized in Iran between 1933 and 1937 clearly receded into tradition. Although water courses, pools, terraces, and trees were components characterizing Persian classicism, these designs were neither re-creations of luxuriant paradise gardens nor transformations of the Persian heritage into a more modern idiom.[85] The intrigue of distorted perspectives, juxtaposed paving patterns, and earth fragmentations had vanished. In lieu of overscaled triangular icons, Guevrekian now drew parterres that resembled gallicized simplifications of a Persian vocabulary.[86]

The Jardin d'eau et de lumière and the Noailles garden were indisputably, and deservedly, seen as his most brilliant interpretations of contemporary Persian miniatures. They also were frequently labeled cubist. In examining this assertion, Richard Wesley described the Jardin d'eau et de lumière as the first attempt to equate the aesthetic of modern art with landscape design.[87] For its sharp outline, shallow depth, compressed space, and inclined surfaces, Wesley compared the exposition garden to *Man with a Mandolin,* painted by Picasso in 1912. Similarly, he extended a parallel between the sequence of terraces of the Villa Heim and the cubist technique of collage Picasso used in his 1914 *Glass Pipe and Lemon.* Despite these possible resemblances, Wesley was justly reserved in accepting the successful application of cubist principles to the garden and suggested that "the fundamental paradox of the Cubist garden remained unresolved." "How could Guevrekian have translated the spatial conception implied in a Cubist painting into a tridimensional art?" questioned the author, since cubism "dealt essentially with the bidimensional articulation of an opaque surface."[88]

In fact, Guevrekian used the third dimension only sparingly. His triangular gardens were fabricated as images; although slightly inclined to augment their perception at eye level, they were best viewed from above. The movement of robust volumes such as a stained glass sphere and a statue suggested time—the fourth dimension sought by cubist painters. Paradoxically, Guevrekian's collages of tiles and plants were conferred a sense of reality principally by these alien three-dimensional elements. To cite Apollinaire's description of cubist paintings, these landscape vignettes appeared "more cerebral than sensual."[89] As vegetation competed with mineral elements in these architectonic landscapes, the cyclical transformation of nature—roughly equivalent to the cubist concern for time—was actually repressed. Guevrekian realized gardens of a single instant. In these exercises, whether cubist or simply formal, nature was neither re-created nor idealized; it was abstracted. As expressions of a garden design aligned with aesthetic trends, these tableaux-jardins also exemplified a "Cubism [that was] not an art of imitation, but an art of conception rising toward creation."[90]

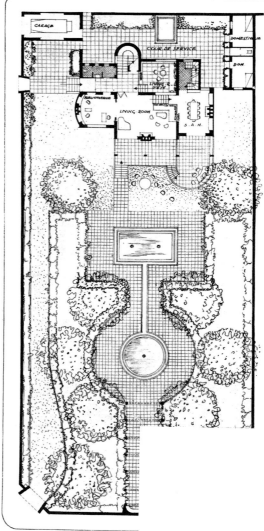

7-27

146

LE CORBUSIER

THE LANDSCAPE VS. THE GARDEN

8-1

Although Le Corbusier's architecture and urbanism have been studied, analyzed, and continuously reevaluated—perhaps more than those of any other twentieth-century architect—his approach to landscape design remains largely unscrutinized.[1] It is not my intention to examine his buildings extensively in relation to site, vegetation, and nature or to trace the sources that influenced his consciousness of landscape. Rather, by studying his writings and the projects he designed with Pierre Jeanneret during the 1920s and 1930s, I hope to situate Le Corbusier's discourse within the prevailing trends in French landscape architecture.

The projects I have selected to illustrate the architects' attitude toward both gardens and landscape follow an almost chronological order: the Pavillon de L'Esprit Nouveau, the Villa Meyer, the Villa "Les Terrasses," the Villa Church, the Villa Savoye, and the Beistegui Penthouse. Although the Villa "Le Lac" was realized earlier than these designs, it is studied

8-1 PAVILLON DE L'ESPRIT NOUVEAU.
Exposition Internationale des Arts Décoratifs et Industriels Modernes. Paris, 1925.
Le Corbusier and Pierre Jeanneret. The statue in front of the pavilion is by Jacques Lipchitz.
[FLC L2 (8) 1-8. © 1993 ARS, N.Y. / SPADEM, Paris]

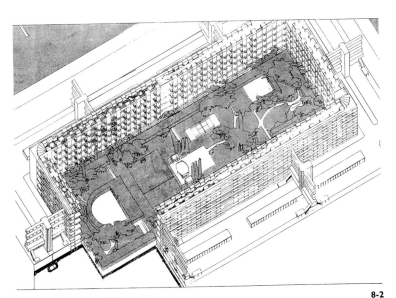

8-2 IMMEUBLE-VILLAS.
AXONOMETRIC
DRAWING SHOWING
PARK AND
RECREATIONAL
FACILITIES.
First presented at the
Salon d'Automne, 1922.
Le Corbusier and
Pierre Jeanneret.
[Le Corbusier,
Urbanisme. © 1993 ARS,
N.Y. / SPADEM, Paris]

8-3 IMMEUBLE-VILLAS.
DETAIL OF THE FACADE
WITH "HANGING
GARDENS."
[Le Corbusier, *Vers une
architecture.* © 1993
ARS, N.Y. / SPADEM,
Paris]

8-4 PAVILLON DE L'ESPRIT
NOUVEAU.
THE "HANGING
GARDEN."
Two of the walls were
painted burnt sienna;
the interior color of the
sliding panels was sky
blue. A circular
opening in the ceiling
accommodated an
existing tree.
[FLC L2 (8) 1–19.
© 1993 ARS, N.Y. /
SPADEM, Paris]

8-2

here in light of Le Corbusier's later reassessment. Paralleling this progression in time is his expanding vision of the site. The Esprit Nouveau Pavilion represented a reduced version of both its architectural matrix and the landscape surrounding it; the Villa Meyer was simply placed against an existing eighteenth-century park; at Garches, Le Corbusier manipulated the landscape to offer the best views of the Villa "Les Terrasses"; the Villa Church was immersed in a naturalistic park in Ville-d'Avray; the Villa Savoye stood as a twentieth-century folly in the rural countryside of Poissy; and the Beistegui rooftop commanded views of the city, selectively framing the archetypical monuments of Paris. Finally, in the modest house for his parents Le Corbusier appears to have justified several unbuilt projects that would have framed, enhanced, or honored his native Swiss landscape.

THE ESPRIT NOUVEAU PAVILION

PARIS, 1925. Le Corbusier (1887–1965) and Pierre Jeanneret (1896–1956) conceived the Pavillon de L'Esprit Nouveau as a monument to standardization. Built for the Exposition des Arts Décoratifs, it was intended to represent the cell of a housing unit, the Immeuble-villas (Villa-Apartment Block), a fragment of a greater urban scheme.[2] The pavilion was formulated as a product of industry; composed of standardized elements, it addressed both the intimate scale of interior design and the broader question of urban planning.[3] The *maison-outil,* or house as tool, denied both specificity and regionalism. Whether rented or sold, housing had to answer *besoins-types,* or typical needs, with unrelenting practicality.[4] In an attempt to demonstrate the validity of the pavilion as a ubiquitous housing type, Le Corbusier planned to transplant the Esprit Nouveau unit to a garden city after the exposition. Had the imposing trees not blocked its removal, the *machine à habiter* would have left the exposition one evening at midnight, rolled up the Champs-Élysées, crossed the Seine, and landed in the suburbs, intact, at dawn.[5] The notion of a generic site concluded a succession of studies at increasing scale, from furniture (*meuble-type*) to the house (*maison-type*). Architecture was placed in what I consider a *paysage-type,* a generic landscape framed by calculated openings; its shaping was less important than its evocation of nature. Seldom were the scenery and vegetation more than an unaltered backdrop. Thus the architectural frame defined the vista. Ideally, the Pavillon de

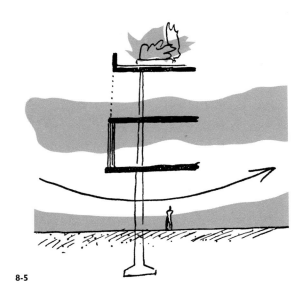

8-5

8-6

8-5 DIAGRAM
ILLUSTRATING THE
TRILOGY
SUN-AIR-VEGETATION.
Le Corbusier.
[Le Corbusier, "Unité"]

8-6 "THE ESSENTIAL
PLEASURES HAVE
ENTERED THE
DWELLINGS."
Le Corbusier.
[Le Corbusier, "Unité"]

L'Esprit Nouveau should have looked out on its site in the same way that a cell of the Immeuble-villas would look on its central naturalistic landscape.

In its style the Esprit Nouveau appeared entirely alien to the public attending the exposition. This white modular structure adjacent to the Grand Palais stretched the limits of any system of architectural reference. The design of its landscape further removed Le Corbusier's project from the general trends of the fair. In marked contrast to the prevalent *style régulier,* the garden consisted of a few hardy shrubs scattered about the site, which J.C.N. Forestier described as being "without any apparent order."[6] Although the program announcing the Esprit Nouveau credited Forestier as the garden designer, Le Corbusier's correspondence fails to substantiate any active participation by the landscape architect.

In an early letter, the architects stated their preference for the building to be placed on a large expanse of lawn, adorned only by a statue by Jacques Lipchitz. Although Forestier was entrusted with the design of the "hanging garden," Le Corbusier himself specified the various shrubs and flowers to be planted in the containers.[7] He sought vegetation that provided texture or a touch of color, as if plantings were another standardized component of the housing system. The architect suggested Chinese thujas, evergreen euonymus, for its round and thick foliage, and variegated gold-and-green spindle trees; color would be provided by potted flowers and oleanders.[8] But the planting schedule did not proceed according to Le Corbusier's strict instructions: less than ten days before Anatole de Monzie, the Minister of Fine Arts, inaugurated the pavilion, the architect was still crying for turf and shrubs.[9] Insisting on the hanging garden as the "keystone" of the proposal, he lamented the absence of flowers and trees.[10]

The Immeuble-villas project opened its internal facades onto an enclosed landscape. Each cell or "villa" included a hanging garden. The dwelling units overlooked a central park of 400 by 1000 feet that featured a soccer field, tennis courts, playgrounds, and a sports clubhouse. These facilities for hygiene and recreation were set in an essentially timeless naturalistic landscape of "free clumps of trees and lawns."[11]

Although the Plan Voisin for Paris, presented as a diorama inside the pavilion, created the illusion of dense groves of trees by using only a few shrubs, the evocation of a grand landscape surrounding the cell itself was undermined by the scale of the adjacent gaslights and low wire fence.[12] Within the enclosure of the terrace, the shrubs were domesticated and controlled; the surrounding landscape was left virtually untouched. When Le Corbusier finally obtained, with Forestier's help, the necessary "masses of turf, flowers and shrubs," he attempted to re-create a miniaturized image of a naturalistic landscape. The sculpture by Lipchitz provided a counterpoint to the rustic variegation of shrubs and front lawn of the Esprit Nouveau; its abstraction scandalized conservative viewers. "Even Negro fetishes," a critic wrote, were preferable to this modern art, because they were at least modeled upon a concept, "primitive, perhaps, but sincere."[13] If the modernity of a renewed style régulier was balanced by the neoclassical figures evident in most of the exposition gardens, Le Corbusier reversed this paradox in his juxtaposition of contemporary art and rustic landscape.

Concluding his report on the section Art du jardin, Forestier praised "the flexibility of talent, the spirit of invention, [and] the ingeniousness of artists," who have seldom had the opportunity to express themselves in garden design, that "amiable and important section of this field curiously termed decorative arts."[14] The garden classified as a decorative product might explain Le Corbusier's assertion that gardeners were "untouched by grace." Probably directing this criticism at the exterior decorators of the fair, he excluded Forestier, whom he later described as "dispersing the charm of plantings with an inventive grace."[15]

To Le Corbusier, gardens and landscape were green abstractions that belonged to the trilogy of "Sun-Air-Vegetation."[16] For the urban landscape, the "encounter between the geometric elements of buildings and the picturesque elements of vegetation" was both "necessary and sufficient." With regard to hygiene and aesthetics, he described the Immeuble-villas as breathing; as to form, the "round volumes of foliage and the arabesques of the branches" played against the architectonic prism. The generalized categories of plantings and vegetation were picturesque and graceful simply as natural entities.[17] If given shape, greenery would appear as decoration. Furthermore, such calculated vegetal composition might detract from the impact of the pure architectural volumes, whose uniform facades constituted a

"trellis against which the tree branches [were] advantageously silhouetted."[18]

Linking architecture and urbanism, the Pavillon de L'Esprit Nouveau superimposed the concept of the garden upon that of landscape. When Le Corbusier insisted on the significance of the hanging garden—in reality a terrace with a few planters—he revealed his ambiguous attitude toward nature. The use of vegetation within the architectural frame was inherently constricted by technical limitations. The greater landscape, on the other hand, was left untouched, as a stage on which sun, air, and rain were the principal actors. The garden in the air is the "modern recipe for ventilation," Le Corbusier declared. Easily accessible, it is protected from harsh sunlight and rain, and its dry paving prevents rheumatism. Hygienic, it transformed the usually inert apartment building into a breathing sponge that integrated air and greenery within its concrete structure. Such a garden was convenient for city dwellers because it was "efficient and maintenance-free." Atop the Immeuble-villas one would find the "solariums, the swimming pool, the exercise rooms and the promenades amid the greenery of the hanging gardens."[19] This displacement of the ground level upward became an architectural dictum that Le Corbusier applied, with modifications, to several of his residential designs.

VILLA MEYER

NEUILLY, 1925. The Villa Meyer, an unrealized project designed for "a client without scruples," appeared to be a reduction of the grand ideas first expounded in the project for the Immeuble-villas.[20] Enshrining a domesticated garden, the house was set within, or against, a naturalistic landscape from the late eighteenth century. As if expressing the contrast between the picturesque vegetation and the pure prism seen in the 1922 proposal for the apartment block, the Villa Meyer was described by Le Corbusier as a smooth volume, standing nobly against the foliage of the adjacent park.[21] The house in Neuilly was to overlook La Folie Saint-James, an estate laid out in the Anglo-Chinese style by François Bélanger around 1778 for Baudard de Vaudésir, baron de Saint-James.[22] In a letter to Mrs. Meyer, Le Corbusier described the setting as a "wild copse" whose ancient trees conjured the illusion of being far removed from Paris. Although not intended to stand on *pilotis,* the living room

was raised above the ground floor, leaving the shaded first floor for service.[23]

Le Corbusier and Jeanneret proposed several variations for a vertically organized *parti* that captured both nature and views of the park. Only the first of these schemes included a horizontal interaction with the site, using a terrace to extend the house into the garden. Like the Immeuble-villas, the domesticated nature of the roof garden played against an architecturally framed view that treated the park's vegetation as only a backdrop. Three of Le Corbusier's seven perspective sketches depicted the gardens as an integral part of the villa. There was little evidence, however, of extending the landscape design outward from the architectural shell. A sunken vegetable garden, which would have been doomed to failure for lack of sun, and the implication of a path meandering through a few clumps of trees were the only allusions to a developed backyard. In almost direct conceptual opposition to the shaded, damp soil of the garden were the rooftop solarium and swimming pool, open to the sun and stars. Placed above the "somber mass of the trees," they collectively comprised a tribute to hygiene.[24]

The upper terrace selectively controlled the views onto the park through sliding panels similar to those enclosing the terrace garden of the Pavillon de L'Esprit Nouveau. This restraint on openness and protection from "surrounding tumult" echoed René-Louis de Girardin's assertion that "every sort of pleasure is destroyed by distraction; that's why sight, the most vagabond of our senses, needs to be fixed in order to experience pleasure without weariness; that's why every decoration requires a foreground to enhance the perspective effect; that's why every picture requires a frame to control view and attention."[25]

In his plea to Mrs. Meyer, Le Corbusier explained that with such sliding panels one could be completely isolated. The architect compared the effect to the atmosphere of a painting by Carpaccio or that of Robinson— a popular restaurant amid trees, outside Paris.[26]

Planted in the eighteenth-century manner, the trees in the parc Saint-James followed a naturalistic pattern; amid the vegetation the architect Bélanger had arranged a variety of *fabriques*. A bridge, a kiosk, and a belvedere all exuded a Chinese air.[27] The most remarkable construction in the park, however, was the imposing rustic-classical Grand Rocher, a mass

8-7

8-7 VILLA MEYER. DETAIL OF A LETTER TO THE CLIENT DESCRIBING THE FIRST PROJECT. October 1925. Le Corbusier and Pierre Jeanneret. [© 1993 ARS, N.Y./ SPADEM, Paris]

8-8 VILLA MEYER. SECOND PROJECT. SKETCHES. [© 1993 ARS, N.Y./ SPADEM, Paris]

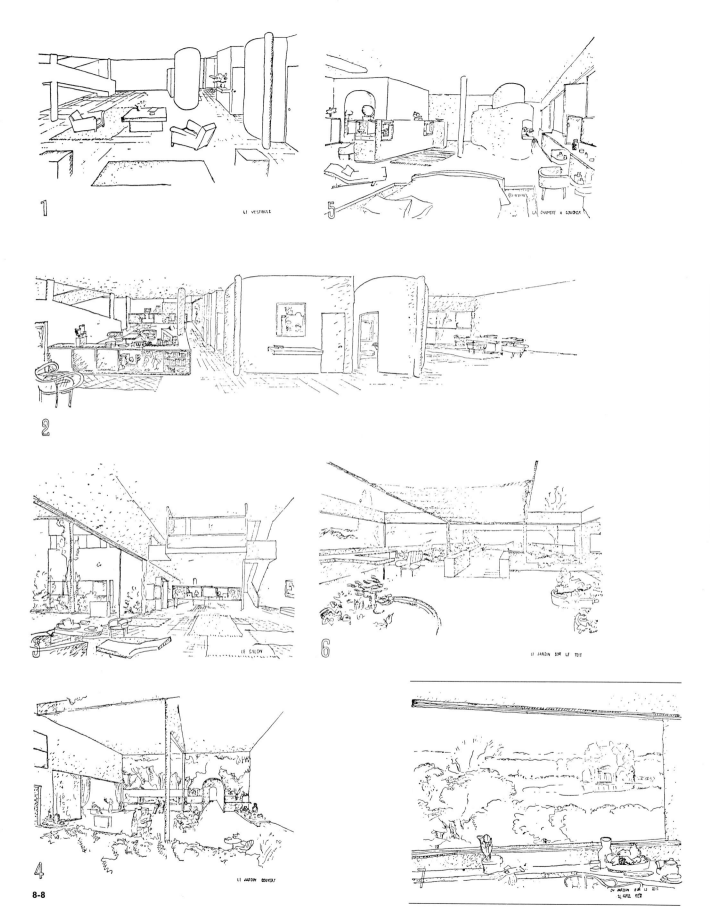

1

5 LE VESTIBULE

LA CHAMBRE A COUCHER

2

3 LE SALON

6 LE JARDIN SUR LE TOIT

4 LE JARDIN COUVERT

DU JARDIN SUR LE TOIT
LE JARD. 1937

8-8

8-10

8-9 VILLA MEYER.
SECOND PROJECT.
AXONOMETRIC VIEW
OF THE SOUTH
FACADE, TOWARD
THE PARK.
Neuilly-sur-Seine, April
1926. Le Corbusier and
Pierre Jeanneret.
[Dorothée Imbert, based
on FLC 31538]

8-10 VILLA MEYER.
VIEW FROM THE ROOF
TERRACE TOWARD LE
GRAND ROCHER.
[© 1993 ARS, N.Y. /
SPADEM, Paris]

8-11 LE GRAND ROCHER.
La Folie Saint-James,
Neuilly-sur-Seine, circa
1782. François Bélanger.
[Photo: Dorothée
Imbert, 1991]

of large boulders forming a vault over the facade of a Doric temple.[28] The mysterious mood it conveyed was intensified by its reflection in an ornamental lake.

Although Le Corbusier addressed the park as a generic green entity, he selected a specific view of La Folie Saint-James to illustrate the "jardin sur le toit": the walls enclosing the roof garden framed the Grand Rocher and its mirrored image. This last sketch of the series presented a slice of life: a shelf set for tea with implements and fruits, gloves and a flower pot. At the edge of the terrace, the proportionally dominant exterior landscape was presented as a picture, a tableau in which the focal point of the grotto, with its architectural portico, stamped the mock wilderness with the presence of man. As an architectural sign in nature, the rock echoed the Villa Meyer, itself a constructed object floating amid trees. But in a reversal of the eighteenth-century practice of projecting painting onto nature, Le Corbusier recaptured the landscape as an image. Unlike the naturalistic vegetation in the picturesque tableau, nature within the concrete shell was strictly controlled. A potted tulip, gardening gloves, and fruits in a bowl were constant reminders of the human presence. The architect thus countered the romantic tableau of La Folie Saint-James with a Purist composition, playing the contemporaneity of the domestic utensils against the historicism of the temple.

In Neuilly, the architectural machine would have been conceptually immersed in the landscape. A polite nature was returned to the house, however: not in the meager manifestations of the planter boxes, but in the active visual borrowing of scenery.

8-9

8-11

VILLA "LES TERRASSES"

GARCHES, 1927. Le Corbusier and Pierre Jeanneret took a different approach in addressing the site of the Villa "Les Terrasses," which they designed for Michael and Sarah Stein and Gabrielle de Monzie.[29] Like many of their commissions during this period, the villa was located on the outskirts of Paris, in Garches, on a long narrow lot covered with vegetation. Although the architects' process has been precisely recorded and analyzed, these studies have seldom included the garden as part of the project, except for an early site plan dated 13 November 1926, which clearly presented the designed lot.

8-12

8-12 VILLA "LES TERRASSES."
ENTRANCE WITH
GATEHOUSE.
Garches, 1927.
Le Corbusier and
Pierre Jeanneret.
[FLC L2 (5) 3. © 1993
ARS, N.Y. / SPADEM,
Paris]

8-13 VILLA "LES TERRASSES."
SITE PLAN.
Early project, dated
November 1926.
[Dorothée Imbert,
based on FLC 10411]

8-14 VILLA "LES TERRASSES."
GROUND-FLOOR PLAN.
[Dorothée Imbert, based
on FLC 10418 and
contemporary
photographs]

8-15 VILLA "LES TERRASSES."
ROOF TERRACE.
[Lurçat, *Terrasses et
jardins*]

The villa occupied the middle of the site. On the north side, the driveway lined a vegetable garden and orchard; to the south a winding path skirted a pleasure garden of lawn and ended in a grove of trees. Although this particular landscape scheme was not executed, rarely did Le Corbusier draw a garden with such detail—that is, a garden directly on the ground. Accepting the typical model for a country estate, Le Corbusier flanked the forecourt with a gatehouse; an allée lined with plantings led to the formal court, but instead of heading directly to the main entrance, it focused on the garage. Labeled "Jardin," this site plan was an exquisite graphic composition that weighed densities, masses, and voids. The house was barely noticeable, and it served primarily as a limit between the realm of the automobile, with its straight paths and trees planted in lines, and the loosened formality of the secluded backyard. Front and rear were balanced as if equal importance was accorded to driving and strolling.

The poplars along the edge of the site were positioned to screen buildings on neighboring lots rather than to address an aesthetic preference. The dimensions of the other plantings appear to have been generated from the proportions of the golden rectangle that ruled the *tracé régulateur* of the facades. This suggests that although Le Corbusier's method may have had its origins in necessity, it was realized in studied proportions. The contrast between the orthogonal garden of the November 1926 project and the calculated casualness of the realized design remains puzzling. Like the Villa Meyer or the Immeuble-villas, Le Corbusier ultimately brought vegetation into the building. But he also reached outward with the "covered hanging garden," which was balanced on the north side by a modeled carpet of trimmed boxwood, the only remnant of formalism in the final garden design.[30]

A variety of trees and shrubs existed on the site prior to construction. By 31 March 1927, the maintenance and preparation work, including earth removal, weeding, and pruning, was completed.[31] A cost estimate prepared by the landscape contractor Lucien Crépin at the end of 1926 proposed transplanting 70 trees and 300 shrubs; his final report, however, listed 150 trees and 480 shrubs.[32] Crépin supplemented the existing vegetation with an impressive number of new plants. Seasonal color was provided by a few species of annuals, vines, and flowering shrubs, such as forsythias, brooms,

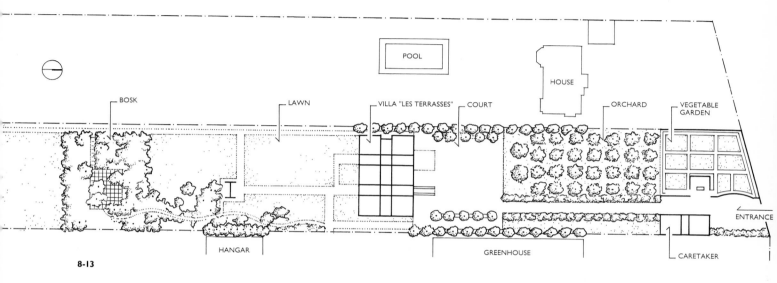

BOSK · LAWN · VILLA "LES TERRASSES" · COURT · POOL · HOUSE · ORCHARD · VEGETABLE GARDEN · ENTRANCE · HANGAR · GREENHOUSE · CARETAKER

8-13

8-14

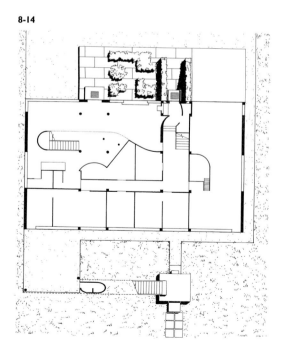

8-15

8-16

8-18

rhododendrons, roses, and hydrangeas, as well as poplars, purple flowering plums, box elders, hawthorns, a crabapple, a weeping willow, and a purple beech. These sparse chromatic accents were overwhelmed, however, by a symphony of evergreens and conifers. Crépin billed the client, Gabrielle de Monzie, for 11 firs, 4 Norway spruces, 11 false cypresses, 7 yews, 4 cedars, 6 pines, 1 larch, 1 cryptomeria, 1 araucaria, 3 junipers, 31 thujas, 150 aucubas, 130 euonymus, 78 privets, 299 laurels, 35 boxwoods, and 8 bamboos. Although such trees and shrubs covered all ranges of greens, from gold to blue, their permanent foliage nevertheless conveyed a certain homogeneity. It is doubly ironic, perhaps, that the image of a naturalistic landscape should be achieved by substantial new planting or by moving existing vegetation on the site.

The tension created by juxtaposing Matisse paintings and Oriental art objects, Renaissance furniture, and the sheer volume of the villa was echoed by the contrast between architecture and landscape. The "pure prism" of the house was set against the loosely defined plantings of the garden, where sinuous paths were anchored by rigorous squares of paving.[33]

A sketch of the final scheme that accompanied the nursery's specifications clearly established the division between the front and back yards and their corresponding design vocabularies.[34] Although the front yard was dominated by a straight access road that neatly dissected the lawn and its scattered vegetation, the rear garden evidenced a delicate balance between paving and planting, hard edge and irregularity. One of the rare photographs of the south portion of the site, in which white concrete tiles played against dark vegetation, illustrates a mirror image of Le Corbusier's framed landscape. The views of nature usually captured within the concrete openings were here translated into perspectives of the villa seen through the vertical lines of trees. Even the sinuous path was calculated to offer the optimal views of the facade.[35] Having successfully reversed the outward-inward borrowing from nature to building, Le Corbusier would later write, "This week, I saw Garches again, after 32 years, white . . . behind the trees: an exquisite vision."[36]

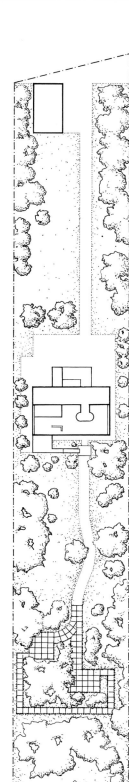

8-17

VILLE-D'AVRAY, 1928.   The Villa Meyer borrowed its landscape scenery from the parc de la Folie Saint-James, setting architecture against a distant natural background. The Villa "Les Terrasses" was centered between front and back gardens carpeted with lawn and planted with various exotic species. The expanse of the Church estate in Ville-d'Avray, on the other hand, allowed Le Corbusier and Jeanneret to establish yet a third relationship between architecture and site while operating on a landscape of a different scale. This project, designed between 1928 and 1929, included the remodeling of a nineteenth-century house and the conversion of its stables into guest facilities. On the adjacent lot, an existing building was to be transformed into a music pavilion. The two estates would be united by gardening, wrote Le Corbusier.[37]

To redefine the existing landscape, the architects cleared its shady groves, pruned the crowns of trees, and regraded the terrain. In fact, Le Corbusier's axonometric view of the Church estate shows that all buildings, new or old, exerted little impact on the landscape. In the upper right-hand corner of the drawing are the "château" and transformed stables, while the "villa" remodeled into a music pavilion floats within the expanse of the park to the lower left. Curvilinear paths and roads connect these two architectural poles. Le Corbusier viewed the proposed modernist syntax— whether applied to the music pavilion or the new guesthouse—as a device to homogenize the variety of historical styles that he considered of dubious taste.[38] The park contained trees of many species planted a century earlier, whose informal arrangement was apparently not considered by the architects to be anachronistic with the new buildings. As a "sumptuous oasis" on the outskirts of the "giant city," the park would provide the perfect foil for the Corbusian pavilions. In front of the château, a central expanse of lawn created the setting for select tree specimens; elsewhere, paths meandered through clumps of vegetation, occasionally skirting a building as if by accident. Through manipulation of the grade, the bean-shaped island of lawn flowed smoothly into the orchard, formerly part of the neighboring estate. The combined orangerie-greenhouse was neatly defined by the retaining walls supporting its terrace. The music pavilion, however, seemed to be the only building that truly engaged the site. A catwalk con-

8-16 VILLA "LES TERRASSES." THE REAR GARDEN. [*L'Architecture d'Aujourd'hui,* December 1933]

8-17 VILLA "LES TERRASSES." RECONSTITUTED SITE PLAN. [Dorothée Imbert, based on FLC HI (4) 201 and contemporary photographs]

8-18 VILLA "LES TERRASSES." VIEW FROM THE REAR GARDEN [FLC L2 (5) 62. © 1993 ARS, N.Y. / SPADEM, Paris]

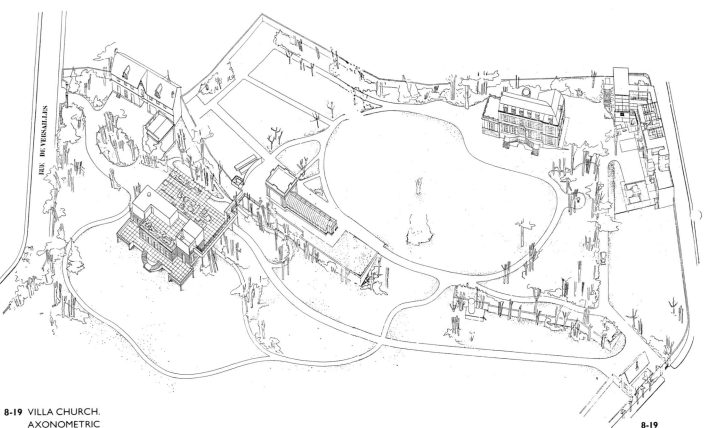

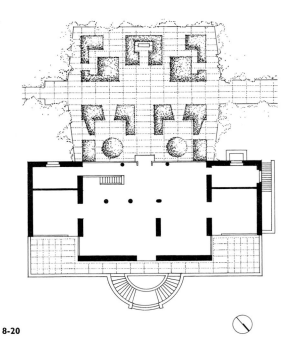

8-19 VILLA CHURCH.
AXONOMETRIC
DRAWING OF THE
ESTATE.
The music pavilion is in
the northeastern corner,
the château and guest-
house diametrically
opposite; in between the
two is the *orangerie*.
Ville-d'Avray, 1928.
Le Corbusier and
Pierre Jeanneret.
[Le Corbusier, "Une
ancienne maison
transformée par MM.
Le Corbusier et
Jeanneret"]

8-20 VILLA CHURCH.
MUSIC PAVILION.
GROUND-FLOOR PLAN
WITH SYMMETRICAL
PARTERRE.
[Dorothée Imbert,
based on FLC 8166]

8-21 VILLA CHURCH.
THE *PARTERRE
DE BRODERIE*, BEFORE
THE MUSIC PAVILION.
[Lurçat, *Terrasses et
jardins*]

8-19

8-20

8-21

8-22

8-22 VILLA CHURCH.
PERSPECTIVE SKETCHES,
LOOKING TOWARD
THE CHÂTEAU AND
THE PAVILLON
DES AMIS.
[FLC 8186. © 1993 ARS,
N.Y. / SPADEM, Paris]

nected the grade level of the orangerie to the upper terrace of the pavilion; this aerial access overlooked a concrete terrace slab inlaid with patterns of low shrubs. Facing south, these brightly colored geometric figures were conceived as a *parterre de broderie*.[39] Recalling the Purist shapes used by Le Corbusier for planters on several roof terraces, this configuration also appeared as an enlargement of the vegetal forms set before the entrance to the Villa Stein—de Monzie. Perhaps Le Corbusier juxtaposed this Purist tableau against the naturalistic park as a gesture toward the nineteenth-century *style composite,* itself a hybrid of the formal and informal models.[40]

Édouard André had defined the style composite as the perfect union of architecture and landscape; the immediate surroundings of buildings acknowledged the laws of architecture and geometry and gradually dissolved into areas of unshaped nature.[41] The two winglike terraces of Le Corbusier's pavilion, however, did not fade into a softer formality; rather, they sharply delineated the designed object against the site.

A swimming pool, solarium, exercise room, and open-air shower were proposed for the roof of the Villa Meyer. And in the 1926 scheme for the Villa "Les Terrasses," the ascending *promenade architecturale* led to a 255-foot running track. Sun, hygiene, and sports also met on the roof of the *pavillon des amis,* where, for his documentary on Le Corbusier, director Pierre Chenal filmed Church and his guests exercising.[42] The ground level of the estate, however, seems to have been assigned no particular function other than to accommodate the automobile—a signature of several of Le Corbusier's projects at that time. In photographs of the Villa Stein—de Monzie the automobile and the machine à habiter are juxtaposed; in addition, the curvature of the ground-floor wall of the Villa Savoye was determined by the turning radius of a car. Likewise, the only suggestion of human life in the axonometric drawing of the Church estate was a departing automobile.

Le Corbusier minimized the human element in his drawings for the site, but he stressed the importance of vegetation in his written account of the Church design. He spoke of the mature trees, the parterre de broderie, the roof terrace "glistening with flowers," the "salon d'hiver with large plants and even exotic trees." Of all landscape schools, the *style paysager* seemed to be most appropriate; as André wrote, "Its aim is always the same. There is neither epoch to comply with, nor memories to keep, nor past styles to imitate."[43] Le Corbusier's intervention in the landscape, or the lack of it, further reinforced the concept of the park as a verdant backdrop for white architecture.

Throughout the project, Le Corbusier and Jeanneret underlined the play among the nineteenth-century mansion, the neoclassical fragments, and the modernist additions. In a series of perspective sketches, the lines of tree trunks and a winding path set off the modernist guesthouse. The neoclassical birdbath or fountain, which Le Corbusier also included in his aerial view, belonged to the past and anchored the foreground of one of these landscape vignettes. The base of the music pavilion—a remnant of a previous building—was painted dark green in stark contrast to the white of the new second floor, and the twin helix stairs—uncharacteristic of Le Corbusier's repertoire—linked the concrete terrace on pilotis to the grass below.[44]

Timeless was the image of a nature untouched, as modernist architecture sat lightly amid its vegetation.

VILLA SAVOYE

POISSY, 1931. Of all the residential projects, the Villa Savoye best expressed the Corbusian relationship between architecture and nature. The house at Poissy, designed between 1929 and 1931, was free of the constraints imposed on the Villa Stein—de Monzie by its suburban lot, and on the Villa Church by its existing architecture. Placed unobtrusively on a softly crowned pasture and orchard, the villa conveyed the image of a modernist fabrique set in a Virgilian landscape.[45]

Throughout his projects, Le Corbusier displaced the center of gravity upward in the search for air and light. A valid argument for the urban villas, it hardly seemed relevant to the broad expanse of meadow at Poissy.[46] Here, Le Corbusier used the *fenêtre en longueur* on all four sides and floor-to-ceiling glass panes on the terrace, which flooded the living spaces on the second floor with light. At the Villa Savoye, the demands of biology converged with those of construction, stated Sigfried Giedion. In addition to functioning as "a breathing sponge," the hanging garden and roof terrace provided "distant views on the horizon" unavailable from the ground.[47] Because grass was "unhealthy and damp," the

garden was planted eleven feet above the soil—on a terrace.[48] A "generator for sunlight," this garden in the air verified the experimental model first presented at the Pavillon de L'Esprit Nouveau.[49] So dominant was the garden of the Villa Savoye that the critic Julius Posener described it as the main space, of which the living room was only a covered extension.[50]

Whether placed on the roofs of villas, apartment blocks, or towers, these terraces in the air were consistently described by Le Corbusier as magnificent compositions recalling the hanging gardens of Semiramis.[51] Roof gardens crowned the skyscrapers of the Plan Voisin; 650 feet above the trees, they resembled an "undulating flock of green sheep," wrote Le Corbusier. He described these gardens as "paved with stone, planted with spindle trees, thujas, laurels, ivy, enameled with tulips or geraniums in parterres de broderie, or woven with paths bordered by a medley of flowering perennials."[52] Vacillating between a grand formalism and the intimacy of herbaceous wildflower beds, these clichés underline Le Corbusier's ambiguous approach to the designed landscape. As drawn or photographed, however, his rooftop designs seldom offered such an abundance of vegetation. The hanging garden of the Villa Savoye was no exception. Areas of paving far outweighed plantings; like discrete pieces of furniture with green tops, two planters held a meager mixture of shrubs. In a photograph of the living room, the plant container appears behind the glass curtain as a mirror image of the interior carpet.[53]

Using principles similar to the Japanese concept of *shakkei*, Le Corbusier composed certain points of terrace plantings in reference to an element in the distant landscape, usually the crowns of mature trees.[54] Immersed in nature and isolated from other buildings, the Villa Savoye needed only to frame the landscape to compose a most picturesque tableau. With a painterly vision, Le Corbusier described the siting of the villa: "The view is very beautiful, grass is a beautiful thing, and so is the forest—to be barely touched. The house will be placed on grass, like an object, disturbing nothing."[55] Such statement of nonintervention appeared to echo the "improvements" of Capability Brown, whom Uvedale Price praised not for 'what *had*, but [for] what had *not*, been done; . . . [As] the eyes and the footsteps were equally unconfined."[56] At Poissy, only a few fruit trees and a central expanse of lawn com-

8-23

8-24

plemented the peripheral shrubbery, poplars, and pines.[57] The only apparent points of contact between the raised white frame and the earth were thin concrete pillars, or pilotis. The receding core of the ground floor was painted green, and as a result the house hovered above the grass dome.[58] Its facades uniformly divided, its surfaces flat and without texture, the villa appeared as a pristine shell detached from its surroundings. Subtly contrasting with this sheer white envelope was the tinted curved wall of the solarium on the upper terrace, a shelter against the prevailing winds and an alcove to trap the sun.[59] A perspective sketch of the hanging garden illustrates Le Corbusier's incorporation of politely tamed vegetation within the hygienic open-air living room.[60] As a line of interaction or caesura between the two realms, the sliding panels shown on the original sketch—but never realized—would have revealed or closed off the views of the meadow and trees beyond the wall.[61]

To define his concept of a promenade architecturale, Le Corbusier cited Arab architecture, the essence of which was comprehended through walking.[62] The dynamic spatial sequence and the varied perception of the volume of the Villa Savoye led Sigfried Giedion to write that "it is impossible to comprehend the house by a view from a single point; quite literally, it is a construction in space-time."[63] If the perception of interior spaces relied on the walking figure, the landscape was to be traversed at the higher speed of the automobile. In spite of its label as a country residence, the villa joined nature through the sky rather than across the land.

The house was elevated, thus erasing any division between front and back yards, argued the architect: one garden was planted on the roof, and another was slipped beneath the house.[64] Although seductive as a concept, the garden below the Villa Savoye never materialized. Instead, this space was devoted to a driveway paved with gravel, which prevented the grass meadow from continuing under the house. The Villa Savoye appeared to be accessible by car alone, and given the visual interaction with the site from the raised terraces, there was no need to circumambulate the site on foot. The city dweller does not seek the proximity of trees and plants, commented Giedion, but "aspires to dominate the landscape." In contrast with Frank Lloyd Wright's symbiosis of earth and architecture, at the Villa Savoye Le Corbusier rejected any "passive adaptation to the

8-23 VILLA SAVOYE.
Poissy, circa 1931.
Le Corbusier and
Pierre Jeanneret.
[*L'Architecture
d'Aujourd'hui,*
December 1933]

8-24 VILLA SAVOYE.
VIEW FROM THE
LIVING ROOM
TOWARD THE
HANGING GARDEN.
[FLC L2 (2) 2-73. © 1993
ARS, N.Y. / SPADEM, Paris]

8-25 VILLA SAVOYE.
RAMP LEADING TO
THE SOLARIUM.
The window frames a
view of the surrounding
landscape.
[FLC L2 (2) 2-26. © 1993
ARS, N.Y. / SPADEM, Paris]

8-25

8-26 VILLA SAVOYE.
PERSPECTIVE SKETCH.
Cross section through
the exterior landscape
—framed by a window
and sliding panels
—and the domesticated
hanging garden.
[FLC 19425. © 1993 ARS,
N.Y. / SPADEM, Paris]

8-27 SITE PLAN
ILLUSTRATING A
DEVELOPMENT OF
VILLA SAVOYE CLONES
OUTSIDE BUENOS
AIRES.
Le Corbusier and Pierre
Jeanneret.
[Le Corbusier, *Précisions*.
© 1993 ARS, N.Y. /
SPADEM, Paris]

8-26

8-27

ground" as the means to realize a unity of sky and air.[65]

In fact, so divorced in formal language was the building from its surroundings that Le Corbusier proposed the villa as a new, universal type: "Perfectly fit for the rustic landscape of Poissy; it would also be magnificent in Biarritz."[66] The house could even be transplanted beyond the Basque countryside, beyond the Atlantic, even as multiple units on a patch of land in Argentina. The Corbusian dream evoked "twenty houses rising from the tall grasses of an orchard where cows will continue to graze. . . . Grass will flank the paths, nothing will be troubled, neither trees, nor flowers, nor herds. The inhabitants will . . . contemplate [a countryside], left intact, from their hanging garden or from the four sides of their fenêtres en longueur. Their domestic life will be inserted in a Virgilian dream."[67]

In spite of the inherent contradiction between tall grasses and their antagonists, grazing cows, Le Corbusier played the pastoral cliché to the extreme. The imprint of man, whether orchard, herd, house, or road, left the natural order undisturbed. The tableau remained intact for the gentle viewer. And "if the [prime] view were elsewhere, on another side, or if the orientation were different, the hanging garden would simply have to be modified."[68]

The Savoye family, "neither modern nor old-fashioned, . . . just wanted to live in the country."[69] Juxtaposed to, rather than interacting with, nature, the house could indeed belong to any idyllic, atemporal paysage-type. The model constructed at Poissy, like the Immeuble-villas project, sought a certain synthesis of "nature-architecture" or more precisely, an antithesis that was "as majestic as [it was] unexpected."[70]

Of the five points of a new architecture proposed by Le Corbusier, the first two—pilotis and roof gardens—effaced the imprint of the building and garden on the surrounding landscape.[71] Historically, gardens, regardless of style, occupied the point of contact between architecture and site. The planted terrace did not complement the garden, in spite of Le Corbusier's polemical advertisements, but replaced it with a new, architectonic device. Once the specific identity of the garden was removed and the landscape typified, all sites became interchangeable, allowing architecture to assume a universal form.

Posener judged the overall proportions of the Villa Savoye awkward for the exaggerated spaces of its interior garden, terrace, hall, and living room, but he nevertheless saw this very "fault" as the trademark of a "perfect" house.[72] And although one might regret Le Corbusier's lack of direct attention to garden design, perhaps the natural countryside best complemented the style of this architectural monument. The classic setting of the Villa Savoye expressed the architects' "violent desire . . . to play a game of 'affirmation-man' against or with 'presence-nature.'"[73]

Like William Kent, who "leaped the fence and saw that all nature was a garden,"[74] Le Corbusier was characterized as wanting to see "the whole garden vanish, to see the fields sweeping right up to the side walls, or the house on stilts rising out of a sea of grass," in a "curious reversion to eighteenth-century romanticism."[75] Disengaged from the ground, like a sanatorium reaching toward the sun and pure air, the villa interacted with a natural, almost cosmic, order.

THE BEISTEGUI ROOFTOP

PARIS, 1930. The terraces that Le Corbusier and Pierre Jeanneret designed for the comte Charles de Beistegui's penthouse spiraled upward as an homage to the sky and the monuments of Paris. Like the Pavillon de L'Esprit Nouveau, the Beistegui project joined two extremes: decorative art and urban design.[76] For this architectural prototype overlooking the Champs Élysées, Le Corbusier and Jeanneret proposed "a solution for the roofs of Paris," a "pure, invincible, correct" design.[77] Intentionally deviating from custom, the client furnished the rigorously modern apartment in the rococo style.[78] Given this unpredictable juxtaposition of elements, the critics felt the ensemble displayed an "esprit de surréalisme"—the ultimate "cadavre exquis."[79]

An implicit reference to La Ville radieuse of 1930, the penthouse design explored modern technology but was hardly a sample of social and urban reform.[80] It was conceived, instead, to entertain "in a setting recalling the interiors of days past when the chandeliers scintillated with the light of innumerable flames." Thus, the apartment was designed as the frame for a divertissement.[81] Practicality was subordinated to the general mise-en-scène. The contradictions were not limited to questions of style alone. Although the interior was illuminated exclusively by candles, electricity was used to

8-28 PENTHOUSE FOR CHARLES DE BEISTEGUI. OVERALL VIEW WITH THE ARC DE TRIOMPHE IN THE BACKGROUND. Paris, circa 1931. Le Corbusier and Pierre Jeanneret. [FLC L2 (4) 9-7. © 1993 ARS, N.Y. / SPADEM, Paris]

8-28

move screens, open windows, project movies, and broadcast radio, music, and drama. In a letter/storyboard to Mrs. Meyer, Le Corbusier had provided instructions for using part of her villa as a theater; similarly, in the Beistegui apartment he assigned different functions and times of use to different sights and terraces. [82] Although summarized in the introduction to the second volume of his *œuvre complète* as a "roof over the Champs Élysées with gardens and sound proofing of exterior noise," the sequence of exterior spaces and their scenic arrangement seemed to exemplify the terrace ideals described in *Précisions*.[83] Here, on the terrace, the "solarium brings health. At night, people dance to the music of a gramophone. The air is pure, the sound muffled, the view distant, the street far away. If trees are nearby, you are above their canopy. The sky shimmers with stars . . . you see all of them."[84]

"Instead of [using] M. Umbdenstock's patriotic roof tiles and slates," Le Corbusier crowned the building with "three hanging gardens" carpeted with "flowering meadows."[85] This vivid evocation of nature was not sustained, however, in his later description of the Beistegui belvedere. The succession of terraces instead represented the Corbusian ideal of the hanging garden as a lookout. Whereas the Villa Savoye surveyed the "agrarian landscape of Poissy," the Beistegui apartment contemplated the urban panorama and selected fabriques from its dense fabric. To counter the "turbulence" of the inebriating vastness of the city and to obliterate the "morose desert of the roofs and chimneys," Le Corbusier and Jeanneret created "an architectural center of stones, gardens, and sky," focusing on the essence of Paris: the Arc de Triomphe, the Tour Eiffel, the Sacré-Cœur, and Notre-Dame.[86]

The hedge on the eastern edge of the third level grew in movable containers, which, at the push of a button, withdrew electrically to unveil the occluded view. The uppermost stairway led to the solarium, a white enclosure carpeted with grass from wall to wall. It was, in effect, a monastic cell, equipped with a fireplace for chilly evenings, with the sky as its ceiling. The purity was interrupted only by the spire of a yew and the periscope of a functioning camera obscura. Even the placement of the fireplace—"dressed by the owner in the Spanish Louis XV style"—against the similar shape of the Arc de Triomphe seen "at point-blank range" was hardly a coincidence.[87] There, one was reunited with the elements of nature: sun,

8-29 BEISTEGUI ROOFTOP, TERRACES AND SOLARIUM FURNISHED BY THE CLIENT WITH PAINTINGS AND CAST STONE FURNITURE. Paris, circa 1934. [Watt, "The Surprising Apartment of M. Carlos de Beistegui"]

8-29

air, fire, and earth. This space concluded the cadavre exquis, an open-air extravaganza that subsumed the rococo taste of Beistegui within the pristine yet odd simplicity of its frame.

Despite all the luxurious contrivances that characterized the design, Le Corbusier evoked austerity in his description of the Beistegui apartment, which "compris[ed] only one large living room, a dining room, a bedroom and its dependencies and utilitarian spaces: kitchen, servants' rooms, etc. . . . The whole interior is, with extreme care, painted with white mat varnish and sanded with stone pumice."[88] But while the owner "greatly admired" Le Corbusier and Jeanneret's architecture, he intended to maintain total control over the design of his apartment.[89] Beistegui mixed rococo and Napoléon III styles with twentieth-century technology in a cerulean ensemble whose description betrays a craving need for every conceivable variety of blue.[90] On the other hand, the color scheme of the exterior, if not its decoration, was left untouched. Black-and-white photographs seem the perfect medium to represent the monochromatic roof terraces. The dark green hedges reinforced the outline of the white stone terraces against the backdrop of the milky Parisian sky. Not only was the Beistegui landscape entirely green—composed of lawn, thuja, boxwood, yew, ivy, and ruscus—but its parts also shared a homogeneous density. Boxwood and yews of the desired height were sheared as walls or pruned as potted specimens, although even the simplest hedge had to be layered with a screen of ivy as protection against strong winds.[91] Ruscus was tied to the green lattice protecting the taller hedges with patinated brass, providing a temporary vegetal screen until the ivy had grown.[92] When closed, the vegetal partitions blocked any unplanned glimpses of the surrounding cityscape and arrested the horizontal flow of the terraces.

The architects assumed an attitude toward nature of both denial and illusion. The poetry and picturesqueness Le Corbusier saw in the distant canopies of trees was nullified by the pruned boxwood abstractions of his design for Charles de Beistegui. Although the spatial configurations of terraces changed with the movement of the hedges, there was little seasonal transformation in the evergreen vegetation.

To substantiate the planting of terraces, Le Corbusier invoked the insulating properties of the vegetation, which mitigated the deteriorat-

8-30 BEISTEGUI ROOFTOP. FIRST LEVEL OF TERRACES, EXTENDING THE LIVING AND DINING ROOMS. [*L'Architecte*, 1932]

8-31 BEISTEGUI ROOFTOP. ANNOTATED ROOF PLAN. [Dorothée Imbert, based on FLC 29863, 17445, 17539 and 17598]

8-30

8-31

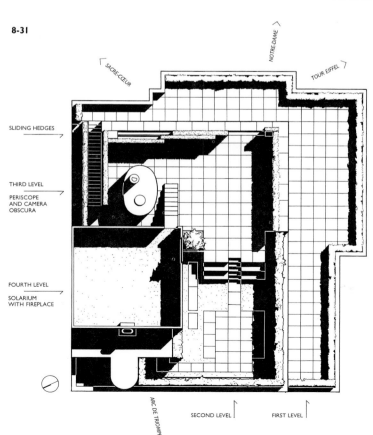

ing effects of expansion and contraction on the reinforced-concrete frame.[93] Leaving aside such technical justifications, the architectonic landscape of the Beistegui penthouse was a nearly perfect example of the garden as viewing platform. In architectural scenery, Le Corbusier explained, "the elements of the site intervene according to their [volume], their density, the quality of their material; they carry definite and various sensations (wood, marble, tree, turf, blue horizon, close or distant sea, sky). The elements of the site stand like . . . the walls of a room. Walls and light, shade or light, sad, gay or serene, etc. One has to compose with these elements." "Le dehors" (the outside) always being also "un dedans" (an inside), the architect manipulated the views from each of the terraces.[94]

Although it was intended as a "first-class architectural laboratory," the construction of the Beistegui penthouse was nevertheless hampered by numerous technical shortcomings.[95] The client described his apartment as a Tower of Babel, where miscommunication reigned and all the work was done twice.[96] The accounts of Toutin & Roussel, the landscape contractors, reveal a sequence of mishaps.[97] A month after a hedge of boxwood was planted, it was "carefully" uprooted to build the protective ruscus screen and then replanted; vegetation was also removed to allow for modifications to the masonry. An invoice for May 1931 lists the replacement of a boxwood hedge with thujas, and the twelve-foot yew ("specimen extra") with a *Cupressus lawsoniana*. In October the grass carpet of the solarium was dug up to allow for work on the electrical system, and a new set of boxwood hedges and ivy in containers was installed. In addition, the Lawson cypress planted in May died; it was uprooted and replaced.[98] In fact, photographs of the penthouse published in the 1932 issue of *L'Architecte* show a rather limp tree. Beistegui was billed for 550 hours of labor for this columnar specimen alone. Although intended as the design's principal vertical accent, it did not survive: by 1936, the tree had become a support for ivy.

8-32

8-32 BEISTEGUI ROOFTOP, VIEW TOWARD THE THIRD LEVEL.
The mobile hedge in the open position, revealing a Parisian panorama. The tree at left is still struggling to live.
[FLC L2 (4) 9-1. © 1993 ARS, N.Y. / SPADEM, Paris]

As the containers began to show signs of leakage, soil and plants were removed and restored. The mobile planters, whose watertightness was problematic, required frequent repairs amounting to 40 percent of their initial cost.[99] In a letter dated 31 January 1931, Beistegui reminded Jeanneret and Le Corbusier of the monetary discrepancy between their 400,000-

8-33

8-33 BEISTEGUI ROOFTOP.
VIEW FROM THE
SECOND LEVEL.
The cypress has died
and is covered with ivy;
the sliding hedge is ajar.
[FLC L2 (4) 9-12. © 1993
ARS, N.Y. / SPADEM,
Paris]

franc estimate for the construction of the penthouse and the actual price tag of nearly 1,000,000 francs.[100] Beistegui's anger was perhaps aggravated by the fact that he had selected the landscape contractor himself; Toutin & Roussel had considered the project "perfectly and easily feasible," in spite of the predictable expenses of hoisting the plants, containers, and soil by crane.[101] In contrast to these verbal assurances, the price of the hanging gardens had increased from 17,614 to 97,377.50 francs.[102] If the vegetation had withered, the expenses had flourished.

With the possible exception of the solarium, the Beistegui apartment was a belvedere rather than a true garden, and yet the promenade architecturale across the rooftop was admirably choreographed. In executing this seemingly minor space, Le Corbusier transformed his ideas for the Palace of the League of Nations, conceived as a "deferential act of devotion toward nature," into this "act of devotion toward Paris." "The unexpected effects of perspectives" were "firmly framed" not by "polished stone" but by vegetal partitions. In spite of the transformation in materials, the "sudden indentations in the landscape" of Switzerland were directly translated into a spliced urban skyline, using the techniques and tricks of "true scenography."[103]

On fine summer nights, one dined in the close paved with stones and lawn and outlined with boxwood and yews, glimpsing the silhouette of Notre-Dame in the distance. To reveal Paris, "the palisade of greenery . . . to the east, slowly disappeared." The esplanade on the third level was used for dancing; ascending a few steps, one "[bumped] into a door made from a stone slab: this door opened slowly to reveal an all-white enclosure, entirely carpeted with lawn. The door [closed]: silence. One saw only the sky and the play of clouds and the shimmering azure." This final stage of the architectural promenade excited the feeling of being on the open sea.[104]

Le Corbusier proposed a nautical analogy in several of his projects and descriptions. From the rooftop of his parents' house, the Villa "Le Lac," one contemplated Lake Léman as if "leaning against the railing of a ship"; the roof terrace of the later Unité d'Habitation in Marseilles resembled an ocean liner with a landscape of concrete chimneys and hull shapes floating high above the horizon of the Mediterranean.[105] At a simpler level, the surreal quality of the Beistegui project was akin to the

Savoye solarium, in which freestanding walls were also open to the sky and seemed to have no other function than to enclose or frame the surroundings visually.

Such tension between the terraces of the Beistegui penthouse and the cityscape was not as obvious in early stages of the design process. In these studies, the outdoor spaces appeared as mere extensions of the interior rooms, opened to the views, with the generically informal Corbusian shrubbery contained in planters set in a crossword-puzzle pattern.[106] An axonometric view dated 4 June 1929 featured a sheltered rooftop room that replicated the lower salon, without windows, down to the very furniture. From this first project to the final design, vegetation was pushed progressively outward, from the center to the edge of the terrace.[107] Whether or not this arrangement was a result of Beistegui's influence, its simplicity was enhanced by the sophistication of the details, both formal and technical. The rails of the movable planters were sunken, for example, to conceal the cable-driven system even when the ivy partitions were slid open. On the seventh floor, the bases of the wooden planters set against the white tile floor were covered with *lierre des bois,* while the concrete containers of the intermediate terrace adjacent to lawn were clad with a white stone veneer.[108]

The ambiguity of the penthouse could be summarized in the juxtaposition of the clean line of electrically displaced vegetal screens and the kitschy allure of a topiary rooster. As "night deepened the calm" and the boxwood edges disappeared in the darkness, the white slabs appeared to float in the sky, recalling the "hanging platters of gold" 650 feet above the ideal urban Plan Voisin.[109] A prototype of a *toit-jardin,* the ensemble was nevertheless a technological and decorative extravaganza. As witnessed in various photographs, the overlay of Beistegui's style complemented this fascinating "paysage architectural créé de toute pièces."[110]

Catherine Courtiau has summarized Le Corbusier's manipulation of garden, sky, light, and panorama as equivalents to walls, windows, and roof in the concept of a "denatured nature."[111] The roof garden and pilotis, axioms of a landscape extended across architecture and even upward, essentially severed the horizontal relationship established among building, garden, and nature. Two types of nature recur throughout these projects: the generic landscape, the paysage-type that often constitutes a background, and the immediate vegetation found in the hanging garden. Between these two "dehors," or exterior entities, Le Corbusier stretched calculated lines of sight.

In the Beistegui penthouse, the urban landscape was further distilled. Architecture provided the means to refabricate the ideal perspectives, whether through obstruction or selection. The open-air solarium, totally enclosed, was both acoustically and visually silent, as if an homage to the skies; the periscope and the sliding hedges, on the other hand, kinetically reframed the surroundings. The normal order of things was reversed: the panorama of Paris selectively or temporarily blocked from view was brought back inside the camera obscura, restoring its vastness in portions, while all the interior utilities—telephone, fireplace, and record player—were brought to the outdoor rooms.[112]

No transparency or change of color enriched the design; hedges resembled walls; trellises created the "illusion of nature" until, in time, they too came to resemble hedges.[113] Technology dominated the rhythm of natural process, as electricity powered the green partitions in an ultimate attempt to *forcer la nature*.[114] The hedges also marked the limits between the private roof garden and the urban realm beyond, and with the architectural elements, framed the panorama into discrete images.[115] Selecting four essential features from the Paris skyline, Le Corbusier laid a tracé régulateur over the city, as if it had been ordered by his proposed —yet unrealized—urban plans.

8-34 BEISTEGUI ROOFTOP. THE GRASS-CARPETED SOLARIUM WITH A ROCOCO FIREPLACE; THE ARC DE TRIOMPHE EMERGES BEHIND THE WALL. [*L'Architecture d'Aujourd'hui,* December 1933]

8-35 BEISTEGUI ROOFTOP. EARLY SCHEME. Perspective dated 4 June 1929. [FLC 17435. © 1993 ARS, N.Y. / SPADEM, Paris]

8-34

8-35

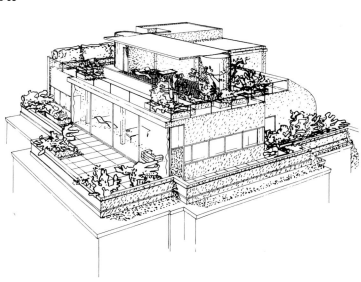

8-36

8-37

THE LITTLE HOUSE ON THE LAKE

LES CORSEAUX, 1923; 1953.   Thirty years after he built the house for his parents near Vevey, Switzerland, Le Corbusier reevaluated its design in a book titled *Une petite maison*. He argued for the 1923 Villa "Le Lac" as a paradigm of architecture against nature. Situated between the road and the shoreline, this simple box, only one room deep, modestly confronted the grandeur of Lake Léman and the Alps.

To protect "la petite maison" from the intense summer sun and the power of the nearly overwhelming views, Le Corbusier carefully planned trees and an exterior wall. This design clearly reveals another expression of the architect's view of landscape: that the presence of nature should be modulated. A landscape that is "omnipresent" and "omnipotent," he wrote, ought to be "limited and dimensioned. . . . Walls are raised to block the horizons, which are to be revealed only in strategic points."[116] He offered a similar approach for the Palace of the League of Nations in Geneva, where "a magnificent portico" was intended to frame the lake and passing boats; the Alps were segmented into panels, "as in a museum."[117] The design for the house of Hélène de Mandrot in Toulon (1930), on the other hand, was a paroxysm of this attitude. There, Le Corbusier obliterated the splendid view in order that it be revealed only through the opening of a door, in an "explosion" of landscape.[118] In comparison to an extreme statement like this, the facade of his parents' house appeared vulnerable to light and surroundings, its thirty-five-foot-long ribbon window capturing the Alps and flattening the perspective into a panoramic view.[119] In addition, photographs taken on the roof and published in *Une petite maison* look down, not outward, as if to avoid the openness of the horizon unprotected by Le Corbusier's usual architectural partitions.

The membrane between architecture and site not only regulated the views but also established a critical distance between man and nature. Le Corbusier seemed to dislike grass as well as the shade created by trees, and on the Léman the trees around the house were periodically thinned. Each element of a mixed planting scheme had been carefully specified: one tall poplar, one weeping willow, one flowering acacia, one fruit-bearing cherry, one conifer, and a single broad-leafed paulownia. But no matter how picturesque the effect, uncontrolled growth necessitated their removal. Thirty years after the building was

8-38

8-36 VILLA "LE LAC."
VIEW OF THE HOUSE
FROM THE LAKE.
Les Corseaux,
Switzerland, 1923.
Le Corbusier and
Pierre Jeanneret.
[FLC L2 (4) I-33. © 1993
ARS, N.Y. / SPADEM,
Paris]

8-37 VILLA "LE LAC."
VIEW FROM THE
ROOFTOP,
OVERLOOKING THE
LAKE, AS IF ONE WERE
"LEANING AGAINST
THE RAILING OF
A SHIP."
[Photo: Dorothée
Imbert, 1991]

8-38 VILLA "LE LAC."
SKETCH OF A
LANDSCAPE FRAMED
BY ARCHITECTURE.
1945. Le Corbusier.
[Le Corbusier, *Une
petite maison.*
© 1993 ARS, N.Y. /
SPADEM, Paris]

8-39 PALACE OF THE LEAGUE
OF NATIONS.
THE PORTICO
STRUCTURES THE
PANORAMA OF
LAKE LÉMAN.
Geneva, 1927.
Le Corbusier and
Pierre Jeanneret.
[Le Corbusier, *Une
maison—un palais.*
© 1993 ARS, N.Y. /
SPADEM, Paris]

8-39

completed and the site planted, Le Corbusier's account stated:

> Reader, in 1923 the site was stark naked; only a staked cherry tree showed a few hairs at the end of a stick. Today, shade abounds and the sun is well distributed. We had built. And we had immediately planted a pine, a poplar, a weeping willow, an acacia, a paulownia — all puny saplings. The sun beats down, the soil is warmed, the water is tepid, the trees move on. . . . The cherry tree has grown into a big boy. My mother makes jam from it for the whole winter. The pine? It needed to be cut, for it cast an evil shadow on the poplar. The poplar? It became formidable. We sawed it in half. Then we tore it out entirely, as its roots tickled the modest . . . foundations of the little house. The acacia? It stole the sun from the neighbor's salad patch. It was removed. The weeping willow? It wept too much, keeping the sun from reaching the bedroom. It dipped its leaves in the lake; it was poetic and everything! Cut down, the weeping willow! Thus the paulownia remained with its big dumb leaves. Its trunk is huge, covered with lichens as a meadow is covered with dandelions. Its intrepid limbs grow in every direction. . . . Every year we cut "the" branch, that is, the one that has become intolerable.[120]

Having corrected the predominance of the tree within the equation of sun-air-greenery, it seemed that any vegetation not contained within the roof terrace was to be kept at a distance. To accomplish this, Le Corbusier rearranged the Swiss landscape into a pictorial panorama, much like his intention for the site of the Cité mondiale of Geneva, which he compared to an Acropolis overlaid with the pastoral vision of Rousseau. There, the "touching agrarian scene" of vast rolling meadows and grazing sheep would be left undisturbed by construction. Le Corbusier orchestrated "prisms and spaces" and "composed atmospherically" with "flocks, grasses, and flowers in the foreground," and with "the lake, the Alps, the sky . . . and the divine proportions" beyond. And "thanks to the pilotis," he concluded, "the natural ground remains untouched [and] the poetry is intact."[121] From a higher eye level, this panoramic view encompassed an idealistically distant horizon, whose meadows, mountains, and water gave no indication of scale. The middle ground, defined vaguely by the presence of sheep (and recalling Humphry Repton's use of cattle), merged with the background, implying an infinite continuation of the landscape.[122]

8-40

8-41

Le Corbusier argued that with the near-greenhouse conditions that rooftops offered—pure air, intense light, and warm damp soil—vegetation would grow more beautifully above the ground than on it.[123] Although he played the vegetal elements of his rooftops against the framed scenery, almost in a Japanese manner, Le Corbusier seldom attempted to shape the landscape immediately surrounding the pilotis. The house no longer divides front from back; elevated, it allows the continued passage of the automobile, air, and even greenery.[124] He dismissed the very conception of baroque architecture because it revolved around a fixed theoretical point.[125] Similarly, the architect avoided the decorative figure of a regular garden, which established a directional view. A strongly defined foreground would have distracted the inhabitant from the carefully orchestrated horizon.

When built, the little house was condemned by its neighbors for having committed a crime of *lèse-nature*.[126] Today, it appears only humbly assertive, playing its diminutive measurements against the majestic scenery. But if the Alps are partially tamed by the interior view through the fenêtre en longueur, the impact of the lake seen through the square opening in the exterior wall is intensified. In its modulation of the landscape, the little house arrests the human eye—"always roaming" in its "investigations"—and eloquently makes the view a part of the architecture and architecture a part of the view.[127]

8-42

Although a denial of the physical (as opposed to visual) connection between architecture and landscape was apparent in most villas and projects of the 1920s and 1930s, Le Corbusier's office brochure of a decade earlier offered architectural, interior, and garden design services.[128] Arguing for an asymmetrical planting scheme at the Villa Schwob (1916), Le Corbusier wrote to his client, "I have examined the question of gardens in depth,"[129] partly a reference to the summer of 1915, which he spent at the Bibliothèque Nationale studying several landscape treatises.[130] Le Corbusier drew from these an eclectic knowledge of the French formal garden vocabulary. His compilation of garden elements included the reproduction of several assemblages of *boulingrins* illustrated in *La théorie et la pratique du jardinage,* the eighteenth-century treatise by Antoine Dezallier d'Argenville.[131] The young architect complemented his interest in vegetal patterning with a glance at botany, by copying those pages treating the seasonal decoration of parterres.[132] Although Le Corbusier researched the landscape tradition of the Grand Siècle, he was also aware of André Vera's writings on the new garden. One of Le Corbusier's index cards captures the essence of order pervading *Le nouveau jardin,* published in 1912: "André Vera insists x times . . . [on the fact] that we are a generation that loves and desires *order,* cleanliness, and clarity in everything, order at work, in spirit, in exterior things."[133]

8-43

Although Le Corbusier's published writings seldom touched on the garden, except in the case of existing entities like the Tuileries or the Palais Royal, he apparently intended to use a photograph of André Vera's work in a proposed "Garden chapter."[134] In fact, the table of contents for the manuscript *La construction des villes* included a chapter titled "On the Constituent Elements of the City" and contained section headings such as "On Trees" and "On Gardens and Parks." The text ended, however, with the section "On Enclosing Walls" and left Le Corbusier's distillation of his research on gardens unrecorded.[135] Traces of these notes surfaced in the later *Propos d'urbanisme* (1946), in which he described and illustrated the bosquets and boulingrins copied from *La théorie et la pratique du jardinage.* He enumerated "cabinets et salons, petites salles et grandes salles, petits cloîtres en lattis de verdure et grands cloîtres, labyrinthes etc." to present the aspect of formal gardens as an out-

8-44

8-43 ANNOTATED SKETCH OF A JAPANESE HOUSE. "From within the very spacious room . . . one sees the immense panorama, the black pines . . . the sea, the volcano, the rice fields." Le Corbusier. [FLC B2-20, 224. © 1993 ARS, N.Y. / SPADEM, Paris]

8-44 UNITÉ D'HABITATION. BORROWED SCENERY FROM THE ROOFTOP. Marseilles, 1947–52. Le Corbusier. [Photo: Marc Treib, 1991]

8-45 COMPARATIVE SECTIONS THROUGH TRADITIONAL AND MODERN BUILDINGS. "Reinforced concrete allows pilotis. The house is in the air, far from the ground; the garden slides beneath the house; the garden is also above the house, on the roof." Le Corbusier. [Dorothée Imbert after Le Corbusier]

8-46 VILLA COOK. THE PILOTIS SUPPORT — ACCORDING TO FLETCHER STEELE — A "GARDEN CEILING." Boulogne-sur-Seine, 1927. Le Corbusier and Pierre Jeanneret. [Lurçat, *Terrasses et jardins*]

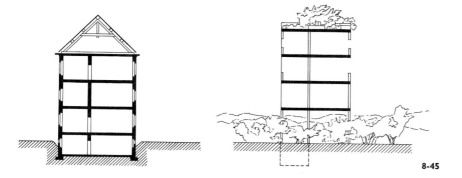

8-45

8-46

Grand Boulingrin comparti avec de la Broderie

fig. 2.

8-48

door extension of interior decoration.[136] Certainly this terminology had "grace, style and class," but it also signaled the beginning of a decadence that encouraged decoration for the sake of decoration, whether it be applied to the centerpiece of a table or to a palace. As the last link of this infernal chain came the parterre, curse of the gardener who "will spend his life defending this senseless haberdashery against weeds and slugs." If these compositions belonged to the "admirable" past of kings, concluded Le Corbusier, the aerial view of Vaux-le-Vicomte nevertheless "provoked several anxious questions," which, typically, he left unanswered.[137]

In spite of his interest in formal gardens, he believed that the city of tomorrow should be set amid greenery, because "trees are accepted by everyone"—"they leave you alone."[138] A "necessity for the lungs, a token of affection for our hearts," trees were arranged as "a condiment for the . . . modeled geometries" of contemporary architecture.[139] Nonetheless, Le Corbusier criticized the vegetal camouflage of garden cities for simply perpetuating an illusion. He argued that garden maintenance not only burdened the worker with an additional chore but also required *bad movements* that "deformed" and "wore down" the body. Claiming that it caused only "illusions and rheumatism," he denounced the campaign to "cultivate one's garden" promoted in "numerous leaflets" and in "billboards dripping with colors."[140]

Le Corbusier's references to gardens, hanging or otherwise, did not systematically preclude a specific style. Ahistorical, they could embrace strict regular figures as well as Robinsonian rusticity.[141] But the garden he promoted for the base of the Villa Meyer was not à la française; rather, it recuperated "the wild copse" of the parc Saint-James. The Palace of the League of Nations set its polished geometry against the "landscape arabesques" whose groves and shrubbery were barely manipulated to flatter the massive walls of gray granite.[142] If he omitted a horizontal junction between landscape and architecture on the ground plane, Le Corbusier envisioned a modernist symbiosis on a grander order. The alliance between man and nature took place in the city, a symphony composed of glass, iron, stone, concrete, and trees, grasses, flowers, sky, and clouds.[143] Ideally the ground plane of the Ville contemporaine would resemble the parc Monceau.[144] Although the roof garden belonged to the geometric realm of

8-47 *BOULINGRIN* WITH *BRODERIE.*
Le Corbusier copied this design during his studies at the Bibliothèque Nationale. The drawing was later published in his *Propos d'urbanisme.*
[Dezallier d'Argenville, *La théorie et la pratique du jardinage.* Courtesy Dumbarton Oaks, Washington, D.C.]

8-48 VILLE CONTEMPORAINE. SKETCH OF THE GROUNDS WITH SKYSCRAPERS RISING FROM CLUMPS OF VEGETATION.
1922. Le Corbusier.
[Le Corbusier, *Précisions.* © 1993 ARS, N.Y. / SPADEM, Paris]

8-49 PALACE OF THE LEAGUE OF NATIONS.
The polished granite architecture sets off the untouched Swiss landscape. Geneva, 1927. Le Corbusier and Pierre Jeanneret.
[Le Corbusier, *Une maison—un palais.* © 1993 ARS, N.Y. / SPADEM, Paris]

8-49

architecture, the landscape best appeared naturalistic. Architecture composes a "circus of geometry" that "contains the delightful picturesqueness" of the landscape, while "the sky rests . . . on the horizon."[145] Le Corbusier most often resorted to a varied palette of plants, a combination of individual specimens grouped with little apparent concern for mass, texture, or color. His preference for evergreen species was certainly evident on the terraces for Beistegui, and there are no apparent traces of the interest in floral decoration manifested in his writings. Perhaps a variable such as the seasonal colors that bloomed on the roof of the little house on the lake actually completed the unpredictable natural tableau set against the fixity of architecture:

> It's the end of September. The autumn flora wakes up; the roof is green again: a thick carpet of wild geraniums covers all. It is very beautiful. In spring, the new grass and wild flowers. In summer, a meadow of tall wild grasses. The roof garden lives on its own, responding to the sun, rain, wind and seed-carrying birds. (Last hour, April 1954: the roof is entirely blue with forget-me-nots.)[146]

The planted roof terrace replaced the earthly garden; the ground was taken over by sports facilities or automobile circulation; and the distant landscape was borrowed visually. Unlike his contemporaries, who fashioned *tableaux-jardins*, Le Corbusier modeled only slightly the *tableau-paysage* in the background, instead elevating the garden toward the sky, "high above the lake, freed from the groves of trees, far from the noise of the road . . . in the air, amid azure, under the sun, in total bliss, in full light."[147] In the pursuit of the trilogy of sun-air-greenery, he gave predominance to the sun.

Although he congratulated Le Corbusier for "extending the natural garden style to its logical conclusion," Christopher Tunnard mitigated his praise, because

> few people want to be condemned to languish at a window and exercise exclusively on a roof garden. . . . Most of us soon find that Nature unadorned (even with the alternative of a roof garden by Le Corbusier) is not enough: that the landscape or at any rate the surroundings of the house must be planned in accordance with human needs. Certainly the old conception of the garden designed as a series of pretty pictures must be put aside and a new and economical technique be used. The garden as an organization, whether that organization be only a path and a plant, must exist and can be ordered into a perfect and satisfying relationship with the house and the landscape.[148]

To Le Corbusier, the vegetation of the Virgilian landscape needed little shaping. "The plan [was developed] from the inside to the outside; the exterior [resulted] from an interior"; and the hanging garden created its landscape principally by means of the facade through which it looked.[149] Like the Beistegui camera obscura, the landscape of Le Corbusier followed the view. Wrapped around an existing tree, the Pavillon de L'Esprit Nouveau literally appropriated the scenery.[150] Rarely, however, did Le Corbusier engage the landscape other than visually.

8-50

8-51

8-50 PARC MONCEAU.
"The ground of the
large city could look
like this." (Le Corbusier,
Urbanisme).
[Photo: Marc Treib,
1992]

8-51 VEGETATION SAMPLING:
"THE PACT WITH
NATURE IS SIGNED."
[Le Corbusier, "Unité"]

8-52 ROOF TERRACE.
Weissenhof-Siedlung.
Stuttgart, 1927.
Le Corbusier and
Pierre Jeanneret.
[Lurçat, *Terrasses et
jardins*]

8-52

ANDRÉ LURÇAT

THE OUTDOOR ENSEMBLE

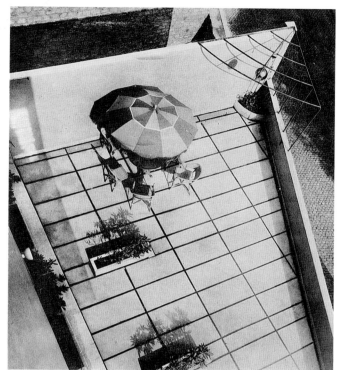

9-1

The master of heights finds the world
simplified. For form he sees a great flatness,
and for line the horizon. All else is but
pattern. We may safely expect new patterns.
Fletcher Steele,
"New Styles in Gardening"

The gardens designed by André Lurçat
(1894–1970) were contemporaneous with, and
situated between, the classical modernity of
Paul Vera and Jean-Charles Moreux and the
Virgilian landscape of Le Corbusier.[1] Lurçat
sought a harmony between building and site
through the "exploitation and provocation" of
natural elements. By manipulating vegetation
and water into an infinite variety of combinations, he wrote, one effected the imperceptible
and gradual transition from human creation to
natural milieu.[2] Such a belief evidenced the
continuing tradition of the *style composite*; it
also revealed the divergence in approach to site
and garden between two architectural modernists. Le Corbusier allowed his buildings
minimal contact with the earth and considered
vegetation a green abstraction, a visual compo-

9-1 HOUSE FOR WALTER
GUGGENBÜHL.
VIEW OF THE LOWER
TERRACE FROM ABOVE.
Paris, 1927.
André Lurçat.
[Lurçat, *Projets et
réalisations*]

9-3 HOUSE FOR MR.
HEFFERLIN.
ROOF TERRACE.
Ville-d'Avray, 1932.
André Lurçat.
[Lurçat, *Formes,
composition et lois
d'harmonie,* III]

9-2

nent of the *paysage-type.* In contrast, the geometric base upon which Lurçat set his villas was articulated with water and plants, materials he considered sources of "life, color, texture, contrast, and light."[3]

The five volumes of Lurçat's *Formes, composition et lois d'harmonie,* published between 1953 and 1957, included a chapter entitled "Nature," which spanned several centuries of garden history.[4] A repudiation of early modernism, this text—written almost thirty years after his most compelling garden designs—nevertheless confirmed Lurçat's affinity for plants, both their morphology and their cultural associations. The palette of trees he selected to illustrate the interrelation between architecture and nature was almost classical. To provide a vertical counterpoint to the dominant horizontals of a building, he recommended the Italian poplar, cypress, and thuja. The linden, horse chestnut, elm, sycamore, birch, or even cedar, on the other hand, could be used to screen an edifice.[5] Allying a horticultural to the sculptural concern, he specified trees based on climatic conditions. For the transparent light and constant humidity of the Parisian atmosphere, he advised the subtlety of deciduous foliage; but the "brutality and intensity" of southern light required the rough silhouette and intense value of the cypress or Italian stone pine.[6] Although Lurçat refrained from expressing any aesthetic bias toward either the *styles régulier* or *paysager,* he illustrated the text predominantly with photographs of formal gardens, French or Italian. Almost buried among images of Versailles, Villandry, and Villa Marlia was a picture of the exuberantly planted roof terrace he had designed in Ville-d'Avray, the sole trace of modernist landscape architecture in his entire compilation.

TERRACES AND GARDENS

In *Architecture,* which was published in 1929, Lurçat asserted that modernist houses had undergone several transformations in response to technical innovations and contemporary necessities. Two new components of these "monoliths" of modernist architecture, *pilotis* and roof terraces, were to shape the structure of the modern garden. In Lurçat's view, the evolution of "eternal" real estate into the standardized movable house was coincidental with the appearance of a "lighter" connection between architecture and the earth: the pilotis. The argument against a damp and unhealthy ground surface warranted lifting the living functions upward, toward the sky, where the sun reigned with its "light and benefits."[7] The space below the house was thus available for a garage, a shelter, or a covered garden—although vegetation seldom grew in such recessed shade. It was this separation of the main living activities from the soil, however, that conferred a new status upon the garden.

Because there was no direct horizontal connection with the landscape at ground level, the garden was essentially composed to be viewed from above. The interrelation of interior and exterior spaces on the upper-floor terraces, on the other hand, was achieved by installing hygienic facilities such as the solarium, swimming pool, exercise room—or garden. To the technical, economical, practical, and sentimental reasons for the use of terraces advocated by Le Corbusier, Lurçat added an aesthetic motive.[8] The roofs of historical cities, he wrote, were blemished by chimneys, dormers, and balconies, architectural features with neither order nor any apparent beauty.[9] Predicting the soaring interest in air travel, and thus the advent of a new point of view, he reconceived the terrace not only as an extension of the floor surface but also as a horizontal facade. The garden would bestow a new charm to the roof: intimate in scale, it was also an unexpected source of delight, with its flowers, shrubs, and fountains. Such a facade to the sky, Lurçat suggested, completed the "orthogonal and organized" harmony of the house and further linked building and surroundings.[10]

But while Le Corbusier set a pure architectural prism against a naturalistic landscape, Lurçat extended the geometric order of the building into the garden at ground level. In the introduction to *Terrasses et jardins*—published the same year as *Architecture*—he insisted on the importance of framing the house with a garden that followed similar compositional rules, more specifically, the rules of geometry. Lurçat thus verbally shaped the garden into a reinvigorated regular style, citing those great eras in which architecture and landscape were in complete accord. Whether Indian, Persian, Gothic, Renaissance—Italian or French—the most beautiful gardens of the world had been "governed by order and strict disposition." This pronouncement was followed by the implication that English or romantic gardens, on the other hand, were guilty of "imitating nature and artificially re-creating its disorder" and thus did not belong to contemporary life. They

9-3

reflected "those times during which the literary mind took precedence over the formal and analytical spirit." Having lost its status as a necessity and having been diminished by budgetary limitations, the garden in the modern era had become a rarity, conceded Lurçat. As the locus for vegetation and cleaner air, the roof terrace could reestablish the link between the architectural interior and nature that had been attenuated at ground level.[11]

In *Terrasses et jardins*, a critical record of modern landscape design, Lurçat illustrated early twentieth-century gardens on the ground and in the air. Selections ranged from the organic models of Frank Lloyd Wright's Taliesin and Prairie School Coonley House to the minerality of Vera and Moreux's *tableau-jardin* for the hôtel de Noailles. The photographs represented all schools of thought, and the subsequent relation between nature and architecture was addressed in a variety of ways. Tony Garnier integrated landscape within the frame of the courtyards at his own house in Saint-Rambert, whereas Ernst May and Ludwig Mies van der Rohe used the retaining wall to express the continuation of the architectural module into the landscape. As a counterpoint to this horizontal extension, nature was elevated, reappearing on rooftops by André Lurçat and Le Corbusier. Inside the house, Mallet-Stevens provided a true *jardin d'hiver*, and Raoul Dufy, Nicolau Rubió, and Llorens Artigas arranged bonsai specimens within painted ceramic shells to create ironic "apartment gardens." The imprint of architectural lines on the garden ranged from geometric compositions—as seen in Guevrekian's design for the Noailles or for Jacques Heim—to the quietly reformed Gothic scheme of Josef Frank or the tiled pools of Moorish inspiration by Moreux. The scale and degree of innovation varied, but the projects Lurçat chose as representations of modern landscape architecture were consistently drawn with regular lines.

The roof terrace, a vital element of the modern dwelling, overlooked the distant landscape and—at times—a garden below. In spite of urban lots of meager dimensions, several of the houses André Lurçat built between 1924 and 1926 for the artists of the Cité Seurat in Paris included minuscule geometric gardens, compared by one eulogistic critic to the gardens of Pompeii.[12] If space limitations precluded a terrace, flower boxes lined the large windows. The house he designed for his brother, the painter Jean Lurçat, formed an L around an entrance

9-4

9-5

9-4 *JARDIN D'HIVER.*
Paris, 1927.
Robert Mallet-Stevens.
[Lurçat. *Terrasses et jardins*]

9-5 BONSAI COMPOSITION.
Circa 1926.
Raoul Dufy, Nicolau
Rubió, and Llorens
Artigas.
[Lurçat, *Terrasses et jardins*]

9-6 GARDEN FOR
JACQUES HEIM.
Neuilly, 1928.
Gabriel Guevrekian.
[Lurçat, *Terrasses et jardins*]

9-6

and courtyard facing south. Of roughly square proportions (17 by 18 feet), the tiny "garden" was edged by a rustic stone path; simple brackets of flowers defined the exterior green room that extended the minute "greenhouse." Because the entrances of the houses for Mrs. Bertrand and the sculptor Arnold Huggler faced north, Lurçat oriented the living quarters and gardens southward, toward the sun. Larger in scale than Jean Lurçat's miniature landscape, these outdoor rooms displayed the garden elements characteristic of André Lurçat.

In spite of ground-level connections between inside and outside, these gardens seem to have been conceived primarily as a decoration for the upper floors. A caption to a photograph of the Bertrand house in *Projets et réalisations* described the geometric design of this garden as "easily readable from above." This image of nature recalled the accounts of "synthetic" compositions of André Vera.[13] Such similarity with the classical modernity of Vera's "new garden" of the early 1920s was furthered by the regular order of evergreen lines throughout the seasons and the division of its plan into "rectangular spaces comparable to the rooms of an apartment."[14] Already limited in surface area, the Bertrand and Huggler gardens were further reduced by paths and changes in level. The sitting area of the Bertrand house was sunken, and its sense of seclusion reinforced by the contrast between white paving and a dark vegetal frame. The Huggler garden, on the other hand, balanced the light stone of the raised terrace with the geometrically planted surfaces, reversing the ratio between pavement and vegetation from one platform to the other. Simple in layout, these two little gardens presented a graphic composition in accord with the restrained modernism of the building facades. Notwithstanding the sober proportions and triangular shapes of contemporary garden design, traces of classicism remained apparent throughout Lurçat's gardens: symmetry ruled the design, at least partially; axes led from door to fountain, even if cast in concrete.

9-7 CITÉ SEURAT. GROUND-FLOOR AND GARDEN PLANS.
A) house for Jean Lurçat;
B) house for Arnold Huggler;
C) house for Mrs. Bertrand;
D) house for Pierre Bertrand;
E) house for Mr. Bachelet.
Paris, 1924–26.
André Lurçat.
[Dorothée Imbert]

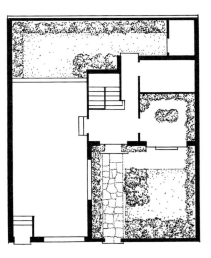

A

9-7

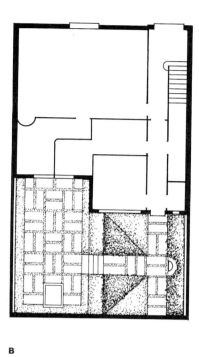

B

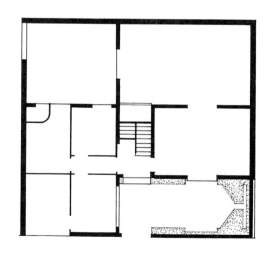

C

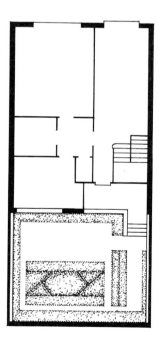

D

E

0 1   5   10   20

9-8 HOUSE FOR
ARNOLD HUGGLER.
GARDEN.
Cité Seurat. 1925–26.
[Lurçat, *Projets et
réalisations*]

9-9 HOUSE FOR
MRS. BERTRAND.
GARDEN.
Cité Seurat. 1925.
[Lurçat, *Projets et
réalisations*]

9-8   9-9

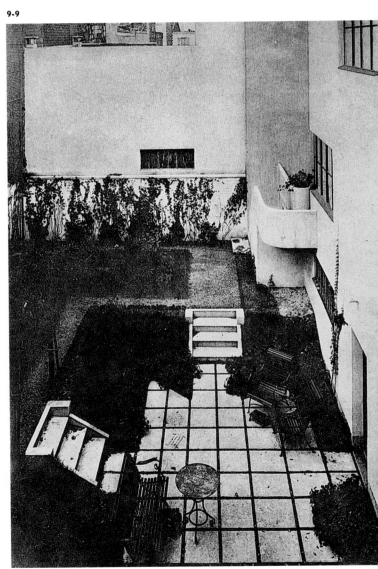

VILLA BOMSEL; VILLA MICHEL

VERSAILLES, 1926.   André Lurçat had served as a juror for the Austrian section of the 1925 Exposition des Arts Décoratifs; his widely publicized Bomsel garden was not presented in the section Art du jardin, although it was designed at almost exactly the same time as the landscape of the fair. Commissioned in 1924 and completed two years later, the villa and garden for Edmond Bomsel received equal critical acclaim—an unusual phenomenon in design publications. The garden was essentially a suburban enlargement of the miniature frames of nature composed by Lurçat for the houses in the Cité Seurat. Published in France around 1926, and shortly thereafter in England, Germany, and the United States, the landscape design was celebrated for being in perfect harmony with its modernist villa.[15] To a large degree, this accord was based on proportions that corresponded to the architectural plan of the house. In no way were the outdoor spaces a direct continuation of the interior, however. Lurçat raised the living quarters above the servants' rooms and garage in order to remove them physically from the dank soil of Versailles. By so doing, he severed any direct connection between ground floor and garden. "Enriched with various architectural elements," the garden was "geometrically composed" to function as an appropriate view from several points within the house; it could be entered from the second floor, and the most striking perspective was from the intermediate and rooftop terraces.[16] From the highest level, almost aerial photographs recorded a planar design, where volume was suggested by concrete elements, and thickness by variations in texture.

A skewed historicism simultaneously conferred both a familiar and innovative appearance to the garden. The cross-axial system was weighted toward the west in order to align the water channel—the main feature of the design—with the first-floor corridor and the protruding bay, the conceptual spine of the facade. This barely perceptible imbalance was countered by an almost total symmetry along the east-west axis. The central motif comprised a square parterre, two corners of which were cut by the respective radii of the *salle fraîche* at the southeastern edge of the lot and the second-floor terrace. Each of these coordinate axes—or given their modest dimensions, exterior corridors—focused on an accent such as a fountain, a plant container, an indentation in a hedge, or

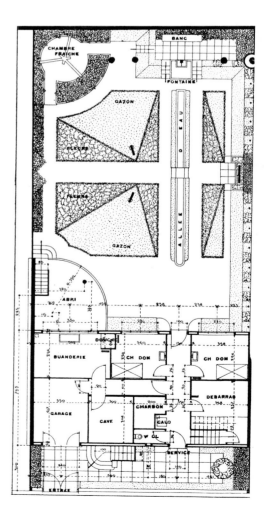

9-10 VILLA BOMSEL. GROUND-FLOOR AND GARDEN PLAN. Versailles, 1925. André Lurçat. [*L'Architecte*, 1926]

9-10

9-11

9-12

9-11 VILLA BOMSEL.
THE GARDEN SEEN
FROM THE ROOF
TERRACE.
[Photo: Therese Bonney;
© 1993 ARS, N.Y. /
SPADEM, Paris]

9-12 VILLA BOMSEL.
THE GARDEN,
LOOKING TOWARD
THE HOUSE.
The Villa Michel is
discernible to the left.
[Photo: Therese Bonney;
© 1993 ARS, N.Y. /
SPADEM, Paris]

a door. The "water allée," with jets at either end, established a north-south axis, enhancing the perceived depth of the garden as the light liquid accent reflected the dark leaves of sword lilies along the edge of the pool.[17] The cruciform parti provided a focus to the view from the corner terrace.[18]

All of these elements were part and parcel of the classical vocabulary. To achieve a sense of modernity, Lurçat sheathed the axial composition and traditional garden elements, such as the salle fraîche, linear pool, and fountain, with a contemporary veneer. "His patterns do not follow the old conventional lines," wrote Fletcher Steele, "yet, on the other hand, they rarely show the more extreme complications of certain of the modernists."[19] Unlike those "more extreme modernists," Guevrekian and Legrain, for example, Lurçat retained traces of the classical past. Extending an architectural hand into garden details, he simply interlocked parts of concrete, gravel, grass, and glass, rescuing the ensemble from the suburban mundane. A raised sitting terrace integrated a fountain of cast cement, which spilled water down a vertical pane of glass. Instead of framing a classical *boulingrin*, the *glacis* was transferred to the western edge of the garden to articulate the transition between the horizontal planes of lawn and gravel and an enclosing wall, which wrapped whimsically around a tree growing on the property line. The triangle, a nearly ubiquitous motif in the modern gardens of other designers, appeared only in the quietly outlined rectangular parterres that contained alternating panels of turf and flowering perennials. Light blue "monuments" visually anchored the triangular panes of lawn and appeared to have no other function than to support climbing roses and perhaps recall the color scheme of the villa.[20] Purely architectonic, these concrete slabs established a correspondence with the building, as if to echo the plant containers—the "fixed elements of life"—that Lurçat had placed within the villa.[21]

Despite the volume of its concrete furniture, the Bomsel garden was essentially two-dimensional. Gravel and vegetation played equal roles in defining this graphic composition: the view from the upper terrace of the new villa afforded a glimpse of a more traditional garden on the adjacent lot, where the ratio of circulation to planting differed strikingly. A frame to the green and yellow parterres, the small pebbles also covered the

semicircular second-floor balcony, creating a visual link between the two levels of the Villa Bomsel.[22] Although conceived essentially as a tableau-jardin, the garden nevertheless addressed functionalism, both through the spaces created and through the use of plants. Espaliered fruit trees lined the western wall, and several seating areas, raised above the dampness, highlighted the design. An English periodical described the salle fraîche as a "diminutive terrace . . . which, when covered with its gaily colored awning and surrounded by the dark green leaves of the rhododendron, must form an enchanting spot of colour against the trees beyond."[23] The shape of the green room echoed the half-raised circular terrace, which a German critic saw—perhaps in a desperate search for any trace of function—as a shelter for warm rainy days. In spite of these numerous amenities for rest and contemplation, a photograph shows the garden disturbed from its prescribed order: table and chairs were scattered across gravel and lawn rather than stiffly arranged in their specified places, as in Lurçat's design.

In answer to the "ingeniously divided and enclosed space" of the Bomsel house, in which the use of reinforced concrete paid a tribute to the "essential," Lurçat planned a similarly "clear image" for the garden, as a reflection of the "sharpness, precision and economy" so admired during the period.[24] In a 1930 issue of *Gartenschönheit,* critic Lonia Winternitz praised Lurçat's plant selection and design as indicative of an up-to-date, maintenance-free garden. A plan and photographs of the Bomsel garden illustrated her article.[25] Her approbation of this design was countered by another German critic, the landscape architect Wilhelm Hübotter, who analyzed the garden in writings and drawings in a concurrent issue of *Die Gartenkunst.*[26] Hübotter argued that Lurçat's garden should be "analogous to architecture," since its scheme derived from the conception of the house. Didactically, he presented an alternative design that expressed "his inner feelings." In Hübotter's proposal, elements such as the pool and salle fraîche were shifted in position and reshaped. At the risk of being criticized for having no "artistic imagination," he suggested a broad expanse of lawn, which would be "implemented and maintained with all the technical resources available to contemporary landscape architects."[27] Not unlike the advocates of the style régulier, however, Hübotter invoked the sensitivity of "modern man" combined with the "thorough knowledge of

9-13

9-13 VILLA BOMSEL.
VIEW OF THE GARDEN
FROM THE SECOND-
FLOOR TERRACE.
A concrete-and-glass
fountain terminates the
line of the water trough,
and the cross-axis is
marked by concrete
"monuments."
[Lurçat, *Terrasses et
jardins*]

9-14 VILLA BOMSEL.
COUNTERPROPOSAL
FOR THE GARDEN.
1930. Wilhelm
Hübotter.
[*Gartenkunst,* July
1930]

9-15 VILLA BOMSEL AND
VILLA MICHEL.
AXONOMETRIC
DRAWING.
Versailles, 1925.
André Lurçat.
[Delisle, "André
Lurçat"]

9-15

both gardener and artisan" to determine the shape of the future landscape.[28]

Corroborating Fletcher Steele's allegation that "now, as formerly, the French intellect is easily dissociated from human needs, instincts and senses," Lurçat avoided Hübotter's "sensitive" inspiration and built another variation of the geometric theme on the grounds across the street from the Villa Bomsel. There, he erected a house and garden for his father-in-law, Auguste Michel, in 1926. The axonometric view presents the similarly scaled Bomsel and Michel buildings as mirror images. Like the Bomsel scheme, the garden for the Michel house reflected the simplicity of its architectural matrix. A trapezoidal plan of nearly square proportions and symmetrical along the north-south line, the garden almost completely denied the positions of openings in the facade it addressed. The first floor of the Villa Michel, like that of its neighbor, housed services, but as a reverse image, all the southerly facing living spaces of the upper levels viewed the street rather than the garden. Accessible only through elements marked on the plan as "service stairs" or a "passage" adjacent to the garage, the garden does not relate to the interior in any direct way. Apparently, the layout of the backyard was determined by the projected shadow of the building.[29] The triangle became the dominant module of the plan, governing the form of a central shaded platform as well as the parterres, which were further subdivided by triangles of lawn and rose bushes.[30] Framed by lines of euonymus and flower beds, the decorative garden continued a plot for growing vegetables. Perhaps designed to match the austerity of the architecture—which was supposedly conceived as a reproducible unit—Lurçat's landscape design bordered on the banal and failed to attract as much attention as the garden of the Villa Bomsel.[31] The contradictions inherent in a decorative kitchen garden and a flat pattern hardly visible from the upper floors were evident in the published photographs illustrating the facade but little of the garden space it addressed.

In a 1929 issue of *House Beautiful*, Fletcher Steele reported that "one would look in vain to such architects as Le Corbusier, Pierre Jeanneret, Mallet-Stevens, André Lurçat, for the modernistic touch in gardens to match their extraordinary buildings." Their little courts and gardens, he continued, "might have been carried out by the most commonplace and conventional of garden makers" were it not "for a

9-14

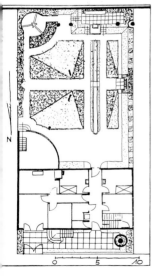
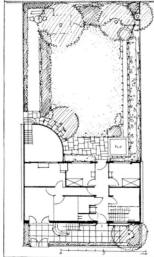

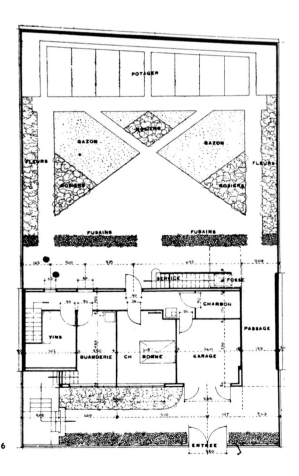

9-16 VILLA MICHEL. PLAN.
The ground floor with
the service areas and the
garden. Versailles, 1926.
André Lurçat.
[Delisle, "André Lurçat"]

9-16

sign of the same hand in architectural detail and pattern."³² A sweeping condemnation such as this begs for exceptions, but the allegation is certainly valid when applied to the Michel garden. Here, triangular shapes and the juxtaposition of utilitarian and pleasure areas merely hinted at a modernist architectural hand. Nevertheless, a year later Steele refuted his opinion in the article "New Pioneering in Garden Design," in which he cautiously stated that "far from being an extremist," Lurçat nevertheless belonged to the "contemporary school." He saw this affiliation manifested in the "picturesqueness" the architect achieved "through simple, yet careful, relations between garden and details."³³ Perhaps the Bomsel garden was both better and worse than Steele alleged. Extending the interior ensemble outward, Lurçat anchored the contemporary patterns of his garden scheme with architectonic details, even if the whole remained less than the sum of the parts.³⁴ Steele had condemned modernist architects for showing "an utter lack of interest or understanding of plant life and the myriad ways it might reënforce their ideas and lend them a charm now usually lacking." He later contradicted this sentence, asserting that "horticulture [played] a large part in M. Lurçat's gardens."³⁵ Indeed, the design for the Villa Bomsel reflected both Lurçat's hand and traces of a revised French tradition. While order prevailed, the drawn line did not completely subjugate vegetation. The order that structured the garden was softened, and its clarity obscured, by the plantings as they matured and by such dissonant elements as a concrete and glass fountain set in a rustic frame of *rocaille*.

The 1925 exposition had confirmed the uselessness of decorators, who "were born from a dearth of architects," wrote André Lurçat in *Architecture*. Instead of merely refurbishing the form of a product, he believed that one "must above all transform the spirit, by starting from the utilitarian and not . . . from a concern for beauty."³⁶ This comment about furniture could also be applied to the modernist concept of landscape design. Lurçat created an outdoor ensemble, bypassing the landscape architect as exterior decorator or horticultural consultant. Warranting Christopher Tunnard's assertion that "an architect would rather tackle the grounds himself with the help of a horticultural expert than call in a landscape architect unsympathetic to his ideas," Lurçat attempted to conflate landscape and architecture.³⁷ Avoiding the "direction of loose garden design" that Hübotter ascribed to "modern architects who place their buildings very happily in orchards or undisturbed landscapes," Lurçat, like them, appeared to "mistrust the landscape architect [who chose] to design a strict architectonic garden."[38] It is difficult to ascertain, however, whether Lurçat's transformation of garden forms probed any deeper than the surface. In *Projets et réalisations* (1929), Lurçat discussed the Cité Seurat and the gardens in Versailles as visual compositions; yet in the more analytical *Formes, composition et lois d'harmonie* (1955), he essentially reverted to presenting historical examples of landscape architecture.

However simple and limited, Lurçat's gardens were expressions of both the modern and French landscape traditions. Steele saw the architect's awareness of the horticultural dimension of the garden as utterly Gallic. His selection and arrangement of plants were impervious to any English or American influence, concluded the critic, noting that "even his vines [grew] in different patterns on the walls."[39] The prostrate nature of the Versailles compositions also responded to the new "commonplace point of aeroplane vantage." Steele's argument that the "satisfaction in exact parallels, squares and circles" was "a resource of mere two-dimensional creatures" might justify the preponderance of such planar gardens over the volumetries of plants.[40]

After the Bomsel and Michel projects, geometric patterns almost completely disappeared from Lurçat's garden designs. Triangular motifs resurfaced in the flower beds of a 1926 villa development in Parma, Italy, which also juxtaposed the ornamental garden with utilitarian vegetable plots and vineyards. But following his gardens in Versailles, Lurçat essentially raised his focus upward. As facades to the sky, the roof terraces of his architectural designs borrowed the depth they lacked from adjacent trees. Although constructed several years before the publication of Henry-Russell Hitchcock and Philip Johnson's *The International Style* (1932), Lurçat's Guggenbühl and Froriep de Salis houses seemed to exemplify the premises of this book: "Terraces may extend the house outside its own boundaries, but beyond the terraces the reign of nature should clearly begin."[41] Lurçat appeared to join with Le Corbusier in a policy of nonintervention between landscape and buildings. The Guggenbühl house (1926–27), in Paris, included an open-air exercise room and several terraces, but practically no garden at ground level. Lurçat composed the plan around views of the parc Montsouris across the street. To compensate for the lack of vegetation on the lot, each window was positioned to frame the trees and lawns of the park landscape. His assertion that "the park must be part of the house" was verified in details such as the two steps that elevated the living room, allowing a full view over the balustrade of the terrace.[42] Jean-Louis Cohen considers the Guggenbühl house the first Lurçat building in which the relationship between interior and exterior is conceived not as planar geometry extended to the garden but rather as a spatial relationship engaging the park.[43] Expressing a shift from the garden into a low-maintenance dry landscape—all mineral, apart from a few plant containers—the architect consciously severed architecture from nature.[44] Despite the inert character of the first-floor terrace, P. Morton Shand saw the two steps leading to the living room as "a window-box . . . effecting an intimate and immediate union between house and garden," the ultimate rationalization of the modernist concept interrelating building and landscape.[45]

The house for the painter Froriep de Salis (1927), in Boulogne, also established a diagonal link between terrace and the grounded landscape. The pattern of the little garden was transferred to the roof terrace, which overlooked the large trees of neighboring estates.[46] Like Le Corbusier, Lurçat explored the tension between the built surface of the new roof terrace and the surrounding elements—air, sun, and vegetation. His project for the Beistegui penthouse in 1929, however, remained a rather mundane planted terrace, complete with circular pool, flagpole, and panoramic table, far behind Le Corbusier's realized design.

Lurçat's career coincided with the paradoxical development and dissolution of the new jardin régulier. The little courtyard and hygienic roof terrace, the decorative geometric patterns, and the functional and social landscape accompanied the shift from bourgeois villa to communal housing project. The latter type, an urban garden city, was often set amid shrubbery and scattered clumps of trees interlaced with meandering paths.[47] By the end of the 1920s, Lurçat saw the architect dealing with corporations and the state rather than with the private client, fulfilling comfort and well-being for the masses through planning rather than addressing the personal needs of beauty and material wealth.[48] The harmony previously associated with the composition of a villa, hôtel, or château now resulted from the planning of streets and neighborhoods. "All the eternal laws directing the play of proportions, surfaces and volumes would remain" and bring the "calm and happiness infallibly produced by geometry, rhythm, and beautiful proportions," concluded Lurçat.[49] This was a reassuring statement of a new order, although it did not preclude the disappearance of the garden by the systematic landscape that became synonymous with modernist planning. An economy of means and materials had supposedly brought the rational garden to its developed modern state. Validating Lurçat's statement that "social and moral parameters shape the plastic values of an era," Henri Achel proposed "mass-produced architecture in vast, airy, and sunlit expanses" as the ideal economic solution for modern life.[50] But if, as Achel predicted, the private house became "anachronistic," the formal garden, however small, was doomed to be replaced by a roof terrace, to be transformed into a vegetable garden, or to have its patterns metamorphosed into a naturalistic format—all prescriptions offered by modernism. Steele referred to such an ambiguous stance when he wrote, "What a modernistic garden may be is everybody's guess. The reason is that it does not yet exist as a type."[51]

The Bomsel garden did possess both a classical structure and the balance in scale between outdoor and indoor living spaces—which Tunnard considered a requisite of modern landscape design.[52] The garden's axiality simply expressed the overlay of modernism on academicism, also evident in the partially symmetrical facade. It was thus more a product of expediency than the "unfortunate fixation" that Tunnard believed imparted a "rigid dullness" to any contemporary scheme.[53]

Perhaps Lurçat at least partially succeeded in resolving the inherent dichotomy between the elevated modernist villa and the landscape when he transferred his architectonic order to the immediate surroundings. With a limited number of elements reset in various combinations, he composed gardens of delineated surfaces rather than of volumes. Seen from above, the conventional parterres of Vera's Garden for the Aviator were actualized by Lurçat through the vehicle of roof terraces.

Lurçat himself had predicted "a high degree of expression and beauty" for the garden to parallel the "noble and pure style" of modernist architecture.[54] The outburst of creativity in the field of landscape architecture that characterized the 1920s and 1930s proved to be brief, however. Gardens in the style régulier, or with a certain degree of formality, were the product of modern decorative aesthetics. Linked to the bourgeois house of the period, they revealed the designer's total control over the ensemble, from the architecture to the furnishings, whether interior or exterior. As emphasis shifted from aesthetic to practical concerns, the scale of investigation expanded from architecture to urban planning, and the decorative garden—despite arguments for its rationality—lost its raison d'être.

9-17

9-17 VILLA BOMSEL.
The concrete-and-glass
fountain in a subsequent
rocaille dressing.
[Steele, "New
Pioneering in Garden
Design"]

9-18 HOUSE FOR MRS.
FRORIEP DE SALIS.
THE PLANTED ROOF
TERRACE.
Boulogne-sur-Seine,
1927. André Lurçat.
[Lurçat, *Projets et
réalisations.*]

9-18

202

EPILOGUE

10-1

The two international expositions held in Paris
in 1925 and 1937 bracketed the years in which
the French modern garden developed and
waned. If the Exposition Internationale des
Arts Décoratifs et Industriels Modernes witnessed the advent of a garden with affinities
toward architecture, design, and the decorative
arts, the succeeding Exposition Internationale
des Arts et des Techniques dans la Vie Moderne marked its dissolution. Jacques Gréber,
the chief architect of the 1937 exposition—
himself a garden designer—seemed at a loss to
discern any significant innovation in the garden
section. His introduction to *Jardins modernes,*
the pendant to Marrast's *1925 Jardins,* directed
praise mostly toward floral decoration rather
than toward the design of gardens per se. Gréber glowingly reported that the varieties of
annuals, rock plants, cacti, conifers, fruit trees,
the *floralies,* and the dahlia parterres formed
an admirable "collection of small picturesque
ensembles."[1] In describing these variegated
compositions as appropriate and harmonious
frames for the buildings of the fair, he inadver-

10-1 *FLORALIES* AT THE
GRAND PALAIS.
Exposition
Internationale des Arts
et des Techniques. Paris,
1937. Lambert and
Bertrand-Arnoux.
[Gréber, *Jardins
modernes*]

10-2 GARDEN OF TOMORROW FOR A FAMILY OF ARTISTS. Four freestanding pavilions for sculpture, painting, music, and literature; an open-air theater; and gardens for birds and bees. Aerial perspective, circa 1927. Achille Duchêne. [Duchêne, *Les jardins de l'avenir*]

tently revealed a widespread retreat from original and inventive design. From an aesthetic entity, conceived almost independently of its architectural surroundings, the garden had evolved into a mere accompaniment to building.

Fletcher Steele, still an essential voice for publicizing French garden design abroad, expressed his disappointment in the exposition works illustrated in *Jardins modernes*:

> The latest French gardens at the Exposition Internationale de 1937 . . . exhibit the dangerous tendency of all but the greatest modern art. Sharp, thin, and anaemic, they quite fail to make up in originality what they lack in charm and elegance. There has always been a certain stiffness and precision about good French parterres. It was appropriate to the design. The horticultural variety was brilliantly arranged. In these new parterres one is persuaded that everything is forced and an attempt to be merely original replaces soundness of plan. . . . Some of the earlier modernistic gardens by Guévrékian, the Veras, Pierre Legrain, etc., done ten years or more ago, seemed to promise a great future along lines that had scarcely been developed hitherto. We can only feel disappointment in knowing that these strong, fine new ideas withered before they came to flower.[2]

In 1937, with Pierre Legrain deceased, Gabriel Guevrekian just returning from Iran, and Robert Mallet-Stevens involved with the design of several pavilions, only Jean-Charles Moreux and Albert Laprade remained as principal actors on the garden scene of the exposition.[3] Achille Duchêne, another survivor from the initial cast of characters, played a prominent role in the first International Congress of Garden Architects, also held in Paris in 1937. In his report to the meeting, he developed, and paraphrased, issues he had addressed throughout earlier writings.

Duchêne had witnessed a disturbing trend: "For many reasons . . . great domains do not appeal to the younger generation and are being cut up, parcelled out in a dismal and uninspired manner, to build *bourgeois* villas or working-class dwellings."[4] With these words he bemoaned the demise of garden art in the service of the wealthy individual: *"The Art of Gardens is dying away."*[5] In spite of this glum perspective, Duchêne saw some small hope that with "the rise of democracy . . . one day art will be at the service of the community."[6] The destiny of the garden, he believed, depended upon economic as well as aesthetic factors. As taxes on unbuilt property rose to 12 percent, private gardens became more functional, leaning toward such utilitarian purposes as recreational facilities and producing orchards.[7] Ever the optimist, Duchêne appeared to answer the question raised in a 1928 issue of *L'Architecte:* "Will the garden emerge victorious over sports facilities and vegetable gardens?"[8] Recalling the theme he had developed in *Les jardins de l'avenir,* his modern garden, both aesthetic *and* functional, should epitomize "logic, order, clarity, and hierarchy."[9] The public park, on the other hand, should educate the masses to the nature of beauty. Only then, concluded Duchêne, would the working class be offered the "impression of serenity and order," and thereby would "its senses be refined and its . . . critical abilities developed."[10]

If modernist architecture drew its force from an almost utopian social program, perhaps it was achieved to the detriment of garden design. As the collective organization replaced the great art patron, the unique *tableau-jardin* rapidly faded away, becoming a luxurious and superannuated artifact. The garden section of the 1937 international exposition already suggested a return to horticultural order: modernity was reserved for public squares, such as Moreux's jardin des Gobelins or Gréber's parc Kellerman.

In place of gravel and mosaics, faceted spheres and rotating statues, there remained only photographs and writings—a loss Christopher Tunnard underlined as he wrote: "The mirrors of the Paris gardens will then long-since have been shattered, the trellis-work dismantled; but *Le Nouveau Jardin* will be there to remind us of a transitory movement of great interest and vitality."[11] Ironically, by eluding the fashionable modernity and formal aspects of the reinvigorated *style régulier,* architects like Le Corbusier adopted the look of an untempered landscape. This was not by default, however. The choice was purposeful. When Henry-Russell Hitchcock enunciated the factors governing landscape design in his influential *The International Style,* the geometry of the previous *jardin régulier* was not among them: "The elaborate formal garden has no place in connection with the international style. An aesthetic of right angles derived from architecture cannot be generally applied to landscape design without diminishing the reposeful contrast of the natural background." He clarified his pronouncement: "Natural surroundings are at once a contrast and a background emphasiz-

ing the artificial values created by architects. . . . As far as possible the original beauties of the site should be preserved. Mere open spaces are not enough for repose; something of the ease and grace of untouched nature is needed as well."[12] Unfortunately, Hitchcock failed to provide axioms for improving sites with no "original beauty."

A cycle in garden design history had been completed. Viewed pessimistically, the pictorial compositions of the 1920s and early 1930s may appear only as signs of tasteful decadence. Despite their reduced size and artistic self-consciousness, the formal research and reformation involved in their design nevertheless challenged the received definition of the garden. Whether cubist, modernist, or traditional, these landscape compositions, perhaps victims of a subsequent "horticultural revenge," were followed by a period of sobriety and predictability that has only recently shown signs of abating.[13]

10-3

10-4

PLATE I
"VIEW IN A *PARC
PAYSAGER.*"
1875. Alfred Darcel.
[Darcel, *Étude sur
l'architecture des
jardins.* Courtesy
Association Henri
et Achille Duchêne]

PLATE II
PARQUE DE
MARÍA LUISA.
THE LINEAR POOL
EXTENDING THE
FOUNTAIN OF
THE LIONS.
Seville, 1914.
J.C.N. Forestier.
[Photo: Jeff Stone, 1989]

PLATE III
PERGOLA AND POOL
ON MONTJUÏC.
Barcelona, circa 1916.
J.C.N. Forestier.
[Photo: Luc Imbert,
1990]

PLATE IV
GARDEN ON THE
COURS-LA-REINE.
Exposition
Internationale des Arts
Décoratifs et Industriels
Modernes, Paris, 1925.
Joseph Marrast.
[Autochrome Auguste
Léon; Collection Albert
Kahn, Département des
Hauts-de-Seine]

PLATE V
COURTYARD FOR THE
MANUFACTURE
DE SÈVRES.
In the background are
the vases that were
highly criticized for
their grandiose
dimensions. Exposition
Internationale des Arts
Décoratifs et Industriels
Modernes, Paris, 1925.
Henri Rapin.
[Marrast, *1925 Jardins*]

PLATE VI
JARDIN D'EAU ET
DE LUMIÈRE.
Exposition
Internationale des Arts
Décoratifs et Industriels
Modernes, Paris, 1925.
Gabriel Guevrekian.
[Autochrome Auguste
Léon; Collection Albert
Kahn, Département des
Hauts-de-Seine]

PLATE VII
FLOWERING COLUMNS
FOR A GARDEN OF
LIMITED DIMENSIONS.
Albert Laprade and
Léon Bazin.
[*L'Illustration*,
28 May 1932]

PLATE VIII
LA THÉBAÏDE.
THE FLOWER GARDEN.
Saint-Germain-en-Laye,
circa 1920. Watercolor.
Paul Vera.
[*L'Illustration*,
28 May 1932]

PLATE IX
PROMENOIR WITH
FLOWER BEDS AND
HEDGE PARTITIONS.
Watercolor and pencil
sketch. Paul Vera.
[Collection of Cooper-
Hewitt Museum,
New York.
Courtesy Yu-Chee Chong
Fine Art, London]

PLATE X
GARDEN FOR
PAUL-ÉLIE GERNEZ.
Honfleur, circa 1923.
Paul Vera.
[Photo: Dorothée
Imbert, 1989]

PLATE XI
"JARDIN D'AMOUR."
Watercolor, gouache,
and ink study for *Les
jardins*. Paul Vera.
[Collection of Cooper-
Hewitt Museum,
New York.
Courtesy Yu-Chee Chong
Fine Art, London]

PLATE XII
GARDEN DECOR FOR
MR. AND MRS. ANDRÉ.
Watercolor. Paul Vera.
[Musée d'art et
d'histoire, Saint-
Germain-en-Laye]

PLATE XIII
BOOKBINDING FOR
LE CORNET À DÉS
(Max Jacob, 1916).
1924. Pierre Legrain.
[*Les Arts de la Maison,*
Autumn 1924]

PLATE XIV
JARDIN D'EAU ET DE
LUMIÈRE.
Gouache. 1925.
Gabriel Guevrekian.
[Marrast, *1925 Jardins*]

PLATE XV
GARDEN FOR THE
VILLA NOAILLES.
MODEL.
1926. Gabriel
Guevrekian.
[*Les Arts de la Maison,*
Autumn 1926]

PLATE XVI
VILLA NOAILLES.
THE GUEVREKIAN
GARDEN RESTORED.
VIEW FROM THE
LAWN TERRACE.
Hyères.
[Photo: Marc Treib,
1991]

PLATE XVII
VILLA HEIM.
AXONOMETRIC
DRAWING.
Neuilly-sur-Seine, 1927.
Gabriel Guevrekian.
[*Art et Décoration*,
January 1929]

All translations from the French are my own; I have attempted to capture what I consider to be the sense of the writings rather than follow the text word for word.

PREFACE

1. "Au jardin régulier, on affirme, on formule, on précise on achève. . . . Par raison sociale, mon jardin au surplus ne sera point paysager. Bourgeois je ne dois offrir le désordre en délectation." André Vera, "Lettres sur les jardins," pp. 27–28.

2. Mrs. Howard Robertson, "Two Views against the Geometric Garden," p. 5.

3. Baker, "Equivalent of a Loudly-Colored Folk Art Is Needed," p. 66.

4. Shepheard, *Modern Gardens,* pp. 106–07. For example, the misinterpretation apparent in the Vera entry (written by Catherine Royer and Sarah Zarmati) of *The Oxford Companion to Gardens* continued in *Denatured Visions: Landscape and Culture in the Twentieth Century,* edited by Stuart Wrede and William Howard Adams (New York: The Museum of Modern Art, 1991).

5. "En tempérant de fantaisie les rigueurs du cubisme, tout l'art français s'achemine d'une manière assez imprévue . . . vers un baroque renouvelé, modernisé et relativement tempéré. . . . C'est un difficile problème que de rester Latin en classique et de vouloir en même temps faire surgir une esthétique nouvelle, reposant sur une discipline fortement motivée qui conduit l'artiste à se complaire dans le dissymétrique, non pour satisfaire à une mode, mais parce que des besoins nouveaux appellent des formes et des formules nouvelles. Gaston Varenne cited by Delisle, "André Lurçat, 1924–1925," pp. 92, 94.

6. Walpole, *On Modern Gardening,* p. 22.

1. For a brief summary of Dezallier d'Argenville's treatise, see Ganay, "Le XVIII° siècle: Jardins à la française," in *Les jardins de France et leur décor,* pp. 133–34.

2. The baron Haussmann, préfet de la Seine, described the project for the Bois de Boulogne as "exceeding the competence" of the "jardinier paysagiste" Varé. Also in his memoirs, he ambiguously praised "this poor Barillet-Deschamps" with his "great qualities and little defects." Haussmann thought his work expressed "une entente parfaite de la distribution du sol en pelouses vallonnées, en massifs d'arbres ou d'arbustes rares, en corbeilles de plantes vertes et de fleurs; mais un certain abus de détails et un peu trop d'allées." *Mémoires du baron Haussmann: Grands travaux de Paris, 1853–1870,* vol. 1, pp. 122 and 129, respectively.

3. According to several nineteenth-century landscape treatises, the design of a *jardin paysager, paysagiste,* or *d'agrément* "in good taste" should follow certain rules: views of the garden should induce a promenade and use monuments to entice curiosity. Trees must serve as foils to buildings and enhance vistas: near the residence one should plant species with dark foliage, the height and color intensity of the trees should decrease from foreground to background to obtain the effect of a painted picture. Any suggestion of geometric figures is to be avoided; paths should not zigzag as if following "the tracks of a slug" but should follow the line of ample curves. Boitard, "Des jardins paysagers," in *Traité de la composition et de*

l'ornement des jardins, pp. 58–60. For several of his rules, Boitand cited Thouin's introduction to his *Plans raisonnés de toutes les espèces de jardins* (n.p.).

4. "À mon avis, c'est [au style composite] que l'avenir de l'art des jardins appartient. C'est de l'union intime de l'art et de la nature, de l'architecture et du paysage, que naîtront les meilleures compositions de jardins que le temps nous apportera maintenant en épurant le goût public." André, "Principes généraux de la composition des jardins," in *L'art des jardins,* p. 151.

5. Vitet, "De la théorie des jardins," in *Études sur l'histoire de l'art,* vol. 4, p. 25. Cited by André, *L'art des jardins,* p. 152. Ganay described Vitet as a prophet who daringly rehabilitated the jardin à la française at a time when this fashion was "universally spurned." Ganay, "Les jardins romantiques," in *Les jardins de France,* pp. 255–56.

6. "L'arrangement général comporte une multiplication de détails et de reliefs; ils sont aménagés pour permettre aux dispositions des plantes et des fleurs de donner au jardin une magnifique décoration florale, à la vérité un peu clinquante, qui semble pour ainsi dire quelque feu d'artifice comme immobile, gerbes et fusées se dressant sur un tapis diapré où se jouent de savantes combinaisons de couleurs au dessin souvent maniéré." Ganay on the jardin régulier at the end of the nineteenth century, *Les jardins de France,* p. 295.

7. "Il me resterait à examiner une autre question intéressante, la *restauration des anciens jardins.* . . . Les cas où cet art peut s'excercer sont rares. . . . Il faudrait à un artiste la science et l'art mélangés dans les plus heureuses proportions, la possession entière et le respect de l'histoire des jardins, des connaissances architecturales approfondies et une longue pratique des choses de l'horticulture. Difficile assemblage, qu'il sera peut-être donné à quelqu'un de nos successeurs de réaliser, si l'art des jardins se dégage enfin comme un idéal digne de tenter les esprits élevés." André, "Division et classification des jardins," in *L'art des jardins,* pp. 198–99.

8. Henri Duchêne re-created formal gardens like those at Vaux-le-Vicomte and Champs-sur-Marne but also designed parks in the style paysager, such as Bois-Boudran. Ernest de Ganay dedicated his book *Les jardins de France et leur décor* to "the memory of his admired and sorely missed master in gardens: Achille Duchêne." For a description of Henri and Achille Duchêne's work, see the chapter entitled "Jardins, du second empire à nos jours," pp. 295–98.

9. Duchêne, "Formal Parks and Gardens in France," p. 275.

10. Ganay, "Jardins, du second empire à nos jours," in *Les jardins de France,* p. 297.

11. Duchêne, "Formal Parks and Gardens in France," p. 278.

12. Duchêne, "Jardins d'hier et rénovation des jardins à la française, 1880 à 1900," in *Les jardins de l'avenir, hier, aujourd'hui, demain,* pp. 7–9.

13. For a description of the château de Voisins see Duchêne, "Jardins d'aujourd'hui dits jardins d'architecture, 1900 à 1934," in *Les jardins de l'avenir,* p. 11; and "Formal Parks and Gardens in France," p. 273.

14. "Up to the beginning of 1902 the constructors of gardens continued mainly to follow the so-called 'landscape' school; nevertheless this school had already begun to plan gardens of a so-called 'mixed style'; that is to say, they were eliminating the four grass sweeps leading up to the façade and replacing them by geometrically designed plots parallel to the main lines of the house; flower beds on geometrical lines were introduced in the lawns, opposite the façade. Unfortunately, the relation between the formal garden and the garden treated in the landscape manner was not particularly good." Duchêne, "Formal Parks and Gardens in France," p. 275.

15. Ibid., p. 278.

16. "L'état d'esprit des propriétaires s'est modifié: leurs exigences augmentent, ils demandent des projets d'une composition irréprochable; les décorations de treillage, les parterres de broderies sont toujours à la mode. On donne encore de grandes fêtes. Pour l'exécution des travaux, l'architecte doit fournir des devis détaillés et éviter de dépasser les crédits accordés sous peine d'éprouver des ennuis. Bref, on dépense encore, mais on discute les prix et on exige que la réalisation donne l'impression d'une dépense supérieure à la réalité." Duchêne, "Jardins d'aujourd'hui dits jardins d'architecture, 1900–1934," in *Les jardins de l'avenir,* p. 10.

17. Duchêne, "Jardins d'aujourd'hui," pp. 12–14.

CHAPTER 2:
J.C.N. FORESTIER

18. Duchêne, "Jardins de demain," in *Les jardins de l'avenir*, pp. 16–20.

19. Duchêne, two projects entitled "Jardin pour la demeure d'une famille sportive" and "Jardin destiné à la culture des fleurs et à l'horticulture ménagère," in *Les jardins de l'avenir*, pp. 18–19 and 19–20, respectively.

20. Duchêne, "Les jardins de l'avenir," in *Les jardins de l'avenir*, pp. 21–42.

21. "La création des parcs privés aura vécu, mais, en œuvrant pour des collectivités, on disposera peut-être alors de moyens de réalisation plus puissants que jadis; on pourra, grâce à eux, concevoir des projets plus grandioses, sur des programmes entièrement nouveaux, qui ne laisseront subsister que des artistes assez grands pour s'élever et se maintenir à la hauteur de cette tâche." Duchêne, "Jardins de demain," in *Les jardins de l'avenir*, p. 20.

22. Duchêne, "Jardins modernes," in *Les jardins de l'avenir*, p. 15.

1. Corpechot, "J.-C.-N. Forestier," p. 17; Forestier, *Gardens: A Note-book of Plans and Sketches*, p. 11. The project of gardens for the power plant of the Central Tèrmica de l'Energia Elèctricas de Càtalunya, "La Catalana," was dated 1916.

2. See Achille Duchêne's *Les jardins de l'avenir* and his address at the Premier Congrès International des Architectes de Jardins.

3. Forestier, cited by Varenne, "Les jardins de J.-C.-N. Forestier," p. 89.

4. Forestier, *Gardens*, p. 12.

5. Forestier, cited by Varenne, "Les jardins de J.-C.-N. Forestier," p. 90.

6. Forestier, *Les gazons*, p. 11.

7. Humphry Repton, cited by Édouard André in his preface to *L'art des jardins*, p. vii. "Ce n'est qu'au goût et au sentiment à donner la raison des choses qui échappent à toutes règles" (Forestier, *Jardins: Carnet de plans et de dessins*, n.p.).

8. Forestier graduated from the École Polytechnique in 1880 and studied forestry in Nancy. In her obituary of Forestier, Morgenthau Fox attributed his shift in career to a horseback riding injury. Previously destined for the navy, he had to modify the course of his studies because of a paralysis of the right arm. Morgenthau Fox, "Jean C. N. Forestier," p. 93.

9. The estate had been remodeled by Lord Seymour, Marquis of Hertford, who purchased it in 1835. His descendant, Sir Richard Wallace, a noted art patron, bequeathed Bagatelle to his wife, who in turn willed it to their secretary, Murray Scott.

In financial straits at the turn of the century, Scott attempted to develop the sixty-acre estate for housing. Forestier was credited with effectively negotiating between Scott and the préfet de la Seine. The year 1905 thus marked the end of English ownership of Bagatelle. See Barozzi, *Bagatelle*, pp. 15–23.

10. The comte d'Artois, brother of Louis XVI, commissioned Thomas Blaikie to design the gardens for Bagatelle. Completed in 1786, the grounds contained many exotic species of plants set among picturesque lakes and meandering walks. In 1793, following the Revolution, Bagatelle entered the public domain. Napoléon used the estate as a hunting lodge.

11. For a description of the different constructions at Bagatelle, see Andia, *De Bagatelle à Monceau*, pp. 20–24.

12. Both the term and concept of *fabrique* are borrowed from eighteenth-century painting. Simply phrased, a fabrique is an ornamental construction set in a picturesque landscape.

13. "L'erreur des jardins romantiques n'aura pas été sans conséquence heureuse. Elle a ravivé la certitude que l'aspect de beauté artistique n'est possible à atteindre qu'en se soumettant aux lois du rythme, tout en évitant de se restreindre au seul dessin et de négliger la nature." Forestier, "Les jardins modernes," pt. 1, n.p.

14. In the same text Forestier recommended the use of China drawing ink for the crispness of its lines and the contrast between the lightness of the lawns and the weight of the

212

mosaic-paved alleys. Ibid.

15. Forestier, "The Gardens of France," p. 60.

16. On the north side of Bagatelle, Forestier arranged a water garden using various species of nympheas. Contemporary writers suggest a similarity and respective influence between the composition of these water lilies and those at Giverny (Leroy, *Bagatelle et ses jardins*, p. 88; Barozzi, *Bagatelle*, p. 23); H. Morgenthau Fox asserted that Forestier sent these nympheas to Monet ("Jean C. N. Forestier," p. 95). No documentation clearly supports the connection, however.

17. Haussmann entrusted Alphand—then an Ingénieur Ordinaire des Ponts et Chaussées—with the Service des Promenades et Plantations. "Quand l'Ingénieur-Jardinier eut graduellement grandi, comme sa mission même, la raillerie fit place à l'envie." *Mémoires du baron Haussmann*, vol. 1, p. 127.

18. Alphand, "Tracé des jardins irréguliers," in *Les promenades de Paris*, p. liii.

19. "Il ne suffit pas que [l'arbre, la prairie et la fleur] soient rapprochés dans les hasards de la nature pour constituer un jardin. Ils doivent être contenus par l'ordre précis et très apparent de la composition du jardin." Forestier, "Les jardins modernes," pt. 1, n.p.

20. See Forestier, *Gardens*, pp. 142–88.

21. Forestier, *Jardins: Carnet de plans et de dessins* (translated by Helen Morgenthau Fox as *Gardens: A Note-book of Plans and Sketches*).

22. In his homage to Forestier, Henri Prost characterized "Les espaces libres et les jardins publics à créer," drafted in 1911, as an excellent report that greatly influenced the works of French architect-planners like himself. Upon Forestier's recommendation, Prost went to Morocco in 1913, to be joined by Albert Laprade in 1915 and Joseph Marrast in 1916. The Agence Prost planned several Moroccan cities (Prost, "Hommage à Forestier," pp. 74–75; Marrast, "Maroc," pp. 51–117). Forestier's gardens for the sultan are illustrated in his *Gardens*, pp. 152–53.

23. Forestier, "Les jardins arabes en Andalousie," pp. 32, 34.

24. Ibid., p. 32; and Forestier, *Gardens*, p. 151.

25. For a description of Forestier's urban projects, see Prost, "Hommage à Forestier," pp. 74–75; Leclerc, "Jean Claude Nicolas Forestier (1861–1930)," pp. 24–29; Lejeune, "The City as Landscape," pp. 50–67; and the proceedings of the Colloque Forestier (Paris: Picard, in press).

26. Forestier has been credited with importing wisteria, mock orange, pittosporum, lilac, pyracantha, and certain varieties of roses. See Morgenthau Fox, "Jean C. N. Forestier," p. 97.

27. The military site had served as an exposition ground since the first fair of French industrial products, the Exposition des Produits de l'Industrie Française, in 1798.

28. Founded by Émile Deutsch de la Meurthe in 1922, and later expanded with funds from John D. Rockefeller, Jr., the Cité universitaire houses today six thousand French and foreign students in thirty-seven residence halls. Forestier drew the initial master plan with Lucien Bechmann and Léon Azema. Modeled after American campuses, the cité featured a *parc de sports*, an essential element in the new hygienic student life. Almost every residence represents a different nationality. Among its architects were Le Corbusier, Lucio Costa, Willem Dudok, Albert Laprade, and Jean Prouvé. See A. P., "La cité universitaire de Paris," pp. 38–41; Honoré, "Une ville nouvelle dans Paris: Les agrandissements de la cité universitaire," pp. 463–65; and Ragot, "La cité universitaire internationale de Paris," pp. 76–80.

29. A project for the Hispano-American Exposition appeared as early as 1909, and King Alphonso XIII approved Seville as its site in 1910.

30. In 1530, Isabel the Catholic had established on the Guadalquivir the Casa de Contratación, a commercial institution organized to stimulate and protect trade with America.

31. With the Arreglo para la Unión de María Luisa y Mariana of 1915, Forestier proposed a compromise to adjust the axiality of the park and the rose garden to González's Plaza de América. His contemporaneous Extensión del Parque de María Luisa incorporated the Plaza de España within the park.

32. As the site of several royal betrothals, the lake and the Oriental pavilion had to be preserved. Forestier, *Gardens*, p. 186.

33. The permanent pavilions—to be used later as consular offices for the country they represented—were located in the central area that included the Parque de María Luisa, the Plazas de España and América, and the San Telmo, Eritaña, and Las Delicias gardens. See Trillo de Leyva, *La exposición iberoamericana: La transformación urbana de Sevilla*; and *Libro de oro ibero americano*.

34. Forestier, cited by Varenne, "Les jardins de J.-C.-N. Forestier," p. 90.

35. See Forestier, *Gardens*.

36. Forestier designed the grounds of the marqués de Castilleja de Guzmán's estate on the outskirts of Seville. In Ronda, he created a garden for the duchesse de Parcent. Although a modern interpretation of a Moorish idea, this garden for the Casa del Rey Moro is often described as "genuinely Andalusian."

37. "But gardens are ephemeral and most of them have disappeared. If some survived, it was due to the durable materials used in constructing features that marked the principal outline." Forestier, *Gardens*, p. 143.

38. The nymphea garden was, according to Forestier himself, a reference to the Patio de la Alberca (Court of the Cistern, today Court of the Myrtles) at the Alhambra in Granada; the rose garden framing the Fountain of the Lions resembled the Patio de los Leones (Court of the Lions), also at the Alhambra. See Trillo de Leyva, *La exposición iberoamericana*, p. 170.

39. *Azulejos*, or colored tiles, were frequently used in Seville, Triana, Valencia, Tunisia, Algeria, and Morocco. See Forestier, *Gardens*, p. 150.

40. Ibid., p. 151.

41. Gromort, "Le parc Maria Luisa et le jardin Murillo à Séville," in *Jardins d'Espagne*, vol. 2, pp. 140–41.

42. Forestier, *Gardens*, pp. 151–55.

43. During the 1920s the Parque de María Luisa also functioned as an outdoor reading room, complete with books, a concept promoted by Aníbal González. The glorietas were dedicated to Sevillian authors such as the poet Gustavo Bécquer and the brothers Àlvarez Quinteros. A statue also honored Miguel de Cervantes, whose stay in the Seville prison qualified him as a local figure.

44. In 1922, Portugal was accepted as a member; the exposition was thus renamed Ibero-Americana.

45. The first Barcelona Universal Fair was celebrated in 1888. One of the principal instigators in reviving such an event was the architect-politician Josep Puig i Cadafalch. His address "A votar! Per l'exposició universal" was published by *La Veu de Catalunya* (1 November 1905). See Hernández-Cros, "L'exposició internacional de 1929 a Barcelona," p. 24; and Solà-Morales, "The 1929 International Expo," p. 17.

46. The Feria de Industrias Eléctricas was actually inaugurated in 1923. A royal decree published in the *Gaceta de Madrid* of June 1914 validated the project of the park as well as the coupling of a Spanish exposition with an electrical fair. This intervention clearly appeared as a means of controlling Catalan nationalism. See Hernández-Cros, "L'exposició internacional de 1929 a Barcelona," pp. 26–27.

47. In the 1859 scheme for the expansion of Barcelona by Ildefons Cerdà, the Plaça de les Glòries Catalanes was conceived as the city's center. With the planning of the exposition, the center was shifted to the Plaça d'Espanya, at the foot of Montjuïc.

48. Forestier's project of the gardens for the banker Ferrer-Vidal i Güell was published in *Jardins;* the plans, sections, elevations, and perspective are dated January 1919. That same year, the estate was transformed into a residence for the Spanish royal family. The renovated gardens of the Palau Reial de Pedralbes, dated 1925, are attributed to a collaborator of Forestier, Nicolau Maria Rubió i Tudurí. See Forestier, *Gardens*, pp. 167–69, and Hernández-Cros, Mora i Gramunt, and Pouplana i Solé, *Guia de arquitectura de Barcelona*, p. 118.

49. Cambó described in his memoirs the different tasks he had assigned to his collaborators: Rubió i Tudurí was his right arm; the architect Amargós was in charge of expropriations; the marquès de Camps was responsible for forest plantations; Puig i Cadafalch was one of the principal architects, but the one who shaped the park of Montjuïc was the architect-gardener Forestier. See Cambó, *Memòries*, p. 223.

50. See Hernández-Cros, "L'exposició internacional de 1929 a Barcelona," p. 27; and Solà-Morales, "The 1929 International Expo," pp. 19, 21.

51. Long a proponent for the development of Montjuïc, Josep Amargós i Samaranch had submitted in 1894 an "Avantprojecte de Passeigs i

Urbanització Rural de la Muntanya de Montjuïc." See Hernández-Cros, "L'exposició internacional de 1929 a Barcelona," p. 26. His parti featured an avenue, the Passeig Central K, which girdled the steep topography and led to Forestier's gardens for Miramar.

52. Forestier converted an old quarry into an open-air theater, later to become the Teatre Grec. The project was completed in 1929 by his collaborators Nicolau M. Rubió i Tudurí and Ramon Reventós i Farrarons. Forestier designed two projects for Miramar (1919, 1923). The perspective of the second scheme is attributed to Rubió i Tudurí.

53. Forestier, *Gardens*, p. 18.

54. Prost, "Hommage à Forestier," p. 74.

55. Forestier designed a garden for Joseph Guy in Béziers and one for the comte and comtesse de Polignac at La Bastide du Roy in Biot. Both gardens, which are extremely fine examples of Forestier's southern strain, still exist. The plans for plots measuring 90 by 210 feet and gardens of 54,000 square feet published in *Jardins* were supposedly preparatory studies intended for Forestier's friends. See Morgenthau Fox, "Jean C. N. Forestier," p. 94.

56. See Forestier, "Pergolas, Posts and Arches," in *Gardens*, pp. 29–46.

57. Ibid., p. 13.

CHAPTER 3:
GARDENS AT THE EXPOSITION

1. Steele, "New Pioneering in Garden Design," p. 165.

2. In 1906, Senator Couyba proposed the concept of an international exposition of decorative arts as the means to revitalize the art industry. Roger Marx, Inspector of Museums, furthered the call and urged a *modern* international exposition, an event by which France would cease to "profess its fear of originality" by engaging in a display worthy of the twentieth century. See Marx, "De l'art social et de la nécéssité d'en assurer le progrès par une exposition," p. 55. For a history of the 1925 exposition and its definition of modern, see Nancy Troy, "Reconstructing Art Deco: Purism, the Department Store, and the Exposition of 1925," in *Modernism and the Decorative Arts in France*, pp. 159–226.

3. Italy had taken a more active role in promulgating modern design, convening, in 1902, the first International Exposition of Modern Decorative Arts in Turin. See Guilleré, *Rapport sur une exposition internationale des arts décoratifs modernes: Paris 1915*, dated 1 June 1911. Furthermore, the French representation at the Turin exhibit was so poor that the editors of *Art et Décoration* suggested that France's reputation might have fared better had the country not submitted any display. See "L'exposition de Turin," p. 1. For a study of the Turin exposition and its rules, see Fratini, *Torino 1902: Polemiche in Italia sull'arte nuova.*

4. See the chart comparing the importations and exportations between 1892 and 1908 for markets such as furniture, costume jewelry, and leather goods. Guilleré, *Rapport sur une exposition internationale*, p. 5.

5. Article 2 of the proposal read: "On n'acceptera que les ouvrages originaux qui montreront une tendance bien marquée au renouvellement esthétique de la forme. Les imitations d'anciens styles et les productions industrielles dénuées d'inspiration artistique ne seront pas admises." Marx, "De l'art social," p. 55; Guilleré, *Rapport sur une exposition internationale*, p. 3. See also Chapsal, *Rapport à M. le ministre du commerce, de l'industrie, des postes et des télégraphes*, dated 23 May 1913, p. 2.

6. For an excellent account of the rivalry between France and Germany in its artistic manifestations at the outbreak of the First World War, see Silver, *Esprit de Corps.*

7. "L'exposition de 1922," pp. 1–2.

8. Comparable situations had occurred before: the 1819 Exposition of Industrial Products took place when the country had barely recuperated from the Napoleonic wars, invasions, and the restoration of the monarchy; the 1878 Universal Exposition closely followed the Franco-Prussian War and the Paris Commune; the 1889 fair was planned during the crisis of the Third Republic. Vaillat, "Un siècle d'expositions d'art décoratif—ce que furent les expositions d'art décoratif de 1798 à 1900." See also Silverman, "The 1889 Exhibition: The Crisis of Bourgeois Individualism." For a description of the context of several Universal Expositions up to 1878, see *L'encyclopédie de l'archi-*

tecte, 1878, p. 33, cited in Gilbert Cordier's "À propos des expositions universelles," p. 6.

9. Ligne, "L'exposition internationale des arts décoratifs et industriels modernes de Paris —1925," p. 148. For an account on the influence of the Paris exposition on American commerce see Davies, "Promoting Modern Design," in *At Home in Manhattan: Modern Decorative Arts, 1925 to the Depression*, pp. 83–102.

10. Paul Léon, director of the Beaux-Arts and associate superintendent for the exposition, defined France's contribution to the fair rather bluntly, asserting that decorative arts were to serve a financial cause. "If economy is a virtue," wrote Léon, "it is a negative virtue. . . . It is definitely luxury that France intends to present at this world meeting." Léon, *Art et artistes d'aujourd'hui*, 1925; cited by Guillaume Hebbelynck in "L'exposition internationale des arts décoratifs et industriels modernes de Paris—1925 (suite)," p. 42.

11. With the drastic depreciation of the German mark and Germany's inability to settle its war debt, French and Belgian troops occupied the Ruhr on 11 January 1923, thus creating a further burden on the weakened French economy while increasing tensions in Franco-German relations.

12. Rambosson, "L'exposition des arts décoratifs: La participation étrangère," pt. 1, p. 78

13. "Grand mutilé de guerre, la France est revenue de toute son âme aux arts de la Paix." Dezarrois, "Avant l'ouverture de l'exposition des arts décoratifs: Un magnifique effort," p. 219.

14. *Exposition internationale des arts décoratifs et industriels modernes* (Paris: Imprimerie Nationale, 1922). René Guilleré prescribed a collaboration among the artist, the industrialist, and the artisan, a union that had been attempted almost continually since 1806. In 1798, as a palliative to the exclusion of artisans and industrialists from the Salons, François de Neufchâteau, then Minister of Industry, had instaured the tradition of exhibiting products from French industry. In 1802, following the successful outcome of the third exposition, Chaptal, the current Minister of Industry, founded the Society for the Encouragement of Art and Industry; the next exhibition was inaugurated on 25 September 1806. See Guilleré, *Rapport sur une exposition internationale*, pp. 3–4; and Vaillat, "Un siècle d'expositions d'art décoratif," pp. 309–16.

15. "The invitation to the United States was declined on the grounds that American manufacturers and craftsmen had almost nothing to exhibit conceived in the modern spirit and in harmony with the spirit of the official specifications." *Report of Commission Appointed by the Secretary of Commerce to Visit and Report upon the International Exposition of Modern Decorative and Industrial Art in Paris 1925*, p. 16. See also "L'abstention des États-Unis," p. 3. The Japanese allies were assigned the lot previously designated for the United States.

16. Diplomacy arbitrated the frontiers between pavilions at the exposition: Turkey could not adjoin Greece, and the U.S.S.R. could not be placed next to Poland and Romania. See Dervaux, "L'exposition des arts décoratifs et industriels modernes," p. 49.

17. As an apparently customary practice, construction continued for a few months after the official opening. See "Ouvrira-t-on l'exposition en 1926?" p. 14; and Guilleminault et al., *Les années folles*, p. 290.

18. The commission appointed in 1912 had established the preliminary program. The definite choice of the site was adopted by the City Council on 17 October 1922. See Viée, "L'exposition internationale des arts décoratifs et industriels modernes de 1925," p. 170.

19. Among the site options were the island of Puteaux; the Bois de Vincennes; the Auteuil racetrack; several fortification segments and military zones; and Versailles. The Grand Palais, Petit Palais (with the gardens of the Cours-la-Reine), and esplanade des Invalides had been rejected previously as creating too constricted an enclave within the network of thoroughfares. The three-year occupancy necessary for construction, exposition, and demolition seemed too high a wager. If peripheral sites, such as the fortifications, offered the possibility of permanent structures, the esplanade and its opposite bank compensated with sufficient advantages to merit their selection. See Chapsal, "Emplacement," in *Rapport à M. le ministre*, pp. 6–10; and "Emplacement," in *Exposition internationale des arts décoratifs et industriels modernes* (Paris: Imprimerie Nationale, 1922), pp. 2–3.

20. "Cet emplacement est effectivement un des plus beaux de la Capitale; il a été choisi avec intention; il est tout naturel, en effet, que, pour montrer ce que l'on fait de mieux à notre époque, on l'expose, non seulement dans un cadre qui lui fasse honneur, mais aussi au centre de la vie commerciale; il me semble que là est une des premières conditions de la réussite de cette Exposition." Viée, "L'exposition internationale," p. 169.

21. The *quinconces* owed its name to the trees planted in quincunx that framed the esplanade. Attractions, commercial structures, kiosks, fountains, and statues were located in this area.

22. See Lambert, "Jardins et fontaines," p. 139.

23. See Guilleré, *Rapport sur une exposition internationale*, pp. 8–13.

24. In "De l'art social," Roger Marx credited Léon de Laborde's *Rapport sur l'exposition de Londres de 1851* with first proposing an exposition demonstrating the solidarity of art, life, and science. Laborde predicted the socialization of art as "un art utile."

25. Guilleré, *Rapport sur une exposition internationale*, p. 12.

26. The critic denounced Plumet as having desecrated the vista of the majestic Hôtel des Invalides with four 100-foot-high "tetragonal nightmares" exemplifying "the senile architecture still lingering from 1900." Le Fèvre, "L'architecture," pp. 4–5.

27. Dervaux, "L'exposition des arts décoratifs," p. 50.

28. Lacoste, "L'exposition internationale des arts décoratifs et industriels modernes de Paris—1925 (suite)," p. 161.

29. "Pris dans la tourmente fébrile des villes enrichies, des villes capitalistes, l'art décoratif français, qui domine à Paris, se perd en une débauche captivante et merveilleuse, d'un raffinement exotique mais d'un luxe faux, qui l'éloigne, en une période de démocratie marquée, de la belle santé du labeur et de la vie de l'homme, mais qui lui ouvre des débouchés dans les pays aux dollars enflés, aux pesos redorés." Ligne, "L'exposition internationale," p. 148.

30. Poiret had staged presentations on three canal boats—*Orgues*, *Délices*, and *Amours*—floating on the Seine. Poiret, *En habillant l'époque*, p. 154.

31. Le Corbusier, *L'art décoratif d'aujourd'hui*, p. 98.

32. "The ultimate retreat of ostentation is in polished marbles with disturbing veins, in veneers of rare wood as stupefying as hummingbirds, in glass confections, in lacquers borrowed from *the excesses* of the Mandarins and thence made the starting point for artificial aspirations. Meanwhile, the Prefecture of Police is chasing coke dealers." Ibid., p. 99.

33. "[L'architecture] va sans hésitations, vers une formule nouvelle . . . vers la valeur robuste des surfaces balancées, des volumes équilibrés, débarrassés de l'inutile et superflue ornementation. C'est en somme un retour réactionnaire aux dogmes sains de l'architecture: un luthéranisme architectural. Cette architecture neuve s'élève dans une forme épurée, 'réformée' au dessus du régionalisme sentimental et de la frénésie de luxe des villes." Ligne, "L'exposition internationale," p. 158.

34. Janneau, "Introduction à l'exposition: Considérations sur l'esprit moderne," pp. 147, 150–51; Vera, "Le nouveau style," pp. 21–32.

35. Janneau, "Introduction à l'exposition," pp. 151–52.

36. Francis Jourdain, remembrances on the early movement, in *25 années u.a.m.*, p. 15.

37. Charles Genuys, who directed this section to be designed by "modern" architects (such as Alfred Agache and Hector Guimard), resorted to a picturesque tableau to answer the technical constraints placed upon him by the dense subterranean network of services. "Le peu de développement des emplacements, les restrictions de tous ordres découlant de l'interdiction de toucher aux arbres et à toutes les canalisations souterraines, dont le réseau est si serré dans le sous-sol parisien, ne permettaient point de faire œuvre d'urbanisme. On dut se contenter de recourir au pittoresque." Rambosson, "L'exposition des arts décoratifs. Les pavillons de la province et de l'étranger: Quelques aspects," pp. 38–39.

38. Ibid., pp. 36–37.

39. This type of dedication is found on most French war memorials. Morocco and Tunisia, as French protectorates, and Algeria, as a colony, had provided France with soldiers during the First World War. Praising the upheaval caused by the war and its role as the generator of needed transformations, the critic Chrétien-Lalanne saw the exposition as an hymn to victory, nationalism, and labor:

"The architecture of a vanquished city would be composite, its decor impoverished and uncertain; numb from peace, its arts would collapse under magnificence, bad taste and extravagances." With a reverence to the monarchs of commerce and the industrial powers, he declared, France celebrated with a "perfect purity the virtue of its triumphal arms." Chrétien-Lalanne, "Promenade d'un sceptique à travers l'exposition des arts décoratifs et industriels modernes," p. 112.

40. Le Corbusier attributed the obscure location of the Pavillon de L'Esprit Nouveau between two wings of the Grand Palais, and all the difficulties encountered during its erection, to the ill will of the exposition's board of directors. Le Corbusier, *Urbanisme*, pp. 219–20; *Almanach d'architecture*, p. 151; and "Brève histoire de nos tribulations."

41. Benton, Benton, and Scharf, "Furniture as an Architectural Element in the Avantgarde Interior," in *Design 1920s*, p. 69.

42. Le Corbusier, *Urbanisme*, p. 220.

43. Benton, Benton, and Scharf, "Modernist Tendencies in French Design before 1925," in *Design 1920s*, p. 61.

44. "L'intérêt s'étend du carton à chapeau de la midinette au plan futur de Paris, de Londres ou de Moscou. Le haïssable . . . serait de voir organiser à coups de milliards, sous la législation de l'État, l'exaltation du carton à chapeau à fleurs imprimées." Le Corbusier, *L'art décoratif d'aujourd'hui*, p. 188.

45. Forestier, "Les jardins de l'exposition des arts décoratifs," p. 24, and "Les jardins à l'exposition des arts décoratifs" (22 August 1925), p. 491.

46. One assumes that it was not pure chauvinism that prompted the critic H. de C. to censure the Italian submission; he also extended his sarcasm to a critique of the British pavilion: "The other comes hot from the Architectural Association pantomime; and appears incomplete without the full A.A. Beauty Chorus *rampant* on the front step." H. de C., "A General View," p. 3.

47. K. N. Afanasiev, ed., *Iz istorii sovetskoi arkhitektury, 1917–1925: Dokumenty i materialy* (Moscow, 1963), p. 190; *L'art décoratif et industriel de l'u.r.s.s.* (Moscow: Édition du comité de la section de l'u.r.s.s. à l'exposition internationale des arts décoratifs, 1925). Cited by S. Frederick Starr in *Melnikov*, pp. 87–88.

48. The critic Borissalievitch disassembled the building according to lines of tension and perspective; condemning the unjustified asymmetry, he suggested a parallel between such architectural whims and mental illness. "Mais, lorsque [la symétrie] n'est pas justifiée, elle choque notre sens esthétique. . . . 'L'emploi de l'asymétrie pour l'asymétrie par un jeune architecte m'a permis, dit le Dr Breucq . . . de prévoir longtemps à l'avance l'apparition chez lui d'une *affection mentale* à laquelle il a succombé récemment.'" Borissalievitch, "Promenade esthétique à l'exposition des arts décoratifs," pp. 152–53.

49. Van Montfort, "L'exposition internationale," p. 20; Janneau, "Le cadre de l'exposition," p. 159; Rambosson, "L'exposition des arts décoratifs: La participation étrangère: II," p. 172, respectively.

50. Several other entries countered the primary stream and instead advanced innovative architectural ideas. Kay Fisker, for example, built a monolithic pavilion of alternating red and white brick stripes for Denmark. Although its plan was inspired by the cross of Dannebrog, the Danish pavilion was described as a most remarkable exercise in modernity. Obviously unencumbered by any immoderate fondness for splendor, commented critics, Fisker did not rely on familiar solutions. Mourey, "La section danoise," p. 147; Rambosson, "L'exposition des arts décoratifs: La participation étrangère: II," p. 177.

51. For a plan and description of the greenhouse and its vegetation, see Redslob, "Ein neuer Typ des Wintergartens," pp. 221–23.

52. "On constate ici la différence fondamentale entre l'art allemand et l'art viennois, ce dernier plus souriant et plus souple. Le contraste frappe à un degré plus vif lorsque l'on pénètre dans la salle vitrée composée par M. Peter Behrens et qui, tout en étant fort bien comprise, reste davantage un travail d'ingénieur" (Rambosson, "L'exposition des arts décoratifs: La participation étrangère: I," p. 93). "M. Behrens s'en tenant à des combinaisons de lignes géométriques, à des masses un peu lourdes, sauf pour l'énorme lustre qui emplit tout le centre de la serre de ses pendeloques et de ses boules en cuivre jaune" (Chavance, "La section

217

autrichienne," p. 121). "[L'art viennois] est beaucoup plus près de l'art parisien que de l'art allemand" (Rambosson, "L'exposition des arts décoratifs: Les pavillons de la province et de l'étranger: Quelques aspects," p. 34).

53. H. de C., "A General View," p. 3.

54. In addition to the Pavillon du tourisme, Mallet-Stevens designed a garden, a tourist-information kiosk for the city of Paris, and a hall/*jardin d'hiver* for an ambassador. The importance of these commissions might be explained by the architect's being a relative of Paul Léon, a superintendent for the exposition. See Dominique Deshoulières and Hubert Jeanneau, "The Demands of Architecture," in *Rob Mallet-Stevens, architecte,* p. 47.

55. "Cependant, le béton armé est un moyen, ce n'est pas une fin. . . . Non, cette architecture n'est que de la fausse technique; la technique n'en est que le prétexte" (Hebbelynck, "L'exposition internationale," pp. 48, 50). "Parmi les bâtiments où l'effet décoratif est obtenu par l'accentuation des formes structurales propres au béton armé, . . . l'édifice le plus intéressant . . . est le bureau du Tourisme, où M. Mallet-Stevens a déployé un maximum de virtuosité dans le maniement du béton" (Landry "L'exposition des arts décoratifs. L'architecture: Section française," p. 208).

56. "Je cherche en vain dans ces stabilisateurs pour dirigeables la démonstration d'une technique exceptionnelle" (Hebbelynck, "L'exposition internationale," p. 49). "Ce vitrage même, fidèle aux images du monde tel qu'il

apparaît à ceux qui le parcourent en auto à raison de 120 kilomètres à l'heure, avertit les autres qu'ils peuvent rester chez eux et relire Töpffer" (Landry, "L'exposition des arts décoratifs," p. 208).

57. "It is with great satisfaction that I am taking the opportunity here to testify to the importance of Mallet-Stevens's work. His art—from what I have been able to judge during my personal visit to the international exhibition in Paris—distinguishes itself in a very decided and original way from that of his reactionary compatriots, who are striving to maintain the dazzling Parisian chic. Geometric precision of form, logical constructivism, a desire for a systematic arrangement of the world and volumes, work for the harmonious proportions of the whole, and are in opposition to the luxury inherent to the modern style." Konstantin Melnikov, introduction to *Mallet-Stevens: Dix années de réalisation en architecture et décoration* (Paris: Massin, 1930), cited by Deshoulières and Jeanneau, "The Demands of Architecture," in *Rob Mallet-Stevens, architecte,* pp. 48, 50.

58. There were inherent foundation problems with the pavilions on the eastern section of the esplanade because the Invalides railway station was situated just beneath the surface. Also, lawns and flower beds were laid on beams and had to be watered frequently. See Lacoste, "L'exposition internationale des arts décoratifs et industriels modernes de Paris—1925 (suite)," pp. 175–76.

59. Forestier, "Les jardins à l'exposition des arts décoratifs" (22 August 1925), p. 492.

60. A common feature of the seventeenth- and eighteenth-century French formal garden, the *boulingrin* is an adaptation of the English bowling green, consisting of a rectangular sunken lawn with sloping banks, or *glacis,* on all sides.

61. Apparently, boxwood or yews could not have provided the verticality and density of these green edges in time. Forestier thus resorted to an experiment that proved successful: wooden crates were filled with soil retained by chicken wire and planted with a variety of *Sempervivum.* Forestier, "Les jardins à l'exposition des arts décoratifs" (22 August 1925), p. 492.

62. Bac, "L'art des jardins à l'exposition des arts décoratifs," p. 136.

63. "Représentent dans un paroxysme antiphysique . . . la stylisation du végétal" (Landry, "L'exposition des arts décoratifs," p. 212). "Un placide arroseur municipal, la lance à la main, tombe en arrêt devant un arbre en ciment armé, incertain de savoir s'il requiert, aussi, ses soins" (Beauplan, "À travers la kermesse de Paris"). "Plus loin nous trouvons un jardin très simple, mais assez original, malheureusement orné de quatre palmiers lourdement stylisés, coulés en ciment" (Charensol "La rue—les jardins," p. 326).

64. "Où les frères Martel, hélas! avaient élevé des arbres en béton armé" (Fischer, "L'art décoratif moderne: Les jardins"). "Mallet-Stevens probablement avec une arrière-pensée de blague, voulant à

toute force des arbres, les a imaginés en ciment armé" (Weber, "Les jardins," p. 60). "Il faut bien en parler cependant, ne serait-ce que pour le succès d'hilarité et d'effarement qu'ils ont eu" (Risler, "Les objets d'art à l'exposition des arts décoratifs," p. 418).

65. Morgenthau Fox, "Jean C.N. Forestier," pp. 98–99.

66. Steele, "New Pioneering in Garden Design," pp. 165–66.

67. Forestier, "Les jardins de l'exposition des arts décoratifs," p. 24.

68. Forestier, "Les jardins à l'exposition des arts décoratifs" (22 August 1925), p. 492.

69. "[Une œuvre] intéressante, il est vrai, comme réalisation, mieux que pour son emploi habituel dans les jardins (Forestier, "Les jardins à l'exposition des arts décoratifs" [22 August 1925], p. 492). "Le résultat fut incontestablement intéressant" (Forestier, "Les jardins de l'exposition des arts décoratifs," p. 24).

70. Forestier, "Les jardins de l'exposition des arts décoratifs," p. 20.

71. Morgenthau Fox, "Jean C.N. Forestier," pp. 98–99.

72. Mallet-Stevens in "Frank Lloyd Wright," special issue of *Wendingen* (1925); cited by Banham in *Theory and Design in the First Machine Age*, p. 202.

73. "The Department of Promenades headed by M. Forestier is not easily cheated. All the trees are numbered, the height of the lowest branches and the protruding mass of the foliage are recorded. The guard is keeping a close watch: not a branch will be broken and not

a plant will be torn." Dervaux, "L'exposition des arts décoratifs," pp. 49–50.

74. "Si tous les résultats ne furent pas également heureux, je crois qu'il ne faut pas trop facilement se désintéresser de ces efforts que, pour ma part, je n'avais pas provoqués sans quelque crainte" (Forestier, "Les jardins de l'exposition des arts décoratifs," p. 24). "Mieux que de chercher le cadre impossible du jardin public banal, il y avait à trouver de menus morceaux pour lesquels des artistes ardents aux recherches pourraient, dans des éléments de jardin, donner libre carrière à leurs sentiments, à leur imagination, surtout dans l'emploi des matériaux nouveaux" (Forestier, cited by Marrast in his introductory text to *1925 Jardins*, n.p.).

75. Forestier, "Les jardins de l'exposition des arts décoratifs," p. 24; and "Les jardins à l'exposition des arts décoratifs" (22 August 1925), p. 492.

76. "Entre l'allée du Pavillon de la Ville de Paris et le jardin de Marrast, il y avait un grand espace rectangulaire; la Société 'Pour les jardins' s'est chargée de le décorer; les fleurs qu'elle a apportées sont très belles, mais elles sont arrangées avec une mignardise un peu niaise; que signifient ces corbeilles et ces paniers, posés sur le gazon comme sur un buffet de mariage?" Weber, "Les jardins," p. 60.

77. For a description of the gardens on the Cours-la-Reine, see Forestier, "Les jardins à l'exposition des arts décoratifs," (8 and 22 August 1925).

78. Forestier, "Les jardins de l'exposition des arts décoratifs," p. 22.

79. "Au fond, un bassin terminal en octogone; bancs rouges, jarres pansues et un dallage en opus incertum complètent l'allure très latine de ce jardin" (Lambert, "Jardins et fontaines," p. 139). "Son inspiration, quoique très française de parti général, n'est pas sans rappeler dans ses escaliers un motif cher aux jardins italiens et par ses longs bassins les ingénieux dispositifs d'eau des jardins orientaux" (*L'Architecte*, 1925, p. 96).

80. "Dans le jardin où l'architecte Marrast & l'horticulteur Moser ont si heureusement uni leurs efforts, l'or, le bleu, le vert, les vases pansus, les bancs rouges, les jeux de l'eau & les dalles cernées par les cordons verts ont été associés à l'éclat d'une masse inusitée de fleurs" (Forestier, "Les jardins de l'exposition des arts décoratifs," p. 21). "Le jardin Marrast, dont la parure florale renouvelée à profusion, massifs solides des rhododendrons, nuages épais des hortensias, nappes des bégonias, couvre les deux pentes d'un petit vallon s'enfonçant sous les arbres et que vient animer l'eau jaillissant d'une vasque plate à mosaïque d'or. Un bassin en croissant où dorment des nénuphars la recueille un moment et la laisse fluer dans une longue rigole basse à margelle ponctuée de prismes de marbre, lumineux la nuit et fleuris" (Lambert, "Jardins et fontaines," p. 139).

81. Forestier, "Les jardins de l'exposition des arts décoratifs," p. 21.

82. A replica of the plan was executed immediately after the

fair for one of its visitors, Mr. Ohan Berberyan. The Palm Beach garden featured the same central pool bordered with irregular paving; the principal decorative motifs were also maintained, except that the vases were terra cotta rather than cement and the water allée was framed by a pergola and palm trees. See Rémon, "Un jardin en Floride par M. Marrast, architecte," pp. 33–37.

83. "Mon long séjour au Maroc, les Jardins que j'y ai dessinés ou réalisés m'ont quelque peu influencé, et je rêve toujours de ces 'Riads' où tout est ordre et beauté, luxe, calme et volupté. Bien entendu, il ne s'agit pas de pastiches à réaliser sous le ciel de l'Île-de-France; mais j'avoue avoir un fol amour des fleurs encastrées dans l'architecture, qu'elle soit de gazon, de briques, de marbres ou même de béton." Albert Laprade on the art of gardens, as interviewed by *La Vie à la Campagne* and cited by A. G., "À l'exposition des arts décoratifs: Le bassin des nymphéas," p. 37.

84. "Les jardins les plus réussis de l'Exposition, réalisés par des hommes qui ont fait leurs preuves, au Maroc et ailleurs, se situent de préférence dans ces climats." Bac, "L'art des jardins à l'exposition des arts décoratifs," p. 138.

85. "Le Bassin des Nymphéas nous semble quelque peu nu puisque c'est presque une cour au milieu d'une place publique." A. G., "À l'exposition des arts décoratifs: Le bassin des nymphéas," p. 38.

86. H. de C., "A General View," pp. 6, 10.

87. These vases were frequently criticized for their height. Twenty-three feet tall, they disrupted the perspective of the Dome of the Invalides. See Dacier, "La manufacture de Sèvres à l'exposition des arts décoratifs," pp. 180, 182; Rambosson, "L'exposition des arts décoratifs: La section française," p. 319; Lacoste, "L'exposition des arts décoratifs," December 1925, p. 175.

88. Dacier, "La manufacture de Sèvres," pp. 179–88; Goissaud, "La manufacture nationale de Sèvres," pp. 544–45.

89. "Si l'on critique les vases de M. Laprade, que dira-t-on de ceux dont la Manufacture de Sèvres a orné un de ces jardins 'abotaniques' qu'il vaudrait mieux dénommer cours?" Landry, "L'exposition des arts décoratifs," p. 203.

90. Goissaud, "La manufacture nationale de Sèvres," p. 545; Dacier, "La manufacture de Sèvres," p. 186.

91. "Si J.-C.-N. Forestier, conservateur des promenades de Paris, n'a formellement signé aucun des jardins de l'Exposition tous lui doivent quelque chose, notamment leur caractère méditerranéen." Luc Benoist, "L'exposition internationale des arts décoratifs et industriels modernes: Les arts graphiques. Les arts de la rue et des jardins," p. 262. Perhaps Forestier had exerted an indirect impact on the North African–influenced lanscapes of Marrast and Laprade, having recommended Henri Prost as a planner for Morocco.

92. Forestier, "Les jardins à l'exposition des arts décoratifs" (12 September 1925), p. 526.

93. "Puis les fameuses asperges rouges qui se dressent à droite et à gauche de l'esplanade et qui sont bien la chose la plus ridicule de cette exposition." Charensol, "La rue—les jardins," p. 327.

94. À l'exposition des arts décoratifs: Les jardins," p. 17.

95. Huxley, "Notes on Decoration," p. 239.

96. "On y sentait dominer de multiples influences méditerranéennes, exotiques, persanes, arabes, sans qu'aucune exclût toutefois le sentiment traditionnel" ("Parcs et jardins. Arbres et arbustes, plantes et fleurs," in *Encyclopédie des arts décoratifs et industriels modernes au XX° siècle*, vol. 11, *Rue et jardin*, p. 73). "Et si, avec d'aucuns, on pense à quelque patio d'Alhambra, à certain campo siennois vus à travers une arcade latérale, ce n'est pas pour évoquer une quelconque imitation. . . . Voilà un art moderne dont la France peut être fière" (Dervaux, "L'exposition des arts décoratifs," p. 54). George Rémon described the garden Marrast designed near the Cours-la-Reine as an ensemble "bien français" in inspiration and spirit, despite its borrowed vocabulary (Rémon, "Un jardin en Floride," p. 36).

97. A. G., "À l'exposition des arts décoratifs: Le bassin des nymphéas," p. 37.

98. Forestier, "Les jardins à l'exposition des arts décoratifs" (12 September 1925), p. 526.

99. Ibid.

100. "Aveu de la nécessité qu'il y a à considérer le jardin comme un véritable tableau d'art, à revenir aux saines traditions du dessin." Forestier, "Les jardins de l'exposition des arts décoratifs," p. 19. For a

brief discussion of Simultane-ism, see chapter 4, n. 49.

101. This disgruntled critic denounced Guevrekian for not making his sources obvious and for occupying a prominent site that was initially intended for Mr. Ploquin's "elegant project": a fountain with statues of a reclining woman and a goat. "M. *Guevrékian* ne s'est inspiré d'aucun jardin ancien, c'est certain, et n'a obéi à aucune règle sur les jardins, c'est encore plus certain. . . . Pour permettre à M. *Guevrékian* d'occuper cet emplacement, on a refusé un projet élégant proposé par M. *Ploquin*, architecte paysagiste, lequel devait y placer une charmante fontaine, œuvre d'un sculpteur éminent, M. *Prozinski*, représentant une femme étendue dans un bassin et un bélier, laquelle a été reléguée dans un coin désert du Cours-la-Reine. On nous permettra de le regretter" ("À l'exposition des arts décoratifs: Les jardins," pp. 17–18). Iron-ically, this same sculptural composition was characterized by another critic as "painful." "Quelques sculptures pénibles comme cette femme étendue à plat ventre dans un bassin et qui regarde un bouc penché vers elle" (Weber, "Les jar-dins," p. 61).

102. "Only artists of extraordi-nary talent neglect tradition with impunity." Huxley, "Notes on Decoration," p. 239.

103. Forestier, "Les jardins à l'exposition des arts déco-ratifs" (12 September 1925), p. 526.

104. Forestier, "Les jardins de l'exposition des arts déco-ratifs," p. 21.

105. For a plan of the Grand Palais with the various exhibits, see "Exposition des arts décoratifs et industriels modernes. Intérieur du Grand Palais. Ch. Letrosne, archi-tecte," pp. 76–77.

106. Forestier, "Le jardin mo-derne et l'exposition des arts décoratifs," pp. 92–94.

107. Vera, "Exhortation aux architectes de s'intéresser au jardin," dated 1923, published in *L'Architecte* (1924), pp. 68–71, and in *L'urbanisme ou la vie heureuse* (1936), pp. 169–76.

108. Vera, *Le nouveau jardin*, pp. 9–10.

109. " L'exposition de 1925, en effet, n'entend pas nous mon-trer des œuvres d'exception: elle nous montrera l'art dans la vie, c'est-à-dire dans l'objet d'usage et dans la réalité con-crète." Janneau, "Ce que sera l'exposition de 1925," p. 320.

110. "On fait le reproche à l'exposition des arts décoratifs d'être très peu démocratique. Certes, il aurait été utile pour ce qui nous concerne, de mon-trer un potager, un projet de jardin pour maison ouvrière; mais encore une fois, on man-quait de la place nécessaire et il fallait se contenter de placer d'agréables décorations frag-mentaires, inutilisables ailleurs." Weber, "Les jardins," p. 62.

111. " 'L'avenir est aux *jardins à compartiments*.' . . . En effet, à ce nivellement des fortunes et des conditions correspond un rétrécissement du faste d'autrefois et la transforma-tion de celui-ci va diminuant chaque jour jusqu'à la limite de ces jardins si ingénieuse-ment tracés dans les nouvelles cités ouvrières, distribuant à chacun une petite parcelle de

nature disciplinée. La significa-tion sociale de l'Exposition est immense. L'avenir s'y lit comme dans un livre. La vieille Europe se meurt au seuil de la cité-jardin qui sera le logis-type de la société future. Les meilleurs de nos artistes . . . ont déjà trouvé un terrain de conciliation entre le présent et l'avenir." Bac, "L'art des jardins à l'exposition des arts décoratifs," p. 138.

112. Léon, *Rapport général: Exposition internationale des arts décoratifs et industriels modernes. Paris, 1925*, vol. 9, *Section rue et jardin*, p. 70.

113. Weber, "Les jardins," p. 62.

114. Dezarrois, "Avant l'ouver-ture de l'exposition," p. 219.

CHAPTER 4:
JARDIN RÉGULIER;
JARDIN D'ARCHITECTURE

1. See Pevsner, "The Genesis of the Picturesque," pp. 79–101.

2. Paul Valéry cited by Banham in *Theory and Design in the First Machine Age*, p. 12.

3. Vera, "Le nouveau style," pp. 21–32; "Modernité et tradition: Lettre sur les jardins," pp. 89–97; and "Pour le renouveau de l'art français: Le jardin," pp. 1–4.

4. Vera, "Modernité et tradition," p. 96.

5. "Vera est intelligent de faire un livre dont la teneur et l'esprit s'adressent à 1 seule catégorie de gens." Notes taken by Le Corbusier at the Bibliothèque Nationale during the summer of 1915. Fondation Le Corbusier, Paris, B2–20, 79.

6. Zach, "Modernistic Work and Its Natural Limitations," p. 293.

7. Badovici, "L'art d'Eileen Gray par Jean Badovici, architecte," p. 13.

8. *Le Bulletin de la Vie Artistique* (1 November 1924), cited by Janneau in "Introduction à l'exposition des arts décoratifs: Considérations sur l'esprit moderne," pp. 131–32.

9. Blomfield and Thomas, *The Formal Garden in England*, p. 2.

10. Vera, *Le nouveau jardin*, p. iv.

11. Ibid., p. iii.

12. "Aussi, pour les objets mobiliers ne prendrons-nous conseil ni des Anglais ni des Hollandais, mais continuerons-nous la tradition française, faisant en sorte que ce style nouveau soit la suite du dernier style traditionnel que nous ayons, c'est-à-dire du style Louis-Philippe. Vera, "Le nouveau style," p. 31.

13. "Nous ne ferons point de pastiches. Des chefs-d'œuvre de Le Nôtre, nous retirerons, ainsi qu'il convient, des chose nouvelles et des choses anciennes: des façons autoritaires à transposer en tous lieux, des désirs précis pour les Résidences d'Hiver ou d'Été, comme pour les petits jardins, et de solides préceptes sur la composition" (Vera, *Les jardins*, p. 21). "En un mot la tradition commande de tenir les parties entre elles dans un rapport mathématique" (Vera, "Exhortation aux architectes de s'intéresser au jardin," p. 69).

14. "Nous sommes d'ailleurs, ramenés à la France d'une façon décisive par réaction à l'internationalisme. . . . C'est donc à la fois par un besoin nouveau de notre goût et par une réaction à des influences intérieures que nous nous soumettons à la discipline française." Vera, "Le nouveau style," p. 31.

15. Vera, *L'homme et le jardin*, p. 229.

16. Steele, "New Styles in Gardening: Will Landscape Architecture Reflect the Modernistic Tendencies Seen in the Other Arts?" p. 354.

17. Vera, "Exhortation aux architectes de s'intéresser au jardin," p. 68.

18. Ibid. Exposed concrete in the garden had been used previously at the Vienna Kunstschau of 1908.

19. Ibid., p. 69.

20. See "Contemporary Trends and Future Possibilities in Landscape Design," pp. 288–303; and Steele, "New Styles in Gardening," pp. 350, 352–54.

21. Zach, "Modernistic Work," pp. 293–94.

22. Wheelwright, "Thoughts on Problems of Form," pp. 1–10.

23. *Salle fraîche* generally refers to an exterior "cool room," an architectural or vegetal space, a grotto, a garden lanai, a secluded outdoor room, or an enclosed veranda functioning as a transitional space between indoor and outdoor. One example of a salle fraîche was Moreux's design for the château de Maulny (1930).

24. See the gloriettes Moreux conceived for the square Croulebarbe in 1936, similar to those of the vegetable garden at Villandry, restored circa 1915 after a Renaissance model (chapter 5).

25. Moreux, "Éloge du jardin régulier français," p. 65.

26. Ibid., pp. 65–66.

27. "Pour ce qui est de la coloration propre des plates-bandes, nous tirerons expérience de la coiffure et du costume que porte la femme moderne" (Vera, *Le nouveau jardin*, p. 10). "Le dessin de buis devant la maison a forme de grecque. . . . Il est de circonstance, à l'exemple de ceux que Le Nôtre faisait: on le voit aux vêtements de nos contemporaines, en particulier, à leurs tricots de soie" (Vera, "Jardin dans la banlieue," p. 25).

28. Vera, "Exhortation aux architectes," p. 69; and "Jardin dans la banlieue," p. 24.

29. "La *beauté* sobre et élégante du navire moderne"; "Dans quelque attitude qu'elle soit jetée, avec quelque allure qu'elle soit lancée, une voiture, comme un vaisseau, emprunte au mouvement une grâce mys-

térieuse et complexe très difficile à sténographier." Baudelaire, "Le peintre de la vie moderne," pp. 469, 501, respectively.

30. "Une femme de ménage suffit à l'entretien." Vera, "Promenade à travers siècles et jardins" (1935), in L'urbanisme ou la vie heureuse, p. 244.

31. Vera, "Pour le renouveau de l'art français," p. 1.

32. Vera, Le nouveau jardin, p. 55; and Les jardins, p. 23.

33. Blomfield and Thomas, The Formal Garden in England, p. 2.

34. Vera, "Exhortation aux architectes," p. 70.

35. Vera, Le nouveau jardin, pp. 9–10.

36. Duprat, "Le jardin paysager," p. 44.

37. Vera, Le nouveau jardin, p. 7.

38. Girardin, De la composition des paysages, p. 20.

39. Published in the article "Réponse à l'enquête 'chez les cubistes,'" Bulletin de la Vie Artistique (January 1925); cited by Rosenthal in Juan Gris, p. 166.

40. Deshairs, "L'exposition des arts décoratifs. La section française: Conclusion," pp. 205–17.

41. In 1914, Duchamp-Villon also proposed a Projet d'architecture, which consisted of the ornamentation for the facade of an American college dormitory. For a detailed description of the Maison Cubiste, see Troy, Modernism and the Decorative Arts in France.

42. In his tribute to Duchamp-Villon, Walter Pach recalled the Maison Cubiste as an architecture that was "new, but readable and reassuring in its incorporation of 'cubist'

forms" (Pach, "Raymond Duchamp-Villon," in Raymond Duchamp-Villon, sculpteur [1876–1918], p. 13). The sculptor himself wrote: "C'est, je crois, de cette donnée que nous devons nous inspirer pour établir un décor d'architecture nouveau, non pas que nous essayions d'adapter les formes et les lignes mêmes des objects caractéristiques de notre temps, ce qui ne serait qu'une transposition de ces lignes et de ces formes en d'autre matières, partant une erreur—mais bien plutôt que nous nous pénétrions inlassablement des rapports de ces objets entre eux, pour les interpréter en des lignes, des plans et des volumes synthétiques, qui s'équilibreront, à leur tour, en des rythmes analogues à ceux de la vie qui nous entoure" (Duchamp-Villon, letter dated 16 January 1913, "Extraits de lettres de Raymond Duchamp-Villon," in Raymond Duchamp-Villon, sculpteur [1876–1918], p. 18).

43. Bruno Zevi, 1950, cited by Jorge Romero Brest in "Cubism and Futurism," Encyclopedia of World Art, vol. 4 (New York: McGraw-Hill, 1961), p. 156.

44. "La théorie cubiste se résume donc à une théorie à posteriori qui n'a commencé à prendre figure logique que vers 1918 alors que le cubisme en tant qu'école homogène n'est plus." Ozenfant, "Sur les écoles cubistes et post-cubistes," p. 291.

45. Artists such as Henri Laurens, Jacques Lipchitz, or Alexander Archipenko sculpted according to cubist aesthetics.

46. The fourth dimension was "supposedly generated by the

three known measures: it [represented] the immensity of space eternalized in all directions at a determined moment." Apollinaire, Les peintres cubistes, pp. 61–62.

47. Braque cited by Burgess in "The Wild Men of Paris," p. 405.

48. Cézanne's decomposition of nature into the cylinder, sphere, and cone is often cited as one of the first clues to the emergence of cubism. Ivan Margolius, on the other hand, states that the cubist movement was a reaction against the primacy of the curving lines of those geometric solids. This "move from the appearance to the essence [and] from the natural to the anti-natural" was epitomized in the use of the straight line. Margolius, Cubism in Architecture and the Applied Arts, p. 24.

49. Orphism, or orphic cubism, was a term attributed to and vaguely described by the poet and artist Guillaume Apollinaire. Developed mainly by Robert Delaunay and his wife, Sonia, Orphism considered cubism only as a premise and in its place explored the essence of color. Simultaneism was a term and technique evolved from M. E. Chevrel's theory of Simultaneist contrast. See Chevrel, De la loi du contraste simultané.

50. For a description of the proportional fields of Man in the Café and Smoker, see Rosenthal, Juan Gris, pp. 33–34.

51. V. V. Stech, "Tschechische Bestrebungen um ein modernes Interieur" (Prague, 1915); written for the Deutscher Werkbund Exhibition, Cologne, 1914; cited by Margolius in Cubism in Architecture, p. 82.

223

52. Gabriel Guevrekian's garden for the Villa Noailles in Hyères was recently rebuilt under the supervision of Cécile Briolle, Claude Marro, and Jacques Repiquet.

53. Robert Riley, editor of *Landscape Journal*, describes the architect's plant palette as belonging to the "fragrant I-beam school." Conversation with the author, Champaign, Illinois, summer 1988.

54. "D'autres se sentent plutôt constructeurs et aménagent des . . . lieux de repos maçonnés ou bétonnés dans lesquels la verdure et la fleur jouent un rôle de personnages au milieu d'autres." Rambosson, "Un jardin de Pierre Legrain," p. 1.

55. Giedion, *Space, Time and Architecture*, pp. 381–82.

56. The second maxim advised not to obscure the garden with an excess of vegetation; the third, in contrast, warned against a garden with nothing to arrest the view. The conclusive rule of thumb was to make the garden seem larger than it actually was. Dezallier d'Argenville, *La théorie et la pratique du jardinage*, p. 18

57. Ozenfant, "Sur les écoles cubistes et post-cubistes," p. 295.

58. Clouzot. "L'avant-garde de l'art appliqué," p. 24.

59. Giedion, *Space, Time and Architecture*, p. 416.

60. Ibid., p. 401.

61. Alfred Barr cited by Steele in "New Pioneering in Garden Design," p. 161.

62. Albert Gleizes and Jean Metzinger, *Du cubisme* (Paris: Figuière, 1912); cited by Deshairs in "Pablo Picasso," p. 82.

63. Vera, *Le nouveau jardin*, p. 10.

CHAPTER 5:
ANDRÉ VERA; PAUL VERA; JEAN-CHARLES MOREUX

1. Steele, "New Styles in Gardening," p. 354.

2. Dervaux, "L'exposition des arts décoratifs et industriels modernes," p. 47.

3. Janneau, "Introduction à l'exposition des arts décoratifs: Considérations sur l'esprit moderne," pp. 129–76.

4. Vera, "Paul Vera décorateur," p. 25.

5. Forestier, "Le jardin moderne et l'exposition des arts décoratifs," p. 94.

6. Vera, "Le petit jardin," n.p.

7. Vera, "Modernité et tradition: Lettre sur les jardins," p. 91. The same text was also a chapter in *Les jardins*.

8. "Étant soumis et fructueux, non point indépendants et producteurs exclusivement de feuilles, puissent-ils suggérer aux propriétaires le désir de gagner une valeur sociale!" Ibid.

9. "Pour ce qui est des autres arbres, vous les choisirez d'abord dans la flore régionale, non dans le but de produire des effets pittoresques, mais afin de constituer les témoins de notre attachement à la province que nous habitons: nous nous réjouissons des ressources variées de notre pays. . . . Vous ferez ensuite grand cas des matières brillantes et sompteuses que vous offrent les variétés de thuya, de troène" (Vera, "Modernité et tradition," p. 91). "Plantons . . . non pas des cèdres du Liban ou des catalpas, mais des arbres ou arbrisseaux qui soient de notre pays" (Vera, "Pour le renouveau de l'art français: Le jardin," p. 2).

10. "En élévation, la structure apparaîtra solidement établie, si elle est constituée par des résineux . . . choisis résolument d'origine étrangère pour être sans faute de taille gigantesque, de port régulier, de branchage abondant, de feuillage épais, de matière sompteuse (*Abies pinsapo, Abies grandis, Abies nordmanniana, Picea morinda, Pseudotsuga douglasii, Sequoia gigantea, Thuya atrovirens, Thuya gigantea*)." Vera, "Jardins publics," in *L'homme et le jardin*, p. 189.

11. "'Développez en vous, disait Pie XII, le sens profond de votre passé et de votre terre.' Ce conseil doit nous décider non à l'exotisme, non au dépaysement, non au pastiche, mais au régionalisme et à la modernité." Vera, "Pour le renouveau de l'art français: Le jardin," p. 2.

12. Vera, "Modernité et tradition," pp. 90–91.

13. Vera, *Le nouveau jardin*, p. 56.

14. "Le premier soin serait de n'avoir qu'animaux de pur sang, chefs-d'œuvre de nature, plutôt blancs de couleur, livrée domestique, au plus haut degré, l'acte de mimétisme devenant impossible." Vera, "Lettres sur les jardins," p. 7.

15. *Thébaïde* refers to an area of southern Egypt (the capital of which was Thebes) where early Christian ascetics retired.

16. Vera, "Le jardin de M. André Vera à Saint-Germain-en-Laye," p. 6.

17. Although the species was described as *Euonymus radicans*, today it would be classified as *Euonymus fortunei radicans*. Vera recommended that the lattice structures be painted a different color than the usual dull green. In describing the garden of La Thébaïde, one article

mentioned red, and another mustard yellow. Vera, "Jardin dans la banlieue," p. 25; and "Jardin dans la banlieue—André et Paul Vera," p. 72.

18. Vera, "Le jardin de M. André Vera à Saint-Germain-de-Laye," p. 6.

19. "Ce jardin régulier, aux formes élémentaires, contient les végétaux à feuillage coloré, à floraison prolongée, dûs à la curiosité des ancêtres romantiques; aussi se trouve-t-il posséder plus d'éclat, étant coloré de toutes les couleurs des fanions romantiques, qu'aucun jardin régulier des siècles passés." Vera, "Promenade à travers siècles et jardins" (1935), in L'Urbanisme ou la vie heureuse, p. 243.

20. Vera, "Jardin dans la banlieue—André et Paul Vera," p. 72; and "Jardin dans la banlieue," pp. 24–25.

21. Paul Vera also played tradition against contemporaneity in the garden for Paul-Élie Gernez, situated in Honfleur, Normandy. This design featured modern vernacular ornaments composed of surfaces and volumes of cement inlaid with seashells. See Vera, "Le jardin de Paul Gernez dessiné par Paul Vera," pp. 2–8.

22. "[La cohésion] est obtenue de la même manière, sans pièces superflues, que dans une machine. Ainsi l'ingénieur, l'honnête homme d'aujourd'hui, a satisfaction" (Vera, "Jardin dans la banlieue," p. 24; and "Exhortation aux architectes de s'intéresser au jardin," p. 69). "Tout sur moi est rectangle et rectiligne; tout sur moi est propre, net, exact et comparti. J'ai de cette manière le style d'un paquebot, comme il plaît si fort à nos décorateurs" (Vera, "Le jardin de Paul Gernez," p. 4).

23. Baudelaire, "La Modernité," in "Le peintre de la vie moderne," p. 467.

24. "Vous désirez voir carrés, doubles carrés, rectangles, triangles, multiples communs, le tracé régulateur qui fait un canevas aux formes prochaines, les linéaments devant attacher le jardin à l'habitation" (Vera, "Lettres sur les jardins," p. 4). "Les choses ont ici, sans lourde insistance, un même multiple, un secret commun. La nature est maintenue dans des liens invisibles. Des accords sont réalisés. Les œuvres à ce point, disait Eupalinos, commencent de chanter" (Vera, "Jardin dans la banlieue," p. 24). See Valéry, Eupalinos or the Architect.

25. Vera, "Hommage à Le Nôtre," p. 73. For a proportional decomposition of the parterres and sections of the garden, see Vera, "Modernité et tradition," pp. 93–95.

26. Vera, Le nouveau jardin, pp. 9–10.

27. Vera, "Avec l'aviateur," in Les jardins, p. 136.

28. The title of architecte de jardins was conferred on Paul by André Vera. See Hébert, Mémorial des frères Vera, p. 141.

29. Vera, "Le jardin de Paul Gernez," p. 4. The plan of the public garden in Honfleur is dated 1930 and is at the Musée d'art et d'histoire (Donation Vera), Saint-Germain-en-Laye, 972. 7. 372 ter.

30. Vera, "Le jardin de Paul Gernez," p. 3.

31. See Vera, Le nouveau jardin and Les jardins.

32. Vera, Le nouveau jardin, p. 83.

33. Vera, "Jardin dans la banlieue," p. 24; and "Modernité et tradition," pp. 93–95.

34. "Seulement par l'architecte le jardin peut renaître avec les arts connexes. Au paysager la statue est nudité sortant d'un taillis et gambadant sur l'herbe. . . . Au lieu de l'imprécision, le souci moderne ne cherche-t-il point une évaluation par chiffres ou graphiques? On ne se cache rien. On veut se rendre compte. Des compteurs sont partout." Vera, "Nouvelle exhortation aux architectes de s'intéresser au jardin," in L'Urbanisme ou la vie heureuse, p. 181.

35. Vera, "Modernité et tradition," p. 90.

36. Vera wrote the "Exhortation aux architectes de s'intéresser au jardin" in 1923, but obviously the architects of the time were not listening. In 1924 he tried a second time, publishing—ever optimistically—a "Nouvelle exhortation aux architectes de s'intéresser au jardin."

37. Vera, "Modernité et tradition," p. 90.

38. Vera, "Jardin d'amour," pp. 30–31.

39. Ibid., p. 31.

40. The "Jardin d'amour" was more widely known through the collection of similar hypothetical gardens published in Les jardins.

41. Forestier, "Le jardin moderne et l'exposition des arts décoratifs," p. 94.

42. Vera, "Le jardin rationalisé" (1926), in L'Urbanisme ou la vie heureuse, pp. 213–14.

43. André Lurçat published a photograph of the Noailles garden in Terrasses et jardins. The caption reads: "Jardin de l'hôtel du vicomte de N. à Paris. P. Vera, Architecte à Paris." The anonymous author of the article "Chez le Cte

Charles de Noailles" attributed the design of the stone bench to Paul Vera, although there are no credits for the overall design. Janine Hébert, the keeper of the Veras' memory, includes Moreux as a designer for the Noailles garden. Hébert, *Mémorial des frères Vera*, p. 142.

44. Charles de Noailles eventually became vice-president of the Royal Horticultural Society in London and honorary president of both the International Dendrology Society and the Société Française des Amateurs de Jardins.

45. Pierre Legrain created a garden for Jeanne Tachard's villa in La Celle-Saint-Cloud in 1924. Gabriel Guevrekian designed two pictorial gardens, one for the 1925 Exposition in Paris and the other for the vicomte de Noailles in Hyères, in 1927. See chapters 6 and 7.

46. "Chez le Cte Charles de Noailles," p. 16.

47. See "Chez le Cte Charles de Noailles," p. 16; and Steele, "New Pioneering in Garden Design," p. 164.

48. Vera, "Modernité et tradition," pp. 90-91.

49. Ibid., p. 94.

50. Vera, "Jardin dans la banlieue," p. 25.

51. See Cooper, *The Cubist Epoch*, p. 202; Rosenthal, *Juan Gris*, p. 29; Kahnweiler, *Juan Gris*, p. 125.

52. Berger, "The Moment of Cubism," p. 172.

53. *Papier-collé* (pasted paper) refers to a cubist technique of adding fragments of paper to the painting, either to represent an object or concept, or to establish a connection between two different dimensions—by

the juxtaposition of the real fragment and the illusory medium. The collage technique also involved the use of materials other than paper, such as fragments of oilcloth, caning, or mirror.

54. Chéret, "Il y a un an disparaissait Jean-Charles Moreux, dernier homme de la Renaissance," p. 8.

55. Moreux was chargé de mission au Commissariat à la Reconstruction Immobilière. I am indebted to Gilles Ragot for kindly providing me with his chronology of Moreux's projects and designs, which he established in preparation for a monograph on Jean-Charles Moreux, to be published by the Institut Français d'Architecture.

56. In 1944 Moreux held the position of lecturer (chargé de conférences) on the art of the garden at the Institut des Hautes Études d'Architecture.

57. Moreux joined the U.A.M. in 1931. He was named Architecte en Chef des Bâtiments Civils et des Palais Nationaux in 1944.

58. Champigneulle, "Architecte habile, décorateur raffiné, il était considéré comme un dilettante," p. 8. Jean-Charles Moreux interviewed in "Où va l'architecture. Réponse de J.C. Moreux," p. 132.

59. "Où va l'architecture," p. 132; Champigneulle, "Architecte habile," p. 8.

60. Moreux cited in "Où va l'architecture," p. 132.

61. Both Jean-Marie Dubois, in his article titled "Jean-Charles Moreux" (pp. 30–31), and Gilles Ragot, in his chronology on Moreux, describe the Noailles garden as a collaboration between Moreux and Paul Vera.

62. The date of 1920 is based on the uncertain participation of Moreux in the Vera garden at Saint-Germain-en-Laye; 1924 dates a collaboration of Moreux and Paul Vera on a hôtel and garden project presented at the Salon d'Automne.

63. These were Moreux's own terms.

64. Georges Zezos, "Sous le ciel de Paris en évoquant le jardin du Shepheard's avec l'architecte Moreux," *La Bourse Égyptienne*, 28 May 1947. Fonds Jean-Charles Moreux, Institut Français d'Architecture, Paris, 2-163.

65. Moreux, "Le jardin français du moyen-âge à nos jours," p. 8.

66. Marquetry describes a pattern inlaid with different colors of wood, ivory, or marble. It can refer to floors as well as to pieces of furniture.

67. Moreux, "Éloge du jardin régulier français," p. 62; "Le jardin français du moyen-âge à nos jours," p. 7.

68. Moreux cited in "Où va l'architecture," p. 132.

69. François David-Weill was another supporter of the U.A.M., for whom Jean-Charles Moreux designed a garden in 1934. For a list of the initial members and benefactors, see Herbst, *25 années u.a.m.*, p. 16.

70. See Jacques Rouché, *L'art théâtral moderne*. "Mais ce qui est important encore, et ce que le décorateur ne doit jamais perdre de vue, c'est l'époque même où il vit, l'ensemble des sensations, des idées, des impressions, des notions communes à ses contemporains, et qui constituent la *vision d'art* particulière à chaque génération" (p. 2). "De plus personnage et décor sont inséparables: l'un et l'autre doivent concourir à procurer une impression unique et harmonieuse" (p. 7).

71. Modeled after the creations of the Russian Léon Bakst or the Italian Mario Fortuny, numerous highly pictorial productions followed. Serge Diaghilev directed *Parade* for the Ballet russes, with music by Erik Satie, costumes and sets by Pablo Picasso, and libretto by Jean Cocteau. It premiered in Paris in 1917. Fernand Léger collaborated with Darius Milhaud on the play-ballet of *La Création du Monde* in 1922, a Ballet suédois directed by Rolf de Maré. L'Opéra de Paris produced *David Triomphant* in 1937, with sets by Léger. See Bachollet, Bordet, and Lelieur, *Paul Iribe,* p. 108; Glover, *The Cubist Theater,* pp. 25–35; Cooper, *Fernand Léger et le nouvel espace,* pp. 149–51, 156–57.

72. A full-scale mock-up of the pool's mosaic patterns by Paul Vera is in the collection of Mrs. Janine Hébert, at Saint-Germain-en-Laye.

73. The Moreux archives contain a sketch plan of the côté-cour signed by Vera, while the plan for the other section of the garden is signed by Moreux, which could support the assumption regarding their respective responsibilities.

74. Moreux designed both the house and grounds for the Maison Brugier, in Saint-Cloud, in 1926, and the garden for Eugène Yvon, in Cherbourg, in 1932–33.

75. For a description of the materials and color scheme for this garden see "Jardins de Paris: Chez Mr J. Rouché," pp. 2–6.

76. Rey, "Le XVII° salon d'automne," p. 318.

77. See Baudry, *Petits jardins,* plate 10; Fonds Moreux, 2-203. Descriptions of this garden, apparently designed for Dr. Marthe Jacquelin, can be found in *Gardens and Gardening,* 1939, p. 65; and *Demeures et jardins de France,* p. 234.

78. "Jardins de Paris: Chez le Bon R. de Rothschild," p. 3. A plan, an axonometric drawing, and a photograph of the model for the Rothschild project are found in the Fonds Moreux, 18-120 and 18-122.

79. Moreux cited by Laprade, "L'œuvre de J.-Ch. Moreux," p. 241.

80. Moreux, "Jardins réguliers," p. 20.

81. Moreux, "Éloge du jardin régulier," p. 66.

82. "Mais si . . . plusieurs balcons sont susceptibles d'être traités en jardins, il faudra, tout à l'origine, que l'architecte les considère comme d'importantes composantes de la façade." Moreux, "Éloge du jardin régulier," p. 66.

83. Moreux, "Jardins réguliers," p. 20.

84. A *vertugadin* is an amphitheater formed by inclined planes of lawn. A photograph of the "Jardin fleuriste du XIX° siècle," also part of the grounds of the château de Quintin, is published in *Demeures et jardins de France,* p. 228.

85. A plan of the "Jardin français à perspective accélérée" for César de Hauke in Vignières (1943) is in the Fonds Moreux, 51-340.

86. Jean-Charles Moreux made measured drawings and took photographs of the Orto

Botanico, in Padova; his plan was paired with two views of pools in "Jardins," special issue of *L'Architecture d'Aujourd'hui,* p. 30.

87. Laprade, "L'œuvre de J.-Ch. Moreux," p. 243.

88. Moreux, "Jardins réguliers," p. 20.

89. Vera, *Le nouveau jardin,* p. 6.

90. See the various schemes for the square Foch in "Jardins privés et publics," Fonds Moreux, 2-164.

91. "Remarque importante: Il faut que la même fleur se répète dans chaque massif *uniformément.* Ceci étant conforme à l'esprit de Le Nôtre." Annotated drawing, "Jardins privés et publics," Fonds Moreux, 2-164.

92. "Victorian Curves," *The Glasgow Herald,* 25 February 1952.

93. Moreux, "Le jardin français du moyen-âge à nos jours," p. 8.

94. Vera, "Modernité et tradition," p. 96.

95. Jean-Charles Moreux cited in "Où va l'architecture," p. 131.

96. Vera, "Modernité et tradition," p. 91.

97. Duchêne, "Jardins de demain," in *Les jardins de l'avenir, hier, aujourd'hui, demain,* p. 16.

98. Ganay, "Le jardin de fleurs; Le jardin alpestre; Le jardin d'oiseaux; Les jardins ouvriers," pp. 28, 31.

99. Moreux, "Éloge du jardin régulier," p. 65.

100. Photographs of the projects for the 1937 Exposition are in the Fonds Moreux (29-25) and in the collection of Mrs. Janine Hébert. See "Jar-

dins," the special issue of *L'Architecture d'Aujourd'hui*, pp. 30–31, 55; and Ernest de Ganay's account in "Le jardin de fleurs; Le jardin alpestre; Le jardin d'oiseaux; Les jardins ouvriers."

101. Although Moreux resorted to a rather limited palette of plants, he appears to have mastered an extensive knowledge of vegetation. "Car cet admirable architecte de jardins était aussi jardinier et botaniste" (Champigneulle, "Architecte habile," p. 8). See also Moreux, "De l'utilisation de l'arbre dans le jardin," pp. 24–25.

102. Moreux, "XIXe et XXe siècles," in "Le jardin français du moyen-âge à nos jours," p. 8.

103. Moreux, "There Are Only Two Kinds of Gardens," p. 17.

CHAPTER 6:
PIERRE-ÉMILE LEGRAIN

1. See Bachollet, Bordet, and Lelieur, *Paul Iribe*, pp. 230–31 n. 61. Robert Bonfils dated the beginning of his friendship with Legrain and Robert Delaunay around the year 1904, when they were students at the École des Arts Appliqués Germain Pilon ("Pierre Legrain décorateur créateur," p. xxxv). Legrain worked as an illustrator to support his mother and younger brother.

2. Although most of his drawings for Paul Iribe were unsigned, thirteen of them obviously reflected his hand (Bachollet, Bordet, and Lelieur, *Paul Iribe*, p. 56). Legrain signed a cover for *Le Témoin* (no. 30, 7 August 1909) celebrating Blériot's flight over the English Channel. *Le Témoin* was first published between 1906 and 1910, and later from 1933 to 1935. See Lelieur, Bachollet, and Bordet, "Un joyeux contestataire, 'Témoin' de son temps (1906–1910)," and "Le 'Témoin' de l'affaire Stavisky (1933–1935)," in *Paul Iribe: Précurseur de l'art déco*, pp. 31–40 and 123–30, respectively.

3. See Anthoine-Legrain, "'Souvenirs' sur Pierre Legrain," p. xii.

4. Iribe and his collaborators designed over fifty costumes and two of the three sets for a play whose plot revolved around the world of fashion. *Rue de la Paix*, written by Abel Hermant and Marc de Toledo, was performed at the Theater Vaudeville in 1912. Bachollet, Bordet, and Lelieur, *Paul Iribe*, pp. 108–09.

5. Jean Cocteau also collaborated on *Le Mot*. The first issue was dated 28 November 1914. The twentieth and last was published on 1 July 1915.

Ibid., pp. 145–46; and Lelieur, Bachollet, and Border, "Le caricaturiste de combat (1914–1918)," in *Paul Iribe: Précurseur de l'art déco*, pp. 91–97.

6. Sculptures, furniture, art objects, drawings, pastels, and paintings by Chardin, Watteau, Boucher, and Fragonard were placed on the block. In the aftermath of the great auction, he exchanged his hôtel-museum on rue Spontini and the eighteenth century for the *goût du jour*.

7. In 1912 Paul Iribe and Pierre Legrain also designed the interior of Doucet's apartment on rue du Bois. There, the collector assembled works by Manet, Van Gogh, Cézanne, and Degas, which went on sale at the end of 1917. At his later studio in Neuilly, Doucet displayed works of immense renown, among them, Picasso's *Les demoiselles d'Avignon*, Rousseau's *La charmeuse de serpents*, and Matisse's *Les poissons rouges*. See Revel, "Jacques Doucet, couturier et collectionneur," p. 50; and Joubin, "Le studio de Jacques Doucet," p. 19.

8. Doucet's studio, designed by the architect Paul Ruaud, was situated on rue Saint-James in Neuilly-sur-Seine. André Joubin described the interior in "Le studio de Jacques Doucet."

9. Laurens's sculptures were initially conceived for the unrealized house (1924) for Doucet in Marly, by Robert Mallet-Stevens and Ruaud. It appears that the portico and fountain by Laurens were ultimately photographed in Doucet's garden in Neuilly. These works, termed "Architectures," are illustrated in *Henri Laurens sculpteur, 1885–1954*, pp. 113–16.

10. Doucet's library included French art of all periods, foreign art, classical art and, finally, the arts of the East and Far East. See Revel, "Jacques Doucet," p. 50; and Joubin, "Jacques Doucet, 1853–1929," p. 78. Doucet donated his art library to the University of Paris on 1 January 1918; it was then entrusted to the Fondation Jacques Doucet at the Bibliothèque d'Art et d'Archéologie.

11. The Bibliothèque Littéraire Doucet was later bequeathed to the Sainte-Geneviève Library in Paris. According to one of his secretaries, André Breton, Doucet collected books but did not read any of them. Breton described not only directing Doucet's pictorial tastes but also acting as mediator between the artist and the fashion designer; until 1924, he and Jean Aragon informed Doucet of any new literary movement. Breton cited by Revel, "Jacques Doucet," pp. 51, 81.

12. Rosenthal, "Pierre Legrain relieur," p. 67.

13. Joubin, "Le studio de Jacques Doucet," pp. 18–19.

14. Apparently Legrain conceived bindings and their mock-ups but left the execution to other artisans. See Rosenthal, "Pierre Legrain relieur," p. 67.

15. Outraged at the bookbinding exhibit of the 1925 decorative arts exposition — which he saw as sheer plagiarism of his style — Legrain sent a letter titled "Copier c'est voler" (Copying is stealing) to several artists and critics. Letter dated 17 June 1925, published with several of the responses in Pierre Legrain relieur, pp. xlv–xlvi.

16. Ackerman, "Modernism in Bookbinding," p. 148.

17. "Il a bu à la coupe âpre du cubisme; . . . Il attribue au jeu des lignes, aux angles, aux entrelacs, une vertu permanente; il les admire . . . dans l'art nègre dont la contemplation, il l'assure, a modifié sa sensibilité." Rosenthal, "Pierre Legrain relieur," p. 68.

18. Varenne, "Quelques ensembles de Pierre Legrain," p. 401.

19. Ibid., pp. 401–08. Galuchat is a shark skin whose calcified ruggedness was first smoothed and colored by Mr. Galuchat around 1770. See Bachollet, Bordet, and Lelieur, Paul Iribe, p. 124.

20. Varenne, "Quelques ensembles de Pierre Legrain," pp. 401, 403. For a definition of ensemblier, see Janneau, "Introduction à l'exposition des arts décoratifs: Considérations sur l'esprit moderne," pp. 136, 141–42; and Tisserand, "Feu le salon de réception," p. 340.

21. Legrain, "Introduction," in Objets d'art, n.p.

22. Garner, "Pierre Legrain — Décorateur," p. 134. References to the contemporary perceptions of Jacques Doucet's taste can be found in Joubin, "Le studio de Jacques Doucet," and Chapon, Mystère et splendeurs de Jacques Doucet, 1853–1929.

23. Varenne, "Quelques ensembles de Pierre Legrain," pp. 406–07. Jeanne Tachard established the boutique Suzanne Talbot, whose second proprietor, Mrs. Mathieu-Levy, commissioned Eileen Gray to design several pieces of furniture in 1922–23. See Vaizey, "The Collection of Mr. and Mrs. Robert Walker. Part 2," pp. 232, 242 n. 5.

24. Steele, "New Pioneering in Garden Design," p. 172.

25. Apparently André Breton was a reader for Jeanne Tachard, who introduced him to Jacques Doucet. See Chapon, Mystère et splendeurs de Jacques Doucet, p. 266.

26. One can trace accounts of Figure, a seven-foot sculpture with African-Oceanian connotations, which Jacques Lipchitz modeled in 1926 for Jeanne Tachard's villa in La Celle-Saint-Cloud, outside Paris. It seems, however, that the plaster version of this statue overwhelmed the client's pristine taste. See Patai, Encounters: The Life of Jacques Lipchitz, p. 247.

27. Although Robert Bonfils mentions the grave as one of Legrain's designs, contemporary articles and several books attribute its conception to Henri Laurens. Furthermore, the headstone for the Tachard family bears a strong resemblance to a project Laurens designed for Jacques Doucet's house in Marly. This misattribution might have resulted from the intimate friendship between Pierre Legrain and Henri Laurens. Bonfils, "Pierre Legrain décorateur créateur," p. xxxvii.

28. See Zervos, "Henri Laurens," pp. 11–16; Fiérens, "Henri Laurens," pp. 41–45; and Henri Laurens sculpteur, 1885–1954, pp. 118–19.

29. Legrain, "Introduction," in Objets d'art. Giulia Veronesi saw in the 1922–23 discovery of Tutankhamen's tomb the probable source of the Egyptian style so fashionable during that period (Stile 1925, p. 84).

30. This ebony is from the city of Makassar (Ujung Pandang today), on the main island of the Celebes, in Indonesia. Because of few primary sources, it is difficult to establish whether Legrain was influenced by Paul Iribe or vice-versa. The choice of materials such as Makassar ebony, Chinese galuchat, and oilcloth appeared while Legrain was working with Iribe on the studio for Jacques Doucet. See Bachollet, Bordet, and Lelieur, *Paul Iribe,* pp. 123–24; and Garner, "Pierre Legrain—décorateur," p. 134.

31. See Legrain, "La villa de Madame Tachard à La Celle-Saint-Cloud," p. 68; Varenne, "Quelques ensembles de Pierre Legrain," p. 406; and Bonfils, "Pierre Legrain décorateur créateur," p. xxxvi.

32. Garner, "Pierre Legrain—décorateur," p. 136.

33. The remodeling of the villa was not dated, and the earliest photographs of Legrain's garden I could trace were published in August 1924; I would thus place the date of completion around late 1923 or early 1924.

34. See Rambosson, "Un jardin de Pierre Legrain"; Legrain, "La villa de Madame Tachard à La Celle-Saint-Cloud"; Varenne, "Quelques ensembles de Pierre Legrain"; "An Example of Garden Design in the Modernist Manner at St. Cloud, France"; and Steele, "New Pioneering in Garden Design." Garrett Eckbo traced one of the views of the Tachard garden for his own study. For a discussion of Legrain's impact upon American landscape architects, see Dorothée Imbert, "Pierre-Émile Legrain: A Model for Modernism."

35. Zach, "Modernistic Work and Its Natural Limitations," p. 293.

36. Steele, "New Pioneering in Garden Design," p. 172.

37. Thomas Church, *Gardens Are for People* (New York: Reinhold, 1955), and *Your Private World: A Study of Intimate Gardens* (San Francisco: Chronicle, 1969). See also the Eckbo residence in Berkeley, California.

38. Forestier, "Le jardin moderne et l'exposition des arts décoratifs," p. 94.

39. "Il laisse sous entendue la construction: l'œil en ressent les bienfaits malgré la disparition de la trame" (Rosenthal, "Pierre Legrain," p. 67). Several of Legrain's motifs for book covers relied on a symmetrical structure, however. The majority of his cover designs are illustrated in *Pierre Legrain relieur.*

40. Roland Garros flew across the Mediterranean in 1913. Charles Nungesser and François Coli disappeared on 8 May 1927, while attempting to cross the Atlantic from east to west. Charles Lindbergh successfully flew nonstop from New York to Paris on 20–21 May 1927.

41. Le Corbusier's urbanistic plan for the center of Paris, presented at the 1925 exposition, was baptized Plan Voisin in honor of the airplane and automobile manufacturer Gabriel Voisin. In 1910 Guillaume Apollinaire dedicated his poem "L'avion" to the pioneer of aviation, Clément Ader. Robert Delaunay painted a semi-abstract Simultaneist *Hommage à Blériot* in 1914. Picasso nicknamed Braque "Mon cher Vilbure," in reference to the deceased aviator Wilbur Wright, and cited airplanes or aviators using his stenciled words in paintings such as *The Scallop Shell: "Notre avenir est dans l'air"* (Our Future Lies in the Air), done in 1912.

42. André Vera, with engravings by Paul Vera, *Les jardins,* pp. 136–37.

43. In a bedroom conceived for the vicomte de Noailles, Legrain apparently intended to present the walls as book covers of white oilcloth inlaid with irregular geometric patterns of cork. The appointments—a snakeskin bed, metallic tables, and a leather armchair— composed a "highly original ensemble." See Bonfils, "Pierre Legrain décorateur créateur," p. xxxvii.

44. See Bonfils, "Pierre Legrain décorateur créateur," p. xxxvi.

45. Legrain, "La villa de Madame Tachard à la Celle-Saint-Cloud," p. 68.

46. Rambosson, "Un jardin de Pierre Legrain," pp. 2–4.

47. Steele, "Landscape Design of the Future," p. 301.

48. "Constituer une atmosphère, voilà pour Pierre Legrain la préoccupation dominante, qu'il s'agisse d'une reliure ou d'un intérieur moderne" (Varenne, "Quelques ensembles de Pierre Legrain," p. 401). "*L'œil ne doit rien retenir,* toute recherche n'existe qu'en conformité des recherches voisines" (Legrain, "La villa de Madame Tachard," p. 68).

49. Legrain, "La villa de Madame Tachard," p. 68.

50. Ibid.

51. "Au premier coup d'œil, une reliure de Legrain tranche sur tout ce qui l'a précédée: de grands partis, de larges sur-

faces nues, des oppositions franches de taches, un décor d'une sobriété extrême, des indications elliptiques sous lesquelles on devine des intentions subtiles, quelque chose à la fois d'immédiat et de très distant, tout cela donne une impression forte, celle d'un art qui a réduit ses moyens pour vibrer d'une façon plus intense: sommaire à la surface, au demeurant très raffiné." Rosenthal, "Pierre Legrain," p. 67.

52. Rambosson, "Un jardin de Pierre Legrain," p. 4.

53. "Comme on le voit nulle virtuosité jardinière. De l'architecture d'abord et surtout l'*oubli de Versailles*." Legrain, "La villa de Madame Tachard," p. 68.

54. "Comment Pierre Legrain arrive-t-il à nous donner une telle impression de nouveauté créatrice que ses meubles, au contraire de tant d'autres que l'on voudrait faire passer pour modernes et qui ne sont que du vieux neuf, semblent un point de départ et n'offrent aucune compromission avec les styles anciens?" Varenne, "Quelques ensembles de Pierre Legrain," pp. 404–05.

55. Ibid., p. 407.

56. From Theo van Doesburg's theory of elemental construction formulated in 1924. See "12. *Symmetry and repetition*," in "Towards a Plastic Architecture," in *Programs and Manifestoes on 20th-Century Architecture*, ed. Ulrich Conrads (Cambridge: MIT Press, 1964), pp. 79–80.

57. Legrain, "La villa de Madame Tachard," p. 68.

58. Rambosson, "Un jardin de Pierre Legrain."

59. Legrain, "La villa de Madame Tachard," p. 68.

60. Ibid.

61. Steele, "New Styles in Gardening: Will Landscape Architecture Reflect the Modernistic Tendencies Seen in the Other Arts?" p. 354.

62. Legrain, "La villa de Madame Tachard," p. 68.

63. Partial title of the article describing Legrain's design, "An Example of Garden Design in the Modernist Manner," p. 63.

64. Varenne, "Quelques ensembles de Pierre Legrain," p. 407.

65. "I need not insist here on the prevalence of geometrical motifs in modern decoration, a conception deriving from Cubism, the survival of which —although extinct in the realm of painting—continues in the decorative arts." Georges Cretté, "Distinctive Designs in Hand-Tooled Book-Bindings," p. 379.

66. See Thornton, "Negro Art and the Furniture of Pierre-Émile Legrain," pp. 166–69.

67. Steele, "New Styles in Gardening," p. 354.

68. "L'art de Legrain se rattache à la dernière phase du cubisme, au cubisme synthétique qui use des 'signes' créateurs du réel par allusion lyrique" (Brunhammer, *1925*, p. 145). "Sans avoir jamais été l'esclave d'un système, sans être le disciple de personne, Legrain s'est donc trouvé, plus ou moins volontairement, dans le sillage du cubisme" (Varenne, "Quelques ensembles de Pierre Legrain," p. 408).

69. Legrain, "La villa de Madame Tachard," p. 68.

70. "Les modernes, au contraire, subordonnent l'*écriture* et la proportion du motif décoratif à l'effet total." Janneau, "Introduction à l'exposition des arts décoratifs," p. 145.

71. Legrain, "La villa de Madame Tachard," p. 68.

72. Varenne, "Quelques ensembles de Pierre Legrain," p. 407.

73. Steele, "New Styles in Gardening," p. 354.

231

CHAPTER 7:
GABRIEL GUEVREKIAN

1. A section of this chapter was previously published as a review of *Gabriel Guévrékian (1900–1970): Une autre architecture moderne*, by Elizabeth Vitou, Dominique Deshoulières, and Hubert Jeanneau, *Journal of the Society of Architectural Historians* 49, no. 4 (December 1990): 449–50.

2. Oskar Strnad designed the music room in the Austrian Pavilion by Josef Hoffmann at the 1925 exposition in Paris.

3. Most of Guevrekian's Iranian activity remains unknown. Few of his public buildings, such as the Ministry of War, the Ministry of Foreign Affairs, and the Palace of Justice, were ever published abroad. Perhaps hampered by technical shortcomings, his villas—Panahy (1934), Siassy and Aslani (1935), Khosrovani and Taleghani (1936), Firouze and Mafi (1937)—suggested only the appearance of a modernity suitable for the newly created nation of Iran. The gardens he designed for these villas were little more than a cliché of the Persian garden hybridized with the International Style, thus lacking the originality of his French translations of the paradise garden. Although Guevrekian returned to Europe in 1937, he did not participate in the Paris Exposition des Arts et des Techniques. He lived in London until the outbreak of the Second World War, when he moved back to France. Guevrekian has left practically no traces of these English and French periods. In 1945, with Georges-Henri Pingusson, he participated in the Sarre reconstruction project. Initiated to teaching at the Sarrebrück Beaux-Arts Academy, Guevrekian was invited by architectural historian Turpin Bannister to Auburn University in 1948, and the following year to the University of Illinois at Urbana Champaign, where he remained until 1969. Gabriel Guevrekian died in 1970 in Antibes, France. See the monograph on Guevrekian by Vitou, Deshoulières, and Jeanneau, *Gabriel Guévrékian*.

4. Guevrekian submitted entries to the Salon d'Automne in 1923 and 1924 and participated in an exhibition organized by Robert Mallet-Stevens at the École Spéciale d'Architecture in Paris in 1924.

5. Many of these accounts published in contemporary periodicals can be found in Guevrekian's scrapbooks at the University of Illinois at Urbana Champaign.

6. Apparently, Guevrekian interrupted a musical vocation for his architectural studies. See Zahar, "L'architecture vivante: Gabriel Guévrékian," p. 10.

7. The theory of Simultaneism was elaborated by Chevreul in 1839 and later promoted by Robert and Sonia Delaunay. Simultaneous contrast was achieved by juxtaposing dissonant complementary colors. To explore this principle, Sonia Delaunay experimented with a vibrating palette of reds, blues, browns, and greens in her fabrics, which were displayed in Guevrekian's boutique.

8. A. Loizeau, "Le jardin persan," Guevrekian Archives, University of Illinois, box 2.

9. "Classe 27.—Art du jardin," in *Exposition internationale des arts décoratifs et industriels modernes Paris 1925: Liste des récompenses*.

10. Forestier, "Les jardins à l'exposition des arts décoratifs" (12 September 1925), p. 526.

11. Weber, "Les jardins," p. 60.

12. Both a photograph and the rendering were reproduced by Joseph Marrast in *1925 Jardins*. For a description of the colors in the Jardin d'eau et de lumière, see Charensol, "La rue—les jardins," p. 327; Forestier, "Les jardins à l'exposition des arts décoratifs," p. 526; Weber, "Les jardins," p. 62; Lambert, "Jardins et fontaines," p. 141; Loizeau, "Le jardin persan"; *Revue Horticole*, 16 September 1925, Guevrekian Archives, University of Illinois, box 2.

13. "Les diverses faces des bassins superposés sont, les unes en rouge écarlate et les autres en bleu d'outremer vif, couleur du drapeau" (Forestier, "Les jardins à l'exposition des arts décoratifs," p. 526). "L'eau s'échappe dans ces bassins, sorte de godets à aquarelle, par des tuyaux jumelés comme les canons d'un dreadnought" (Weber, "Les jardins," p. 62).

14. Next to the begonias "flamboyant" were most likely *Ageratum houstonianum* (floss flower) and *Pyrethrum roseum* or *Chrysanthemum coccineum* (painted daisy), all dwarf varieties. See Forestier, "Les jardins à l'exposition des arts décoratifs," p. 526.

15. Although Forestier's description matched the chromatic scheme of Guevrekian's rendering, the photos taken at the fair reveal a garden in which a greater part of the red begonia triangles was replaced by beds of white flowers.

16. Zach, "Modernistic Work and Its Natural Limitations," p. 293.

17. "Les plantations, très diffi-
ciles, de ces triangles, qui
exigeaient des plantes vivement
colorées et très naines, ont
été confiées à la maison
Thiébaud." Forestier, "Les jardins à l'exposition des arts
décoratifs," p. 526.

18. Steele, "New Pioneering in
Garden Design," p. 166.

19. See Robert Delaunay's
notes in Du cubisme à l'art
abstrait, pp. 108–10.

20. Zach, "Modernistic Work
and Its Natural Limitations,"
p. 293.

21. As a frequent collaborator
of Robert Mallet-Stevens,
Louis Barillet also designed the
interior stained glass of the
Pavillon du tourisme at the
1925 exposition.

22. Steele, "New Pioneering in
Garden Design," p. 166.

23. Forestier, "Les jardins à
l'exposition des arts décoratifs," p. 526.

24. See Loizeau, "Le jardin
persan," and Forestier, "Les
jardins à l'exposition des arts
décoratifs," p. 526.

25. The word paradise is
apparently derived from pairi-
daeza, meaning walled garden
in old Persian. See Moynihan,
Paradise as a Garden in Persia
and Mughal India, pp. 1–5.

26. Apollinaire, Les peintres
cubistes, p. 61.

27. See Jullian, "Une des
maisons-clés pour l'histoire du
goût au XXᵉ siècle: L'hôtel du
vicomte et de la vicomtesse de
Noailles, à Paris," pp. 68–91;
Briolle and Fuzibet, "La villa
Noailles: Robert Mallet-
Stevens, 1924," vol. 1.

28. Between 1947 and 1981,
after ceding the Hyères estate
with its numerous gardens to
his wife, Charles de Noailles

created and tended the terraced gardens of his bastide in
Grasse. For a description of
another one of his renowned
landscapes, at the Ermitage de
Pompadour in the forest of
Fontainebleau, see Schneider,
"Charles de Noailles: Master
of Gardens, Life, and Art,"
pp. 74–79.

29. Letter from Charles de
Noailles to Robert Mallet-
Stevens, November 1925, cited
by Briolle and Repiquet, "Une
pièce rare," pp. 38–39. Many
years thereafter, Noailles recalled his "very modern garden
of triangular shape designed by
a pleasant young man, whose
name I forget, but who was
stricken by total alopecia."
Letter to Cécile Briolle and
Agnès Fuzibet dated 30
December 1980, in Briolle and
Fuzibet, "La villa Noailles,"
vol. 1, p. 120.

30. "We liked [Mies van der
Rohe], but he told us he had
other engagements. . . . As we
were young and impatient, we
decided it would be better to . . .
find another architect. . . . I
then thought of Le Corbusier.
Having met Le Corbusier once
or twice and having accompanied him on a visit to the
house which he had built in
Paris for a Swiss banker, I did
not have a very good opinion
of his taste. . . . Even if he did
have imagination and verve, I
did not like his taste." Vicomte
de Noailles, October 1977,
cited by Briolle and Fuzibet,
"La villa Noailles," vol. 1,
p. 119.

31. The château Saint-Bernard
was a feudal castle, razed
under Louis XIII, the only
remnants of which are a few
scattered towers and the surrounding walls. The site was
subsequently used for the convent of the Bernardines. The

Green Drawing Room facing
the garden by Guevrekian is
one of the several rooms
remaining from the convent.
See Deshairs, "Une villa moderne à Hyères," p. 1.

32. For the viscount's garden
log and a plan of the court-
yard, see Racine, Boursier-
Mougenot, and Binet, The
Gardens of Provence and the
French Riviera, p. 201.

33. Maquis refers to the
scrubby thicket found in
southern France and Corsica;
almost impenetrable, it offers a
prime hiding place.

34. Similarly, Charles and
Marie-Laure de Noailles
installed their art collection
inside the villa on movable
racks, which allowed one to
change the decor of the room
by selecting different pictures.

35. The model of the garden
was already published in the
winter 1926 issue of Les Arts
de la Maison.

36. Martet, review of the Salon
d'Automne, Homme Libre,
12–13 November 1927.

37. Fiérens, review of the Salon
d'Automne, Journal des
Débats, 13 November 1927.

38. Les Échos d'Art, 1 March
1927, Guevrekian Archives,
University of Illinois, box 2.

39. Steele, "New Styles in
Gardening: Will Landscape
Architecture Reflect the Mod-
ernistic Tendencies Seen in the
Other Arts?" p. 354.

40. Mallet-Stevens had
intended to construct the villa
in concrete, but because of the
local architect's limited knowledge of this relatively new
building material, the structure
of the villa was executed using
traditional masonry, with the
exception of the beams. As a
result, the villa only looked

like concrete. In 1928, Man Ray filmed *Les Mystères du Château du Dé* at the Villa Noailles. One of the opening sequences showed the modernist villa on the ruins of Saint-Bernard, with this commentary: "Comment deux voyageurs arrivèrent à Saint-Bernard, et ce qu'ils virent dans les ruines d'un vieux château, au-dessus desquelles s'élève un autre château de notre époque."

41. Guevrekian stretched the triangle to allow a glimpse of the Mediterranean Sea inside the "courtyard." Guevrekian cited by Zahn, "Ein geometrischer Garten an der Riviera," p. 223.

42. Jacques Lipchitz conceived the gilded bronze statue *Joy of Life* in 1926. It was cast by Jean Prouvé and without the base measured 89 1/4 inches high. The bronze is currently in the collection of The Israel Museum in Jerusalem.

43. George, "Joie de vivre."

44. Guevrekian cited by Steele in "New Pioneering in Garden Design," pp. 166–67.

45. Rémon, "Jardins de Guevrekian," p. 106.

46. It is unclear from the photographs whether the ground covers planted in the tilted pyramidal beds were in fact two different hues of green.

47. The attempt to reconstruct the sequence of the colored rectangles has proven puzzling. Contradictory evidence and written descriptions lead one to question whether the commentators ever saw the garden as built or whether the architectural and garden critics were frequently mischievous and/or color-blind. The architects restoring the villa adopted the same order as the one represented in the photo of the model (*Les Arts de la Maison*, plate XXVII): the sequence of color planes extending from the drawing room being red-gray-blue-yellow. Guevrekian is cited as describing the order as yellow-blue-red-gray instead. Other accounts throw in some violet ("Originality in Roof Gardens," p. 220; Shand, "An Essay in the Adroit: At the Villa of the Vicomte de Noailles," p. 174). The cast of bricks and foliage in contemporary black-and-white photographs would suggest the use of a red filter. After examining these images with the help of George Waters, I tend to think the tiles at the vertex of the triangular garden —which appear very dark on the photographs—were most likely blue. The order from bottom to top would therefore be red-gray-yellow-blue (or perhaps gray-red-yellow-blue) and was recorded as such by Raymond McGrath in *Twentieth-Century Houses*, p. 44.

48. The pool was described —even though it already appeared on the model presented at the Salon d'Automne —as the "happy result of tapping a spring unexpectedly encountered at this point" (Shand, "An Essay in the Adroit," p. 174). On the other hand, Guevrekian's plan captioned the rectangle where the pool was built as "flower planter" (Rémon, "Jardins de Guevrekian," p. 107). Unfortunately, to my knowledge no description of the color of the tulips exists.

49. The plan published in *Jardins et Cottages* clearly indicates the opening through the southern window as framing the "view towards the sea." See Rémon, "Jardins de Guevrekian," p. 107.

50. See Hope, *The Sculpture of Jacques Lipchitz*, p. 13.

51. Charles de Noailles cited by Schneider, "Charles de Noailles: Master of Gardens, Life, and Art," p. 76.

52. Jacques Lipchitz with H. H. Arnason, *My Life in Sculpture*, p. 96.

53. He also saw the rotation as an evocation of the "less agreeable emotion of a patient's agonized contortions in a dentist chair." Shand, "An Essay in the Adroit," p. 174.

54. As in *Das Kabinett des Doktor Caligari*, a German expressionist film directed by Robert Wiene in 1919, with sets by Hermann Warm, Walter Reimann, and Walter Röhrig.

55. Shand, "An Essay in the Adroit," p. 174.

56. "Originality in Roof Gardens," p. 220.

57. Steele, "New Styles in Gardening," p. 354.

58. Ibid.

59. A reporter described the walls as a protection against the prevailing winds (Mrs. Howard Robertson, "Two Views against the Geometric Garden," p. 6). In fact, the mistral comes from the north, and its course would be interrupted by the hill and dense vegetation; the eastern wind would encounter little resistance from the wide openings at the tip of the triangle; and wind rarely blows from the south in this part of France.

60. Steele, "New Styles in Gardening," p. 354.

61. Fiérens, review of the Salon d'Automne.

62. Van Doesburg's room, which has been re-created, can hardly be perceived volumetrically given its constricted size of 21 square feet.

63. Racine, Boursier-Mougenot, and Binet, *The Gardens of Provence and the French Riviera*, p. 201. I would assume their care was not limited to the walled garden alone but included the other gardens and landscape surrounding the villa as well.

64. The viscount must have appreciated the aloe version of the triangular garden because he had a postcard of the new design issued.

65. See *Sunset New Western Garden Book* (Menlo Park, California: Lane Publishing, 1979), p. 175.

66. Mercer, ed., *Gardens and Gardening, 1934*, p. 26.

67. The renovation began in February 1990 and continues under the direction of architects Cécile Briolle, Claude Marro, and Jacques Repiquet.

68. The replanting of two-tone triangular beds was never attempted. Marigolds fall short of attaining the grace of tulips, but the major loss remains the pair of orange trees that framed the view of *La joie de vivre*. As of June 1991, the side beds were planted with a variety of sedum and the rectangular ones with yellow and orange marigolds. The orange trees were not replaced, and tulips were not planted.

69. "Originality in Roof Gardens," p. 220.

70. Mrs. Howard Robertson, "Two Views against the Geometric Garden," p. 6.

71. Tunnard, *Gardens in the Modern Landscape*, p. 71; and Taylor, *The Modern Garden*, p.

17. Another garden, also in England, bears a striking resemblance to Guevrekian's concept. Designed in 1934 by Amyas Connell for a modernist house in Amersham Hill, Buckinghamshire, the garden is illustrated in Brown, *The Art and Architecture of English Gardens*, p. 183, and also in Taylor, *The Modern Garden*, p. 13.

72. *Les Échos d'Art*, 1 March 1927, Guevrekian Archives, University of Illinois, box 2; Shand, "An Essay in the Adroit," p. 174; "Originality in Roof Gardens," p. 220.

73. The "boutique simultanée" that Guevrekian designed for Sonia Delaunay and Jacques Heim in 1925 led to a few other projects for the fashion designer, such as stores or exhibition spaces, and eventually to the commission of a villa.

74. Zahar, "La maison de Mr et Mme Heim: Morphologie et structure d'une maison," p. 48.

75. The axonometric drawings reinforced this connection, because the terraces and the garden rooms displayed identical paving patterns.

76. Although the terrace pool appears on the plan reproduced in Guevrekian's article "Une villa à Neuilly" (p. 9), it is not shown on the plan redrawn in Vitou, Deshoulières, and Jeanneau, *Gabriel Guévrékian*, p. 44. I am therefore unable to ascertain if this pool was ever built.

77. Guevrekian, "Une villa à Neuilly," p. 8.

78. The remnants of La Folie Saint-James provided a naturalistic backdrop to the 1600 square feet of Guevrekian's garden. Not far from the Villa Heim was the site for which Le

Corbusier and Pierre Jeanneret designed the Villa Meyer.

79. Vera, *Le nouveau jardin*, p. 56.

80. "Le jardin continue le plan de la maison. Des surfaces en briques (gazon, mosaïques et effet d'optique) ont agrandi et enrichi ce jardin si restreint." Guevrekian, "Une villa à Neuilly," p. 8.

81. Marcel Zahar refers to "briques roses et bleues," which were probably pink and deep purple, a common enough color. Zahar, "La maison de Mr et Mme Heim," p. 56.

82. Forestier, "Les jardins à l'exposition des arts décoratifs," p. 526.

83. An axonometric of the penthouse is reproduced in Vitou, Deshoulières, and Jeanneau, *Gabriel Guévrékian*, p. 57.

84. The other contenders were André Lurçat and Le Corbusier, who executed his design in 1932. Jean-Charles Moreux and Robert Mallet-Stevens might also have submitted projects, according to the historian Jean-Louis Cohen. Vitou, Deshoulières, and Jeanneau, *Gabriel Guévrékian*, p. 56.

85. To my knowledge, the remaining black-and-white reproductions and the limited descriptions of these gardens prevent an evaluation of the color schemes.

86. See Guevrekian, "Maisons en pays de soleil," pp. 190–96.

87. Wesley, "Gabriel Guevrekian e il giardino cubista," pp. 17–24.

88. Ibid., p. 21.

89. Apollinaire, *Les peintres cubistes*, p. 63.

90. Ibid., p. 67.

CHAPTER 8:
LE CORBUSIER

1. The following essays and articles are among the exceptions: Mary Patricia May Sekler, "Le Corbusier, Ruskin, the Tree, and the Open Hand"; Caroline Constant, "From the Virgilian Dream to Chandigarh"; Florence Robert, "Le jardin et le paysage dans l'œuvre de Le Corbusier"; Catherine Courtiau, "'Le dehors est toujours un dedans': Tensions entre architecture et nature chez Le Corbusier" (Marc Treib brought this article to my attention; Joachim Wolschke-Bulmahn provided a copy).

2. Le Corbusier, "L'heure du repos," in *Urbanisme,* p. 219 n. 2.

3. "Objet du pavillon: 1° un logement type, de réalisation exclusivement industrielle avec l'emploi systématique d'éléments standards; 2° l'étude de ces principes de standardisation dans leur généralisation urbaine et interurbaine." Fondation Le Corbusier, Paris (hereafter cited as FLC), A2–13, 86.

4. Le Corbusier, "L'heure du repos," in *Urbanisme,* p. 219.

5. Le Corbusier, *Almanach d'architecture moderne,* pp. 130, 148.

6. "Au-devant de la construction de caractère si décidé de *L'Esprit Nouveau*—par Le Corbusier,—intentionnellement quelques arbustes & à peine quelques fleurs avaient été dispersés très irrégulièrement sur les gazons qui l'entouraient. Dans le bâtiment . . . sans ordre apparent, côte à côte étaient plantés des arbustes rustiques & quelques fleurs." Forestier, "Les jardins de l'exposition des arts décoratifs," p. 24.

7. In a letter dated 21 April 1925, Le Corbusier apologized to Forestier for intruding on his terrain, but to avoid any misunderstandings, the architect included a sketch to emphasize his landscape concept. He also reminded Forestier of the garden supervisor's offer to design the terrace for the pavilion. FLC A2–13, 144. Le Corbusier termed his roof gardens and planted terraces *jardins suspendus,* or "hanging gardens," despite the overall paucity of their vegetation.

8. Letter from Le Corbusier to Forestier dated 22 June 1925, FLC A2–13, 150.

9. "Je ne vous cacherai pas que si je devais faire inaugurer le pavillon au milieu des gravois et des terreaux, je ne manquerais pas de protester énergiquement et de faire intervenir le chef de cabinet de Mr. de Monzie. Je suis bien certain que le service des jardins où j'ai toujours rencontré la plus grande bienveillance m'évitera d'avoir recours à ce moyen désagréable; de plus, Mr. Forestier est en nom au Pavillon et au catalogue, et je pense qu'il serait profondément contrarié s'il apprenait à son retour que le pavillon a été inauguré dans de telles conditions" (letter from Le Corbusier to Mr. Bigier, the architect replacing Forestier during his absence, dated 1 July 1925, FLC A2–13, 151–52). The requested vegetation was finally planted on the eve of the inauguration, which Le Corbusier recorded as taking place on 11 July 1925. "Eh bien à ce moment précis où il nous faut des masses de gazon, des masses d'arbustes, de fleurs, M. J.-N.-C. [*sic*] Forestier a dû partir pour l'Espagne. Voilà la guigne! . . . La veille du 11 juillet, on m'avise du retour de M. Forestier. Pneumatique. Il accourt comme un homme généreux. . . . Tout s'équipe. Tout se termine" (Le Corbusier, "Brève histoire de nos tribulations," p. 67).

10. Le Corbusier, "Brève histoire de nos tribulations," p. 67.

11. Le Corbusier, "L'heure du repos," in *Urbanisme,* p. 205.

12. "J'aurais également à vous demander l'installation de quelques arbustes dans l'espace du diorama de façon à créer une illusion de futaies" (letter to Forestier, dated 22 June 1925, FLC A2–13, 150). In an earlier letter to Forestier dated 25 May 1925, Le Corbusier complained about the quality of light the street lamp cast on the hanging garden: "Vous aviez donné ordre de déplacer le bec de gaz dans l'axe de la rotonde de notre pavillon, j'ai répété cet ordre à plusieurs reprises au chef du personnel compétent; rien n'a été fait, au contraire le bec de gaz a été installé, définitivement peint, or, il jette une lumière violente à l'intérieur de notre jardin suspendu en rendant le séjour très désagréable" (FLC A2–13, 146). Forestier expressed his regrets at his inability to please the architect in a reply dated 27 May 1925 (FLC A2–13, 147).

13. "Et que dire de la sculpture s'élevant devant ce pavillon? La pensée peut voyager autour de ce monstre, rien ne peut la retenir. . . . J'aime encore mieux, infiniment, un fétiche nègre parce qu'au moins, dans un morceau de ce genre, il y a une conception, primitive mais sincère." Van Montfort, "L'exposition internationale des arts décoratifs et indus-

triels modernes de Paris—1925 (suite)," p. 18.

14. Forestier, "Les jardins à l'exposition des arts décoratifs," p. 527.

15. Le Corbusier, "Brève histoire de nos tribulations," p. 67.

16. "[Matériaux] de l'urbanisme: Soleil-espace-verdure," Le Corbusier, "Unité," p. 53.

17. Le Corbusier, "L'heure du repos," in *Urbanisme,* pp. 223–24.

18. Ibid., p. 224.

19. Le Corbusier, *Précisions sur un état présent de l'architecture et de l'urbanisme,* p. 99.

20. Le Corbusier captioned this project for Mrs. Meyer "Étude d'un hôtel privé, pour un client sans scrupules. 1925" ("Le Corbusier," special issue of *L'Architecture d'Aujourd'hui,* p. 80). There were three projects for the Villa Meyer, dated October 1925, April 1926, and June 1926, in addition to an earlier project that remained unpublished (see Lucan, "Villa Meyer, 1925–1926," pp. 13–20).

21. Letter from Le Corbusier and Pierre Jeanneret to Mrs. Meyer, October 1925, FLC 31525.

22. The Villa Heim, designed in 1927 by Gabriel Guevrekian, also overlooked the parc Saint-James.

23. Letter from Le Corbusier and Pierre Jeanneret to Mrs. Meyer, October 1925, FLC 31525.

24. Ibid.

25. Girardin, "Du cadre des paysages," in *De la composition des paysages,* p. 39.

26. Letter from Le Corbusier and Jeanneret to Mrs. Meyer,

October 1925, FLC 31525. Robinson is mentioned by Chaney ("Concepts of Nature and Redemption in the Work of Le Corbusier," p. 7) citing Bernard Rudofsky (*The Prodigious Builders*, London: Secker and Warburg, 1977).

27. Extending to the Seine, the garden was much larger than it is today. A river with eighteen bridges ran through the estate, which, in addition to the fabriques, contained greenhouses and a conservatory.

28. Apparently Baudard de Vaudésir, baron de Saint-Gemme (anglicized as Saint-James) and Treasurer of the Navy, was imprisoned in 1787 for the questionable financing of his Folie. The Grand Rocher —inside of which were a salon and a steam bath—alone would have cost 1,600,000 livres. Soon thereafter, the duc de Choiseul Praslin acquired the entire estate for the sum of 200,000 livres.

29. I wish to credit James Ward for the insight provided by his dissertation, "Le Corbusier's Villa 'Les Terrasses' and The International Style," which was brought to my attention by Mary McLeod.

30. Le Corbusier chose the loggia of the Villa Stein–de Monzie as an illustration of the air inlet/hanging garden in the project for the Immeuble-villas. Le Corbusier, *Précisions,* p. 99.

31. This first bill was addressed to Madame de Monzie. FLC H1–4, 101.

32. Crépin was responsible for the plantings at the Villa La Roche–Jeanneret in 1923. His first estimate for the Villa Stein–de Monzie is dated 3 December 1926. FLC H1–4, 97–98.

33. For a description of the Steins' collection and interior, see Lucile M. Golson, "The Michael Steins of San Francisco: Art Patrons and Collectors," p. 46. A sketch by Le Corbusier, dated 1929, compares the plans and volumes of various villas. The house at Garches falls into the category of "composition cubique (prisme pur)" and bears the commentary "très difficile (satisfaction de l'esprit)."

34. A partial paving plan (FLC 10522) and this site plan sketch (FLC H1[4], 201) are, to my knowledge, the only remaining traces of the final design.

35. "Le jardin (côté Sud) est planté d'arbres et ensemencé de gazon sur toute la surface. Un chemin de béton dessine dans sa partie milieu une sinuosité dont le tracé est dicté par les vues les plus favorables et les plus variées sur la façade" (Le Corbusier, "Tracés régulateurs," p. 33). A photograph of the garden bore the caption "Au milieu des pelouses et des futaies, un chemin courbe de béton qui provoque des vues variées, et, sous les arbres, des lieux propices pour se reposer" ("Le Corbusier et P. Jeanneret," p. 50).

36. Presentation drawing for the villa's second project, dated 20 July 1926, annotated 25 July 1959, FLC 31480.

37. "Il s'est donc agi, tout d'abord, de relier les deux propriétés: jardinage" (Le Corbusier, "Aménagement de la propriété de Mr Church à Ville d'Avray," 19 December 1928, FLC H3–3, 1); this text was published as an unsigned article, "Une ancienne maison

transformée par MM. Le Corbusier et Jeanneret," pp. 5–9.

38. [Le Corbusier], "Une ancienne maison," p. 5.

39. Ibid., p. 7.

40. André, *L'art des jardins: Traité général de la composition des parcs et jardins*, pp. 151–52.

41. André, *L'art des jardins*, p. 151.

42. See Benton, *Les villas de Le Corbusier et Pierre Jeanneret, 1920–1930*, p. 107. The film *Architecture* was produced by *L'Architecture d'Aujourd'hui* in 1931.

43. André, *L'art des jardins*, p. 150.

44. In a letter to Jeanneret dated 9 July 1928, Henry Church categorically forbade the architects to paint the music pavilion black. "Il est inutile de vous dire que je ne veux de cette couleur où que ce soit. . . . En principe, si vous le voulez bien, nous allons prendre comme base que ce second bâtiment sera peint en blanc tant au dehors comme au dedans, à moins que d'un commun accord nous ne décidions d'y mettre d'autres tons" (FLC H3–3, 60). Le Corbusier described, both verbally and graphically, the base of this building as dark green rather than black.

45. Le Corbusier, *Le Corbusier et Pierre Jeanneret: Œuvre complète de 1910–1929*, p. 186. There is no evidence that the orchard existed previously. A few young trees, widely spaced, can be seen in contemporary photographs and in Le Corbusier's sketches.

46. "*Le plan est retourné. . . .* On fuit la rue: on va vers la lumière et l'air pur." Le Cor-busier, *Le Corbusier et Pierre Jeanneret: Œuvre complète de 1910–1929*, p. 165.

47. Ibid., p. 186.

48. Le Corbusier, *Le Corbusier et Pierre Jeanneret: Œuvre complète de 1929–1934*, p. 24.

49. Le Corbusier, *Précisions*, pp. 99, 137.

50. Posener, "La maison Savoye à Poissy," p. 21.

51. Le Corbusier, "'Plan Voisin' de Paris 1925," in *Le Corbusier et Pierre Jeanneret: Œuvre complète de 1910–1929*, p. 114.

52. Ibid., p. 115.

53. Le Corbusier, *Le Corbusier et Pierre Jeanneret: Œuvre complète de 1929–1934*, p. 27.

54. *Shakkei*, or borrowed scenery, captures a distant vista as part of the garden through framing and mimesis. See Marc Treib and Ron Herman, *A Guide to the Gardens of Kyoto* (Tokyo: Shufunotomo, 1980).

55. Le Corbusier, *Le Corbusier et Pierre Jeanneret: Œuvre complète de 1929–1934*, p. 24.

56. Uvedale Price, *An Essay on the Picturesque* (London: 1794), p. 277; cited by Michael Symes, "Nature as the Bride of Art: The Design and Structure of Painshill," p. 66.

57. Posener, "La maison Savoye à Poissy," p. 21.

58. The original colors of the Villa Savoye are a source of debate among Le Corbusier scholars; the current restoration appears to contradict the tonality of contemporary photographs. "La maison est une boîte en l'air, percée tout le tour, sans interruption, d'une fenêtre en longueur. . . . La boîte est au milieu des prairies, dominant le verger." Le Cor-busier, *Précisions*, p. 136.

59. "Pour couronner l'ensemble, un solarium dont les formes courbes resistent à la poussée des vents et apportent un élément architectural très riche" (Le Corbusier, *Le Corbusier et Pierre Jeanneret: Œuvre complète de 1910–1929*, p. 187). "Ces parties supé-rieures sont de couleurs très claires: bleu, rose et jaune" (Posener, "La maison Savoye à Poissy," p. 21).

60. FLC 19425.

61. The elongated opening of the terrace was ultimately divided only by the extension of the pilotis.

62. "L'architecture arabe nous donne un enseignement pré-cieux. Elle s'apprécie à la marche, avec le pied; c'est en se déplaçant que l'on voit se développer les ordonnances de l'architecture. . . . Dans cette maison-ci, il s'agit d'une véritable promenade archi-tecturale, offrant des aspects constamment variés, inat-tendus, parfois étonnants." Le Corbusier, *Le Corbusier et Pierre Jeanneret: Œuvre com-plète de 1929–1934*, p. 24.

63. Giedion, *Space, Time and Architecture*, p. 518.

64. "Le béton armé nous do-tant du toit plat nous apporte la libération des sujétions sécu-laires. La maison s'enfonçait dans le sol; le jardin passe des-sous la maison; le jardin est aussi dessus la maison, sur le toit" (Le Corbusier, *Almanach d'architecture moderne*, p. 15). "La lumière, l'air passeront sous la maison. Quelle con-quête! Le jardin de devant et celui de derrière ne font plus qu'un; quel gain d'espace, et quelle sensation de bien-être! Et la maison se présentera en l'air. Quelle pureté architec-turale!" (Le Corbusier, *Précisions*, p. 44).

65. Giedion, "La maison Savoye à Poissy, 1928–1930," p. 212.

66. Le Corbusier, *Précisions*, p. 138.

67. Le Corbusier, "Poésie, lyrisme apportés par les techniques," in *Précisions*, p. 138.

68. Ibid.

69. Le Corbusier, *Le Corbusier et Pierre Jeanneret: Œuvre complète de 1929–1934*, p. 24.

70. Le Corbusier, *Précisions*, p. 101.

71. The other three points being the free plan, the *fenêtre en longueur,* and the free facade. Le Corbusier, "Les 5 points d'une architecture nouvelle," in *Le Corbusier et Pierre Jeanneret: Œuvre complète de 1910–1929*, p. 128.

72. Posener, "La maison Savoye à Poissy," p. 21.

73. Le Corbusier, *Précisions*, p. 236.

74. Walpole, *On Modern Gardening*, p. 22.

75. Adams and Youngman, "Gardens Will Be More Free and Flowing," p. 15.

76. Le Corbusier, "L'heure du repos," in *Urbanisme,* p. 219 n. 2.

77. Letter from Le Corbusier to Beistegui, 5 July 1929; cited by Benton in *Les villas de Le Corbusier,* p. 209.

78. "Il faut rompre avec les habitudes." Beistegui cited by Alexander Watt in "The Surprising Apartment of M. Carlos de Beistegui: Fantasy on the Roofs," p. 155.

79. "Siamo di fronte, in questa architettura delle deformazioni e dell'autopunizione, al *cadavere squisito* di Le Corbusier, Pierre Jeanneret e Charles de Beistegui" (Melis, "Memoria M Memoria," p. 37). "Here is the Twentieth Century Style and Rococo, Napoleon III and *Surréalisme!* . . . This is, indeed, a *Surréaliste* conception of interior decoration. . . . An *esprit* of *Surréalisme* again evinces itself in the invention of this imitation furniture (the *commode,* fireplace and mirror) in stone" (Watt, "The Surprising Apartment of M. Carlos de Beistegui," pp. 155–56, 158). *Cadavre exquis,* or exquisite corpse, refers to a Surrealist game: each participant draws or writes on part of a piece of paper, which is folded so that the next player adds to the drawing or text without seeing the previous part. This is repeated to the end of the sheet of paper, which is then unfolded to reveal an artwork composed by the sum of incidental parts.

80. "Je vous envoie une série de photographies du pavillon de la Cité Universitaire ainsi que d'une installation aux 7°, 8° et 9° étages des Champs-Élysées. . . . Ces deux réalisations se trouvent les deux des facteurs essentiels de l'urbanisation future des villes. . . . Je m'occupe à créer La Ville Radieuse—liberté individuelle, bénéfice de l'action collective, le tout apporté par les techniques modernes" (letter from Le Corbusier to P. M. Bardi dated 25 November 1933, FLC H1–14, 197). Le Corbusier's proposal for a Ville radieuse, or Radiant City, rested on principles similar to those of his Plan Voisin for Paris. Old dwellings in the center of large cities would be replaced with skyscrapers of glass and steel rising from parks and linked by networks of highways. The high-rise apartment blocks, called Unités, provided housing of "human scale" and shared collective services and leisure facilities in an effort to better the living environment of each family. See Robert Fishman, "The Radiant City," in *Urban Utopias in the Twentieth Century: Ebenezer Howard, Frank Lloyd Wright, and Le Corbusier,* pp. 226–34.

81. Watt, "The Surprising Apartment of M. Carlos de Beistegui," p. 156.

82. Letter from Le Corbusier and Pierre Jeanneret to Mrs. Meyer, October 1925, FLC 31525.

83. Le Corbusier, *Le Corbusier et Pierre Jeanneret: Œuvre complète de 1929–1934*, p. 12. See also the description of the Beistegui apartment on pp. 53–57.

84. Le Corbusier, *Précisions*, p. 45.

85. "Au lieu des tuiles et ardoises patriotiques de M. Umbdenstock, ce sont trois jardins suspendus successifs avec des pelouses de fleurs en pleine herbe" (letter from Le Corbusier to Bardi, 25 November 1933, FLC H1–14, 197). In his *Cours d'architecture* (1930), Gustave Umbdenstock expressed the need to maintain social order through an architectural order, in which the roof stood as a symbol of "healthy and moral visions" (cited by Monnier, "Un retour à l'ordre: architecture, géométrie, société," p. 47). See also Umbdenstock, "Le miracle du moyen-âge," *L'Émulation* (1937): 165–67.

86. Le Corbusier, "Appartement avec terrasses, avenue des Champs-Élysées, à Paris," p. 100.

87. Ibid., pp. 100–01.

88. Ibid., p. 101.

89. "Si j'ai une grande admiration pour votre architecture, c'est parce qu'elle nous apporte des choses neuves et belles (et c'est déjà énorme) mais j'entends certaines choses seulement et non pas toutes. Pas une des maisons que vous avez faites ne me conviendrait du tout et c'est pourquoi je n'ai jamais envisagé un instant vous faire faire une construction à votre idée mais bien une maison dont j'aimerais et approuverais chaque partie." Letter from Beistegui to Jeanneret and Le Corbusier, FLC H1–14, 458–59.

90. "Light blue and white is the general colour scheme for the furniture in this room. This applies to the settee and chair. . . . The *commode* . . . is also painted white with gilt arabesque ornamentation, and blue marble slab. The chairs on either side are upholstered in light blue embroidery. The interior of the book-case set in the wall . . . is also painted in light blue. . . . There are even glass studs tacking the tasselled trimming to the ottoman which is also upholstered in light blue. The curtains are of a beautiful pale blue embroidered silk. . . . The very ornate imitation draped curtain over the doorway giving into the dining-room is carried out entirely in light blue glass with a deep blue ribbon *motif*. . . . The Napoleon III table ornament takes the form of a pyramid in blue Dresden china, studded with jewels." Watt, "The Surprising Apartment of M. Carlos de Beistegui," pp. 156, 158.

91. The plan, section, and elevation of a plant container show the layered vegetation. FLC 17437.

92. Ruscus or butcher's broom is usually the name for a small-scale ground cover, but it also frequently refers to a material used in dried floral arrangements and Christmas decorations. The contractor's account described the application of twigs to the screens rather than the planting of ground cover.

93. "D'ailleurs le toit-jardin poursuit un but précis; c'est l'isolant assuré contre la dilatation des terrasses de béton armé. Si vous voulez avoir des plafonds propres sans taches d'eau, *plantez un jardin sur votre toit!*" (Le Corbusier, *Le Corbusier et Pierre Jeanneret: Œuvre complète de 1910–1929*, p. 65). "Le béton armé apporte le toit-terrasse et, avec quinze ou vingt centimètres de terre, le 'toit-jardin.' Nous y voici. C'est en août, en pleine canicule; les herbes sont rôties! Qu'importe! Chaque brin porte ombre, et les racines serrées constituent un épais feutre isolant. Isolant du froid, isolant du chaud. C'est-à-dire un produit isotherme gratuit ne nécéssitant aucun entretien" (Le Corbusier, *Une petite maison, 1923*, p. 45).

94. Le Corbusier-Saugnier, "L'illusion des plans," p. 1776.

95. Le Corbusier, "Appartement avec terrasses," p. 104.

96. Letter from Beistegui to Jeanneret and Le Corbusier, FLC H1–14, 458–59.

97. "Mémoire général des travaux exécutés sur les terrasses," statement from Toutin & Roussel, FLC H1–14, 393.

98. The *Cupressus lawsoniana* was reported dead by 10 July 1932 and was coated with a special paint. Three months later it was removed, along with the infected soil, and replaced with another cypress. See the "Mémoire général," FLC H1–14, 393.

99. The cost was fixed at 14,780 francs. The planters needed to be reinforced against the pressure of the wind: the contractors Dubois & Lepeu did the work for 4,400 francs (estimate dated October 1932) and repaired the mechanical system a few months later for 1,463.50 francs. By 20 February 1933, the driving cable had ruptured. FLC H1–14, 440, 442.

100. Letter from Beistegui to Le Corbusier dated 31 January 1931, FLC H1–14, 459.

101. Letter from Beistegui to Jeanneret dated 21 December 1929, FLC H1–14, 357.

102. Estimate dated 9 January 1930, FLC H1–14, 358–59; report dated 26 May 1932, FLC H1–14, 393 (15 pages).

103. Le Corbusier, "Appartement avec terrasses," p. 100; Le Corbusier, *Une maison—un palais*, pp. 158, 160.

104. Le Corbusier, "Appartement avec terrasses," pp. 100–01.

105. "Appuyé sur la rambarde du navire. . . . Appuyé sur le bord du toit." Le Corbusier, *Une petite maison*, p. 50.

106. FLC 17431 and 17432 (3 June 1929).

107. FLC 17437 and 17438 (30 November 1929); 17443 and 17444 (10 January 1930); 17490 (12 May 1930).

108. Toutin & Roussel described the ivy-dressed plant containers in their account of 21 October 1931. For the plans, sections, and elevations of the containers for the intermediate terrace, see FLC 17514.

109. "La nuit fait plus profond le calme: des fauteuils, des causeurs, des orchestres, des danseurs. A ce même niveau de deux cents mètres, d'autres jardins très loin, partout autour, ont l'air de plats d'or suspendus." Le Corbusier, "'Plan Voisin' de Paris 1925," in *Le Corbusier et Pierre Jeanneret: Œuvre complète de 1910–1929*, p. 115.

110. Le Corbusier, "Appartement avec terrasses," p. 100.

111. Courtiau, "'Le dehors est toujours un dedans,'" p. 35.

112. A schematic plan of the periscope room specified the directions of sight that would frame the various monuments. See Reichlin, "L'esprit de Paris," pp. 55–56. In a previous scheme, the northern side of the solarium was composed of sliding marble panels (FLC 17436).

113. "Garniture des panneaux de treillage . . . en Ruscus destinés à donner l'illusion d'un feuillage naturel." Account of Toutin & Roussel, FLC HI–14, 393.

114. As in the seventeenth-century French concept of "forcing nature," in order to correct its "defects."

115. The vegetation of the apartment overlooking the Champs-Élysées created a green facade yet respected the code restrictions.

116. "La raison d'être du mur de clôture que l'on voit ici est de fermer la vue au nord, à l'est, en partie au sud, à l'ouest; le paysage omni-présent [sic] sur toutes les faces, omnipotent, devient lassant. Avez-vous observé qu'en de telles conditions, 'on' ne le 'regarde' plus? Pour que le paysage compte il faut le limiter, le dimensionner par

une décision radicale: boucher les horizons en élevant des murs et ne les révéler, par interruptions de murs, qu'en des points stratégiques." Le Corbusier, *Une petite maison*, pp. 26–28.

117. Le Corbusier, *Précisions*, p. 49.

118. "La composition est ordonnée sur le paysage. La maison occupe un petit promontoire dominant la plaine derrière Toulon, elle-même barrée par la magnifique silhouette des montagnes. On a tenu à conserver la sensation de surprise qu'offre le spectacle inattendu de cet immense développement paysagiste et pour cela, on a muré les chambres du côté de la vue et l'on a tout simplement percé une porte qui l'orsqu'on l'ouvre, dégage sur un perron d'où le spectacle fait comme une explosion." Le Corbusier, *Le Corbusier et Pierre Jeanneret: Œuvre complète de 1929–1932*, p. 59.

119. See Reichlin, "The Pros and Cons of the Horizontal Window. The Perret–Le Corbusier Controversy," pp. 64–78. The author describes how a vertical opening allows views of foreground, middle ground, and the infinite sky, thus displaying "a detail of maximum perspective depth, an abundance of variety and nuance in respect to the dimensions, colorfulness and brightness of the landscape" (pp. 72–73). In their mature state the trees might have framed the view more effectively, but Le Corbusier had them cut down.

120. Le Corbusier, *Une petite maison*, pp. 52–56.

121. "Le site est une espèce d'acropole, dominant le cirque

de quatre horizons prestigieux, trois horizons de montagnes très diverses, et un autre fait de la fuite du Haut-Lac. Le plateau est en réalité formé de divers vallonnements doux, d'immenses pelouses inclinées tout le tour et parsemées d'arbres gigantesques, objets de la fierté genevoise. Des troupeaux paissent par-ci par-là. Ce touchant spectacle agreste qui nous reporte aux pages attendries de Jean-Jacques Rousseau, je ne veux pas le troubler. . . . Pour l'instant je conserve l'herbe et les troupeaux, les arbres séculaires et toutes les échappées ravissantes du paysage, et, en l'air, à un niveau déterminé, sur un sol horizontal de béton juché au haut des pilotis qui descendent, eux, là où ils trouvent leur base, j'élève les prismes limpides et purs d'édifices utilitaires; je suis soulevé par une intention élevée; je proportionne des prismes et les espaces qui les entourent; je compose atmosphériquement. Tout y participe: les troupeaux, les herbes et les fleurettes du premier plan, que l'on foule du pied et que l'on caresse de l'œil, le lac, les Alpes, le ciel . . . et les divines proportions. Et grâce aux pilotis, sur cette acropole vouée à la méditation et au travail intellectuel, le sol naturel demeure, la poésie est intacte." Le Corbusier, *Précisions*, p. 50.

122. "The eye forms a very inaccurate judgement of extent, unless there be some standard by which it can be measured; bushes and trees are of such various sizes, that it is impossible to use them as a measure of distance; but the size of a horse, a sheep, or a cow, varies so little, that we immediately judge their distance from their apparent diminution, according to the distance at which they are placed; and as they occasionally change their situation, they break that surface over which the eye passes, without observing it, to the first object it meets to rest upon. . . . It has been objected to the slides with which I elucidate my proposed alterations, that I generally introduce, in the improved view, boats on the water, and cattle on the lawns. To this I answer, that both are real objects of improvement, and give animation to the scene; indeed it cannot be too often inculcated that a large lake without boats, is a dreary waste of water, and a large lawn without cattle, is one of the melancholy appendages of solitary grandeur observable in the pleasure-grounds of the past century." Humphry Repton, chapter 5, "Concerning Park Scenery," in *Sketches and Hints on Landscape Gardening*, pp. 81–82.

123. "Le jardin sur le toit. De l'herbe pousse entre les joints des dalles; des tortues se promènent tranquillement; des arbres ont été plantés: thuyas, cyprès, fusains, okubas [*sic*], lauriers de Chine, troènes, tamarins, etc. Six ans ont passé, la verdure est plus belle que dans un jardin: le 'toit-jardin' est un peu dans les conditions d'une serre (car l'air est pur, la lumière intense, et les racines plongent dans un terrain chaud et humide)" (Le Corbusier, *Le Corbusier et Pierre Jeanneret: Œuvre complète de 1910–1929*, p. 65). Although "okuba" appears to be closer phonetically to the botanical *Aucuba japonica*, the Japanese name for this plant is *aoki*. For "tamarin" Le Cor-

busier probably intends "tamarinier," or tamarind, a subtropical evergreen tree.

124. "Je vais élever (les poteaux) à trois mètres au dessus du sol intact et j'accrocherai mon plancher là-haut. *J'ai ainsi disponible tout le sol sous la maison.* Je dessine sur ce sol reconquis une auto, et je fais passer l'air et les verdures." Le Corbusier, *Précisions*, p. 41.

125. Le Corbusier, *Le Corbusier et Pierre Jeanneret: Œuvre complète de 1929–1934*, p. 24.

126. Le Corbusier, notes written on the back of a photograph of la petite maison seen from the lake (FLC L2[4] 1–142). Apparently after the house was built, the Conseil Municipal of the town nearby passed a law forbidding roof terraces as well as buildings painted white.

127. "L'œil humain, dans ses investigations, tourne toujours. . . . Il s'attache à tout et est attiré par le centre de gravité du site entier. D'un coup le problème s'étend à l'entour. Les maisons voisines, la montagne lointaine ou proche, l'horizon bas ou haut, sont des masses formidables qui agissent avec la puissance de leur cube." Le Corbusier-Saugnier, "L'illusion des plans," p. 1775.

128. "Je me charge de la confection des plans et de la construction de villas, de maisons de campagne, de tous immeubles industriels (spécialité de béton armé), . . . ainsi que d'architecture intérieure et d'architecture de jardin." Le Corbusier cited by Robert, "Le jardin et le paysage dans l'œuvre de Le Corbusier," p. 11; see also Sekler, "Le Corbusier, Ruskin, the Tree, and the Open Hand," p. 53.

129. "J'ai tant étudié la question des jardins, et j'en ai tant vu partout, que je suis navré de voir commettre des erreurs capables de nuire si fortement à l'ensemble. . . . D'autre part planter dans les gazons des arbres symétriques à la baie du hall, est, je vous le certifie, une erreur d'architecture capable de compromettre la façade. La maison est toute symétrie, le jardin est au cordeau. Si vous ne coupez pas par une 'asymétrie indispensable', ce sera créer une lassitude réelle, et rétrécir tout le monumental de la façade." Letter from Le Corbusier to Mrs. Schwob dated 30 September 1917, in Robert, "Le jardin et le paysage," p. 93.

130. Among the works Le Corbusier consulted were: Francesco Colonna, *Hypnerotomachie, ou Discours du songe de Poliphile* (Venice, 1499). Although Le Corbusier dated the text 1499, he used the French title, which was first published in 1546; Jacques Boyceau, *Traité du jardinage* (Paris, 1638); André Mollet, *Le jardin de plaisir* (Stockholm, 1651); Antoine Dezallier d'Argenville, *La théorie et la pratique du jardinage* (Paris, 1747); Charles-Antoine Jombert, *Les délices de Versailles et des maisons royales . . .* (Paris, 1766); Jean-Charles Krafft, *Plans des plus beaux jardins de France, d'Angleterre et d'Allemagne . . .* (Paris, 1809); Henri Stein, *Les jardins de France des origines à la fin du XVIII siècle* (Paris, 1913). FLC B2–20.

131. Dezallier d'Argenville, chapter VII, "Des boulingrins," in *La théorie et la pratique du jardinage* (1739, the third of four editions), plates between pp. 78–79, 82–83.

132. Ibid., chapter VIII, "De la place convenable à chaque fleur dans les jardins, & des différentes décorations des parterres suivant les saisons," pp. 306–13.

133. Le Corbusier, FLC B2–20, 55. The argument for order recurred throughout Vera's texts as he invoked morals, religion, or politics. In "Promenade à travers siècles et jardins," of 1935, he extended a parallel between formalism in the garden and the general desire for order, whether witnessed in bolshevism or fascism: "La préoccupation n'est-elle pas encore l'établissement d'un ordre nouveau: bolchevisme, fascisme, un ordre élaboré par la Société des Nations, ou basé sur des principes spiritualistes? Il y a volonté d'instaurer un ordre. N'est-ce pas pour tracer des jardins réguliers un motif de plus?" Vera, L'Urbanisme ou la vie heureuse, p. 243.

134. "Dans chap Jardin mettre 1 cliché de André Vera pour montrer l[e?] mode[rne?] Vera est intelligent de faire un livre dont la teneur et l'esprit s'adressent à 1 seule catégorie de gens." Le Corbusier, FLC B2–20, 79.

135. Chapter II, "Des éléments constitutifs de la ville . . . 5) des murs de clôture; 6) des ponts; 7) des arbres; 8) des jardins et des parcs; 9) des cimetières; 10) cités jardins." Le Corbusier, manuscript for La construction des villes, FLC B2–20, 556.

136. Annotated sketches, FLC B2–20, 225, 257bis; Le Corbusier, Propos d'urbanisme, p. 29.

137. "Le jardinier consacrera sa vie à entretenir contre chiendent et limaces cette gageure de passementerie, toujours défaite par les pousses nouvelles" (Le Corbusier, Propos d'urbanisme, pp. 29–30). "Temps de grands rois. Ce fut une apogée, ce fut tout un temps. Admirable, nous sommes bien d'accord; mais la photo d'avion de Vaux-le-Vicomte provoque un faisceau de questions inquiètes . . . et Monsieur le Surintendant y connut des difficultés financières" (p. 30).

138. Le Corbusier, Urbanisme, p. 72,

139. Le Corbusier, Précisions, p. 154.

140. Ibid., p. 102.

141. As in William Robinson's wild garden; see his "Explanatory," in The Wild Garden, pp. 1–11. "Les 'toits-jardins' des grattes-ciel . . . émaillés de tulipes ou de géraniums en parterres de broderie, ou sillonnés de chemins bordés de la bigarrure des fleurs vivaces." Le Corbusier, "'Plan Voisin' de Paris 1925," in Le Corbusier et Pierre Jeanneret: Œuvre complète de 1910–1929, p. 115.

142. Le Corbusier, Une maison—un palais, pp. 158, 160.

143. Le Corbusier, "Unité," pp. 27–28.

144. Le Corbusier, Urbanisme, pp. 73, 192. The duc d'Orléans had commissioned Carmontelle to design the estate of Monceau in 1778. Confiscated in 1793, the Anglo-Chinese garden was later subdivided and developed. Jean-Charles-Adolphe Alphand remodeled the remaining grounds in 1861.

145. Ibid., pp. 223–24.

146. Le Corbusier, Une petite maison, pp. 48–49.

147. Le Corbusier, Précisions, pp. 48–49.

148. Tunnard, "The Functional Aspect of Garden Planning," p. 199.

149. Le Corbusier, Vers une architecture, p. 143.

150. The director of the Department for Architecture, Parks and Gardens, Louis Bonnier, threatened to withdraw from Le Corbusier his authorization to build for having cut "three important branches of a tree." The magazine L'Esprit Nouveau replied that, oddly enough, Mr. Le Corbusier had just reported the branches missing. The architect then warned the department that if things did not "return to their initial state," he would decline all responsibility for the success of the hanging garden that framed the tree in question. Letter from Louis Bonnier to the director of L'Esprit Nouveau dated 4 April 1925, FLC A2–13, 139; reply from an administrator of L'Esprit Nouveau to the director of the Department for Architecture, Parks and Gardens dated 10 April 1925, FLC A2–13, 141.

243

CHAPTER 9:
ANDRÉ LURÇAT

1. Although both Lurçat (a Catholic) and Le Corbusier (a Calvinist) shared a predilection for an "architectural Lutheranism" (see chap. 3, n. 33), they differed in their conception of how a house should address the site.

2. Lurçat, "La nature," in *Formes, composition et lois d'harmonie*, vol. 3, p. 337.

3. Ibid.

4. This chapter included the topics "vegetation, water, [the] combination of these elements, [the] art of gardens, style adapted to destination." Ibid., pp. 335–62.

5. Ibid., p. 339.

6. Ibid., p. 356.

7. The author listed pilotis, the terrace, the horizontal window, color, and artificial light as "Les éléments nouveaux." Lurçat, *Architecture*, pp. 109–10, 130, 128, respectively. Real estate translates into *propriété immobilière*, as in immobile.

8. "Des raisons techniques, des raisons d'économie, des raisons de confort et des raisons sentimentales nous conduisent à adopter le toit-terrasse." Le Corbusier, "Les 5 points d'une architecture nouvelle," in *Le Corbusier et Pierre Jeanneret: Œuvre complète de 1910–1929*, p. 128.

9. Lurçat, *Architecture*, p. 117.

10. Ibid., pp. 118, 123; and Lurçat, "Introduction," in *Terrasses et jardins*, n.p.

11. "Quelques terrasses sont déjà aménagées, en France en particulier, où la verdure pousse aussi à l'aise qu'au sol, où l'on profite d'un air meilleur, où l'on peut déjeuner, dîner, dormir, prendre des bains de soleil, faire de la cul-ture physique en plein air et pourtant à l'abri des regards des voisins. . . . Ceci n'est pas le seul gain intéressant que nous apportent les terrasses nouvelles; le plus capital est sans doute cette possibilité de lier grâce à elles intimement la vie du bâtiment avec celle du jardin, et par lui avec la nature environnante. Les loggias, les terrasses trouvées aux différents étages et sur les toits plats, et garnies de verdure et d'arbustes, permettent un enchaînement absolu du jardin organisé avec la maison, pour la plus grande joie des yeux et de l'esprit." Lurçat, "Introduction," in *Terrasses et jardins*, n.p.

12. Charles Imbert, "Le quartier artiste de Montsouris," p. 108.

13. Lurçat, *Projets et réalisations*, plate 11; Vera, *Le nouveau jardin*, pp. 9–10.

14. Vera, *Le nouveau jardin*, p. 56.

15. See Delisle, "André Lurçat, 1924–1925," pp. 80–96; "Hôtel particulier à Versailles (S.-et-O.): A. Lurçat, architecte," pp. 78–80, plate 60; "Architectures," p. 224; Mrs. Howard Robertson, "Two Views against the Geometric Garden," pp. 5–6; Achel, "André Lurçat, architecte," pp. 113–16; Steele, "New Pioneering in Garden Design," pp. 159–77; Winternitz, "Ein französischer Hausgarten," pp. 88–89; Hübotter, "An die Schriftleitung der 'Gartenkunst,'" pp. 105–06; *Contemporary Landscape Architecture and Its Sources*, p. 36.

16. Lurçat, *Projets et réalisations*, plate 16.

17. Winternitz, "Ein französischer Hausgarten," p. 88.

18. "Hôtel particulier à Versailles," p. 80.

19. Steele, "New Pioneering in Garden Design," p. 172.

20. "Hôtel particulier à Versailles," p. 80; Winternitz, "Ein französischer Hausgarten," p. 88.

21. Delisle, "André Lurçat," p. 92.

22. Ibid., p. 90.

23. Mrs. Howard Robertson, "Two Views against the Geometric Garden," p. 6.

24. "Hôtel particulier à Versailles," p. 80.

25. The critic mentioned sword lilies, roses, privets, laurels, and poplars. Winternitz, "Ein französischer Hausgarten," p. 89.

26. I wish to thank Jean-Louis Cohen for bringing to my attention the article by Hübotter, "An die Schriftleitung der 'Gartenkunst,'" and Kai Gutshow for his help in translating it. Apparently, in his *Cours d'architecture*, Gustave Umbdenstock had also traced over the photograph of the Villa Bomsel and annotated it with the condemnation "inert character of a geometric layout." Umbdenstock, *Cours d'architecture, École Polytechnique*, Paris, 1930, fig. 362; cited by Cohen, "L'architecture d'André Lurçat (1894–1970): Autocritique d'un moderne," p. 161.

27. Hübotter, "An die Schriftleitung," p. 105.

28. "Nur das Lebensgefühl der modernen Menschen wird uns leiten müssen, verbunden mit einwandfreier gärtnerischer und handwerklicher Sachkenntnis." Ibid.

29. "La façade est orientée au midi. Le jardin attenant est

dessiné en fonction de l'ombre portée par la maison. Le terreplein triangulaire offre un séjour ombreux. Des massifs de rosiers alternent avec des pelouses de gazons; une ligne de fusains et des bordures garnies de fleurs encadrent le jardin." Delisle, "André Lurçat," p. 87.

30. The garden as built appears to have followed an even simpler parti. In the photographs illustrating Steele's "New Pioneering in Garden Design," which show only portions of the garden, roses are arranged in a line and not the wedge shape more characteristic of the 1920s.

31. Apparently, the house could have been built in six months, and very economically. See *L'Organisation Ménagère*, Paris, no. 11 (15 March 1926), pp. 13–15; cited by Cohen, "André Lurçat," p. 164.

32. Steele, "New Styles in Gardening," pp. 353–54.

33. Steele, "New Pioneering in Garden Design," p. 171.

34. See the descriptions of the interior by Delisle, "André Lurçat," pp. 90, 92; and by Cohen, "André Lurçat," p. 160.

35. Steele, "New Pioneering in Garden Design," p. 172.

36. Lurçat, *Architecture*, p. 70.

37. Tunnard, "Modern Gardens for Modern Houses—Reflections on Current Trends in Landscape Design," p. 58.

38. Hübotter, "An die Schriftleitung," p. 105.

39. "In much of the modernistic work in France, one finds what would be expected,—that in the new, the French point of view with regard to the placing and importance of flowers and horticulture remains as in the

old." Steele, "New Pioneering in Garden Design," p. 172.

40. Steele, "New Styles in Gardening," p. 353.

41. Hitchcock and Johnson, *The International Style*, p. 77.

42. Lurçat, "L'hôtel du peintre Walter Guggenbuhl," *Art et Industrie* (10 March 1927): 10; cited by Cohen, "André Lurçat," p. 174.

43. Cohen, "André Lurçat," p. 172.

44. "Nous savons que Lurçat aime ainsi introduire parmi les constructions, sévères à force de roideur, ce qu'il nomme des éléments fixes de vie, massifs ou vases de fleurs, où l'œil du citadin trouve un charme certain. Dans le cas présent, ces éléments servent d'heureuse transition entre le cube de béton et la belle échappée sur le parc voisin." Rémon, "Une villa d'André Lurçat au Parc Montsouris," p. 340.

45. Shand, "André Lurçat's 'Architecture,'" p. 613.

46. Lurçat, *Projets et réalisations*, plate 66.

47. See Jean-Claude Delorme and Jean-Paul Scalabre, "De l'avant-garde fonctionnaliste à la pratique municipale," *Architecture Mouvement Continuité* (special issue on Lurçat), no. 40 (1976): 20.

48. Lurçat, *Projets et réalisations*, pp. 11–12. Although the plans for a floating island in Venice (1931) for Beistegui can be found in the Fonds Lurçat (folder 40) at the Archives de France, in Paris, Lurçat essentially abandoned bourgeois architecture after 1930.

49. Lurçat, *Projets et réalisations*, p. 12.

50. Achel, "André Lurçat, architecte," p. 115.

51. Steele, "New Pioneering in Garden Design," p. 162.

52. "There shall be no incongruity in scale between the arrangements for outdoor and indoor living spaces." Tunnard, "Modern Gardens for Modern Houses," p. 58.

53. Ibid., p. 59.

54. Lurçat, "Introduction," in *Terrasses et jardins*, n.p.

CHAPTER 10:
EPILOGUE

1. See Gréber, "Introduction," in *Jardins modernes: Exposition internationale de 1937*, n.p.

2. Steele, review of *Jardins modernes: Exposition internationale de 1937,* by Jacques Gréber, pp. 117–18.

3. Mallet-Stevens designed the Hygiene, Tobacco, Brazilian Coffee, and National Solidarity Pavilions, as well as the Palace of Light. Moreux is cited as having been the architect of the garden for the U.A.M. Pavilion. The series of decorative and didactic garden projects he had designed with Paul Vera for the parc de Sceaux remained on paper. Albert Laprade and Léon Bazin's courtyard scheme, titled Irak, was illustrated in Gréber, *Jardins modernes,* plate 22.

4. Duchêne, "Formal Parks and Gardens in France," p. 280. There are several passages of this text that reappear word for word in the 1937 report, which is also a promulgation of the social ideas he expressed in *Les jardins de l'avenir* (1935). See Duchêne, "Premier congrès international des architectes de jardins." I wish to thank Caroline Constant for bringing this report to my attention.

5. "Le grand luxe a cessé d'avoir sa fin en soi; en tant que grand art mis au service des puissantes individualités, *l'Art des Jardins se meurt.*" Duchêne, "A. L'art des jardins en 1937," in "Premier congrès international," p. 1.

6. Duchêne, "Formal Parks and Gardens in France," p. 280; "L'Art des Jardins est . . . en train de renaître sous une nouvelle formule, . . . celle de *l'Art des Jardins envisagé du point de vue social. . . .* Son esthétique sera en quelque sorte plus *utilitaire* que par le passé, puisqu'au lieu d'exprimer le raffinement de quelques êtres priviligiés, il devra satisfaire les aspirations esthétiques des foules." Duchêne, "A. L'art des jardins en 1937," in "Premier congrès international," p. 2.

7. Duchêne deplored the decline of luxury; even in his "utilitarian" gardens he sought the satisfaction of "intellectual and artistic pleasures" of a rather elitist nature. Such gardens should "preferably include a green theater, an outdoor cinema, a stage for rhythmic dancing, gushing waters . . . a bird garden, beehives . . . in other words, everything that could delight and enrich thoughts." Duchêne, "C. Les jardins privés dans les conditions de la vie actuelle," in "Premier congrès international," pp. 5–6.

8. "Chaque époque de l'art a eu ses jardins. . . . Aurons-nous les nôtres? L'architecte moderne tend de plus en plus à la suppression de tout ce qui n'est pas, ou ne paraît pas être, simplement utile, par goût et par nécessité: le jardin pourra-t-il lutter victorieusement contre les emplacements de culture physique et les potagers?" "Jardins—J.-C.-N. Forestier, architecte," p. 64.

9. Duchêne, "C. Les jardins privés," in "Premier congrès international," p. 6, italics added.

10. "Tout ce qui s'offrira à la vue du peuple doit lui donner l'habitude du beau, affiner ses sens et développer ses facultés contemplatives ou critiques; tout doit contribuer à lui donner l'impression de la sérénité et de l'ordre." Duchêne, "E. Conception actuelle des parcs de collectivités publiques," in "Premier congrès international," p. 16.

11. Tunnard, review of *L'homme et le jardin,* by André Vera, p. 183.

12. Hitchcock and Johnson, *The International Style,* p. 77.

13. "Monsieur Carel exprime dans son rapport, que l'on revient pour certaines compositions aux jardins naturels avec scènes de fantaisie, avec dessins de buis 'd'avant-garde' et qu'il lui semble que l'horticulture délaissée depuis des années va prendre enfin sa revanche." Carel cited by Duchêne, "C. Les jardins privés," in "Premier congrès international," p. 7.

"À l'exposition des arts décoratifs: Les jardins." *La Construction Moderne* 41, no. 2 (11 October 1925): 16–19.

"L'abstention des États-Unis." In "Chronique." *Art et Décoration* (January 1925): 3.

Ache, Jean-Baptiste. "André Lurçat: Quarante-cinq ans de recherche architecturale." In *André Lurçat architecte.* Paris: Conservatoire National des Arts et Métiers, 1967, pp. 9–25.

———. "André Lurçat: 48 ans d'architecture." *La Construction Moderne* 86, no. 5 (September–October 1970): 52–59.

Achel, Henri. "André Lurçat, architecte." *L'Architecture* 40, no. 4 (April 1927): 113–16.

Ackerman, Phyllis. "Modernism in Bookbinding." *The International Studio* 80, no. 330 (November 1924): 145–49.

Adams, T., and G. P. Youngman. "Gardens Will Be More Free and Flowing." In *Gardens and Gardening, 1939,* edited by F. A. Mercer. London: The Studio Limited, 1939, pp. 14–15.

Alphand, Adolphe. *Les promenades de Paris.* Paris: J. Rothschild Éditeur, 1867–73. Reprint. Princeton: Princeton Architectural Press, 1984.

Andia, Béatrice de, editor. *De Bagatelle à Monceau, 1778–1978: Les folies du XVIII° siècle à Paris.* Paris: Musée Carnavalet, 1978.

André, Édouard. *L'art des jardins: Traité général de la composition des parcs et jardins.* Paris, 1879. Reprint. Marseille: Laffitte, 1983.

"André Lurçat," special issue of *Architecture Mouvement Continuité,* no. 40 (1976).

André Lurçat architecte. Paris: Conservatoire National des Arts et Métiers, 1967.

Les années 25: Art déco/Bauhaus/Stijl/Esprit Nouveau. 2 vols. Paris: Musée des Arts Décoratifs, 1966.

Anthoine-Legrain, Jacques. "'Souvenirs' sur Pierre Legrain." In *Pierre Legrain relieur.* Paris: Librairie Auguste Blaizot, 1965, pp. xi–xv.

Antonetti, Guy. *Histoire contemporaire politique et sociale.* Paris: Presses universitaires de France, 1986.

Apollinaire, Guillaume. *Les peintres cubistes.* Paris: Eug. Figuière, 1913. Reprint. Paris: Hermann, 1980.

L'Architecte. N.s. 1 (1924), 2 (1925), 3 (1926), 4 (1927), 5 (1928), 6 (1929), 9 (1932).

"L'architecture," special issue of *Le Gaz Chez Soi,* n.d. (ca. 1935).

"Architectures." *Cahiers d'Art* 1, no. 8 (October 1926): 220–25.

"L'art des jardins." *Connaissance des Arts*, no. 41 (July 1955): 20–25.

Les Arts de la Maison. Spring–Summer 1924, Autumn–Winter 1924, Spring–Summer 1925, Autumn–Winter 1925, Spring–Summer 1926, Autumn–Winter 1926.

Auböck, Maria. "Teatro natura. La costruzione dei giardini negli anni della Secessione." In *Le arti a Vienna dalla Secessione alla caduta dell'impero asburgico.* Venice: Edizioni La Biennale, 1984.

Bac, Ferdinand. "L'art des jardins à l'exposition des arts décoratifs." *L'Illustration* 166, no. 4301 (8 August 1925): 135–38.

Bachollet, Raymond, Daniel Bordet, and Anne-Claude Lelieur. *Paul Iribe.* Paris: Éditions Denoël, 1982.

Badovici, Jean. "L'art d'Eileen Gray par Jean Badovici, architecte." *Wendingen*, no. 6 (1924): 12–15.

Baker, Geoffrey. "Equivalent of a Loudly-Colored Folk Art Is Needed." *Landscape Architecture Quarterly* 32, no. 2 (January 1942): 65–66

Les ballets suédois dans l'art contemporain. Paris: Éditions du Trianon, 1931.

Banham, Reyner. *Theory and Design in the First Machine Age.* New York: Praeger, 1970.

Barozzi, Jacques. *Bagatelle.* Paris: Association des Amis du Parc et du Château de Bagatelle, 1984.

Barr, Alfred H., Jr. *Cubism and Abstract Art.* Cambridge: Harvard University Press, 1936.

Barré-Despond, Arlette. *Union des artistes modernes.* Paris: Éditions du Regard, 1986.

Baudelaire, Charles. "Le peintre de la vie moderne." In *Curiosités esthétiques: L'art romantique et autres œuvres critiques.* Paris: Éditions Garnier, 1962, pp. 453–502. Originally published in *Le Figaro,* 26, 29 November and 3 December 1863.

Baudry, Jean. *Petits jardins.* Paris: Massin, n.d.

Beauplan, Robert de. "À travers la kermesse de Paris." *L'Illustration* 166, no. 4307 (19 September 1925): 285–88.

Benoist, Luc. "L'exposition internationale des arts décoratifs et industriels modernes: Les arts graphiques. Les arts de la rue et des jardins." *Beaux-Arts,* no. 16 (15 September 1925): 253–64.

———. "Les tissus de Sonia Delaunay." *Art et Décoration* (November 1926): 142–44.

Benoit-Levy, Georges. "Petits jardins au goût du jour." *L'Illustration* 182:1, no. 4656 (28 May 1932): n.p.

Benton, Tim. *Les villas de Le Corbusier et Pierre Jeanneret, 1920–1930.* Paris: Philippe Sers, 1984.

Benton, Tim, Charlotte Benton, and Aaron Scharf. *Design 1920s: German Design and the Bauhaus, 1925–32; Modernism in the Decorative Arts: Paris, 1910–30.* Milton Keynes, England: Open University Press, 1975.

Berger, John. "The Moment of Cubism." In *The Sense of Sight.* New York: Pantheon, 1985, pp. 159–88.

Bizot, Chantal, Micheline Beranger, Marina Urquidi. *Bibliographie 1925.* Paris: Société des Amis de la Bibliothèque Forney, 1976.

Blaizot, Georges. "De Marius Michel à Pierre Legrain: Notes et souvenirs d'un libraire." In *Pierre Legrain relieur.* Paris: Librairie Auguste Blaizot, 1965, pp. xxi–xxiv.

Blanche, J.-E. "H. Sommer, Architecte." *Art et Industrie* (February 1927): 15–18.

Blomfield, Reginald, and F. Inigo Thomas. *The Formal Garden in England.* 1892. Reprint. London: Waterstone, 1985.

Boitard, Pierre. *Traité de la composition et de l'ornement des jardins.* Paris: Audot, Libraire Éditeur, 1859. Reprint. Paris: L.V.D.V. Interlivres, n.v.d.

Bonfils, Robert. "Pierre Legrain décorateur créateur." In *Pierre Legrain relieur.* Paris: Librairie Auguste Blaizot, 1965, pp. xxxv–xxxviii.

Borissalievitch, M. "Promenade esthétique à l'exposition des arts décoratifs." *La Construction Moderne* (December 1925): 151–55.

Boyer, Jacques. "L'exposition internationale des arts décoratifs." *La Nature,* no. 2657 (7 March 1925): 145–47.

Briolle, Cécile, and Agnès Fuzibet. "La villa Noailles: Robert Mallet-Stevens, 1924." 2 vols. Thesis, U.P.A. Marseilles-Luminy, France, 1981.

Briolle, Cécile, Agnès Fuzibet, and Gérard Monnier. *Rob Mallet-Stevens: La villa Noailles.* Marseilles: Éditions Parenthèses, 1990.

248

———. "La villa de Noailles à Hyères, 1923– 1933." *Casabella,* no. 504 (July–August 1984): 44–51.

Briolle, Cécile, and Jacques Repiquet. "Une pièce rare: Le jardin cubiste de Gabriel Guevrekian à Hyères (1926)." *Monuments Historiques,* no. 143 (February–March 1986): 38–41.

———. "La villa de Noailles, style ou liberté. Hyères, 1924–1933." In *Rob. Mallet-Stevens: Architecture, mobilier, décoration.* Paris: Action Artistique de Paris; Philippe Sers Éditeur, 1986, pp. 27–43.

Brown, Jane. *The Art and Architecture of English Gardens.* New York: Rizzoli, 1989.

Brunet, C. "Jardins de la villa Noailles." École Nationale Supérieure du Paysage, Versailles, 1987.

Brunhammer, Yvonne. *1925.* Paris: Les Presses de la Connaissance, 1976.

Burgess, Gelett. "The Wild Men of Paris." *The Architectural Record* (May 1910): 400–14.

Butler, Frances. "Big, Little and Nothing: The Empty Garden." *The Princeton Journal:* Thematic Studies in Architecture. (Landscape) 2 (1985): 70–87.

C., H. de. "A General View." *The Architectural Review* 58, no. 344 (July 1925): 3–19.

Cambó, Francesc de Asís. *Memòries (1876–1936).* Barcelona: Editorial Alpha, 1981.

Cancale, Henri. "Little French Gardens." *House and Garden* (December 1921): 19–21.

Catalogue général officiel. Exposition internationale des arts décoratifs et industriels modernes: Paris, avril–octobre 1925. Paris: Ministère du Commerce et de l'Industrie des Postes et des Télégraphes, ca. 1926.

Champigneulle, Bernard. "Architecte habile, décorateur raffiné, il était considéré comme un dilettante." *Arts; Spectacles,* no. 628 (17–28 July 1957): 8.

Chaney, Fred. "Concepts of Nature and Redemption in the Work of Le Corbusier." Ph.D. dissertation, Cambridge University, 1991.

Chapon, François. *Mystère et splendeurs de Jacques Doucet, 1853–1929.* Paris: Jean-Claude Lattès, 1984.

Chapsal, F. *Rapport à M. le ministre du commerce, de l'industrie, des postes et des télégraphes.* Paris, 23 May 1913.

Charensol. "La rue—les jardins." *L'Amour de l'Art* 6 (August 1925): 324–27.

Chavance, René. "Guévrékian, architecte et décorateur." *Art et Décoration* 55, no. 1 (January 1929): 1–15.

———. "Jean-Charles Moreux, architecte et décorateur." *Art et Décoration* (January 1927): 48–55.

———. "Pierre Legrain." Obituary in "Échos et Nouvelles." *Art et Décoration* 56 (August 1929): viii.

———. "La section autrichienne." *Art et Décoration* (September 1925): 120–32.

Chéret, Yvon. "Il y a un an disparaissait Jean-Charles Moreux, dernier homme de la Renaissance." *Arts; Spectacles,* no. 628 (17–28 July 1957): 8.

Chéronnet, Louis. "Un hôtel particulier au Ranelagh par J.-C. Moreux avec la collaboration de Bolette Natanson." *Art et Décoration* (1932): 331–40.

———. "Principes et orientation des expositions." *L'Architecture d'Aujourd'hui* 11, no. 1–2 (January 1940): 29–30.

Chevrel, M. E. *De la loi du contraste simultané.* Paris: Pitois-Levrault, 1839.

"Chez le Cte Charles de Noailles." *Art et Industrie* (September 1927): 16.

Chong, Yu-Chee. "Natural Order." *World Architecture* (April 1989): 72–75.

Chrétien-Lalanne, M. "Promenade d'un sceptique à travers l'exposition des arts décoratifs et industriels modernes." *L'Architecture* 38, no. 8 (1925): 105–16.

Clouzot, Henri. "L'avant-garde de l'art appliqué." *La Renaissance de l'Art Français* 9 (1926): 219–24.

———. "En marge de l'art appliqué moderne." *L'Amour de l'Art,* no. 4 (April 1924): 105–25.

Cocteau, Jean. *Le rappel à l'ordre.* Paris: Stock, 1918–26.

Cohen, Jean-Louis. "L'architecture d'André Lurçat (1894–1970): Autocritique d'un moderne." Doctorat, École des Hautes Études en Sciences Sociales, Paris, 1985.

———. "L'architecture en France: Entre le spectre de l'urbanisme et le halo des recherches soviétiques." In *Paris-Moscou, 1900–1930.* Paris: Centre Georges Pompidou, 1979, pp. 272–85.

———. "Mallet-Stevens et l'u.a.m.: Comment frapper les masses?" *Architecture Mouvement Continuité,* no. 41 (1977): 19–22.

Colquhoun, Alan. "Displacement of Concepts in Le Corbusier." In *Essays in Architectural Criticism: Modern Architecture and Historical Change.* Cambridge: MIT Press, 1981, pp. 51–66.

Colvile, Georgiana. *Vers un langage des arts autour des années vingt.* Paris: Librairie Klincksieck, 1977.

Constant, Caroline. "From the Virgilian Dream to Chandigarh." *The Architectural Review,* no. 1079 (January 1987): 66–72.

Contemporary Landscape Architecture and Its Sources. San Francisco: Museum of Modern Art, 1937.

"Contemporary Trends and Future Possibilities in Landscape Design." Papers presented at the Annual Meeting of American Society of Landscape Architects, Philadelphia, 25–27 January 1932. *Landscape Architecture Quarterly* 22, no. 4 (July 1932): 288–303.

Cooper, Douglas. *The Cubist Epoch.* London: Phaidon Press, 1970.

———. *Fernand Léger et le nouvel espace.* Geneva: Éditions des Trois Collines, 1949.

Cordier, Gilbert. "À propos des expositions universelles." AMC: Bulletin de la Société des Architectes Diplômés Par Le Gouvernement, no. 17 (1970): 2–69.

Corpechot, Lucien. "J.-C.-N. Forestier." *La Gazette Illustrée des Amateurs de Jardins* (1930): 17.

Cosmi, Brigitte de, and Pierre-Alain Croset. "I clienti di Le Corbusier." *Rassegna* (I clienti di Le Corbusier), no. 3 (July 1980): 89–96.

Courtiau, Catherine. "'Le dehors est toujours un dedans': Tensions entre architecture et nature chez Le Corbusier." *Mitteilungen der Gesellschaft für Gartenkultur* 7, no. 2 (1989): 34–43.

Crane, Walter. "Modern Decorative Art at Turin: General Impressions." *Magazine of Art* 25 (1902): 488–93.

Cretté, Georges. "Distinctive Designs in Hand-tooled Book-bindings." *The Studio* 100, no. 452 (November 1930): 378–81

Croset, Pierre-Alain. "La questione del cliente." *Rassegna* (I clienti di Le Corbusier), no. 3 (July 1980): 5–6.

———. "Il tetto-giardino: 'Ragione tecnica' e ideale estetico." *Rassegna* (La natura dei giardini), no. 8 (October 1981): 25–38.

Crowe, Sylvia. *Garden Design.* London: Thomas Gibson; Chicester: Packard Publishings, 1981.

Dacier, Émile. "La Manufacture de Sèvres à l'exposition des arts décoratifs." *La Revue de l'Art Ancien et Moderne* 48 (1925): 179–88.

Darcel, Alfred. *Étude sur l'architecture des jardins.* Paris: Dunod, 1875.

Daval, Jean-Luc. *Journal des avant-gardes: Les années vingt/les années trente.* Geneva: Éditions d'Art Albert Skira, 1980.

Davies, Karen. *At Home in Manhattan: Modern Decorative Arts, 1925 to the Depression.* New Haven: Yale University Art Gallery, 1983.

Delaunay, Robert. *Du cubisme à l'art abstrait.* Edited by Pierre Francastel. Paris: S.E.V.P.E.N., 1957.

Delisle, B. "André Lurçat, 1924–1925." *Jardins et Cottages* (December 1926): 80–96.

———. "J.-Ch. Moreux." *Jardins et Cottages* (1927): 108–14.

Delorme, Jean-Claude. *Les villas d'artistes à Paris (de Louis Süe à Le Corbusier).* Paris: Les Éditions de Paris, 1987.

Demeures et jardins de France. Plaisir de France. Paris: Les Publications de France, 1953.

Dervaux, Adolphe. "L'Exposition des arts décoratifs et industriels modernes." *L'Architecte,* n.s. 2 (May 1925): 45–54.

Deshairs, Léon. "L'exposition des arts décoratifs. La section française: Conclusion." *Art et Décoration* (December 1925): 205–17.

———. "Pablo Picasso." *Art et Décoration* (March 1925): 73–84.

———. "Une villa moderne à Hyères." *Art et Décoration* (July 1928): 1–24.

Dezallier d'Argenville, Antoine Joseph. *La théorie et la pratique du jardinage.* La Haye: Jean Martin Husson, 1739. Facsimile edition. Milan: L. J. Toth, n.d.

Dezarrois, André. "Avant l'ouverture de l'exposition des arts décoratifs: Un magnifique effort." *La Revue de l'Art Ancien et Moderne* (1925): 209–20.

Dill, Malcolm H. "To What Extent Can Landscape Architecture 'Go Modern'?" *Landscape Architecture Quarterly* 22, no. 4 (July 1932): 289–92.

Dormoy, Marie. "Les meubles de jardin." *Art et Décoration* (May 1930): 129–41.

———. "Pierre Legrain et Jacques Doucet." In *Pierre Legrain relieur.* Paris: Librairie Auguste Blaizot, 1965, pp. xvii–xx.

Dubois, Jean-Marie. "Jean-Charles Moreux (1889–1956)." *Monuments Historiques*, no. 142 (December–January 1986): 30–35.

Dubois, Marc. "2 into 1." *The Architectural Review* 181, no. 1079 (January 1987): 33–36.

Duboy, Philippe. "Architecture de la ville: Culture et triomphe de l'urbanisme. Ch. E. Jeanneret, 'La Construction des villes,' Bibliothèque Nationale de Paris, 1915." Paris: Ministère de l'Urbanisme, du Logement et des Transports. Direction de l'Architecture, 1985.

Duchêne, Achille. "Des changements de styles dans l'art des jardins et la rénovation des jardins à la française." In *Jardins d'Aujourd'hui.* Paris: Studios "Vie à la Campagne," 1932, pp. 25–32.

———. "Formal Parks and Gardens in France." *Journal of the Royal Horticultural Society* (1929): 272–81.

———. *Les jardins de l'avenir, hier, aujourd'hui, demain.* Paris: Vincent Fréal, 1935.

———. "Premier congrès international des architectes de jardins." Paris: Société Française des Architectes de Jardins, 4 June 1937. Typescript.

Dunington-Grubb, H. B. "Modernismus Arrives in the Garden—to Stay? An Inquiry into the Course of Current Trends." *Landscape Architecture Quarterly* 32, no. 4 (July 1942): 156–57.

Duprat, Ferdinand. "Le jardin paysager." In *Jardins d'aujourd'hui.* Paris: Studios "Vie à la Campagne," 1932, pp. 41–46.

Les Échos d'Art. Account of Guevrekian's garden at the Salon d'Automne (1 March 1927).

Encyclopédie des arts décoratifs et industriels modernes au XXe siècle, en douze volumes. Vol. 11: *Rue et jardin.* Paris: Imprimerie Nationale, Office Central d'Éditions et de Librairie, ca. 1926.

Escholier, Raymond. "L'art urbain." *Art et Décoration* (January 1923): 22–24.

"An Example of Garden Design in the Modernist Manner at St. Cloud, France—Cubistic Landscape Architecture on the Outskirts of Paris; Mme Tachard, Owner." *House and Garden,* (August 1924): 62–63.

"L'exposition de 1922." In "Chronique." *Art et Décoration* (September–October 1919): 1–2.

"L'exposition de 1925." In "Chronique." *Art et Décoration* (January 1925): 2–3.

"L'exposition de Turin." *Art et Décoration,* suppl. (June 1902): 1.

"L'exposition des arts décoratifs," special issue. *L'Illustration* 165, no. 4286 (25 April 1925).

"L'exposition des arts décoratifs." In "Chronique." *Art et Décoration* (May 1925): 1–6.

"Exposition des arts décoratifs et industriels modernes. Intérieur du Grand Palais. Ch. Letrosne, architecte." *L'Architecte,* n.s. 2 (1925): 76–79.

"L'exposition internationale des arts décoratifs modernes." In "Chronique." *Art et Décoration* (November 1919): 1.

Exposition internationale des arts décoratifs et industriels modernes. Paris: Imprimerie Nationale, 1922.

Exposition internationale des arts décoratifs et industriels modernes. Paris: Librairie Larousse for *L'Art Vivant,* 1925.

Exposition internationale des arts décoratifs et industriels modernes, Paris 1925: Liste des récompenses. Paris: Imprimerie des Journaux officiels, 1926.

"Exposition internationale des arts décoratifs industriels et modernes." *La Construction Moderne* (30 March 1924): 309–11.

Fauchereau, Serge. *La révolution cubiste.* Paris: Denoël, 1982.

Fiérens, Paul. "Henri Laurens." *Cahiers d'Art* 1 (1926): 41–45.

———. "Jan et Joël Martel." *L'Art et les Artistes* (1935–36): 295–300.

———. Review of the Salon d'Automne. *Journal des Débats,* 13 November 1927.

Fischer, Raymond. "L'art décoratif moderne: Les jardins." *La Liberté,* 5 March 1930.

Fishman, Robert. *Urban Utopias in the Twentieth Century: Ebenezer Howard, Frank Lloyd Wright, and Le Corbusier.* New York: Basic Books, 1977.

Fleg, Edmond. "Nos décorateurs." In *Les Arts de la Maison* (Winter 1924): 17–27.

"Fleurs et parterres: Le parc transformé." *Art et Industrie* (May 1929): 3–12.

Fohlen, Claude. *La France de l'entre-deux-guerres*. Paris: Casterman, 1966.

Forestier, J. C. N. *Gardens: A Note-book of Plans and Sketches*. Translated by Helen Morgenthau Fox. New York: Scribner's, 1924. Originally published as *Jardins: Carnet de plans et de dessins*. Paris: Émile-Paul Frères, 1920.

———. "The Gardens of France." *House and Garden* (October 1924): 58–63, 150, 154, 156.

———. *Les gazons*. Paris: Lucien Laveur, 1908.

———. *Grandes villes et systèmes de parcs*. Paris: Hachette, 1906.

———. "The Greatest Rose Garden in the World: Impressively Arranged with True Gallic Enthusiasm for Orderliness and Effectiveness, the Roserie of L'Hay Stands Unexcelled." *House and Garden* (March 1923): 50–53, 100, 102.

———. "Le jardin moderne et l'exposition des arts décoratifs." *L'Architecte*, n.s. 2 (1925): 92–94.

———. "Les jardins à l'exposition des arts décoratifs." Parts 1–3. *L'Agriculture Nouvelle*, no. 1448 (8 August 1925): 467–69; no. 1449 (22 August 1925): 491–93; no. 1450 (12 September 1925): 526–27.

———. "Les jardins arabes en Andalousie." *La Gazette Illustrée des Amateurs de Jardins* (1921): 25–34.

———. "Les jardins de céramique de MM. Raoul Dufy, N.M. Rubio et Artigas." *Art et Industrie* (August 1927): 27–30.

———. "Les jardins de l'exposition des arts décoratifs." *La Gazette Illustrée des Amateurs de Jardins* (1925): 19–24.

———. "Les jardins modernes." Parts 1–2. *Art et Industrie* (January and February 1911): n.p.

———. "Villes renaissantes et jardins." Parts 1–5. *Revue Horticole* 87, no. 21 (1 April 1915): 439–42; "II. Petites villes et villages" 87, no. 22 (16 April 1915): 452–55; "III. Petites villes et villages" 87, no. 23 (1 May 1915): 472–76; "IV. Villes moyennes et grandes villes" 87, no. 24 (16 May 1915): 484–87; "V. Villes moyennes et grandes villes" 87, no. 25 (16 June 1915): 505–09.

Forster, Kurt W. "Antiquity and Modernity in the La Roche–Jeanneret Houses of 1923." *Oppositions* (Le Corbusier 1905–1933), no. 15–16 (Winter–Spring 1979): 130–53.

Fratini, Francesca R. *Torino 1902: Polemiche in Italia sull'arte nuova*. Turin: Martano, 1970.

Fry, Edward. *Cubism*. New York: McGraw-Hill, 1964.

G., A. "À l'exposition des arts décoratifs: Le bassin des nymphéas." *La Construction Moderne* (25 October 1925): 37–38.

———. "À l'exposition des arts décoratifs: Le jardin des oiseaux." *La Construction Moderne* (13 December 1925): 131–32.

Gambard, Marie-Josèphe. "Jardins des années '30' (entre deux-guerres)." *Paysage Actualités*, no. 105 (June–July 1988): 42–44.

Ganay, Ernest de. *Bibliographie de l'art des jardins*. Paris: Bibliothèque des Arts Décoratifs, 1989.

———. "Le jardin de fleurs; Le jardin alpestre; Le jardin d'oiseaux; Les jardins ouvriers." *Plaisir de France*, no. 9 (1 June 1935): 28–31.

———. "Les jardins d'Achille Duchêne." *Art et Industrie* (August–September 1935): 31–34.

———. *Les jardins de France et leur décor*. Paris: Librairie Larousse, 1949.

———. "La tradition et le XIXᵉ siècle." *L'Illustration* 182:1, no. 4656 (28 May 1932), n.p.

Gangnet, Pierre. "Le sentiment de la nature chez Mallet-Stevens." *Architecture Mouvement Continuité*, no. 41 (1977): 12–13.

Garner, Philippe. "The Lacquer Work of Eileen Gray and Jean Dunand." *The Connoisseur* 183, no. 735 (May 1973): 3–11.

———. "Pierre Legrain—décorateur." *The Connoisseur* 189, no. 760 (June 1975): 130–37.

Gazette des Beaux-Arts. Review of Guevrekian's garden at the Salon d'Automne (December 1927).

George, Waldemar. "Joie de vivre." *Presse*, 20 February 1928.

———. "Les tendances générales." In *Exposition internationale des arts décoratifs et industriels modernes*. Paris: Librairie Larousse for *L'Art Vivant*, 1925, pp. 285–88.

Giedion, Sigfried. "Le Corbusier et l'architecture contemporaine." *Cahiers d'Art* 5, no. 4 (1930): 204–11.

———. "La maison Savoye à Poissy, 1928–1930." *Cahiers d'Art* 5, no. 4 (1930): 212–15.

———. "Le problème du luxe dans l'architecture moderne à propos d'une nouvelle construction à Garches de Le Corbusier et Pierre Jeanneret." *Cahiers d'Art* 3, no. 5–6 (1928): 254–56.

———. *Space, Time and Architecture: The Growth of a New Tradition.* Cambridge: Harvard University Press, 1947.

Girardin, René-Louis de. *De la composition des paysages.* 1777. Reprint. Paris: Éditions du Champ Urbain, 1979.

Glover, J. Garrett. *The Cubist Theatre.* Studies in the Fine Arts. The Avant-Garde, no. 38. Ann Arbor: UMI Research Press, 1983.

Goissaud, Antony. "À l'exposition des arts décoratifs: Le village français et les pavillons régionaux." *La Construction Moderne* 41, no. 1 (4 October 1925): 1–6.

———. "Exposition des arts décoratifs." *La Construction Moderne* 40, no. 31 (3 May 1925): 361–71.

———. "La manufacture nationale de Sèvres." *La Construction Moderne* 40, no. 46 (16 August 1925): 541–46.

Golson, Lucile M. "The Michael Steins of San Francisco: Art Patrons and Collectors." In *Four Americans in Paris: The Collections of Gertrude Stein and Her Family.* New York: Museum of Modern Art, 1970, pp. 34–49.

Gréber, Jacques. "Jardins d'aujourd'hui." *L'Architecture d'Aujourd'hui* (February 1934): 83–87.

———. *Jardins modernes: Exposition internationale de 1937.* Paris: Éditions d'Art Charles Moreau, ca. 1937.

Greentree, Carol. "Parque Maria Luisa: A Public Garden in Seville." *Pacific Horticulture* 52, no. 1 (Spring 1991): 43–49.

Gregotti, Vittorio. "La natura dei giardini." *Casabella,* no. 491 (May 1983): 12–13.

Gresleri, Giuliano. *L'Esprit Nouveau. Le Corbusier: Costruzione e ricostruzione di un prototipo dell'architettura moderna.* Milan: Electa, 1979.

Gromort, Georges. *L'art des jardins.* 2 vols. Paris: Vincent Fréal, 1934.

———. *Jardins d'Espagne.* 2 vols. Paris: A. Vincent, 1926.

Grumbach, Antoine. "The Promenades of Paris." *Oppositions,* no. 8 (Spring 1977): 50–67.

Gueissaz, Catherine. "Les frères Vera et l'art des jardins entre les deux guerres." *Histoire de l'Art,* no. 12 (December 1990): 81–89.

Guevrekian, Gabriel. Description of the Noailles Garden in Hyères following "Ein Geometrischer Garten an der Riviera." *Gartenschönheit* 10 (June 1929): 223.

———. "Maisons en pays de soleil." *Art et Décoration,* no. 2 (1946): 190–96.

———. "Une villa à Neuilly." *Art et Industrie* (July 1929): 7–10.

———. "Villa à Neuilly." *Cahiers d'Art* 4, no. 5 (1929): 227–30.

Guidot, Raymond. "Art et industrie: Tradition et avant-garde." In *Paris-Moscou, 1900–1930.* Paris: Centre Georges Pompidou, 1979, pp. 236–48.

Guignard, Jacques. "Pierre Legrain et la reliure: Évolution d'un style." In *Pierre Legrain relieur.* Paris: Librairie Auguste Blaizot, 1965, pp. xxv–xxxiii.

Guilleminault, Gilbert, et al. *Les années folles.* Paris: Club des amis du livre, 1962.

Guilleré, René. *Rapport sur une exposition internationale des arts décoratifs modernes: Paris 1915.* Paris, 1 June 1911.

Haerdtl, Oswald. "André Lurçat, Paris." *Moderne Bauformen* 26, (1927): 98–112.

Haffner, Jean-Jacques. *Compositions de jardins.* Paris: Vincent Fréal, 1931.

Hamel, M. "Salon d'automne." *Les Arts* (American edition), no. 107 (November 1910): 4–18.

Hebbelynck, Guillaume. "L'exposition internationale des arts décoratifs et industriels modernes de Paris—1925 (suite)." *L'Émulation* (March 1926): 41–56.

Hébert, Janine. *Mémorial des frères Vera: Leurs œuvres, leurs affinités avec leur époque.* Pontoise, Val d'Oise: Graphédis, 1980.

Henri Laurens sculpteur, 1885–1954. Edited and published by Marthe Laurens. Paris, 1955.

Herbst, René. *25 années u.a.m.* Paris: Éditions du Salon des Arts Ménagers, 1956.

Hernández-Cros, Josep Emili. "L'exposició internacional de 1929 a Barcelona." In *El Pavelló Alemany de Barcelona de Mies van der Rohe, 1929–1986.* Barcelona: Fundació Publica del Pavelló Alemany de Barcelona, Ajuntament de Barcelona, 1987, pp. 24–31.

————. "Forestier a Barcelona." *Quaderns d'Arquitectura i Urbanisme*, no. 151 (March–April 1982): 27–39.

Hernández-Cros, Josep Emili, Gabriel Mora i Gramunt, and Xavier Pouplana i Solé. *Guia de Arquitectura de Barcelona*. Barcelona: Ajuntament de Barcelona, 1985.

Hitchcock, Henry-Russell, and Philip Johnson. *The International Style*. 1932. Reprint. New York: W. W. Norton, 1966.

Holme, C. Geoffrey. "Designing the New Garden." In *Gardens and Gardening, 1937*, edited by F. A. Mercer. London: The Studio Limited, 1937, pp. 9–27.

Honoré, F. "Une ville nouvelle dans Paris: Les agrandissements de la cité universitaire." *L'Illustration* 174:2, no. 4521 (26 October 1929): 463–65.

Hope, Henry R. *The Sculpture of Jacques Lipchitz*. New York: Museum of Modern Art, 1954.

"Hôtel particulier à Versailles (S.-et-O.): A. Lurçat, architecte." *L'Architecte*, n.s. 3 (1926): 80.

Hübotter, Wilhelm. "An die Schriftleitung der 'Gartenkunst.'" *Die Gartenkunst*, no. 7 (July 1930): 105–06.

Huxley, Aldous. "Notes on Decoration." *The Studio* 100, no. 451 (October 1930): 239–42.

"L'idée de nature chez Le Corbusier." *Pour: Une ville verte*, no. 25 (January 1972): 56–58.

Imbert, Charles. "Le quartier artiste de Montsouris: La cité Seurat, 101, rue de la Tombe-Issoire (Paris)." *L'Architecture* 40, no. 4 (April 1927): 101–12.

Imbert, Dorothée. "J.C.N. Forestier: Tracé architectonique et poétique végétale." In *Jean C.N. Forestier*, edited by Bénédicte Leclerc. Paris: Picard, 1993.

————. "Pierre-Émile Legrain: A Model for Modernism." In *Modern Landscape Architecture: A Critical Review*, edited by Marc Treib. Cambridge: MIT Press (in press).

"L'inauguration de l'exposition des arts décoratifs." In "Chronique." *Art et Décoration* (April 1925): 1.

Ingalls, George E. "The Maria Luisa Park in Seville." *Landscape Architecture Quarterly* (January 1925): 81–92.

"The International Exhibition." *The Architectural Review* 82, no. 490 (September 1937): 87–89.

Janneau, Guillaume. "Le cadre de l'exposition." *Beaux-Arts*, no. 10 (15 May 1925): 152–60.

————. "Ce que sera l'exposition de 1925." *La Revue de l'Art Ancien et Moderne* 45 (1924): 316–22.

————. "Introduction à l'exposition des arts décoratifs: Considérations sur l'esprit moderne." *Art et Décoration* (May 1925): 129–76.

————. "Le salon d'automne: L'art urbain et l'art décoratif." *Art et Décoration* (December 1924): 173–92.

"Le jardin," special issue of *L'Illustration* 182:1, no. 4656 (28 May 1932).

"Un jardin à la française chez Madame Paul Dupuy à Versailles." *Art et Industrie* (August 1931): 3–7.

"Un jardin moderne." *Vogue* (July 1930): 63. Translated as "A Modern Garden." *Vogue* (20 August 1930).

"Jardins," special issue of *L'Architecture d'Aujourd'hui*, no. 4 (1937).

"Jardins—J.-C.-N. Forestier, architecte." *L'Architecte* (1928): p. 64, pls. 44–46.

Jardins d'aujourd'hui. Paris: Studios "Vie à la Campagne," 1932.

"Jardins de Paris: Chez le Bon R. de Rothschild." *Art et Industrie* (October 1930): 2–8.

"Jardins de Paris: Chez Mr J. Rouché." *Art et Industrie* (October 1931): 2–6.

Jeanneret, Charles-Édouard [Le Corbusier]. *Étude sur le mouvement d'art décoratif en Allemagne*. 1912. Reprint. New York: Da Capo, 1968.

————. Letter to Charles L'Eplattenier, dated 22 November 1908, reproduced in the special issue on Le Corbusier. *Aujourd'hui: Art et Architecture*, no. 51 (1965): 10–11.

Jellicoe, Geoffrey. *Studies in Landscape Design*. 3 vols. London: Oxford University Press, 1960.

Jellicoe, Geoffrey, Susan Jellicoe, Patrick Goode, and Michael Lancaster. *The Oxford Companion to Gardens*. Oxford: Oxford University Press, 1986.

Johnson, Douglas and Madeleine. *The Age of Illusion: Art and Politics in France, 1918–1940*. New York: Rizzoli, 1987.

Joubin, André. "Jacques Doucet, 1853–1929." *Gazette des Beaux-Arts*, ser. 6, vol. 3 (November 1930): 69–82.

———. "Le studio de Jacques Doucet." *L'Illustration* 176:1, no. 4548 (3 May 1930): 17–20.

Jourdain, Francis. Remembrances on the beginning of the U.A.M. In *25 années u.a.m.* Paris: Éditions du Salon des Arts Ménagers, 1956, pp. 15–16.

Juan Gris. Catalog of the exposition held at the Orangerie des Tuileries, 14 March–1 July 1974. Paris: Éditions des Musées Nationaux, 1974.

Jullian, Philippe. "Une des maisons-clés pour l'histoire du goût au XXe siècle: L'hôtel du vicomte et de la vicomtesse de Noailles, à Paris." *Connaissance des Arts,* no. 152 (October 1964): 68–91.

Kahn, Gustave. "Exposition internationale des arts décoratifs et industriels modernes: Paris: MDCCCCXXV." *The Architectural Review* 58, no. 344 (July 1925): 1–2.

Kahnweiler, Daniel-Henry. *Juan Gris: His Life and Work.* Translated by Douglas Cooper. London: Thames and Hudson, 1969.

———. *Juan Gris: Sa vie, son œuvre, ses écrits.* Paris: Gallimard, 1946.

Kassler, Elizabeth. *Modern Gardens and the Landscape,* revised edition. New York: Museum of Modern Art, 1984.

Lacoste, Henri. "L'exposition internationale des arts décoratifs et industriels modernes de Paris—1925 (suite)." *L'Émulation,* no. 11 (November 1925): 161–67.

———. "L'exposition internationale des arts décoratifs et industriels modernes de Paris—1925 (suite)." *L'Émulation,* no. 12 (December 1925): 169–77.

Lambert, Jacques. "Jardins et fontaines." *L'Illustration* 166, no. 4301 (8 August 1925): 139–42.

Landry, Lionel. "L'exposition des arts décoratifs. L'architecture: Section française." *Art et Décoration* (June 1925): 177–212.

Laprade, Albert. "Expositions d'hier et de demain." *L'Architecture d'Aujourd'hui* 11, no. 1–2 (January 1940): 27–28.

———. "Idées générales sur le jardin moderne." *L'Illustration* 182:1, no. 4656 (28 May 1932).

———. "L'œuvre de Jean-Charles Moreux." *L'Architecture* (July 1939): 239–46.

———. "Parcs et jardins de J.-C.-N. Forestier." *L'Architecture* 44, no. 2 (1931): 37–40.

Leclerc, Bénédicte. "Jean Claude Nicolas Forestier (1861–1930), La science des jardins au service de l'art urbain." *Pages Paysages,* no. 2 (1988–89): 24–29.

Le Corbusier. *Almanach d'architecture moderne.* Collection de "L'Esprit Nouveau." Paris: Éditions G. Crès, 1925.

[Le Corbusier]. "Une ancienne maison transformée par MM. Le Corbusier et Jeanneret, propriété de M. Church à Ville-d'Avray." *Art et Industrie* (January 1929): 5–9.

———. "Appartement avec terrasses, avenue des Champs-Élysées, à Paris (1932)." *L'Architecte,* n.s. 9 (1932): 100–04.

———. *L'art décoratif d'aujourd'hui.* Paris: Éditions G. Crès, 1925. Reprint. Paris: Éditions Arthaud, 1980.

———. "Brève histoire de nos tribulations." In "Le Corbusier," special issue of *L'Architecture d'Aujourd'hui* (April 1948): 59–67.

———. *Le Corbusier et Pierre Jeanneret: Œuvre complète de 1910–1929.* Zurich: Éditions Dr. H. Girsberger, 1937.

———. *Le Corbusier et Pierre Jeanneret: Œuvre complète de 1929–1934.* Zurich: Les Éditions d'Architecture Erlenbach, 1947.

———. *Une maison—un palais: "À la recherche d'une unité architecturale."* Paris: Éditions G. Crès, 1928. Reprint. Torino: Bottega d'Erasmo, 1975.

———. "Notes à la suite." *Cahiers d'Art* 1, no. 3 (March 1926): 46–52.

———. *Une petite maison, 1923.* Zurich: Éditions Girsberger, July 1954.

———. *Les plans Le Corbusier de Paris.* Paris: Éditions de Minuit, 1956.

———. *Précisions sur un état présent de l'architecture et de l'urbanisme.* Paris: Vincent Fréal, 1960.

———. *Propos d'urbanisme.* Collection Perspectives Humaines. Paris: Éditions Bourrelier, 1946.

———. "Tracés régulateurs." *L'Architecture Vivante* (1928–29): 12–34.

———. "Unité." In "Le Corbusier," special issue of *L'Architecture d'Aujourd'hui* (April 1948): 5–58.

———. *Urbanisme*. Paris: Éditions G. Crès, 1925. Reprint. Paris: Éditions Arthaud, 1980.

———. *Vers une architecture*. Paris: Éditions G. Crès, 1923. Reprint. Paris: Éditions Arthaud, 1977.

Le Corbusier-Saugnier. "L'illusion des plans." *L'Esprit Nouveau*, no. 15 (April 1922): 1767–80.

"Le Corbusier," special issue of *L'Architecture d'Aujourd'hui* (April 1948).

"Le Corbusier, 1910–1934," special issue of *Architecture Mouvement Continuité*, no. 49 (1979).

The Le Corbusier Archive. 32 vols. Edited by H. Allen Brook. New York: Garland Publishing Co.; Paris: Fondation Le Corbusier, 1982.

"Le Corbusier et P. Jeanneret," special issue of *L'Architecture d'Aujourd'hui* 4, no. 10 (December 1933).

Le Dantec, Denise, and Jean-Pierre Le Dantec. *Reading the French Garden: Story and History*. Cambridge: MIT Press, 1990.

Le Fèvre, Georges. "L'architecture." In *Exposition internationale des arts décoratifs et industriels modernes*. Paris: Librairie Larousse for *L'Art Vivant*, 1925, pp. 3–12.

Legrain, Pierre. *Objets d'art*. Paris: Éditions d'Art Charles Moreau, n.d.

———. "La villa de Madame Tachard à La Celle-Saint-Cloud." *Vogue* (1 June 1925): 68.

Lejeune, Jean-François. "Jean-Claude Nicolas Forestier; The City as Landscape." *The New City* (Foundations), no. 1 (Fall 1991): 50–67.

Lelieur, Anne-Claude, Raymond Bachollet, and Daniel Bordet. *Paul Iribe: Précurseur de l'art déco*. Catalog of an exposition at the Bibliothèque Forney, Hôtel de Sens. Paris: Bibliothèque Forney, 1983.

Léon, Paul. *Rapport général: Exposition internationale des arts décoratifs et industriels modernes. Paris, 1925*. Vol. 9: *Section rue et jardin*. Paris: Librairie Larousse, 1927.

Leroy, André. *Bagatelle et ses jardins*. Paris: Baillière, 1956.

Libro de oro ibero americano: Catálogo oficial y monumentál de la exposición de Sevilla. Santander, Spain: Aldus, 1930.

Ligne, Jean de. "L'exposition internationale des arts décoratifs et industriels modernes de Paris—1925." *L'Émulation*, no. 10 (October 1925): 146–59.

Lipchitz, Jacques, and H. H. Arnason. *My Life in Sculpture*. New York: Viking, 1972.

Loizeau, A. "Le jardin persan." *Le Petit Jardin*, 10 November 1925.

Lucan, Jacques. "Villa Meyer, 1925–1926." *Architecture Mouvement Continuité*, no. 49 (1979): 13–20.

Lurçat, André. *Architecture*. Paris: Au Sans Pareil, 1929.

———. *Formes, composition et lois d'harmonie*. 5 vols. Paris: Vincent Fréal, 1953–57.

———*Projets et réalisations*. Paris: Vincent Fréal, 1929.

———. "Recherche et création." In *André Lurçat architecte*. Paris: Conservatoire National des Arts et Métiers, 1967, pp. 37–42.

———. *Terrasses et jardins*. Collection L'Art International d'Aujourd'hui, no. 4. Paris: Éditions d'Art Charles Moreau, n.d. (ca. 1929).

McCance, William, and A. F. Clark. "The Influence of Cubism on Garden design." *Architectural Design* 30, no. 3 (March 1960): 112–17.

McGrath, Raymond. *Twentieth-Century Houses*. London: Faber and Faber, 1934.

McLeod, Mary. "Le Corbusier and Algiers." *Oppositions* (Le Corbusier, 1933–1960), no. 19–20 (Winter–Spring 1980): 54–85.

Magnol, Véronique, and Georges Weill. *Jardins et paysages des Hauts-de-Seine de la Renaissance à l'art moderne*. Nanterre: Archives des Hauts-de-Seine, 1982.

Mallet-Stevens, Rob. "L'esprit des expositions." *L'Architecture d'Aujourd'hui* 11, no. 1–2 (January 1940): 37.

———. "Frank Lloyd Wright et l'architecture nouvelle par Rob Mallet-Stevens." *Wendingen*, no. 6 (1925): 92–93.

Margolius, Ivan. *Cubism in Architecture and the Applied Arts*. North Pomfret, Vermont: David and Charles, 1979.

Marrast, Joseph. *1925 Jardins*. Paris: Éditions d'Art Charles Moreau, 1926.

———. "Maroc." In *L'œuvre de Henri Prost*. Paris: Académie d'Architecture, 1960, pp. 51–117.

Martet, Jean. Review of the Salon d'Automne. *Homme Libre*, 12–13 November 1927.

Martinie, A. H. "Deux récentes réalisations de J.-Ch. Moreux." *Art et Décoration* 59 (January–June 1931): 59–64.

Marx, Roger. "De l'art social et de la nécessité d'en assurer le progrès par une exposition." *Idées Modernes*, no. 1 (January 1909): 46–57.

Maumené, Albert. "Le jardin, cadre de la maison." In *Jardins d'aujourd'hui*. Paris: Studios "Vie à la Campagne," 1932, pp. 11–23.

Mauricheau-Beaupré, Ch. "Les jardins et les peintres de jardins à Bagatelle. À propos d'une exposition récente." *L'Architecture* 41, no. 12 (1928): 399–406.

Melis, Paolo. "L'Attico Beistegui." *Domus*, no. 625 (February 1982): 3–7.

———. "Memoria M Memoria." *Controspazio* (September 1977): 32–37.

Mémoires du baron Haussmann: Grands travaux de Paris, 1853–1870. 2 vols. Paris, 1893. Reprint. Paris: Guy Durier, 1979.

Mercer, F. A., editor. *Gardens and Gardening, 1934.* London: The Studio Limited, 1934.

———. *Gardens and Gardening, 1937.* London: The Studio Limited, 1937.

———. *Gardens and Gardening, 1939.* London: The Studio Limited, 1939.

Meyer, Elizabeth. "The Modern Framework." *Landscape Architecture Quarterly* (March 1983): 50–53.

Migennes, Pierre. "Jardins d'aujourd'hui." *Art et Décoration* 63 (June 1934): 201–10.

"Moderne Fantasietuinen." *De Telegraaf,* 28 June 1931.

Molinier, Jean-Christophe. *Coup d'œil sur les jardins de l'histoire du XVe au XXe siècle.* Paris: Association Henri et Achille Duchêne, 1989.

———. "Les Duchêne ou les jardins réinventés." *Vieilles Maisons Françaises*, no. 120 (December 1987): 50–57.

———. "Une dynastie de jardiniers: Henri et Achille Duchêne." *Monuments Historiques*, no. 142 (December–January 1986): 24–29.

———. *Jardins de ville privés, 1890–1930.* Association Duchêne–Musée Albert Kahn. Paris: Éditions Ramsay/de Cortanze, 1991.

Monnier, Gérard. "Un retour à l'ordre: Architecture, géométrie, société." In *Le retour à l'ordre dans les arts plastiques et l'architecture, 1919–1925.* Université de Saint-Étienne: Centre Interdisciplinaire d'Études et de Recherche sur l'Expression Contemporaine, 1974, pp. 45–54.

———. "La villa des Noailles à Hyères: Un regard neuf sur l'œuvre de Rob. Mallet-Stevens." *Techniques et Architecture*, no. 331 (July 1980): 60–62.

Moreux, Ch. "Un hôtel à la Muette." *Art et Industrie* (June 1930): 9–10.

Moreux, Jean-Charles. "De l'utilisation de l'arbre dans le jardin." *Plaisir de France*, no. 168 (March 1952): 24–25.

———. "Éloge du jardin régulier français." *Élites Françaises*, no. 14–15 (April–May 1947): 58–66.

——— "Une gloriette dans un jardin." *La Demeure Française*, no. 3 (Spring 1925): 57–58.

———. "Un hôtel particulier à Saint-Cloud." *Art et Industrie* (March 1929): 8–10.

———. Introduction to "Grandes Demeures." In *Demeures et jardins de France.* Plaisir de France. Paris: Les Publications de France, 1953, pp. 95–96.

———. "Le jardin français du moyen-âge à nos jours." In *De Franse tuin van middeleeuwen tot op onze dagen.* Exhibition catalog. Rotterdam, 11 June–1 September 1948, pp. 5–8.

———. "Jardins réguliers." *Art et Industrie* (November 1934): 20–22.

———. *J.-Ch. Moreux.* Geneva: Éditions "Biblos," Les Archives Internationales d'Architecture, 1932.

———. "Quelques nouveaux modes de construction." *Art et Industrie* (May 1929): 13–16.

———. "There Are Only Two Kinds of Gardens." In *Gardens and Gardening, 1939,* edited by F. A. Mercer. London: The Studio Limited, 1939, p. 17.

Morgenthau Fox, Helen. "Jean C. N. Forestier." *Landscape Architecture Quarterly* (January 1931): 93–100.

Mosser, Monique. "Henri and Achille Duchêne and the Reinvention of Le Nôtre." In *The Architecture of Western Gardens*, edited by Monique Mosser and Georges Teyssot. Cambridge: MIT Press, 1991, pp. 446–50.

Mourey, Gabriel. "La section danoise." *Art et Décoration* (October 1925): 147–56.

Moussinac, Léon. *Mallet-Stevens*. Paris: Éditions G. Crès, 1931.

Moynihan, Elizabeth B. *Paradise as a Garden in Persia and Mughal India*. New York: George Braziller, 1979.

Newton, Norman T. "Landscape Architecture Today—A Biological View: What Points Really Matter?" *Landscape Architecture Quarterly* 32, no. 1 (October 1941): 18–21.

Nicolau M. Rubió i Tudurí (1891–1981): El jardí obra d'art. Barcelona: Fundació Caixa de Pensions, 1985.

"Notice historique." *Annuaire de l'Union centrale des arts décoratifs*, 1904, pp. 1–9.

Ollivier, Félix. "Le domaine de Sceaux." *L'Architecture* 44, no. 1 (1931): 1–10.

L'œuvre de Henri Prost. Paris: Académie d'Architecture, 1960.

"Originality in Roof Gardens." *The Ideal Home* (September 1929): 220.

Otin, A. Guy. "Le jardin moderne." In *Jardins d'aujourd'hui*. Paris: Studios "Vie à la Campagne," 1932, pp. 53–60.

"Où va l'architecture? Réponse de J. C. Moreux." In "L'architecture," special issue of *Le Gaz Chez Soi*, n.d. (ca. 1935).

"Ouvrira-t-on l'exposition en 1926?" *La Construction Moderne* 41, no. 2 (11 October 1925): 13–16.

Ozenfant, Amédée. *Foundations of Modern Art*. New York: Dover, 1952. Reprint.

———. "Sur les écoles cubistes et post-cubistes." *Journal de Psychologie Normale et Pathologique*. Paris: Librairie Félix Alcan, 1926. Reprint. Turin: Bottega d'Erasmo, 1975.

P., A. "La cité universitaire de Paris." *L'Architecture d'Aujourd'hui* 7, no. 6 (June 1936): 38–41.

Paris 1937 Arts et Techniques dans la vie moderne, January 1937.

Paris 1937: Exposition internationale arts et techniques. Paris: Imprimerie Reboul, 1937.

Patai, Irene. *Encounters: The Life of Jacques Lipchitz*. New York: Funk and Wagnalls, 1961.

Péan, Prosper. "La technique et la pratique de l'art des jardins." *La Construction Moderne* (20 January 1924): 181–83.

Pechère, René. *Petits jardins d'aujourd'hui*, vol. 2. Paris: Éditions d'Art Charles Moreau, n.d.

Pevsner, Nikolaus. "The Genesis of the Picturesque." *The Architectural Review* 96 (1944): 79–101.

Pierre, José. "1925 ou la quadrature du cercle." *L'Œil*, no. 192 (December 1970): 44–53.

Pierre Legrain relieur: Répertoire descriptif et bibliographique de mille deux cent trente-six reliures. Paris: Librairie Auguste Blaizot, 1965.

Pillard-Verneuil, Maurice. "Le salon d'automne." *Art et Décoration* (July–December 1910): 129–60.

Pingusson, Georges-Henri. "Une exposition dirigée." *L'Architecture d'Aujourd'hui* 11, no. 1–2 (January 1940): 35.

Poiret, Paul. *En habillant l'époque*. Paris: Éditions Grasset, 1930.

Porcher, Jean. "La maison nouvelle en France." *Art et Décoration* (January 1928): 1–16.

"Un port-folio de documents d'architecture, de décoration et de jardins modernes." *Vogue* (1 June 1925): 37–39.

Posener, Julius. "La maison Savoye à Poissy." *L'Architecture d'Aujourd'hui*, no. 2 (December 1930): 21.

"Progress in Garden Design." In *Gardens and Gardening, 1939*, edited by F. A. Mercer. London: The Studio Limited, 1939, pp. 9–20.

Prost, Henri. "Hommage à Forestier." *Urbanisme*, no. 3–4 (1952): 74–75.

Racine, Michel. *Le guide des jardins de France*. Paris: Hachette, 1991.

Racine, Michel, Ernest Boursier-Mougenot, and Françoise Binet. *The Gardens of Provence and the French Riviera*. Cambridge: MIT Press, 1987.

Ragot, Gilles. "La cité universitaire internationale de Paris: Un musée d'architecture en plein air." *Monuments Historiques*, no. 148 (December 1986): 76–80.

Rambosson, Yvanhoé. "L'exposition des arts décoratifs: La participation étrangère: I. Tchécoslovaquie, Pays-Bas, Pologne, Suède, Autriche, Principauté de Monaco." *La Revue de l'Art Ancien et Moderne* 48 (1925): 77–93.

———. "L'exposition des arts décoratifs. La participation étrangère: II. Japon, Belgique, Angleterre, Italie, Russie, Yougoslavie, Espagne, Luxembourg, Suisse, Grèce, Danemark, Turquie." *La Revue de l'Art Ancien et Moderne* 48 (1925): 156–78.

———. "L'exposition des arts décoratifs. La section française: Quelques aspects." *La Revue de l'Art Ancien et Moderne* 47 (1925): 313–22.

———. "L'exposition des arts décoratifs. Les pavillons de la province et de l'étranger: Quelques aspects." *La Revue de l'Art Ancien et Moderne* 48 (1925): 30–40.

———. "Un jardin de Pierre Legrain." *Jardins et Cottages* 1, no. 1 (April 1926): 1–7.

Rapin, Henri. "L'art décoratif." *La Construction Moderne* (10 April 1927): 321–22.

Raymond Duchamp-Villon, sculpteur (1876–1918). Paris: Jacques Povolzky, Éditeur, 1924.

Redslob, Edwin. "Ein neuer Typ des Wintergartens: Peter Behrens Bau für die Pariser Ausstellung." *Gartenschönheit* 6 (December 1925): 221–23.

Reichlin, Bruno. "L'esprit de Paris." *Casabella*, no. 531–532 (January–February 1987): 52–63.

———. "La 'petite maison' à Corseaux: Une analyse structurale." In *Le Corbusier à Genève, 1922–1932: Projets et réalisations*. Lausanne: Éditions Payot, 1991.

———. "The Pros and Cons of the Horizontal Window. The Perret–Le Corbusier Controversy." *Daidalos* 13, no. 15 (September 1984): 64–78.

Rémon, Georges. *L'art des jardins*. Paris: Flammarion, n.d.

———. "Un jardin en Floride par M. Marrast, architecte." *Jardins et Cottages* (1926): 33–37.

———. "Les jardins d'Albert Laprade." *Jardins et Cottages* (1927): 65–79.

———. *Les jardins de l'Antiquité à nos jours*. Paris: Librairie d'Art R. Ducher, 1929.

———. "Jardins de Guevrekian." *Jardins et Cottages* (1927): 106–07.

———. "Une villa d'André Lurçat au parc Montsouris." *La Construction Moderne* 43, no. 29 (15 April 1928): 337–42.

Répertoire du goût moderne. 5 vols. Paris: Éditions Albert Lévy, 1928.

Report of Commission Appointed by the Secretary of Commerce to Visit and Report upon the International Exposition of Modern Decorative and Industrial Art in Paris 1925. Washington, D.C.: 1926.

Repton, Humphry. *Sketches and Hints on Landscape Gardening*. London, 1794. Reprinted by J. C. Loudon in *The Landscape Gardening and Landscape Architecture of the Late Humphry Repton, Esq*. London, 1840. Reprint. Westmead, Farnborough, Hants., England: Gregg International Publishers, 1969, pp. 23–116.

Le retour à l'ordre dans les arts plastiques et l'architecture, 1919–1925. Université de Saint-Étienne: Centre Interdisciplinaire d'Études et de Recherche sur l'Expression Contemporaine, 1974.

Revel, Jean-François. "Jacques Doucet, couturier et collectionneur." *L'Œil*, no. 84 (December 1961): 44–51, 81, 106.

Reverdy, Pierre. "L'imperméable." In *La peau de l'homme*. Paris: Flammarion, 1926, pp. 97–134.

Rey, Robert. "Le XVII salon d'automne." *L'Architecture*, no. 23 (1924): 315–32.

Riousse, André. *Petits jardins d'aujourd'hui*, vol. 1. Paris: Éditions d'Art Charles Moreau, n.d.

Risler, Ch. "Les objets d'art à l'exposition des arts décoratifs." *L'Architecture* 38, no. 23 (1925): 413–24.

Ritter, Raymond. "À Barcelone: Aspects de l'exposition." *L'Illustration* 174:1, no. 4510 (10 August 1929): 132–35.

———. "À l'exposition de Barcelone: Le village espagnol." *L'Illustration* 174:1, no. 4514 (7 September 1929): 227–31.

——— "L'Amérique à Séville." *L'Illustration* 173:2, no. 4502 (15 June 1929): 726–28.

———. "Jeux de lumière et d'eau." *L'Illustration* 174:1, no. 4511 (17 August 1929): 152–53.

Rob Mallet-Stevens, architecte. Brussels: Archives d'Architecture Moderne, 1980.

Robert, Florence. "Le jardin et le paysage dans l'œuvre de Le Corbusier." Thesis, École d'architecture de Versailles, 1988.

Robertson, Howard. "Some Recent French Developments in Domestic Architecture." *The Architectural Review* 61, no. 362 (January 1927): 2–7.

Robertson, Mrs. Howard. "Two Views against the Geometric Garden." *The Queen*, 12 December 1928, pp. 5–6.

Robertson, Howard, and F. R. Yerbury. *Examples of Modern French Architecture*. New York: Scribner's, 1928.

Robinson, William. *The Wild Garden*. London, Melbourne: Century Hutchinson / The National Trust, 1983. Reprint.

Rosenthal, Léon. "Pierre Legrain relieur." *Art et Décoration* (January–June 1923): 65–70.

Rosenthal, Mark. *Juan Gris*. Exhibition catalog. University Art Museum, Berkeley. New York: Abbeville Press, 1983.

Roubaud, François. "Politique culturelle à Hyères, Var: Réhabilitation de la Villa Noailles, 1924, Rob. Mallet-Stevens." Thesis, UPA 1, Paris, 1984.

Rouché, Jacques. *L'art théâtral moderne*. Paris: Édouard Cornély, 1910.

Roux-Spitz, Michel. "L'architecture moderne et l'exposition des arts décoratifs et industriels." In *Bâtiments et jardins à l'exposition des arts décoratifs*. Paris: Éditions Albert Lévy, 1925.

Rowe, Colin. *The Mathematics of the Ideal Villa and Other Essays*. Cambridge: MIT Press, 1976.

Rubin, William. *Picasso and Braque: Pioneering Cubism*. New York: The Museum of Modern Art, 1989.

Rubió i Tudurí, Nicolau M. "Forestier." *Quaderns d'Arquitectura i Urbanisme*, no. 151 (March–April 1982): 17–18.

———. *El jardí obra d'art*. In *Nicolau M. Rubió i Tudurí (1891–1981): El jardí obra d'art*, pp. 17–27.

S.,L. "L'exposition internationale des arts décoratifs et industriels modernes." *La Construction Moderne*, no. 49 (7 September 1924): 577–79.

Sabatier, Pierre. "Le salon du jardin." *Art et Industrie* (July 1929): 19–22.

Saddy, Pierre. "Le Corbusier e l'Arlecchino." *Rassegna* (I clienti di Le Corbusier), no. 3 (July 1980): 24–31.

———. "Le Corbusier chez les riches: L'Appartement Charles de Beistegui." *Architecture Mouvement Continuité*, no. 49 (1979): 57–60.

———. "L'exposition des arts décoratifs 1925." *Signatures*, no. 33 (20 November 1966): n.p.

Saint-Sauveur, Hector. *Architecture et décor des jardins*. Introduction by Henri Clouzot. Paris: Ch. Massin, n.d.

Salles, G. "Un artisan amoureux de son métier" *Arts; Spectacles*, no. 628 (17–28 July 1957): 8.

Salmon, André. "L'exposition Nancy-Paris." *L'Art Vivant*, no. 34 (15 May 1926): 371–73.

Schneider, Pierre. "Charles de Noailles: Master of Gardens, Life, and Art." *Vogue* 162, no. 1 (July 1973): 74–79.

Segre, Roberto. "La Habana de Forestier." *Quaderns d'Arquitectura i Urbanisme*, no. 151 (March–April 1982): 19–26.

Sekler, Mary Patricia May. "Le Corbusier, Ruskin, the Tree, and the Open Hand." In *The Open Hand: Essays on Le Corbusier*, edited by Russell Walden. Cambridge: MIT Press, 1982, pp. 42–95.

Shand, P. Morton. "André Lurçat's 'Architecture.'" *The Architects' Journal* (29 April 1931): 611–14.

———. "An Essay in the Adroit: At the Villa of the Vicomte de Noailles." *The Architectural Review* 65 (April 1929): 174–75.

Shepheard, Peter. *Modern Gardens*. London: Architectural Press, 1953.

Silver, Kenneth E. *Esprit de Corps: The Art of the Parisian Avant-Garde and the First World War, 1914–1925*. Princeton: Princeton University Press, 1989.

Silverman, Debora L. "The 1889 Exhibition: The Crisis of Bourgeois Individualism." *Oppositions*, no. 8 (Spring 1977): 70–91.

Solà-Morales, Ignasi de. "The 1929 International Expo." *Rassegna* (Barcelona), no. 37 (March 1989): 16–21.

"Un square aux Gobelins réalisé par Jean Ch. Moreux." *Art et Décoration* 67 (July–August 1938): 278–79.

Starr, S. Frederick. *Melnikov: Solo Architect in a Mass Society*. Princeton: Princeton University Press, 1978.

Steele, Fletcher. *Design in the Little Garden*. Boston: Atlantic Monthly Press, 1924.

———. "Fine Art in Landscape Architecture." *Landscape Architecture Quarterly* 24, no. 4 (July 1934): 177–79.

———. "French Gardens and Their Racial Characteristics." *Landscape Architecture Quarterly* 12, no. 4 (July 1922): 211–23.

———. *Gardens and People.* Cambridge: Riverside Press, 1964.

———. "Landscape Design of the Future." *Landscape Architecture Quarterly* 22, no. 4 (July 1932): 299–302.

———. "New Pioneering in Garden Design." *Landscape Architecture Quarterly* 20, no. 3 (April 1930): 158–77.

———. "New Styles in Gardening: Will Landscape Architecture Reflect the Modernistic Tendencies Seen in the Other Arts?" *House Beautiful* 65, no. 3 (March 1929): 317, 352–54.

———. "Private Delight and the Communal Ideal." *Landscape Architecture Quarterly* 31, no. 2 (January 1941): 69–71.

———. Review of *Jardins modernes: Exposition internationale de 1937,* by Jacques Gréber. *Landscape Architecture Quarterly* 28, no. 2 (January 1938): 117–18.

———. " 'The Voice Is Jacob's Voice, but the Hands . . .' " *Landscape Architecture Quarterly* 32, no. 2 (January 1942): 64–65.

Strong, William A. "It Is Modern If It Cares Well for Basic Necessities." *Landscape Architecture Quarterly* 32, no. 2 (January 1942): 66–68.

Symes, Michael. "Nature as the Bride of Art: The Design and Structure of Painshill." In *British and American Gardens in the Eighteenth Century,* edited by Robert P. Maccubin and Peter Martin. Williamsburg, Virginia: The Colonial Williamsburg Foundation, 1986, pp. 65–73.

Tafuri, Manfredo. " 'Machine et mémoire': La città nell'opera di Le Corbusier." *Casabella,* no. 502 (May 1984): 44–51.

Tériade, E. *Fernand Léger.* Paris: Éditions Cahiers d'Art, 1928.

"Terrasses." *Art et Industrie* (July 1931): 9–11.

Thornton, Lynne. "Negro Art and the Furniture of Pierre-Émile Legrain." *The Connoisseur* 181, no. 729 (November 1972): 166–69.

Thouin, Gabriel. *Plans raisonnés de toutes les espèces de jardins.* Paris: Imprimerie de Lebégue, 1820.

Tisserand, Ernest. "Feu le salon de réception." *L'Art Vivant,* no. 33 (1 May 1926): 338–41.

Traz, Georges de [François Fosca, pseud.]. *Bilan du cubisme.* Paris: Bibliothèque des Arts, 1956.

Treib, Marc, editor. *Modern Landscape Architecture: A Critical Review.* Cambridge: MIT Press, in press.

———. "Postulating a Post-Modern Landscape." *Process Architecture,* no. 61 (1985): 10–24.

———. "Traces upon the Land: The Formalistic Landscape." *Architectural Association Quarterly* 11, no. 4 (1979): 28–39.

Trillo de Leyva, Manuel. *La exposición iberoamericana: La transformación urbana de Sevilla.* Sevilla: Ayuntamento, Servicio de Publicaciones del Excmo, 1980.

Troy, Nancy J. *The De Stijl Environment.* Cambridge: MIT Press, 1983.

———. *Modernism and the Decorative Arts in France: Art Nouveau to Le Corbusier.* New Haven: Yale University Press, 1991.

———. "Toward a Redefinition of Tradition in French Design." *Design Issues* 1, no. 2 (Fall 1984): 53–69.

Tunnard, Christopher. "Asymmetrical Garden Planning: The Oriental Aesthetic." *The Architectural Review* 83, no. 498 (May 1938): 245–48.

———. "The Functional Aspect of Garden Planning." *The Architectural Review* 83, no. 497 (April 1938): 195–99.

———. "The Garden in the Modern Landscape." *The Architectural Review* 83, no. 496 (March 1938): 127–32.

———. *Gardens in the Modern Landscape.* London: Architectural Press, 1938.

———. "Modern Gardens for Modern Houses—Reflections on Current Trends in Landscape Design." *Landscape Architecture Quarterly* 32, no. 2 (January 1942): 57–64.

———. Review of *L'homme et le jardin,* by André Vera. *Landscape Architecture Quarterly* 41, no. 4 (July 1951): 183–84.

———. "Science and Specialization: The Conventional Garden of Today." *The Architectural Review* (February 1938): 85–87.

Ulpts, Jürgen. "Quelques remarques sur l'architecture de jardin de Le Corbusier." In *Le Corbusier et la nature: Rencontres des 14–15 juin 1991.* Paris: Fondation Le Corbusier, 1991.

Vago, Pierre. "Les expositions de Paris." *L'Architecture d'Aujourd'hui* 11, no. 1–2 (January 1940): 31–32.

———. "La leçon de 1937." *L'Architecture d'Aujourd'hui*, 11, no. 1–2 (January 1940): 34.

———. *Robert Mallet-Stevens, l'architetto cubista*. Bari: Dedalo Libri, 1979.

Vaillat, Léandre. "Le nouveau visage de Paris." *L'Illustration* 200, no. 4969 (28 May 1938): n.p.

———. "Un siècle d'expositions d'art décoratif—ce que furent les expositions d'art décoratif de 1798 à 1900." *La Revue de l'Art Ancien et Moderne* 45 (1924): 309–16.

———. "Le village français à l'exposition." *L'Illustration* 166, no. 4301 (8 August 1925): 131–34.

Vaizey, Marina. "The Collection of Mr. and Mrs. Robert Walker. Part 2." *The Connoisseur* 182, no. 734 (April 1973): 230–42.

Valéry, Paul. *Eupalinos or the Architect*. London: Oxford University Press, 1932.

Van Montfort, H. "L'exposition internationale des arts décoratifs et industriels modernes de Paris—1925 (suite)." *L'Émulation* (February 1926): 17–28.

Varenne, Gaston. "L'art urbain et l'art appliqué." *L'Amour de l'Art* (1926): 382–84.

———. "L'art urbain et le mobilier au salon d'automne." *Art et Décoration* (July–December 1923): 161–84.

———. "Les jardins de J.-C.-N. Forestier." *Art et Décoration* 53 (March 1928): 89–96.

———. "Quelques ensembles de Pierre Legrain." *L'Amour de l'Art* 5, no. 12 (December 1924): 401–08.

———. "La section de l'Union des Républiques Soviétistes Socialistes." *Art et Décoration* 48 (July 1925): 113–19.

Vaudoyer, Jean-Louis. "Le salon d'automne: II. L'art décoratif." *Art et Décoration* (December 1919): 173–92.

Veissière, Gabriel. "Le salon d'automne." *L'Architecture*, no. 23 (1923): 371–86.

Vera, André. "Exhortation aux architectes de s'intéresser au jardin." *L'Architecte* (1924): 68–71. Reprinted with "Nouvelle exhortation aux architectes de s'intéresser au jardin" in *L'Urbanisme ou la vie heureuse*. Paris: Éditions R. A. Corréa, 1936, pp. 169–82.

———. "Hommage à Le Nôtre." *Urbanisme*, no. 3–4 (1952): 72–73.

———. *L'homme et le jardin*. Paris: "Présences," Librairie Plon, 1950.

———. "Jardin d'amour." *La Gazette Illustrée des Amateurs de Jardins* (Winter 1914): 30–31.

———. "Jardin dans la banlieue." *L'Architecture Vivante* (Spring–Summer 1924): 24–25.

[Vera, André]. "Jardin dans la banlieue—André et Paul Vera." *L'Architecte* (1924): p. 72, pls. 41–42.

[Vera, André]. "Le jardin de M. André Vera à Saint-Germain-en-Laye." *Art et Industrie* 4, no. 8 (10 August 1928): 3–7.

———. "Le jardin de Paul Gernez dessiné par Paul Vera." *Art et Industrie* (January 1930): 2–8.

———. *Les jardins*. Paris: Émile-Paul, 1919.

———. "Lettres sur les jardins." Parts 1–2. *La Demeure Française*, no. 1 (Spring 1925): 23–32, and no. 4 (Winter 1925): 3–12.

———. "Modernité et tradition: Lettre sur les jardins." *Les Arts Français* (Les Jardins), no. 30 (1919): 89–97.

———. *Modernités*. Paris: Librairie de France, 1925.

———. *Le nouveau jardin*. Paris: Émile-Paul, 1912.

———. "Le nouveau style." *L'Art Décoratif* (1912): 21–32.

———. "La nouvelle architecture." Parts 1–2. *L'Architecte* (September 1912): 65–67 and (October 1912): 73–75.

———. "Paul Vera décorateur." *Art et Industrie* 4, no. 3 (10 March 1928): 25–29.

———. "Le petit jardin." *L'Illustration* 182:1, no. 4656 (28 May 1932): n.p.

———"Une phase nouvelle dans l'évolution du jardin." In "Jardins," special issue of *L'Architecture d'Aujourd'hui* (April 1937): 3.

———. "Pour le renouveau de l'art français: Le jardin." In "Jardins et espaces verts," special issue of *Urbanisme*, no. 86 (January 1943): 1–4.

———. *Urbanisme*. Collection Initiations, no. 13. Paris: Éditions de la Revue des Jeunes, 1946.

———. *L'urbanisme ou la vie heureuse*. Paris: Éditions R. A. Corréa, 1936.

Verne, Henri, and René Chavance. *Pour comprendre l'art décoratif moderne en France*. Paris: Hachette, 1925.

Veronesi, Giulia. *Stile 1925: Ascesa e caduta delle "Arts Déco."* Florence: Vallecchi Editore, 1966.

Viée, M. "L'exposition internationale des arts décoratifs et industriels modernes de 1925." *La Construction Moderne* (13 January 1924): 169–70.

Vienot, J. "La leçon de 1925." *L'Architecture d'Aujourd'hui* 11, no. 1–2 (January 1940): 33.

"Une villa à Hyères appt. au Ve et à la Vtesse de Noailles." *Art et Industrie* 4, no. 9 (10 September 1928): 2–10.

Vitet, Ludovic. "De la théorie des jardins." In *Études sur l'histoire de l'art*. Vol. 4. Paris: Michel Levy, 1864, pp. 1–25.

Vitou, Elizabeth, Dominique Deshoulières, and Hubert Jeanneau. *Gabriel Guévrékian, 1900–1970: Une autre architecture moderne.* Paris: Connivences, 1987.

Vitry, Paul. "Avant l'exposition des arts décoratifs." *Beaux-Arts*, no. 7 (1 April 1925): 97–99.

————. "Conclusion." *Beaux-Arts*, no. 16 (15 September 1925): 265–68.

————. "L'exposition internationale des arts décoratifs et industriels modernes: Introduction." *Beaux-Arts*, no. 10 (15 May 1925): 145–51.

————. "Le village français." *Art et Décoration* (August 1925): 57–71.

Vriesen, Gustav, and Max Imdahl. *Robert Delaunay: Light and Color.* New York: Harry N. Abrams, 1967.

Walpole, Horace. *On Modern Gardening.* In *Anecdotes of Painting in England.* Vol. 4. 1780. Reprint. London: Brentham Press, 1975.

Ward, James. "Le Corbusier's Villa 'Les Terrasses' and the International Style." Ph.D. dissertation, New York University, 1984.

Watt, Alexander. "The Surprising Apartment of M. Carlos de Beistegui: Fantasy on the Roofs." *The Architectural Review* (April 1936): 155–59.

Weber, Marcel. "Les jardins." In *Exposition internationale des arts décoratifs et industriels modernes.* Paris: Librairie Larousse for *L'Art Vivant*, 1925, pp. 59–62.

Weelen, Guy. "Robes simultanées." *L'Œil*, no. 60 (December 1959): 78–85.

Weiser, Partick. "L'exposition internationale, l'État et les beaux-arts." In *Paris 1937–1957: Créations en France.* Paris: Centre Georges Pompidou, 1981, pp. 56–63.

Wesley, Richard. "Gabriel Guevrekian e il giardino cubista." *Rassegna* (La natura dei giardini), no. 8 (October 1981): 17–24.

Wheelwright, Robert. "Thoughts on Problems of Form." *Landscape Architecture Quarterly* 21, no. 1 (October 1930): 1–10.

Winternitz, Lonia. "Ein französischer Hausgarten." *Gartenschönheit* 11, no. 5 (May 1930): 88–89.

————. "Terrassenanlagen." *Gartenschönheit* 11, no. 10 (October 1930): 184–85.

Woodbridge, Kenneth. "The Nomenclature of Style in Garden History." In *British and American Gardens in the Eighteenth Century*, edited by Robert P. Maccubin and Peter Martin. Williamsburg, Virginia: Colonial Williamsburg Foundation, 1986, pp. 19–25.

Zach, Leon Henry. "Modernistic Work and Its Natural Limitations." *Landscape Architecture Quarterly* 22, no. 4 (July 1932): 292–95.

Zahar, Marcel. "L'architecture vivante: Gabriel Guévrékian." *L'Art Vivant* (January 1929): 10–13.

————. "L'hôtel de Mr Reichenbach." *L'Art Vivant* (1932): 507.

————. "La maison de Mr et Mme Heim: Morphologie et structure d'une maison." *La Renaissance de l'Art Français* (February 1931): 48–56.

————. "Quelques jardins construits par Albert Laprade." *Art et Industrie* (March 1930): 6–8.

————. "Le salon des artistes décorateurs." *Art et Industrie* (June 1930): 22–26.

Zahn, Leopold. "Ein geometrischer Garten an der Riviera." *Gartenschönheit* 10 (June 1929): 222–23.

Zervos, Christian. "Henri Laurens." *L'Art d'Aujourd'hui* (Fall–Winter 1924): 11–16.

————. "Les tendances actuelles de l'art décoratif: I. Le mobilier: Hier et aujourd'hui." *La Revue de l'Art Ancien et Moderne* 47 (January–May 1925): 68–75.

INDEX

Numbers in italics indicate figures.